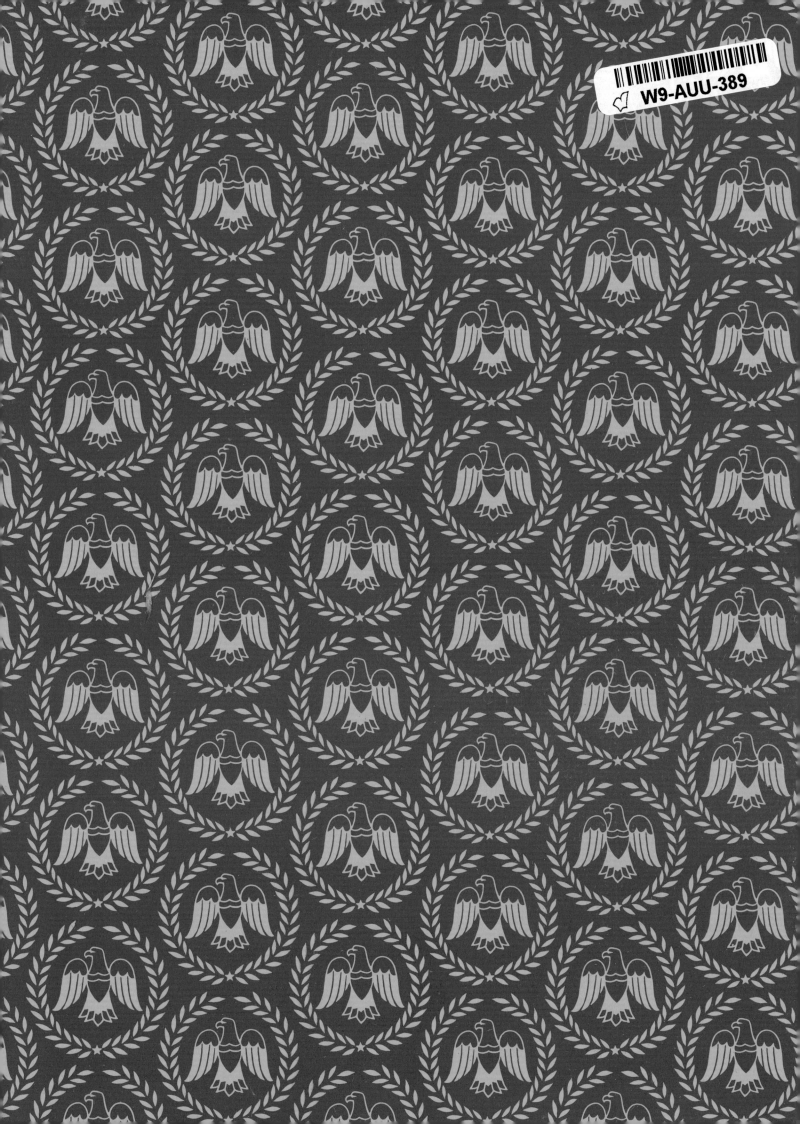

Treasury of American Design

TREASURY

OF

TWO VOLUMES IN ONE

A Pictorial Survey of Popular Folk Arts

Based upon Watercolor Renderings in the

Index of American Design, at the

National Gallery of Art

AMERICAN DESIGN

by *Clarence P. Hornung*

FOREWORD by J. CARTER BROWN
Director, National Gallery of Art, Washington, D.C.
INTRODUCTION by HOLGER CAHILL
Formerly National Director, Index of American Design

HARRY N. ABRAMS, INC., *Publishers*, NEW YORK

The design as well as the text of this volume
is the work of Clarence P. Hornung, who also created
the typographic format, marginal decorations,
and binding design. The type is set in Times Roman
with initial letters and book titles in the author's Georgian
initials; the chapter headings were hand-set by him
in Caslon italic swash letters.

The introduction to this book is reprinted from Holger Cahill's
introduction to *The Index of American Design* by Erwin O. Christensen,
published in 1950 by Publication Fund, National Gallery of Art

Standard Book Number: 8109–0501–9
Library of Congress Catalogue Card Number: 76–142742

To

SARA

CONTENTS

Book Three: AROUND HOUSE AND GARDEN

Book Four: WOMAN'S WORLD

AUTHOR'S NOTE

SINCE MY FIRST VISIT in the mid-1930s to the New York City Federal Art Project on King Street, I have been intrigued with the Index of American Design as a great national heritage. Here in one vast collection of over 17,000 carefully documented drawings is the depository of our country's tradition of fine craftsmanship. Executed by American artists under the Works Progress Administration, these full-color watercolor renderings depict designs in decorative, folk, and popular arts from the early days of colonization to the last decade of the nineteenth century. Among the many categories represented are furniture, ceramics, glass, silver, pewter, textiles, and innumerable objects of daily use. The objective of the program was to create a record of our design heritage which could be used for research purposes and would be available for exhibitions or publication in book or periodical form.

Thirty-five states participated in the program, and supervisory staffs were set up in key cities of these states. While this was one of the most ambitious undertakings ever conceived in the realm of the arts, it unfortunately did not include many areas of culture beyond the reach of urban centers. A number of southern and midwestern states were not represented in a program which should have been nationwide in scope. It is the fervent hope of many scholars and educators that this deficiency may someday be corrected, but even with these regional omissions the pictorial and research material in the Index is a major source of information about our artistic history.

The collection, deservedly, has won national recognition. It constitutes a powerful and moving document of the skill, taste, and creative vigor which characterized the life of our preindustrial and early industrial communities and has established a high place for our native arts among the folk cultures of the Western world.

A major value of the Index is the vitalizing influence it can have upon the communities of today and tomorrow. The vigorous traditions of our country's early cultural life can be active agents in the areas of education, home and community planning, contemporary craftsmanship and industrial design, and in the conduct of our daily affairs.

My idea of making the plates of the Index available to the public in book form impelled me to seek a publisher as early as 1936. Between 1936 and 1938, I had discussions with a number of publishers who shared my interest but who felt disinclined to proceed because of the very magnitude of the project and the staggering costs involved. One publisher even pleaded for a Congressional subsidy, but with the advent of World War II this remote possibility quickly evaporated. Years passed, and the material remained locked away, first at the Metropolitan Museum of Art in New York City, and later at the National Gallery of Art in Washington, D.C., where it is now housed. Finally, in 1950, Erwin O. Christensen, then curator of the Index of American Design, published a volume of text and plates. The book's appearance represented a major breakthrough. Excellent as it was, however, less than 3 percent of the renderings were included, an inadequate representation of so extensive a collection.

It has taken four years of constant work to write and design this book and select the pictures for it. It has been a gigantic task, challenging from every aspect. The unbounded enthusiasm of the publisher, Harry N. Abrams, and the generous cooperation of all concerned have served to sustain the author's interest at times when seemingly insurmountable obstacles stood in the way. The choice of illustrations is entirely my responsibility, and I alone am responsible for any omissions and inadequacies.

I cannot begin to express my thanks to those who reviewed the manuscript for their time and patience. I am particularly indebted to Erwin Christensen for his critical suggestions; to Dr. Grose Evans, the present curator of the Index, for his analytical reading of the text; and to Marvin D. Schwartz for the scholarly insight with which he scrutinized the manuscript.

A special word of appreciation is due various members of the staff at the National Gallery of Art. First, my warmest thanks to J. Carter Brown, its director, for his deep understanding as expressed in the foreword to these volumes. I also want to thank Dr. Grose Evans and his capable associate Lina Steele, who showed endless patience in ferreting out needed illustrations, and Henry Bevil, staff photographer, who provided the color transparencies. Special thanks are due Edgar William and Bernice Chrysler Garbisch for granting permission to use a number of paintings by American primitives owned by the National Gallery.

Without the generous assistance of many institutions a compilation such as this would have been virtually impossible. I am greatly indebted to Colonial Williamsburg and its friendly trustees and staff who helped in supplying photographic illustrations. Jane Abbot Tyler and Hugh DeSamper of the Press Bureau filled every request, and Peter A. G. Brown and Jean C. Hildreth, curator and registrar, respectively, of the Abby Aldrich Rockefeller Folk Art Collection at Williamsburg, were most accommodating. Thanks are also due to the staffs of the Henry Francis du Pont Winterthur Museum, Winterthur, Delaware; the Peabody Museum, Salem, Massachusetts; the Sandwich Glass Museum, Sandwich, Massachusetts, and its director, Mrs. J. Robert Kershaw; the Shelburne Museum, Shelburne, Vermont, and its director, Sterling C. Emerson; the Bennington Museum, Bennington, Vermont, and its director-curator, Richard Carter Barret; the Eleanor and Mabel Van Alstyne Collection of American Folk Art at the Smithsonian Institution, Washington, D.C.; the Mount Vernon Ladies Association, Mount Vernon, Virginia, and the association's curator, Christine Meadows. My gratitude also goes to countless friends who have given valuable assistance, especially Albert Steinhacker, Louis Grudin, Fridolf Johnson, and the late Albert Schiller.

For permission to reprint the late Holger Cahill's essay as it originally appeared in Erwin Christensen's book, I am grateful to his widow, Dorothy C. Miller Cahill. Mr. Cahill was the director of the Index program and one of its prime movers, and his story of the project is the official account of its inception and operation.

The wholehearted cooperation of the entire staff of the publisher is a unique experience for one who has authored many books with many publishers. I cannot begin to express my gratitude to Harry N. Abrams for the foresight and enthusiasm he showed in supporting this project. In seeking to maintain the high standards of excellence for which the Abrams imprint has won renown throughout the world, I have tried to give my utmost. Special thanks are due to the late Milton Fox for his sympathetic understanding, to Paul Anbinder for his help in cutting through difficulties at every stage, to Margaret Kaplan for her keen perception and sensitivity concerning problems of text and unity, and to all the other members of the staff whose fine teamwork has contributed immeasurably toward making what could have been an arduous task a most pleasurable one.

A note of accolade is due the hundreds of gifted men and women whose magnificent work constitutes the Index of American Design. Theirs is the real creative contribution. Unfortunately, the limits of space prevented listing the names of the artists next to their renderings, but a roster of artists appears in the appendix.

And finally, how does one acknowledge the debt to one's life partner, who has had to endure with infinite patience the endless trials and vicissitudes of a most difficult period? There is no special "thank you" known to man that can repay a woman for such fortitude.

C.P.H.

FOREWORD

I MUST EXPRESS my great pleasure in the publication of this splendidly illustrated book, which will make available to a very wide audience so large a number of the magnificent watercolor renderings from the Index of American Design at the National Gallery of Art. Over 2,900 illustrations, some 850 in color, present a previously unsurpassed panorama of American crafts and folk arts. Clarence Hornung is to be congratulated not only for the informative text he has written, but also for his handsome and imaginative design for this project. The publishers must be equally saluted for their support and encouragement of a project of this magnitude.

The collection in the Index of American Design contains over 17,000 renderings of American decorative arts ranging from before 1700 to about 1900. The selections in this book have been carefully made to show the most representative specimens of these works from various regions and cultures of our country. The watercolors here reproduced were rendered with astonishing skill by American artists in many states during the years 1935–41 under grants from the Federal and State governments. These painters compiled a visual archive of remarkable beauty recording in a form far less perishable and more sensitively interpretive than the color photograph, these American objects, many of which have since disappeared.

The renderings at the Gallery are consulted here frequently, especially by designers and scholars. In addition, special exhibitions from the Index are shown in the Gallery building, and traveling exhibitions of original renderings as well as sets of color slides are circulated without charge by the Gallery across the nation.

It is my hope that this publication will make many aware of the richly varied and accomplished American works which are so important a part of our heritage.

J. Carter Brown, *Director*
National Gallery of Art
Washington, D.C.

INTRODUCTION

THE INDEX OF AMERICAN DESIGN is a record made by artists of a chapter in American history which is largely anonymous. It is the story, told in pictures, of articles of daily use and adornment in this country from early colonial times to the close of the nineteenth century. In the main it is devoted to the craft traditions which dominated American production for more than two hundred years and left their heritage to our developing mass-production technology which has impressed its forms upon our contemporary culture. Phases of this technology are represented in the Index, especially from the second half of the nineteenth century when mass-production methods were in the making and the machine was taking over even the more complicated handicrafts.

The Index is the result of a conjunction of circumstances during the depression of the 1930's. It was organized in response to several needs: the need of artists for employment, the need of the Government work program to devise projects which would maintain the skills of the unemployed, and public need for pictorial information on American design and craftsmanship. Demand for information on this phase of our history had been growing for some years before the Index came into being. It made itself felt insistently during and after the First World War, partly because of the rapid expansion of visual education, partly because American industry realized during the war its too close dependence on European design.

Behind these developments and sustaining them was a wide interest in American decorative and domestic art which had been steadily building up since the seventies and eighties when the work of early American craftsmen began its journey from farm sheds, town attics, and secondhand dealers' storerooms toward the art museum. The Centennial Exposition at Philadelphia in 1876 had something to do with it, but its contribution was in the spirit of the log cabin tradition fixed in popular consciousness since the campaign of the first President Harrison. The Centennial, like most American fairs, was devoted to contemporary enterprise and "modern improvements." In a period when the design of articles of everyday use was at a low ebb it is not surprising that the American artifacts most admired at the Exposition were trotting wagons, agricultural implements and clocks, all of which were more clearly related to handicraft traditions than to our rapidly developing machine technology. There were some exhibits of early American furniture and utensils. A house, built in "imitation of a New England log house" of 1776, contained, among other things, Peregrine White's cradle, John Alden's desk, Governor Endicott's folding chair, chests of drawers, bedsteads, quilts and kitchenware. Twenty ladies in costumes of the Revolutionary period conducted visitors through the house "explaining with courtesy the wonderful articles of furniture and cooking utensils whose very simplicity made them incomprehensible to the victims of modern improvements."

Interest in early American craftsmanship was not altogether new in the 1870's. Museums had concerned themselves with it to a degree, though the primary interest of most was history, natural history, or ethnology. Among these institutions one may mention the Charleston (South Carolina) Museum founded in 1773, the oldest institution of its kind in the country, the Massachusetts Historical Society (1790), the Albany Institute of History and Art (1791), the New-York Historical Society (1804), the American Antiquarian Society in Worcester (1812), the Peabody Museum and the Essex Institute in Salem, the Pennsylvania Historical Society, in Philadelphia, and various state and city museums and historic houses.

Pioneers in the late nineteenth century development were such men as Dr. Henry Chapman Mercer of Doylestown, Pennsylvania, who gave up archaeology and began collecting early American material in the 1880's; Dr. Edwin Atlee Barber, early writer on ceramics and glass, effective discoverer of Pennsylvania German pottery and Bennington Ware and founder of the collections that bear his name at the Philadelphia Museum of Art; John Cotton Dana, founder of the Newark (New Jersey) Museum and of the first library picture collections in this country;

Mr. and Mrs. Robert W. De Forest, founders of the American Wing of the Metropolitan Museum of Art; Henry W. Kent, of the Metropolitan staff, who was behind most of the Museum's activities in the early American field; R. T. Haines Halsey, Henry W. Erving, Eugene Bolles, and other collectors and writers who were calling attention to the American tradition in design before the turn of the century.

In the early 1900's great impetus was given by such events as the Boston Museum's important exhibition of colonial silver in 1906; the Hudson-Fulton celebration in New York in 1909 when the Metropolitan Museum exhibited a collection of early American decorative art; the foundation in 1910 of the Society for the Preservation of New England Antiquities, whose editor, George Francis Dow, did pioneering studies of arts and crafts; the *Werkbund* exhibitions at the Newark Museum (1912 and 1922) that brought to this country the message of an organization which was one of the most important links in the progression from William Morris to modern design; and the activities of collectors like Mr. and Mrs. De Forest, Francis H. Bigelow, Howard Reifsnyder, Judge Alphonso T. Clearwater, and Henry F. du Pont. The "manufacturer and designer" exhibitions begun in 1917 at the Metropolitan Museum under the direction of Richard F. Bach, and the survey of American resources in industrial art by Charles Russell Richards at the beginning of the twenties, while they took note of all resources no matter what their origin, served to call attention to the quality of the indigenous contributions. In 1924 when the American Wing of the Metropolitan was founded the most conservative museums were beginning to see that early American furniture, ceramics, glass, silver, metalware, textiles, tools, and utensils were worthy of serious attention. The tricentennials beginning with that of Jamestown in 1907, and the New England tricentennials of the twenties and thirties, projects like Henry Ford's Wayside Inn, opened in 1928, and the important Williamsburg restoration begun by John D. Rockefeller, Jr., in 1927 were high points in the development. In the late 1920's it was not unusual to see early American furniture which had been disregarded two generations before sold for many thousands of dollars. At a New York sale in April, 1929, three eighteenth century Philadelphia pieces were bid up to $103,000 by collectors. Another New York event of 1929 more appealing to the general public was the exhibition of early American art held for the benefit of the Girl Scouts.

Appreciation of American folk and popular art, which forms one of the major categories of the Index of American Design, grew more slowly. It has two main sources: the ethnological collection which has made us aware of design horizons beyond our own Western tradition, and the rise of modern art. Each is involved to some extent in the other. Modern artists helped educate ethnologists and the museum public to the esthetic quality of primitive, folk and popular art. The ethnological collection exerted an influence on the early development of modern art. Study of the art of primitive peoples led to an interest in the art of peasants, artisans and amateurs. These ideas made themselves felt in the United States in the second decade of this century in the work and writings of artists returning from European study, in small collections, and in the pages of such magazines as R. J. Coady's *The Soil*, and *The Arts* founded by the painter Hamilton Easter Field, one of the early collectors of American folk art. Between the mid-twenties and the mid-thirties folk and popular art was brought into the focus of national consciousness through such notable collections as those of Mr. and Mrs. Elie Nadelman, Mrs. Isabel Carleton Wilde, and Mrs. John D. Rockefeller, Jr., and through a series of exhibitions at the Newark Museum, the Whitney Studio Club, the Museum of Modern Art, the Whitney Museum of American Art, and Colonial Williamsburg.

These various developments provided a matrix for an index of American design. They also pointed up the need for it. Despite the enthusiasm of collectors, and possibly because of it, American material in the arts has always been widely scattered. No really comprehensive collections exist here such as one found in Germany before World War II and may still find in Sweden. The scattering of American material is due in part to the factor of distance, the extent of the country as compared with European nations, the wide separation of the Colonies, and transportation difficulties in early days. More fundamental reasons were the comparatively broad base of patronage in colonial times and the diversity of traditions that existed here at one and the same time.

The rapid growth of interest in visualization around the turn of the century led public libraries to gather pictorial information to meet the needs of education and industry. The first of these public library collections of documentary pictures was organized by John Cotton Dana at Denver in 1891, and later at Springfield, Massachusetts, in 1898, and at Newark, New Jersey, in 1903. In 1916 the New York Public Library set up its Picture Collection following Mr.

Dana's ideas. Though not devoted exclusively to American subjects these picture collections were called upon to answer questions similar to those asked in the preface of this book: "What is American? Is there anything recognizably American aside from Indian material? Where can I see it? Have you a picture of it?" European visitors had been asking such questions for a long time. It seems probable that some of our self-consciousness about what is American, aside from the stream of fashions which we have imported and appropriated as our own, has been stimulated by questions asked by European visitors from the middle of the nineteenth century and repeated with growing insistence after the First World War. During the 1920's more and more Americans were asking them, not only collectors, artists, designers and educators, but also manufacturers made keenly aware of the drying up of European design sources during the war. The New York Public Library Picture Collection in its reports during the early 1930's makes note of the increasing demand for American material and the difficulty in meeting it.

The idea for an Index of American Design crystallized into a plan in the spring of 1935. It was not a new idea. European nations had made large collections of their native design material and published richly illustrated books on the subject. With us well-illustrated publications have been few until recent years. Pioneers in this type of publication in the United States were historical museums, private collectors, and amateurs. Some of the earliest documentary drawings of American artifacts—of Benjamin Franklin's stove, for instance—were published in *The Transactions of the American Philosophical Society* in the last quarter of the eighteenth century. A hundred years later one finds William C. Prime writing on pottery and porcelain (1878); John H. Buck on old silver in 1888; Dr. Edwin Atlee Barber, writing on American ceramics, glass, and the tulip ware of the Pennsylvania German potters as early as 1893; Irving W. Lyon on colonial furniture in New England, 1891; R. T. Haines Halsey on pottery, 1899, and on silver, 1906; Luke Vincent Lockwood on furniture, 1901; Frances Clary Morse; and Alice Morse Earle, who began writing in the nineties and probably did more to popularize early New England than any other writer. N. Hudson Moore and Clarence C. Cook also were writing on American domestic art, and many of those named were collecting it before the turn of the century. One of the important collectors and writers of the early 1900's was Alexander Wilson Drake, who wrote on American copper and brass in 1907 and showed a collection of samplers at the Cincinnati Museum of Art in 1909. Frederick William Hunter's book on Stiegel glass, which had wide influence, was published in 1914.

Among the historical societies, that of Bucks County in Doylestown, Pennsylvania, brought out pioneering illustrated books on the decorative stove plates of the eighteenth century, the art of illuminated writing among the Pennsylvania Germans, and ancient carpenter's tools. These books, written by Dr. Henry Chapman Mercer, were published in the twenties. Also published in the twenties were Albert H. Sonn's work on early American wrought iron, J. B. Kerfoot's book on American pewter, and the early writings of Mrs. Rhea Mansfield Knittle on handicrafts west of the Alleghenies. These and other admirable publications brought into view neglected chapters in the history of the useful and popular arts in the United States and called attention to what still needed to be done in research, in education, and in the organization of collections. Important contributions in these various fields were made by such men as Fiske Kimball, Royal Bailey Farnum, Leon L. Winslow, Valentine Kirby, Henry Turner Bailey, Theodore S. Woolsey, Howard D. Eberlein, William Laurel Harris, George Leland Hunter, and others.

When the Civil Works Administration was set up in 1933 unemployment in many professions was severe and nowhere more severe than in the arts. The first large Government project for artists, organized in December, 1933, and directed by Edward Bruce under the Treasury Department through a grant of funds from the Civil Works Administration, employed mainly painters, sculptors, and printmakers. Although it also employed designers and craftsmen the basic problem of unemployment among commercial artists remained. The Civil Works Administration and various State Emergency Relief Administrations tried to meet it through setting up handicraft and recording projects. The most valuable recording projects were the Historic American Buildings Survey carried out under the direction of the Department of the Interior through a grant of funds from CWA and later from WPA; and a record of American Indian design begun by Frederick Douglas at the Denver Art Museum in 1932 which employed Government project artists from 1933 until its work was completed in 1938. Another recording project, planned before the Index but organized later, was the Historic American Merchant-Marine Survey, which was under the joint direction of the Smithsonian Institution and WPA. Other similar projects were proposed in 1935.

One such project, for recording decorative iron and bronze in New York, was put before Mayor La Guardia's Municipal Art Committee by Peter Larsen, who later carried it on under the Index of American Design.

These projects were the immediate forerunners of the Index, but it did not grow out of them. The Index idea as it was later developed by the WPA Federal Art Project resulted from discussions between Romana Javitz, head of the New York Public Library's Picture Collection, and artists who came to the Library for research. This was in the early spring of 1935. Miss Javitz and the Picture Collection staff had recognized for some time the need for a comprehensive source record of American design. Prominent among the artists who participated in the discussion at the Library was Ruth Reeves, a textile designer and painter. She brought the Index idea to Mrs. Frances Pollak, head of Educational Projects for the New York City Emergency Relief Administration, and suggested that artists employed on Government projects carry it out. Later Miss Reeves, who was the missionary of the Index idea, brought it to the attention of WPA officials in Washington and to Edward Bruce, head of the Section of Painting and Sculpture. Mrs. Pollak immediately saw the Index as a solution for the problem of commercial artist unemployment and asked Miss Javitz to formulate a plan. This plan was completed in July, 1935, but because of difficulties in finding public sponsorship, the Index remained largely in the planning stage until after the organization of the Federal Art Project in October, 1935.

The Index of American Design was organized as a nationwide activity in two meetings of the Federal Art Project national staff, December 7 and 8, 1935. Certain activities of the nascent Index in New York City were ruled out. It was felt that Indian Arts should be left to the ethnologists who had been making pictorial records in that field. The Index was limited to the practical, popular and folk arts of the peoples of European origin who created the material culture of this country as we know it today. Architecture had to be ruled out because two other Government projects were concerned with it, the Historic American Buildings Survey and the Historic American Merchant-Marine Survey. The Index was placed under the direction of the Washington staff of the Federal Art Project. Constance Rourke was appointed national editor and Ruth Reeves national co-ordinator. A small central research staff was set up in Washington. A larger research staff had already been set up under the New York City project. In the spring of 1936 C. Adolph Glassgold succeeded Ruth Reeves as national co-ordinator of the Index and he was succeeded by Benjamin Knotts in 1940.

State Index projects of any size set up their own research staffs made up of persons familiar with the history of American crafts or expert in some particular field. Where employment was small the research was done by the project supervisor or by the artists themselves. It was the function of research staffs to make surveys of local material, to select from it the objects to be recorded, checking on their history and authenticity. Before an object was assigned to an artist for recording it was examined by the research supervisor and all information concerning it entered on the data sheet which would be pasted on the back of the completed drawing. The Washington Index office checked on the quality of local project work and assisted in co-ordinating research. It might be found, for instance, that objects of the same kind were duplicated over wide areas and it became necessary for the state projects to determine whether material which they planned to record had been recorded elsewhere, whether the objects were the best available examples, and if any good purpose would be served by the duplication. Considering the extent of the Index, it is surprising how little duplication took place. In choosing objects for recording priority was given to material of historical significance not previously studied, which, for one reason or another, stood in danger of being lost. Regional and local crafts were emphasized; for instance, crewel work, Shaker design and the early colonial crafts in New England; the folk crafts in Pennsylvania and in the Southwest; pioneer furniture, tools, and utensils in the Middle West and in Texas; early Mormon textiles in Utah, and various community crafts in Ohio, Illinois, Iowa, and other states. In carrying on their work, research staffs received generous help from museums, private collectors, and dealers who owned the material recorded by the Index.

In January, 1936, a preliminary Index manual was issued by the Washington office of the Federal Art Project outlining the scope of the new activity, its purpose, plan of organization, methods of recording, research, classification and filing, together with specimen copies of data sheets to accompany each drawing. The research methods and data sheets were drawn up by Phyllis Crawford, research director of the New York City project, in collaboration with Miss Javitz. Two months later a supplementary bulletin on techniques was issued. This was based on the teaching of Suzanne Chapman who was loaned to the

Massachusetts Index project by the Boston Museum of Fine Arts. Miss Chapman had studied methods worked out by Joseph Lindon Smith, who made pictorial records of the Museum's Egyptian expedition. Mr. Smith had devised a meticulous technique of documentary painting in water color. Miss Chapman taught Index artists this "Egyptologist's technique."

The Index plan as finally worked out in its objective and techniques of recording and research proved well suited to the program of the Federal Art Project. The Project was charged by the Government with finding useful employment for thousands of artists referred to the WPA by local agencies throughout the country. What work the Project could carry on depended on the skills of these artists, or skills which they might acquire through in-service training. The basic directive of the whole WPA program was maintenance of skills. There were other directives. Congress did not approve projects which were in competition with private enterprise. Some project supervisors found this opposition irksome, but it was, in fact, wise. Unemployment would scarcely have been relieved if Government employees had engaged in competition with others employed at higher wage levels in commerce, industry or the professions. It was in these circumstances that the Index came into existence. Here was a job that needed doing. The doing of it would maintain and improve skills. It would not compete with private enterprise but would, and in fact did, benefit private enterprise through providing it with a reservoir of pictorial and research material on American design and craftsmanship.

The Index of American Design as it exists today was produced by a great collaborative enterprise to which hundreds of persons contributed talent, ideas, techniques, research methods, and persevering, devoted effort. . . . In its early stages the Index met with many difficulties. Since its drawings were to remain Federal property they could not be allocated in the states where they were made. This virtually eliminated local sponsorship. No Federal project could be set up in the states without the consent of the WPA administrations involved and so it became necessary to win the support of the state administrations for a project which would show no contribution to their sponsor's funds. WPA was required by law to show local contributions in cash or kind ranging from 10 per cent in 1935 to 25 per cent in 1939. Projects which had a high percentage of sponsors' contributions had to support projects which had little or none. This difficulty was considerably aggravated when the Federal program came to an end and the states took

over administrative control of the Arts Projects. It must be said, however, to the great credit of WPA State Administrators, that with few exceptions they agreed to carry the Index both in its early stages in 1935–1936 and after the close of the Federal period in 1939.

Another difficulty was with museums, dealers, and private collectors who owned material which the Index sought to record. At first many of them were sceptical of Government projects and saw little value in the Index. Even when they admitted its worth they thought it might better be carried out by what they considered the cheaper and more expeditious method of photography. Museums were won over when they became convinced of the sound purpose of the Index, the quality of its drawings and its careful research methods. Dealers and collectors followed. Important in winning this support for the Index were Constance Rourke, Ruth Reeves, Mildred Holzhauer, Nina Collier, C. Adolph Glassgold, Thomas C. Parker, Pauline Pinckney, and Katherine Caulkins from the Washington office of the Federal Art Project; Richard C. Morrison and Gordon W. Smith in Massachusetts; Phyllis Crawford, Helen McKearin, Janet Rosenwald, Aline Bernstein, Carolyn Scoon, Millia Davenport, Elizabeth T. Riefstahl, Scott Graham Williamson, and Charles O. Cornelius in New York. Many of these were expert in various fields of American design. A strong supporter who helped convince collectors of the value of the Index was the late Homer Eaton Keyes, editor of the magazine *Antiques*, which he founded in 1922.

A third difficulty was with the artists. In the beginning many artists felt that the Index was dead copying. Index artists had to discipline themselves to meticulous rendering techniques and to the objects they recorded. They could not express themselves through the free use of form and color and so felt cheated of the creative assignments they had expected from the Federal Art Project. But they discovered that documentary art may become a free creative activity even within severe discipline and limitations. This change in the artists' attitude was brought about by the steady improvement of project standards and the missionary work of supervisors on the Washington staff of the Federal Art Project and in the states: Richard C. Morrison, Gordon W. Smith, Suzanne Chapman, Elizabeth Moutal, Ingrid Selmer-Larsen, Lawrence Peterson, and Alfred Smith in Massachusetts; Dorothy Hay Jensen in Maine; Donald Donovan in Rhode Island; William Warren in Connecticut; Lou Block, Lincoln Rothschild and Tillie G.

Shahn in New York; Frances Lichten in Pennsylvania; Hildegarde Crosby Melzer in Illinois; Sylvester Jerry and Paul McPharlin in Michigan; Elzy J. Bird in Utah; Donald Bear in Colorado; R. Vernon Hunter and E. Boyd in New Mexico; and Warren Lemmon in California.

The Index prospered in New England and the Middle Atlantic states where a great deal of early American material was available for recording and artists of the highest competence could be employed. It lagged in the South and some parts of the West because of lack of material to record, but mainly because personnel trained in the techniques which the Index required could not be employed under Government regulations. The situation was improved somewhat by lending artists from Massachusetts, New York, and other northeastern states to teach Index techniques in the South and West. This was a complicated procedure involving the agreement of two state administrations, problems of quota, per diem and travel allowances, and rates of pay which differed considerably in various parts of the country. Another reason why the Index developed slowly in the South was that states like North and South Carolina, Virginia, Tennessee, Mississippi, and Florida were leaders in the Community Art Center movement. Most of their artists were employed in teaching and in bringing art to the general public. Because of these circumstances some states in the South had no Index projects. However, excellent Index drawings were made in Virginia, Kentucky, Louisiana, and Texas. In the West and the Middle West where problems of quota and pay rate were not so difficult many states benefitted by the eastern experience. Others did not, either because trained personnel could not be hired or because their Index material was duplicated in other states. The Index project was finally set up in thirty-five states and employed an average of three hundred artists from the time it was organized in December, 1935, until it was closed down shortly after the United States entered the war in 1941.

While expert supervisors from the metropolitan centers assisted many Index projects throughout the country, the best results achieved often depended on purely local developments. An example of this is Utah, a state with a small art project and a good source of material in the Relic Halls founded by the Daughters of the Utah Pioneers. The story is told by Elzy J. Bird, under whose direction the Index did some of its best drawings:

"When I became director of the project I had been working on an Index plate and I remember the amount of sweat that went into the finished product. Most of the artists seemed to feel as I did, that it was merely copy work and didn't give free rein to anything creative.

"At first I think the only artist who took the Index seriously was William Parkinson. I remember one artist doing a remarkable textile piece— just one. He said he'd sooner starve than do another. Finally I raided our silk screen department and found some of the boys who were very skillful with their hands. Frank Mace, Frank Maurer and Paul Vaughn were the ones who really enjoyed doing Index drawings. Mace was a journeyman printer, Vaughn a metal craftsman, Maurer a carpenter and ex-Marine. I put them to work with Parkinson and together they developed the wonderful painting of textiles, working from dark to light with transparent and opaque water color. Another of the group was Florence Truelson who devised her own method of producing textile textures. From time to time others came and went. There were, for instance, several cowboys who could sit down for days over a drawing of leatherwork or an old spur or gun. They were the saddle and spur type; wouldn't be caught dead doing a textile but you could certainly keep them out of trouble with something of the old West."

The Federal Art Project tried to channel Index techniques in the direction of quality, but no one technique was insisted upon. What was insisted upon was strict objectivity, accurate drawing, clarity of construction, exact proportions, and faithful rendering of material, color and texture so that each Index drawing might stand as surrogate for the object. This ideal was not always carried out in practice. The best drawings, while maintaining complete fidelity to the object, have the individuality which characterizes works of art. To find their peers in American art we must go back to the still-life of William Harnett and the *trompe-l'œil* painters of the nineteenth century. The lesser drawings represent steps in the training of artists who later produced better work. This training was carried on by expert supervisors, in Boston, New York, Philadelphia, Chicago and the larger Index projects generally. Miss Chapman and her pupils in Boston taught their technique throughout New England and were called upon to teach it in other parts of the country. Techniques were also taught through touring exhibitions of the best drawings, and of drawings in various stages of completion illustrating the method step by step.

The technique recommended in the Index manual

(WPA Technical Series, Art Circular No. 3) for most categories of objects was a transparent water-color method. The object was first carefully studied and a light outline drawing made. The lighter passages of color were then washed in, gradually working up to the darkest passages. One wash might be applied directly over another, allowing the first wash to dry thoroughly, or a glaze might be applied and new washes of color laid in over the glaze. High lights and shadows were simplified and accidental reflections and cast shadows eliminated. Another method described in the Index manual was the opaque water-color method in which the darkest undertone passages were laid in first, then the lighter tones, with the darkest and lightest accents picked out last. This was the technique of the Utah artists. New York used a variant of this method, underpainting in Chinese ink and laying in the color over this monochrome wash. Oil technique was preferred for certain types of objects. Michigan used it in recording tobacconists' signs and Pennsylvania in recording Pennsylvania German folk art. Another method favored in New York and New Jersey for certain kinds of textiles was scratchboard done by scratching with a steel pen through a water-color wash into the soft chalk and wax surface of a prepared drawing paper. Pen and ink, and pencil were used where color was not important. Photography was also used. Some critics argued that photography should have been employed exclusively. However, aside from the fact that the Index was part of an employment program for artists, there were many reasons why photography did not become its leading technique. The camera, except in the hands of its greatest masters, cannot reveal the essential character and quality of objects as the artist can. Problems of distortion and of lighting are difficult. The camera cannot search out the forms of objects deeply undercut or modeled in high relief, match color as closely as the artist, or render the subtle interplay of form, color and texture which creates the characteristic beauty of so many products of early American craftsmen. Color photography approximating the quality of Index drawings is an expensive process with many problems which have not been fully solved. The color photograph is perishable, while water color is one of the most durable of art media. . . .

The Index, in bringing together thousands of particulars from various sections of the country, tells the story of American hand skills and traces intelligible patterns within that story. In documenting the forms created by the tastes, skills, and needs of our ances-

tors it brings a new vitality and warmth into their everyday history, whether they were the founders of colonies and states, or political, religious, or economic refugees who came here to find a new free way of life, "a chapter of harmony and perfection" in the relations of men.

In one sense the Index is a kind of archaeology. It helps to correct a bias which has tended to relegate the work of the craftsman and the folk artist to the subconscious of our history where it can be recovered only by digging. In the past we have lost whole sequences out of their story, and have all but forgotten the unique contribution of hand skills in our culture. As early as the eighteenth century little remained above ground of seventeenth century Jamestown. When the Williamsburg restoration began in 1927 a good deal of the research into that eighteenth century town had to be done by digging in old sites. These excavations recovered more than forty tons of material other than brick, including fragments of ceramic ware, glass, bone, iron, brass and pewter. Colonial Williamsburg is authority for the statement that an accurate reconstruction "would not have been possible without this very intensive archaeological exploration, just as it could not have been done without the most intense sort of research work with surviving documents and records." "Artifacts are of inestimable value in giving us a broad over-all impression of the culture and taste of colonial people." In the damp earth of the peninsula between the York and the James rivers, wood, textiles, leather, clothing, and floor coverings disintegrate quickly. Consequently some of the history of Jamestown and Williamsburg is lost and can be reconstructed only from conjecture and analogy supported by surviving written documents. The same may be said of other early towns. Some of the houses in Plymouth, before they could be restored, had to be freed from constructions laid over them through the generations. This sort of digging into the American past has been necessary not only for the early period but even for developments in our machine technology in the nineteenth century. Siegfried Giedion and John Kouwenhoven in their researches into the history of mechanization and mass-production methods have shown how much we have forgotten about the development of techniques which have given contemporary American civilization its character.

As we study the drawings of the Index of American Design we realize that the hands that made the first two hundred years of this country's material culture expressed something more than untutored creative instinct and the rude vigor of a frontier civilization. This need surprise us only if we forget the ageless tradition that may lie behind the making and decoration of the simplest article of everyday use. The artifacts recovered at Jamestown are far from crude. The earliest houses at Plymouth have a direct and simple manner of construction which shows that they were built by men who knew exactly what they were about. While the tradition of the early American craftsman is basically English, it shows in its beginnings an interweaving of influences made more complex by immigration and intercolonial migration. This helps to explain the variety of handicraft and popular art styles in certain sections, in Pennsylvania, New Jersey, New York, Virginia, the Carolinas and the settlements to the west. Pennsylvania Germans settled some towns in New England. The Moravians and other Palatine Germans followed the Shenandoah Valley through Virginia and into North Carolina and the Ohio River Valley to the west, carrying with them their typical handicraft skills.

The English tradition itself is far from single, even in the work of the artisans and craftsmen who came from Britain before the middle of the seventeenth century. These men were trained in ways of doing things that go back through late medieval times in Britain, France, and The Netherlands into Gothic and even Romanesque times. This medieval tradition lived a long time in Britain. Some phases of it were in existence in the hill towns of Gloucestershire as late as the twenties of this century; in the United States it lasted well into the nineteenth century. The men who carried this tradition in early colonial times and through the recurring primitivisms of the expanding frontier were sometimes specialists and sometimes jacks-of-all-trades not only because of the exigencies of life in a new land but also because their training made for flexibility. Joiners and shipwrights could turn their hands to architecture, the making of furniture, and the carving of tools and utensils. Some of the carvings which they made as shop signs and ship's decoration we now recognize as our earliest sculpture. Carriage makers and house and sign painters knew how to design and paint coats of arms, shop signs, portraits, and landscapes, some of which may still be found on the overmantels of eighteenth century houses. There is small question that the portraits of the 1670's which began the development that culminated in the eighteenth century came out of this anonymous and sturdy craftsmanship. Like early American articles of everyday use these portraits reflect a tradition of shop practice which looks back

through Tudor painting to medieval manuscripts and Books of Hours. But they look forward also to our eighteenth century masters, Feke, Copley and Earl.

There is this double aspect in the work of the craftsman who is the bearer of folk memory in the arts. This folk memory, which is amazingly tenacious, is a storehouse of the technical and symbolic innovations of the past, and on more than one occasion has prepared the way for new developments. For this reason the Index of American Design which records American craftsmanship is more than a backward look. There is in it also the Davy Crockett "go ahead principle." It tells the story of creativeness and inventive change when traditional design failed to meet new problems. Dr. Henry Chapman Mercer, in his valuable study of early carpenters' tools, says that American tools do not appear as inventions but as European heirlooms "modified rather than transformed by a new environment." And yet the book in which he makes this statement gives evidence of real transformations. One is that of the American ax whose quality, both as tool and as design, was admired by European visitors to the Philadelphia Centennial in 1876. As early as 1828 Fenimore Cooper had noted the superior form, neatness and "precision of weight" of the American ax. In all previous European axes, with their heavy bits, the weight was poorly distributed so that the ax wobbled in delivering oblique blows and was both tiring and dangerous for the woodsman. Some time between 1744 and 1776 there developed the American ax in which the weight has been distributed so that the poll is heavier than the bit. This new "precision of weight" made the ax steady and much more effective. The thinning of the blade made it easier to withdraw after the blow. Later, in the first half of the nineteenth century came the lean and delicately curved handle. How did these changes come about? Undoubtedly they were stimulated by the needs of an agricultural civilization in a forest frontier where every acre of farmland had to be cleared of trees. Possibly useful hints came from the eastern Pennsylvania wedge-ax which had no cutting edge. Perhaps the two developments came independently. In any event we have here a tool transformed into something more useful and beautiful than anything in its ancestry.

The inventiveness that reshapes forms in response to the needs of a changing environment and the stimulating influence of one tradition upon another is reflected many times in the Index. The Shakers, most austere of our eighteenth and nineteenth century craftsmen, were English immigrants. Their design may be traced to English sources but in its severe integrity in handling materials, its discarding of ornament in favor of unadorned surface and its sense of fitness and function it is as much a forerunner of modern ideas as it is a reflection of the past. Pennsylvania German and Spanish Colonial which are related to peasant art seem further away from us. Yet, in their feeling for surface and their stimulating influence upon our all but lost sense of vivid and clear color in articles of everyday use they have much of value for contemporary designers and craftsmen.

Today we are surrounded by so many and such powerful evidences of mass-production technology that we are apt to forget that this technology was born in a handicraft tradition. The forgetfulness may be an expression of our passion for obsolescence. It is one of the accidents of our history that modern design in the United States has developed in almost complete isolation from traditional craftsman's skills. Here the Index serves in the role of interpreter, calling our attention to the unique and irreplaceable contribution which these skills have made, and may still make, in our culture. We can see many ways in which contemporary design has been influenced by the hand skills of the past. Perhaps we may even be permitted to wonder if in the design of such modern things as the steamboat and the automobile, lustiest offspring of our mass-production economy, we have improved upon the work of the shipwrights and the wagonmakers whom Horatio Greenough admired a hundred years ago. Nikolaus Pevsner has pointed out our tendency to overestimate the contribution of the engineer and underestimate the craftsman and the artist as factors in modern design. We need not follow William Morris and Walter Crane and insist that handicraft is the one true root and base of the arts. But it is no mere Luddism to maintain that the hand skill is one of the main roots. This is true today not only in broad areas of industry which have a craft base, textiles, furniture, ceramics, glass, utensils, printing, and the building trades, but also in design for mass production and in the making of the machine itself.

The wide interest in American craftsmanship that developed in the last quarter of the nineteenth century, and which is part of the ancestry of the Index, was not antiquarian. Men like John Cotton Dana and Henry W. Kent made no separation between the machine and the hand tool but insisted that the machine could become an instrument of man's creative skill in making articles of everyday use—one as sensitive as the hand tool and much more powerful, after it had been fully mastered. But they felt that we must not forget what the craftsman had learned in the dialectic of shop practice, his sympathy with materials and his knowledge of their possibilities and limitations. The Index of American Design is a repository of the skills of craftsmen who thought out their design in the material itself; it may well become a steadying influence and a source of refreshment to the designer who brings his ideas to life on the drawing board and the craftsman who models and tools the pattern.

The Index, as it stands, is the largest and most nearly comprehensive collection of its kind in the world. But it is not complete. The Second World War brought the activities of the project to an end before its work was done in any state and before much had been accomplished in the South. The first need of the Index is completion. The second is a wider distribution of its pictorial information. . . .

The Index has value not only for the designer, the craftsman and the manufacturer, but even more for the historian, the educator, the student and the general public. As the late Constance Rourke, one of the soundest students of American culture, has phrased it: "Not the least of the revelations of the Index may be those offered to the student of American social history. Fresh light may be thrown upon ways of living which developed within the highly diversified communities of our many frontiers, and this may in turn give us new knowledge of the American mind and temperament. Finally, if the materials of the Index can be widely seen they should offer an education of the eye, particularly for young people, which may result in the development of taste and a genuine consciousness of our rich national inheritance."

HOLGER CAHILL

VOLUME

ONE

BOOK ONE

On Land & Sea

BOOK ONE: *On Land & Sea*

Forgotten Figures, Fore & Aft

3

IN COLONIAL TIMES, shipbuilding was vital to maintaining the lifeline between America and England. The industry began in 1607, when the thirty-two-ton pinnace *Virginia* was built at the mouth of the Kennebec River in Maine. The next thirteen years saw only occasional construction of some small craft; but in 1620 the Virginia Company —realizing that this slow progress meant the hiring of foreign hulls, which would considerably diminish profits—decided to import twenty-five professional shipwrights from England. Within eight years, the colony of Massachusetts Bay welcomed a group of six ship carpenters. Similar steps were taken by the French in Canada, the Dutch in New Amsterdam, the Swedes in Delaware, and the English in other ports along the eastern seaboard. By about 1700 the American merchant fleet numbered some fifteen hundred vessels, most of which made their home port in Boston and nearby waters.

1 *The art and skill of the wood-carver are seen in this collection of ships' figureheads, carrousel animals, cigar-store Indians, and other colorful trade characters dating from the last half of the nineteenth century. Photograph by Arnold Newman, courtesy the Smithsonian Institution, Washington, D.C.* **2** *Figurehead, carved of oak, from the American barque* Edinburgh, *by John Rogerson, 1883* **3** *Three quarter-length figure from the clipper ship* Rhine, *c. 1850* **4** *Female bust surmounting scroll and acanthus leaves to form a terminal for the bow of a ship, c. 1790*

4

7

5

5 Carved and painted by Isaac Fowle, noted ship carver of Boston, c. 1850 6 This elaborate bow treatment on the U.S.S. Cincinnati displays the figure of Winged Victory holding above her head an eagle representing Freedom. Figure and eagle are of bronze; arabesque scrolls and dolphins are carved of wood. Late nineteenth century. Photograph courtesy Peabody Museum, Salem, Massachusetts

At the time, no captain would have considered sailing the seven seas in a vessel that did not carry a handsome figurehead at its prow. People of seafaring nations had always demonstrated a desire for this symbolic protection, as if it would appease the fury of the wild seas and the gods above. Egyptian, Phoenician, and Viking craft as well as Roman and Grecian vessels carried these figureheads, which often took the form of animals and serpents, heads of state, or gods and goddesses. Pliny the Elder, the celebrated Roman author, had declared: "A storm may be lulled by a woman uncovering her body at sea."

Early figureheads in the Colonies followed English designs. The majestic British lion, which had decorated such prominent English ships as *Henri-Grace-à-Dieu*, the galleon of Henry VIII, was especially popular.

After 1776 our native carvers, who made their headquarters in the major shipbuilding centers—near the waterfront of India Wharf in Boston, on South Street in New York, or on Front Street in Philadelphia—needed a new vocabulary to express their new-found spirit of independence. The British lion, the coiled serpent, or the fire-breathing dragon gave way to the proud eagle. The figures of Miss Liberty and Columbia replaced the mythological gods and goddesses. Figures of presidents and statesmen, characters from literature and history, as well as ordinary men and women, were placed at the bow.

The carving of figureheads was a highly skilled craft, the training for which was rooted in the old guild system of master, journeyman, and apprentice. The length of the apprentice's service depended upon how quickly he learned and his value in the shop. Most figurehead

6

7

8

7 *Unusually realistic modeling distinguishes this formally gowned female figure from the sloop* Postmaster 8 *Three-quarter-length figure posed in an attitude popular with ship carvers, c. 1840* 9 *Elegantly costumed girl with flowers from the* Creole, *built in 1847* 10 *Female tar holding straw sailor hat and an oar and gowned in Classic costume with finely scrolled bodice, c. 1850*

9   10   11

11

11 *Figurehead of a woman holding a corsage from a West Coast clipper ship, c. 1860. Photograph courtesy Portland Art Museum, Portland, Oregon* 12 *From the sailing ship* White Lady, *this figurehead with pronounced drapery folds is attributed to Charles A. L. Sampson, of Bath, Maine, c. 1870*

carvers whose names have come down to us served an apprenticeship and in turn trained eager youngsters. A list of more than seven hundred carvers has been compiled and authenticated, and, as research continues, more names will undoubtedly be added.

The attitude, size, and position of a ship's figurehead was determined by the limited space under the bowsprit. The early figureheads were almost perpendicular to the water line, whereas in the clipper-ship era the angle of the bowsprit and the water line, and thus of the figurehead, was acute.

The specifications for the figurehead sometimes required that it measure as much as eight feet in height and at least three feet in diameter at its widest point. The mechanical problems presented by such requirements were solved quite ingeniously. Since no single tree trunk could be found which was sufficiently large to enable the carving to be done from a single piece, the block was built from many smaller sections and then carefully joined together by means of trunnels (wooden pegs). The pieces had to be studied to make certain that the grain always ran in the same direction to prevent splintering and facilitate the carving of details.

If a plan called for a figure with outstretched arms, rather than search the forest for a satisfactory trunk and limbs, it was more practical to carve the arms separately and dowel them to the main body with dovetail slip joints. Sometimes these outstretched arms were detachable to avoid damage by storms. They could be removed when the vessel left port and replaced before it entered the next harbor. When ships were eventually broken up for salvage and their fittings sold, arms and other parts of the figureheads were often lost, and many a full-length figure was turned into a three-quarter-length one or truncated torso. Many of the surviving figures now on view at museums take on the appearance of *Venus de Milo*.

In his treatment of figures, particularly of the female figure, the American wood-carver was influenced by the Classic Revival of the early nineteenth century, when Greek and Roman gods and kindred mythological heroes

12

14

13

15 16

13 *From the ship* Indian Princess, *this seven-foot figurehead strikes a pose favored by ship carvers. Tilted head and forward step result from angular position under the bowsprit* **14** *White painted figure for the* Rembrandt *depends on costume for period suggestion.*

15 *American ship carvers were at their best when modeling the female figure* **16** *The Classical pose is based on the marble statue of Artemis at Versailles; from the ship* Cassandra Adams, *built in 1876*

17

18

19

16

17 *This doll-like head from a schooner built at Haverhill, Massachusetts, in 1815, rests on an acanthus scroll* 18 *Female bust, c. 1850 featuring high-styled coiffure. Photograph courtesy New York State Historical Association, Cooperstown* 19 *Severe dress and hairdo of mid-nineteenth-century figurehead* 20 *Despite contemporary costume, this austere beauty is reminiscent of Classical Greek and Roman statuary; from the ship* Henrietta Francis, *built in 1883* 21 *Half-length female figure, carved in Maine between 1825 and 1840*

were in vogue. Many figures were draped in toga-like costumes. Sometimes a head was derived from one Classic type and the pose of the body from another. The soft edges and rounded forms of the drapery of Neoclassical marbles became sharpened edges when carved in the soft-grained pine used for the figureheads. Working with the grain, the carver used his chisels and gouges to perfect a linear pattern of swirls and folds.

If the figure was full length, it was generally detached from the hull and often depicted in an attitude of stepping forward, head erect, with the wind blowing the drapery into graceful folds.

Figureheads were often images of the wife or daughter of a shipowner. The following is an extract from Longfellow's poem "The Building of the Ship":

And at the bows an image stood,
By a cunning artist carved in wood,
With robes of white, that far behind
Seemed to be fluttering in the wind.
It was not shaped in a classic mould,
Not like a Nymph or Goddess of old,
Or Naiad rising from the water,
But modelled from the Master's daughter!

In addition to those wearing Classical costumes, there were figures dressed in the most up-to-date fashions of their time and adorned with the latest coiffures as illustrated in *Godey's* or *Sartain's* magazines.

The figures were robust and buxom, in keeping with the sturdy vessels for which they were designed, and were given a proud patrician bearing. With raised chins and upright postures, they gazed straight ahead at the distant horizon.

Male figureheads depicted presidents, celebrated statesmen, military heroes, shipowners, or Indians. Many of the images of George Washington, Andrew Jackson, Daniel Webster, Benjamin Franklin, and Commodore Perry are superb examples of folk-art carving carried out with skill and taste.

A figurehead of Tamanend, the chief of the Delaware tribe, was carved for the U.S.S.

20

21

22

23

22 *Mid-nineteenth-century female bust* 23 *This head, with its extreme forward thrust, avoids the static pose of upright figures* 24 *Decorative effect in this female portrait bust is enhanced by hairdo, jewelry, and supporting structure* 25 *Ornamental details of coiffure, dress trimmings, and scroll enrich this female figure* 26 *Forward motion is strongly suggested in the attitude of this head* 27 *Half-length figure from the whaler* Marcia, *built in 1832, suggests Classical inspiration* 28 *Unusual drapery treatment characterizes this half-length figure* 29 *A type of female figurehead that was a great favorite with sailors*

24

25

26

27

28

29

Delaware in 1820 by William Luke of Portsmouth, Virginia. This half-length figure rises out of a decorative scroll and a wreath of ivy. The carving of the bust shows a strong and masterful technique, in character more like academic sculpture than folk art. The forcefully delineated figure is thoroughly American, an impression that is reinforced by the inclusion of the sheath of arrows and pipe and dagger placed in the belt. The Massachusetts-built frigate *Boston* had at its prow an Indian holding a bow and arrow.

Many of the figures, especially those of three-quarter length, called for a transitional base, as the head could not spring directly from the cutwater. Scrolled volutes well clothed in floriated acanthus leaves seemed to offer the most acceptable foil between figure and hull. This type of transition became a standard device of the period.

Bustheads seem to have developed from leaf-and-scroll decoration. Carved drapery often served as the transition between the bust and the scroll. In some works, no transitional device was needed because the drapery provided a finish to the arms below the shoulders.

An excellent bust of Benjamin Franklin is attributed to William Rush (1756–1833), the son of a carver. Rush also carved a magnificent statue of George Washington, which is now in Independence Hall, Philadelphia. A life-size wooden bust of Captain Morris, the only piece bearing Rush's signature, shows superior detailing of the facial features.

While wandering along the wharves near Joshua Humphrey's shipyards, Rush saw two French frigates undergoing repairs, *La Danaë* and *La Gloria*. In France at the time of Colbert, a school with a distinguished staff had been organized for the training of ship carvers. The school's standards and tradition, of which the figureheads on these vessels were examples, were considered especially fine. Rush was deeply impressed by the gay and lifelike quality of the heads. The influence these notable French carvings had on him can be clearly seen in his figurehead of George Washington for the ship *Washington*. The figure has been described as "large as life . . . exhibiting a

capital likeness . . . in full uniform as commander-in-chief, pointing with his finger at some distant object and holding a perspective glass grasped in his left hand." Another of Rush's figureheads, an Indian trader made for the ship *William Penn*, created a great stir when viewed at the London wharves. Rush's complete mastery of his medium marks him as America's pioneer sculptor in wood, an honor recognized by his contemporaries who selected him to be the first president of the Pennsylvania Academy of Fine Arts.

Simeon Skillin, Sr. (1716–1778), of Boston, was another noted figurehead carver. In 1767 Skillin carved a fine head of William Pitt for the Sons of Liberty in Dedham, Massachusetts. Skillin's sons, John, Samuel, and Simeon, Jr., also became carvers, as did his grandson, who in 1808 was a partner in Skillin & Dodge in New York, carving trail boards for the U.S.S. *Constitution*.

One of the great names among American carvers is that of Samuel McIntire (1757–1811) of Salem, Massachusetts. McIntire was also a trained architect and cabinetmaker. The homes he built in Salem, many of which can still be seen today, attest to his skill, taste, and versatility. By virtue of his technical background, he was a precise and meticulous craftsman, exhibiting none of the spontaneous traits of the folk artist. Today we have only one piece of ship carving that can be ascribed to McIntire, although many of his sketches and designs for stern decorations have been preserved. Many eagle figureheads were undoubtedly his handiwork; they exhibit characteristics similar to those seen in the fine detailing of his architectural decorations.

John Bellamy (1836–1914), a carver who had a shop at Kittery, Maine, across the river from the busy seaport of Portsmouth, New Hampshire, is famed for glorifying our national

30 *Carved by Charles A. L. Sampson, of Bath, Maine, this full-length figurehead from the* Belle of Oregon *is a companion in style to that of the* Belle of Bath **31** *In 1877 ship carver Sampson modeled this figure for the* Belle of Bath, *dressing his lady in modish Victorian costume. This fashionplate in wood created a sensation in its day*

30

31

21

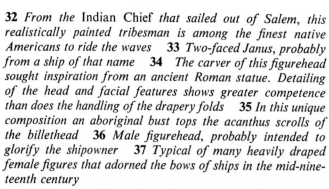

32 *From the* Indian Chief *that sailed out of Salem, this realistically painted tribesman is among the finest native Americans to ride the waves* **33** *Two-faced Janus, probably from a ship of that name* **34** *The carver of this figurehead sought inspiration from an ancient Roman statue. Detailing of the head and facial features shows greater competence than does the handling of the drapery folds* **35** *In this unique composition an aboriginal bust tops the acanthus scrolls of the billethead* **36** *Male figurehead, probably intended to glorify the shipowner* **37** *Typical of many heavily draped female figures that adorned the bows of ships in the mid-nineteenth century*

32

33

34

35

36

37

38   39

38 *From the packet* Commodore Perry, *built in
New York in 1832, this portrait bust of Perry
shows the hand of a competent craftsman* 39 *Indian chieftain Tamanend was mounted at the prow
of the U.S.S.* Delaware, *launched at Norfolk in
1820. The unusually fine characterization and
detailing are the work of William Luke of Portsmouth, Virginia* 40 *Half-length figurehead enriched by the detailing of costume and waistcoat*
41 *Portrait bust, probably representing the shipowner, and featuring an unusually handsome
combination of tastefully modeled decorative
volutes and leaf forms*

symbol, the American eagle. He made hundreds of fine eagles for the navy and commercial shipbuilders, each bearing his unmistakable marks: finely chiseled head and beak,
stylized feather forms, and concave wings often
adorned with flowing ribbons, pennants, and
shields. Bellamy's masterpiece is the gigantic
(eighteen-foot wingspread) eagle for the U.S.S.
Lancaster, now at the Mariners' Museum,
Newport News, Virginia.

The design of a figurehead usually involved
elaborate discussions between carver and shipbuilder. Instructions and sketches were sent
through the mails if the builder was not in the
immediate vicinity. An enlightening piece of

40   41

correspondence concerning the figurehead for the clipper ship *Western World* is included among the papers of the Boston shipbuilders Fernald and Pettigrew. On March 6, 1850, S. W. Gleason and Sons, ship carvers, wrote as follows:

Gentlemen

Your favor of the 5th inst is at hand together with the sketch of the head of the *Western World*, for which we are greatly obliged to you & which no doubt will be of some assistance to us in regard to thickness of cut water &c &c. You have sent us the rake of the stem & steve of bowsprit: if you will

please let us know about the distance you want the upper-side of lower cheek from the underside of bowsprit on the line of the stem, & the distance you want the figure to set out on the line of the bowsprit, and the distance out on the bowsprit of the inner bobstay, we shall be able to furnish a draft on a scale to set the head by: or perhaps it would be better if you would lay the model on a sheet of paper & mark the line of the stem & the shear of the wale streak, this is necessary as the butt end of the lower cheek should start on a parallel line, & for billet heads generally starts from the same line but may be carried lower, where a greater distance is

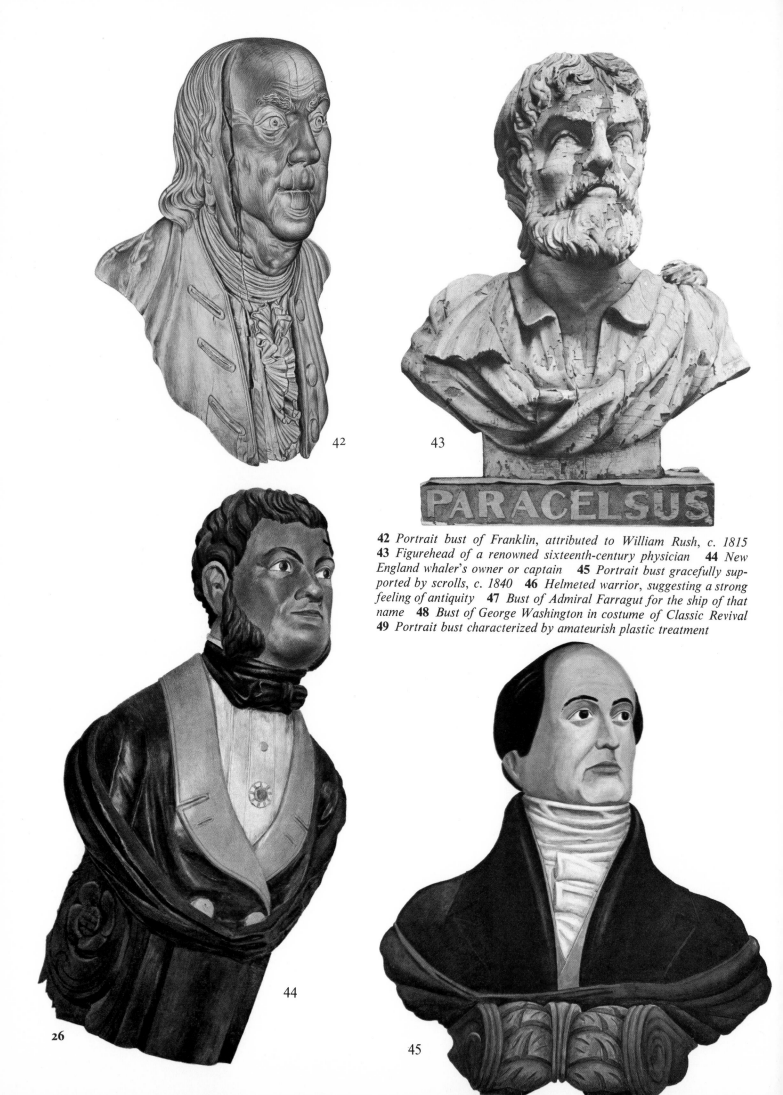

42 *Portrait bust of Franklin, attributed to William Rush, c. 1815*
43 *Figurehead of a renowned sixteenth-century physician* 44 *New England whaler's owner or captain* 45 *Portrait bust gracefully supported by scrolls, c. 1840* 46 *Helmeted warrior, suggesting a strong feeling of antiquity* 47 *Bust of Admiral Farragut for the ship of that name* 48 *Bust of George Washington in costume of Classic Revival* 49 *Portrait bust characterized by amateurish plastic treatment*

42

43

PARACELSUS

44

26

45

46

47

48

49

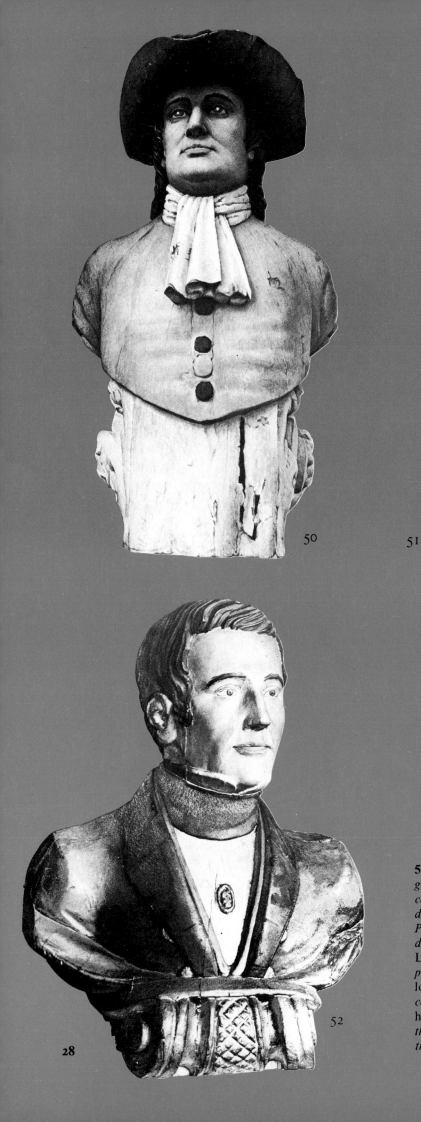

50   51

52

50 *Quaker portrait bust in which features and costume suggest an appropriate sternness*   **51** *Figure of an Elizabethan courtier with strong period connotation in the decorative details of costume*   **52** *Portrait bust of the shipowner Solomon Piper, exemplifying straightforward portraiture except for decorative treatment of the hair*   **53** *Huge head for the ship Lord Percy, built in 1848, featuring a decorated crown and plumes*   **54** *Figurehead for the New Bedford whaler Bartholomew Gosnold; a small vessel, the whaling ship often carried a bust or half-length figure*   **55** *From the ship Abraham Lincoln, c. 1860. While the bust fails in portraiture, the speaker's upraised arm and scroll succeed in conveying the orator in action*

53

54

wanted for a figure. In answer to your question about the size of the figure we would say that the figure should look the size of life after it is on & would have to be in reality 3 or 5 in taller, the standard height among Artists is for a female 5 feet 3 in—suppose we make the figure 5 feet 6 in & the block or scroll as small as possible say 7 in—extreme length of whole 6 feet 1 inch; how will that do? We can furnish you with a beautiful stern piece of shell work similar to the one you saw us at work upon, & if you wish for extra work in the centre—figures or any thing of that kind, we can substitute them for a part of the shell work—unless you should, we shall go right at work upon the stern as soon as we get the dimensions. We have no doubt that you can have the figure before the first of July.

By the closing years of the nineteenth century, the need for figurehead carvers had diminished, and many of these men turned to carving cigar-store Indians, shop and tavern signs, cabinets, picture frames, and architectural details.

55

From Stem to Stern,

the Skill of the Craftsman

57

58

MARINE DECORATION encompasses a multitude of ship parts beyond the figurehead, including sternpieces, taffrails, trail' boards, paddle-wheel covers, billetheads, catheads, and gangway boards.

The huge galleons, frigates, and men-of-war of the European navies were heavily orna-mented, in keeping with naval traditions, and this practice was followed in this country through the middle of the eighteenth century. Studies of records, models, and ship plans indicate that such ships as *America, Raleigh, Hancock, Rattlesnake,* and *Confederacy* were richly adorned.

The galleries, transom, and quarters at the

56 *Carved and gilded stern decorations of the U.S.S.* Raleigh, *one of thirteen frigates ordered by the Continental Congress and built in Portsmouth, New Hampshire, in 1776. Ornamental details were probably carved by Thomas Deering, who portrayed Sir Walter Raleigh in the* figurehead. *Photograph by Mark Sexton, courtesy Peabody Museum, Salem, Massachusetts* **57** *Trail-board decoration for the U.S.S.* Constellation, *built in 1794–95* **58** *Gangway board carved from an oaken plank*

56

sterns of eighteenth-century ships were given lavish ornamental treatment. The areas above, below, and around the fenestrated sections of the stern were carved with allegorical figures entwined with festoons, scrolls, and assorted flora and fauna.

Eventually the gallery and fenestration were replaced by the solid stern, providing the carver with a large flat area for ornamentation. Typical subjects depicted on sternpieces included an allegorical figure in a sculptural setting with minor accessories, a statesman surrounded by his tools of office, a shipowner's wife dressed in her Sunday best, and an American Indian with trophies of the hunt. The border of the decorated sternpiece was lightly ornamented with scrolls and acanthus leaves. Occasionally architectural devices were employed, such as the egg and dart or beaded borders as moldings for outer edges.

Throughout the nineteenth century, the most popular motif used on sternpieces was the American eagle. It stood alone or was combined with ribbons, sunbursts, crossed flags, or shields. The shield consisted of a star-studded field with alternating red and white stripes below. The number of stars did not correspond to the number of states in the Union; their function was purely decorative. The formal pose of the eagle followed that on the Great Seal, with wings raised, the talons clutching arrows and the olive branch, and the accompanying ribbon bearing the legend *E Pluribus Unum* or the name of the vessel. The spread-eagle pose was wonderfully adapted to the shape and form of the horizontal stern, the average width of which ranged from eight to ten feet. A famous eagle sternpiece, carved by J. Nabor in 1870 for the sailing vessel *Columbia*, measured twenty feet across.

The eagle was also often placed on top of a ship's pilothouse as a freestanding element. Pilothouse eagles became so popular that eventually there was large-scale production of the birds in varying sizes, and they were kept in stock by many carvers. Eagles decorated pilothouses until well into the twentieth century, when they were replaced by the electric searchlight.

The trail boards, long, narrow boards on the sides of the cutwater near the figurehead, were decorated with scrolls and leafy foliations

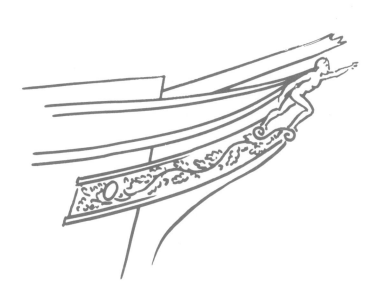

and were carved with the vessel's name. The lettering was usually incised below the surface and gilded to contrast with the black background for greatest legibility.

The end of the cathead, the member projecting out from the ship's forward quarters to which the anchor is hoisted and secured, was also ornamented, generally with a lion's head. This ornament was first carved in wood and later cast in iron.

The paddle wheels of the steam-propelled riverboats of the mid-nineteenth century were covered to prevent water from being thrown on the deck. At first, only the vessel's name ornamented the paddle-wheel cover, but soon other motifs came into use, including sunbursts, radial designs emanating from the center of the lunette, and, in more ambitious compositions, themes using groups of allegorical figures. Eagles, peacocks, and other birds were also used.

The billethead, a graceful scroll not unlike that found on Ionic and Corinthian capitals, was sometimes used instead of the figurehead at a ship's prow. The largest ones were six feet long, or longer, while those made for smaller vessels, such as the bark, brig, or cutter, might be less than a foot in length. The terminal of the scroll was usually embellished with a rosette or quatrefoil, while out of its deep grooves there sprouted smaller scrolls or a flowering of acanthus leaves.

The billethead often replaced a ship's original figurehead after it had been damaged at sea or lost in a naval engagement. When the frigate *Constitution* fought Barbary pirates off the coast of Tripoli in 1803, she was damaged and her figurehead was shattered. Commodore Preble ordered his ship put in for repairs at Malta, where "nine carpenters came on board . . . employed this forenoon in taking down the figurehead which is cut to pieces and thrown away as useless." Shortly thereafter, the first lieutenant reported to his superior that "the cutwater and billethead will be finished within six or seven days."

As we view these relics from famous ships, we are better able to comprehend the spirit of the nation and its naval heroes and to more clearly understand our maritime past and the part that vessels of all kinds have played in the creation of the American free-enterprise system.

59

Proud Symbol
at the Prow

60

61

59 *Flat board treatment shows unusual twist to eagle's head, enriched by stylized feather detailing* **60** *Gigantic eagle head carved of pine* **61** *Pine eagle figurehead from the schooner Nellie G., in posture of a Gothic gargoyle* **62** *Decorative effect achieved by deep cutting and styling of neck feathers* **63** *Eagle figurehead from the* Great Republic, *launched at Boston in 1853. Carved by either S. W. or William B. Gleason* **64** *In this eagle figurehead the neck feathers terminate abruptly with scroll decorations extending to the trail board*

62

63

64

65

66

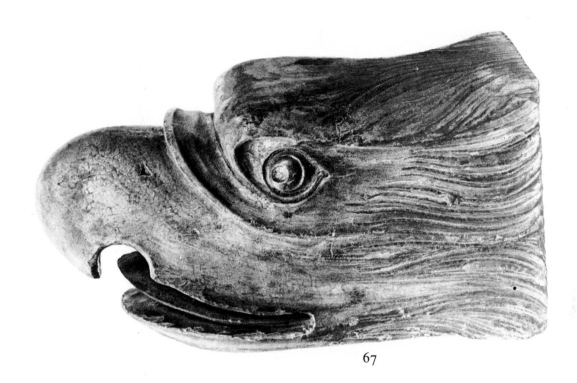

67

65 *Huge eagle head, carved of pine in 1850* **66** *Eagle head with unusually long, sharp beak, carved in 1850* **67** *Carved pine eagle head with distinctive eyes and short beak* **68** *Figurehead of the late clipper-ship era, in which the scroll, extending from the lower beak, introduces a graceful, flowing line*

68

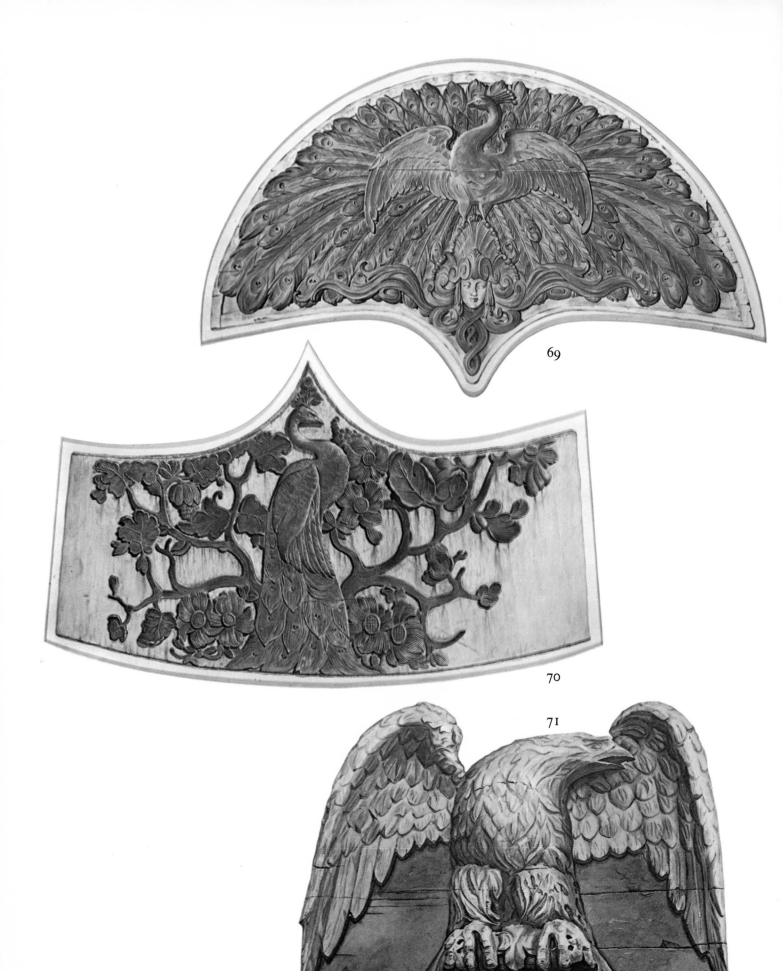

69

70

71

38

72

73

74

69 *Gracefully shaped panel typical of decorations on many sterns and steamboat paddle boxes, c. 1865–90* **70** *Peacock and surrounding embellishment form unique stern piece* **71** *The eagle was the ship carver's favorite motif* **72** *Stern board decoration, attributed to John Bellamy, noted wood-carver of Kittery, Maine, whose eagle carvings reduce the bird's anatomy to a decorative shorthand* **73** *Eagle, flags, and shield were a collective motif popular with carvers of stern pieces* **74** *Pine planks of great width provided the ideal carving surface for the eagle motif, which was invariably gilded and polychromed*

75

76

77

78

79

80

75 Mammoth stern-board eagle and shield, measuring twenty feet across, from the sailing vessel Columbia. *Carved in 1870 by J. Nabor of New Orleans* **76** *Semicircular paddle-wheel case from the vessel* Our Island Home **77** *Spread eagle with ribbon in its beak functioning as background for motto* E Pluribus Unum **78** *Stern piece from the U.S.S.* Enterprise, *carved in 1881* **79** *Pine stern piece or paddle-wheel case measuring seven feet across* **80** *Stern piece of shallow proportions necessitated this squatty composition*

81

82

83

84

85

86

87

88

81 *Spread eagle with scroll decoration on the stern piece of a small late nineteenth-century schooner*
82 *Realism rather than stylization characterizes the feather treatment of this eagle* **83** *Pilothouse eagle perched on high, with huge and dominating wingspread* **84** *Curvilinear lines of wings add grace to this pine eagle, c. 1875* **85** *Unusually sharp, pointed wings accentuating width* **86** *Fully modeled feather details and talons* **87** *Eagle of unusual design with wings as mere appendages* **88** *Downward thrust of eagle's head simulates attack in this cast-iron specimen, c. 1860*

89

90

91

89 *Pronounced feather delineation marks this pilothouse eagle from the Hudson River steamboat* Mary Powell. *Carved by J. Bowers in 1861. Photograph courtesy New York Historical Society, New York City* 90 *Pilothouse eagle, 1850–60, from the Great Lakes steamer S.S.* Anderson 91 *Front view of figure 90* 92 *Pilothouse eagle, perched on beehive, with sharp, V-cut incisions typical of the wood-carver's technique* 93 *Such a spread eagle's structure required reinforcements on the upper wing side* 94 *Eagle's body carved from a solid piece of pine, wings inserted as separate members and reinforced with iron bars*

92

93

94

95

Billetheads

&

Fiddleheads

96

97

98

99

95–102 The billethead, a piece of ornamental wood carving usually fitted into the stemhead of the bow under the bowsprit, has been an integral element in marine decoration for centuries. Its use probably came about when time or cost did not permit the design of a figurehead. It was referred to as a fiddlehead when the scroll turned upward, and as a scrollhead when the volute turned outward. Billethead decoration includes dominant scrolls or volutes, C-curves, acanthus-leaf foliage, and rosettes. These elements were often beautifully arranged and vigorously carved in a Baroque manner, then gilded and polychromed. Billetheads were in general use from 1830 to 1880

100

101

102

103

104

105

103 *Stern-board decoration from the ship Po-cohontas* **104** *Stern piece with pictorial composition indicating that the shipowner was a scholar* **105** *Stern-board decoration combining symbols of antiquity and floral elements* **106, 107** *Scrimshaw, the scratching or engraving of designs on the surface of a whale's tooth, was practiced by seafaring men on long voyages.*

Nineteenth-century New England whalers, especially those from Nantucket and New Bedford, brought back engravings depicting foreign ports, ships, and marine subjects. Indigenous to America, the technique is regarded as a unique whaling folk art **108–111** *Whalers and whaling scenes, clipper ships, side-wheelers, and seacoast towns, all popular subjects in scrimshaw*

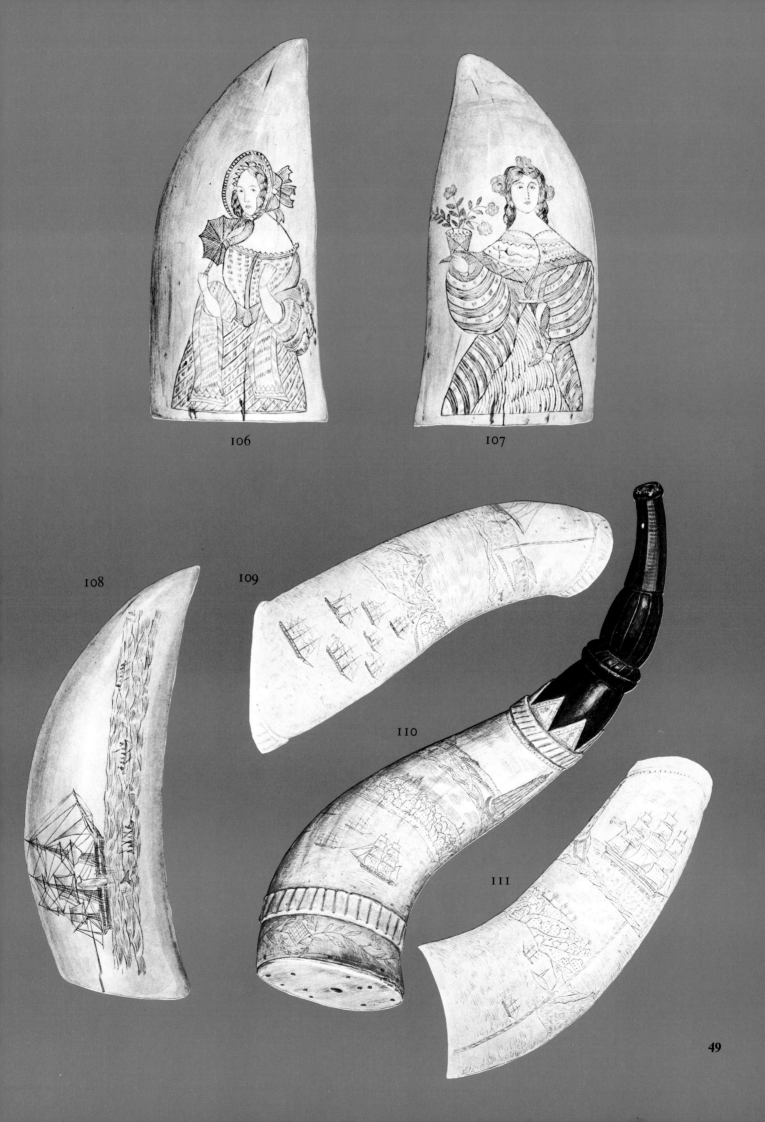

106

107

108

109

110

111

49

112

113

The Tobacconists' Tribe
of Braves & Squaws

TRADESMAN'S SIGNS and symbols, designed as eye-catchers to lure the passerby into shop or tavern, have been with us as long as recorded history. The familiar barber pole, whose spiraling red and white stripes originated in the Middle Ages, the pawn-broker's sign of three balls, the hanging shoe to mark the cobbler's shop, and the watch to show the jeweler's establishment—all indicate the power of symbols over words. The earliest American signs are also interesting visual reminders of how branded merchandise, which has so strongly molded our present-day buying

112 *Indian princess wearing a costume typical of the cigar-store Indian: feather headdress and girdle and a fringed buckskin tunic, to which a beaded necklace and metal breast plate add color. In her right hand she holds a plug of tobacco and in her left, a bunch of cigars*

113 *In contrast to the mild-mannered face of the squaw, there was often a suggestion of feroc-ity in the face of a chieftain* 114 *Modeling of the face and headdress represented the carver's greatest opportunity to demonstrate his skill*

114

habits, had its humble origins.

Carved wooden figures of tradesmen existed in the Colonies as early as 1720, when there appeared a shop figure of a short, stocky gentleman clad in blue coat, red vest, knee breeches, and buckled shoes. His belt, which is inscribed "1720," shows that he antedates by more than a half century the ubiquitous cigar-store Indians who later proclaimed the tobacconist's wares. This early figure was the work of a professional craftsman who, judging from the competence of his handiwork, had evidently received some academic training. Another noted figure of the eighteenth century was the so-called Little Admiral of 1770, who marked the establishment of William Williams, a maker of mathematical instruments in Boston. Frequent reference is made to a 1770 tobacconist figure that stood outside the shop of Christopher Demuth in Lancaster, Pennsylvania. There is no firm description available of its appearance, and indeed, it was described quite differently by several noted writers. One wrote of the figure as "a mild-mannered savage that did not inspire terror"; another, of a "delicate Colonial gentleman tendering a snuff box." Whatever the facts about the gentleman's features, the date, although isolated, is important in our story.

When and where the first cigar-store figure appeared has not been accurately determined. Well-founded conjecture seems to point to a London tobacconist's shop early in the eighteenth century, when the growing habit of taking snuff brought prosperity to the tobacco trade. (Tobacco did not become an important article of commerce until long after Sir Walter Raleigh introduced it into England by way of the Colonies, and snuff could only be bought in an apothecary shop.) With the establishment of the Virginia plantations and the West Indies

trade, the tobacco habit caught on, and many retail shops were opened during the reign of Queen Anne.

At this time the first wooden Indians in England, used to designate tobacco shops, were called "black boys" because of their resemblance to the young black slaves imported to her colonies from Jamaica. It may be that these wooden figures were never intended to represent Indians at all, for the tobacco industry in America depended heavily on the work of slaves imported from Africa.

As the tobacco trade between the United States and Britain grew, British retailing and merchandising techniques were introduced to American tobacconists. The "black boy" became a full-blooded American Indian, starting a clan whose progeny were to dot the streets of American towns and villages. As the smoking of "segars" by men grew more popular, thousands of retail shops sprang up, each displaying some form of wooden Indian. Many of these figures were permanently bolted into position at the shopfront; others were mounted on wheels so that they could be rolled in at night, because vandals singled out these Indians as special targets.

The use of Indians as the most accepted advertising symbol for retail tobacconists began in the 1840s. The first one of undisputed pedigree stood at the shopfront of D. H. McAlpin, on Catherine Street in New York City, in 1840. Squat and swarthy yet impressive in mien, this figure was removed by its owner when he relocated in 1866. For many years it withstood the vicissitudes of time, hail, rain, snow, and Civil War draft riots, ending its career as the tutelary spirit of the cigar counter at the Hotel McAlpin.

In 1856 an advertisement placed in a New York newspaper by Edward Hen, a tobacconist, shows him to be the first to stock Indian figures as part of his inventory. Dozens of figures, the work of various carvers, were sold by his store on Liberty Street.

Eventually the wooden figures followed the westward movement to distant points across the nation. In the Midwest, particularly Wisconsin, Illinois, and Michigan, Germans, Swiss, and Danes developed a considerable industry supplying the needs of tobacconists. Julius Theodore Melchers of Detroit, father of the painter Gari Melchers, became well known in this new field. Julius had learned the trade of ship carver in his native Denmark and produced a few figureheads for the dwindling Great Lakes trade before realizing that greater opportunities existed. His early carvings of Indian figures soon caught the attention of buyers and brought premium prices, for they showed outstanding strength and character.

The craft of carving tobacconist Indians fell naturally into the hands of ship carvers, whose figurehead business all but disappeared toward the close of the nineteenth century with the end of the clipper-ship era. One of the earliest accounts of the making of cigar-store figures, based largely on the reminiscences of S. A. Robb, who conducted a successful business in carving, was written by Frank Weitenkampf for the *New York Times* of August 3, 1890. This was Robb's procedure:

The wood used is generally white pine, which is bought in logs of various lengths at the spar yards. The artist begins by making the roughest kind of an outline—a mere suggestion of what the proportions of the figure are to be. In this he is guided by paper patterns. The log is blocked out with the axe into appropriate spaces for the head, the body down to the waist, the portion from

there to the knee, the rest of the legs (which are at once divided), and the feet.

A hole is now bored into each end of the prepared log about five inches deep; into each of these holes an iron bolt is placed, the projecting parts of which rest on supports, so that the body hangs free. The carver now goes from the general to the particular. The surface of the wood soon becomes chipped up by the chisel, and the log generally takes on more definite form. Then, when the figure is completely evolved, the finishing touches are put on with finer carving tools. Detached hands and arms are made separately and joined on to the body by screws. Then the various portions of the figure are painted, the whole is set upon a stand running on wheels, and it is ready for delivery.

How did the wood-carver arrive at his interpretation of the facial features? What were his models and techniques? This interesting query cannot be answered fully, for diaries and anecdotal references provide only sketchy information. Fine Indian photographs were not available in numbers, and living Indians were seldom seen in the cities except in an occasional traveling circus. Crude engravings in the popular magazines, such as *Harper's, Leslie's*, and *Ballou's*, were based on reportorial sketches and were rarely accurate. Few books or portfolios of illustrations existed, although George Catlin's lithographic gallery of Indian portraits did run into many editions and could be consulted at leading libraries in the larger cities. Thus we must conclude that the carvers arrived at a stereotype by experimenting until they hit upon a successful image, and then repeated it. What the face may have lacked in ferocity was often compensated for in buckskin costume, dagger, tomahawk, or other accou-

115

116

117

115–126 *The variety of wooden Indian types was greatly influenced by the romantic image created in popular nineteenth-century prints, engravings, and lithographs, and especially by the novels of James Fenimore Cooper. Indian tribes such as the Pequot and the Iroquois of New England, the Shawnee and Chippewa of the Midwest, and the Shoshoni and Navajo farther west contributed to the iconographic lore available to the carvers. Documentation on these figures is vague; rarely is the date or make's name known. Although they were made from about*

118

119

120

121

122

123

1850 to the close of the century, it is generally agreed that the carving of tobacconists' Indians reached its peak in the 1890s. Some cast-metal figures appeared in the late eighties; they were expensive but, because of their weight, were not as easily stolen as the wooden Indians. Figure 124 is of cast zinc, with a wrought-iron bow. The heroic pose of the chieftain returning from the hunt (119) is unique

124

125

126

55

127

128

129

130

131

132

133

134

135

127–136 *The catalog of Indian types advertised by the carvers included scouts, hunting chiefs, or "Captain Jacks," whose heads were shaven except for a scalp lock. Figures* **128, 133,** *and* **134** *show scouting chiefs;* **127,** *called "Chief with Musket," is from a series made in Marion, Ohio. The cigar-store Indian became so well established as the tobacconist's symbol that it was quite unnecessary to show the product, but a bunch of cigars or a cigar box was generally depicted in an extended hand*

136

137

138

139

137–148 *The popular image created by the carvers in their female figures was a glorified version of the Indian maiden—a stereotype that bore little resemblance to reality. The chubby characters depicted in 138 and 141 depend solely upon headdress and costume for their Indian identity. The shapely squaws in 142 and 147, wearing belted*

140

141

142

143

144

145

dresses and high-button shoes, were not to be found in Indian villages. Occasionally, the squaw was depicted carrying her papoose (144). An unusual pose (139) shows a squaw with crossed legs. The position with the left leg resting on an extra block (148) may be traced to the influence of ship carvers

146

147

148

149

150

151

152

153

154

156

HOUGHTALING SPORTING GOODS

GUNS AND AMMUNITION

155

157

158

149–158 *The technique of chiseling the Indian figure from a large, solid tree trunk necessitated that the arms be kept close to the body. If the design called for an upraised or extended arm, this member was carved as a separate unit and then screwed into position at the shoulder point. In* **150** *and* **152,** *front and profile views of an unusually vigorous figure are shown. Figure* **157** *is dated 1850 or earlier;* **149** *is dated 1875*

terments aimed at heightening credibility. The result was a folklore Indian type, like those immortalized by James Fenimore Cooper and other American writers.

Tobacconist figures fall into four categories: Chiefs, Squaws or Pocahontases, Blackamoors or Pompeys, and White Men. Indians, both male and female, predominated, and thus the term "cigar-store Indian" became the generic name for all types of tobacconist figures. Chiefs appeared in a variety of dress and head-gear, including the fully dressed Seminole type with plumed headdress as seen in George Catlin's portrait of Osceola. Braves were also divided into categories: an Indian with his hand shading his eyes was a "scout"; one holding a gun or bow and arrow was a "hunting chief"; if his head was shaved except for

159

159 *In shops where numbers of cigar-store figures were carved, the trade term White Men was used to designate figures other than Indians. This figure, called "The Dude," was made about 1890* **160** *Highland chief, in tartan kilt, bonnet, brown jacket with gold epaulettes, and fur sporran with animal's head, may have marked the shop of a Scottish tobacconist*

160

161

the scalp lock, he was a "Captain Jack."

The White Men, so called to distinguish them from Red Men, included Scots; British officers with high bearskin shakos or small fatigue caps; heavy swells of Civil War days with long, flowing side whiskers (called dundrearies) and generously wide trousers; Dolly Vardens in skirts with panniers and hats tilted forward on high headdresses; Punches with the hooked nose, protuberant chin, and hump; Columbines with skirts alarmingly short for the times. The list also includes the conventional plantation Negro with a wide expanse of shirt collar; grave Turks and sultanas; Yankee Doodle; Columbia; warlike Zouaves and other American Civil War types, such as cavalrymen; gallants of the period sporting Prince Albert cutaways and marvelous panta-

164

162

163

161 *Belle of the 1890s with lower limbs displayed and skirt uplifted represented a daring departure in its day* **162** *Scotchman in tartan kilt offers a pinch of snuff to the passerby* **163** *Figure of Judy dressed as a clown, with smiling painted face and turned-in toes* **164** *Punch, with jovial expression and gay attitude, wearing a cornucopia hat and clown's outfit with a ruff*

165

166

167

64   168   169

170

171

165 *Tradesman's figure of Henry Clay. Photograph courtesy Downtown Gallery, New York* 166 *The Bandmaster, who stood in front of a cigar store in Coldwater, Michigan, in 1865, was voted first citizen of the town when the village was incorporated* 167 *Made in 1868 by the well-known carver Julius Melchers, this Scotchman stood outside Tom Dick's saloon* 168 *Blackamoor, c. 1870, was a popular subject as were minstrels and jockeys* 169 *Carved in 1770, possibly by Simeon Skillin, Sr., the Little Admiral stood in front of the Crown Coffee House on Long Wharf in Boston* 170 *Navigator, with a huge sextant, is from the shop of nautical instrument-maker James Fales, of New Bedford, Massachusetts, c. 1850* 171 *Figure of a girl c. 1880* 172 *Familiar figure of Punch, rotund and jovial, with hooked nose and protruding chin, and gaily clad in costume with large ruff*

172

65

loons; racetrack touts and Bowery belles equipped with bustles in the height of fashion; baseball players; sailors; firemen; policemen; and even sculptured likenesses of the shop proprietors.

The heyday of the Indian passed with the nineties. Changing fashions and current events fired the carvers with fresh inspiration. There was an outburst of dudes and dandies, and at the time of the Spanish-American War, Rough Riders and statues of Admiral Dewey became popular.

The closing years of the nineteenth century witnessed a gradual decline in the production of wooden figures. New ordinances by meddlesome local governments branded them traffic obstructions and ordered them off the sidewalks. One by one they were hauled inside, where they lost their original purpose; some were carted off to city junkheaps or consigned to log piles for firewood. From an estimated total of about seventy-five thousand, the tribe has now dwindled to a handful of survivors. The wooden Indian, like his prototype, has been put on a reservation—in his case an honored spot in a museum or a treasured position in a private collection. *Requiescat in pace!*

173

175

173–176 Just as the tobacconists adopted the Indian to symbolize cigars and snuff, mid-nineteenth century tea shops and importers used the Chinaman and Oriental women to advertise goods imported from the Orient **177** *Carved figure holding a bunch of grapes, probably used in a wine merchant's shop* **178** *Military and naval men were among the figures used on shop fronts; this one, c. 1870* **179** *Ship chandlers and instrument shops used figures like this to symbolize their trade* **180** *Female figure, probably used in a women's apparel or millinery shop* **181** *Unique among eighteenth-century signboards is this manacled felon (c. 1775) that was placed over the door of a jail in East Greenwich, Rhode Island, serving as a warning that "crime does not pay"* **182** *Minstrel or house servant, used outside a tavern to welcome wayfarers*

Overleaf: GALLERY OF TOBACCONIST FIGURES. *Figures 195, 199, 212, and 221 from photographs*

174

176

177   178   179

180   181   182

183   184   185   186   187

188   189   190   191   192

193   194   195   196   197

198   199   200   201   202

203   204   205   206   207

208   209   210   211   212

213   214   215   216   217

218   219   220   221   222

69

224

225

Signs of the Times
for Shops & Taverns

IT IS DIFFICULT to pinpoint when and where shop signs and trade symbols first appeared on the American scene. As soon as the early settlers established themselves and satisfied their most primitive needs, it was natural for them to open shops and tradesmen's establishments. The first of these appeared in the coastal settlements of New England, in Philadelphia, and in Virginia. A glance down the main street of a typical eighteenth-century town would reveal the apothecary, shoemaker, hatter, and saddler; the joiner, cabinetmaker, barber, and tanner; the grain dealer, ship's merchant, chemist, and tavernkeeper. As a town's population increased, competition set in and people no longer had only a single shopkeeper to whom to turn. As a community developed, it became necessary for tradesmen to announce their locations and, if possible, to attract trade for their goods and services by some distinctive sign or device. The visible sign, symbol, or shop figure thus became a means of bringing the consumer and purveyor together; this was the first step in a merchandising process destined to grow.

223 *Late eighteenth-century signboard outside Chowning's Tavern, a typical Colonial alehouse. Photograph courtesy Colonial Williamsburg* 224 *Shield-shaped medallion with crossed sword and bugle that decorated a gate on Salem common; made by Samuel McIntire, c. 1800* 225

Tavern sign, 1800–1820, features shield and grapevine years before this motif became the Connecticut state seal 226 *Tavern sign suggesting that the proprietor was proud of his membership in the Masons*

226

To the familiar signs of the barber's pole, the optician's eyeglasses, and the apothecary's mortar and pestle were added the vintner's bunch of grapes, the tailor's scissors, the bootmaker's boot, and the butcher's pig and cleaver. All of these recognizable symbols were designed so that anyone, literate or not, could grasp the message. At first it was unnecessary for the shopkeeper to add his name to the sign that hung outside his door, but as other shops in the same line of endeavor appeared in the vicinity, the tradesman had to make certain that his name and whereabouts were remembered. In time, the three-dimensional signs were augmented with flat signboards on which the shopkeeper's name could address itself to a passerby approaching from either direction.

The fully rounded free-swinging symbols that hung from iron brackets over the shopkeepers' doors were the work of America's first carvers. As the signboard replaced the trade symbol, the making and the painting of signs fell into carpenters' hands. Many talented artists became sign painters. Even the great preacher-painter Edward Hicks, known for his many renditions of the "Peaceable Kingdom," began by painting signs for a living. Hicks placed the following advertisement in *The Newtown Journal and Workingman's Advocate*, beginning with the May 9, 1843, issue:

EDWARD HICKS wishes to inform the Supervisors and all others interested in putting up the DIRECTORS on our public highways, according to law, that if they will paint the boards white, to suit themselves, and bring them to his shop in Newtown, he will letter them and ornament them with his own hands etc. on both sides completely, for thirty-five cents per board. Or should he receive orders for forty or fifty in a place, he will deliver the boards ready to put up, at any distance not exceeding fifty miles, for twenty-five cents per board.

At this time, there were a considerable number of artistic craftsmen who performed various jobs, including painting signs and coaches.

The subjects of the signboards varied greatly. They included landscapes, portraits, decorative symbols, animals, and the ever-popular eagle. Many taverns were named "Eagle Tavern" and carried the pictorial symbol of America.

The tavern or inn was usually the most popular rendezvous in a town, even more so than the public meetinghouse, since it was there that social events were scheduled. It was also the gallery where the works of painters might be exhibited. As such, the sign above the tavern entrance was often pictorially elaborate. The innkeeper's taste, prestige, and community standing were reflected in the quality of his signboard. Often he was able to afford the best craftsmen, since a deal might be arranged so that no cash changed hands. In Boston alone, some sixteen hundred stagecoaches arrived and departed each day, invariably leaving from a prominent tavern rather than a depot, as in later railroad days.

Research has revealed the exact age of many tavern signs, but not the names of the men who painted these harbingers of hospitality. The merrymakers at the "sign of the eagle" or the "stag at bay," and those whose attention was captured by some curious or familiar device, are often the source of information, as is shown in informal references in diaries or anecdotal literature. Much can be gleaned from journals and newspaper accounts of tavern meetings. In the New England area, Connecticut is a particularly rich source of detailed information. This small state had a disproportionately large number of inns, which may be attributed to the unusually heavy coach traffic between New York and Boston, and the need for places where both man and beast could find lodging. From the *Connecticut Journal* of October 16, 1797, we learn that "J. GRIMES respectfully informs the public that he continues as usual the branches of House, Ship and Sign Painting, Glazing of Windows of every size and shape, etc." In Hartford, a very modest newspaper advertisement reads: "S. BLYDENBURG, Painter, announces that he continues the business of Ornamental and Sign Painting, Gilding etc. He wants an active, ingenious lad as an apprentice to the above business. Applications will be attended to and orders executed at his usual abode about 40 rods north of John Trumbull's, Esq."

Many such announcements in New England papers tell us about the sign painters of yesteryear. Their handiwork added immeasurably to the allure of the shops they decorated and tells us much about popular meeting places. In-

variably, however, these signs have given us an anonymous legacy that leaves many questions unanswered. Their anonymity is easy to understand when we remember that a sign was merely part of a day's work.

Signboards may be divided into these few categories: trade signs relating to any type of merchant, retail shop, or service; tavern signs; personal house signs providing both the owner's name and address; toll signs listing rates and charges for roads, bridges, and ferry crossings; and roadside signs or directional indicators.

Many pre-Revolutionary tavern signs appealed to popular loyalties by displaying likenesses of a king, queen, or notable political character. From this custom, perhaps, derived the notion of enhancing the attractiveness of proprietary brands of liquors by dispensing them in flasks decorated with portraits or patriotic emblems.

Trade signs might offer either a very obvious symbol of the craftsman's vocation or a whimsical implication of his trade. Signs fashioned to tickle the susceptibilities of men of special trades and occupations were legion. Tavern signs appeared in great variety, some displaying animals and birds, others featuring fanciful designs or rebus arrangements calculated to attract the wayfarer. The tavern or hostelry signs which announced "Entertainment for Man & Horse" or simply "Victuals for Man & Beast" were the forerunners of today's roadside signs that read "Food and Fuel 3 Miles Ahead."

227

229

228

230

227 Inn sign unique for its decorative border treatment **228** Unusually shaped sign with flowers **229** Shield and eagle in an odd design motif **230** Tavern sign of a type painted by itinerant artists **231** Stage depicted in sign of 1828 was superseded by the famous Concord coach that very year **232, 234** Signboard of David Reed's Tavern (established 1797) featuring entertainment and good food **233** Bull's head, painted by a local artist, contrasts with the sign's delicately proportioned architectural framework. It hung in front of Bissell's Tavern in East Windsor, Connecticut, c. 1760

231

232

233

234

235

236

237

238

239

235 Bissell's Tavern sign, depicting the head of Liberty with a circlet of stars; reverse side displayed a gold eagle from an American coin of 1795 236 Tavern sign of 1816, in which entertainment is featured before food 237 Sign from J. Willard's Inn in Colchester, Connecticut, advertised temperance 238 Sign from Windsor Road Tavern, Hartford, Connecticut 239 Black Horse signboard from a tavern at Saybrook Point, Connecticut, late 1700s 240 Carter's sign welcoming travelers with a hospitable slogan

240

241

242

243

244

246

247

245

241–244 *These tavern figures, which reveal the competence of their painters, are strongly reminiscent of eighteenth-century English shop figures* **245** *An outstanding tavern figure of Bacchus, carved in jail at Windham, Connecticut, by John Russell and three assistants in 1776* **246–249** *Signs employing the grape-bunch motif, symbolizing wine and spirits, in a variety of design solutions*

248

249

250

251

252

253

254

255

250 *Ship chandler's sign with figure holding marine telescope. Photograph courtesy New York Historical Association, Cooperstown, New York* 251 *Very early carved shop figure with 1720 on his belt, antedating by a century the vogue for using Indians to mark tobacconists' shops* 252 *Seated Blackamoor was used to advertise an antique shop, although this was not the purpose for which it was made* 253 *Punch—rotund, hunchbacked, and with hooked nose—was a popular figure* 254 *Nubian slave advertising figure of heroic proportions, attributed to Julius Melchers* 255 *Baseball player, made by Samuel A. Robb of New York, a well-known carver of Indians c. 1875*

256

257

258

259

256 *Tailor's shears, a most effective trade symbol* **257** *Fishmonger's sign since time immemorial* **258** *Barber's pole, a shop sign known the world over* **259** *Butcher's sign for slaughterhouse, c. 1830–50* **260, 264, 266** *Cobbler's signs* **261** *Sign with spectacles and eyes, designating an opticians shop, c. 1875* **262, 263** *Glovemaker's signs, c. 1825–50* **265** *Sign of the Bell in Hand, temperance tavern of James Wilson, town crier of Boston, 1795*

82

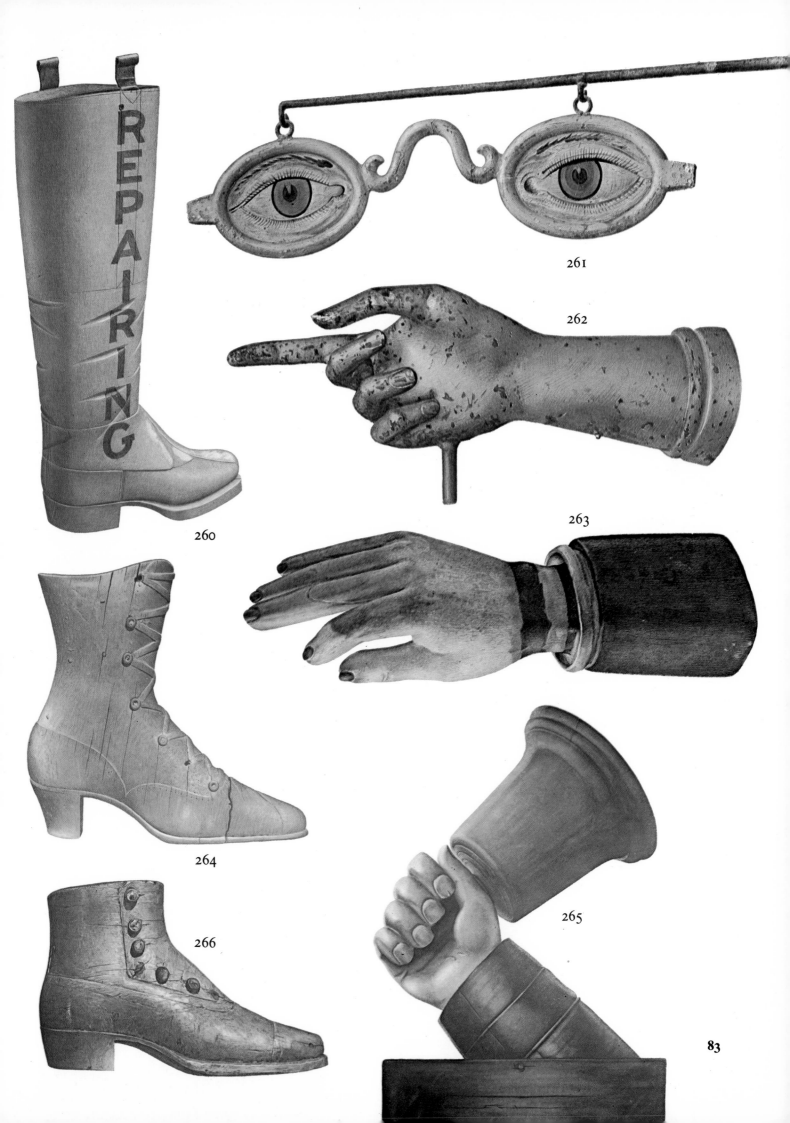

261

262

263

260

264

266

265

83

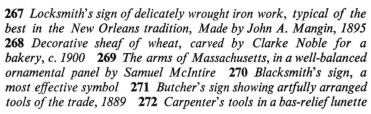

267 *Locksmith's sign of delicately wrought iron work, typical of the best in the New Orleans tradition, Made by John A. Mangin, 1895* **268** *Decorative sheaf of wheat, carved by Clarke Noble for a bakery, c. 1900* **269** *The arms of Massachusetts, in a well-balanced ornamental panel by Samuel McIntire* **270** *Blacksmith's sign, a most effective symbol* **271** *Butcher's sign showing artfully arranged tools of the trade, 1889* **272** *Carpenter's tools in a bas-relief lunette*

267

268

269

270

271

272

273

273 *The Governor's Palace, residence and official seat of the crown's representative in Virginia's capital at Williamsburg, was one of the most truly elegant mansions in Colonial America. It was occupied by seven royal governors, starting in 1716 with Alexander Spotswood, the soldier-architect who supervised its construction. The palace also became the executive mansion for the first two governors of the commonwealth of Virginia, Patrick Henry and Thomas Jefferson. An eighteenth-century carriage stands before the entrance gate. Photograph courtesy Colonial Williamsburg* **274, 275** *Horse heads of cast iron were produced by many iron foundries. The turned wooden post dates from the mid-nineteenth century. It went out of style when solid posts of iron became available*

274

For the Carriage Trade

275

W ITH THE PASSING OF the horse and buggy, the curbside watering troughs and the horse fountains which were located in many town squares or plazas have disappeared, as have the stepping-stones for alighting from high-stepped carriages and the hitching posts.

When farmers drove to town to deliver their produce and purchase their goods, they looked first for a convenient post to hitch their team. The hitching post was the mark of a good store. The main street of a town often re-sembled an illustration in the iron foundry catalogues of J. W. Fiske or Mott Ironworks, who supplied most of the posts used through-out the country in the horse-and-buggy era.

The earliest hitching device was a turned wooden newel post or simple piece of timber with a hitching ring. These were fragile, had to be repainted frequently, and eventually rotted after a few years of exposure. The wrought-iron hitching post which followed was fash-ioned by the village blacksmith from a stout iron bar and given a few twists or spiral turns for decorative effect. He rarely ventured into

276

277

more elaborate designs—these he reserved for grilles and doorway fencing, where his skill commanded a higher price.

The wrought-iron post was succeeded by the cast-iron post, a mass-produced product that readily undersold the handiwork of the blacksmith. These posts came in a variety of designs. Many were designed as fluted columns, sometimes adorned with acanthus leaves at the base. Others were cast in the form of tree trunks. They were invariably topped with a horse's head and a ring for the reins.

In the mid-nineteenth century enterprising iron foundries opened a new field with the introduction of the human figure. Jockeys, Black Sambos, stable roustabouts, liveried footmen, and the like were offered to the carriage trade. Iron-foundry catalogues blossomed with new designs every season until each had managed to copy the other's innovations.

A model was first carved in wood; this model was then reproduced in metal. Often the figures were graceful and naturalistic. Gay colors were painted on the figures of jockeys and footmen. Those who could afford these more expensive posts placed them in front of their homes, thus enhancing their status in the community. A most interesting variation shows the ingenuity of foundries. The cast-iron figure of a white-faced jockey might be darkened to create a Negro liveried servant, thus providing two different figures which had been cast from a single mold.

276–278 *Styles of horse heads varied with the output of each iron foundry. The larger heads, designed to be placed on the wooden post as a cap, often predated 1850 and are marked by realistic equine features* **279** *Stable-boy hitching post, c. 1870* **280** *Hitching post known as "Sambo," second in popularity to the jockey figure. Photograph*

278

279

280

281

282   283

281, 282 *Colorful interpretations of the jockey*
283 *Chinese figures were produced following a wave*
of popular interest in the Chinese railroad workers
of the West, c. 1870 **284, 285** *Negro stable boys*
with polychrome treatment, representing an advance
from the Sambo type (280)

284

285

286 *Unique cast-iron post, a departure from the traditional horse head. From the West Coast, c. 1870* **287–289** *Variants of the typical hitching post* **290, 291** *Earlier horse heads, c. 1850* **292–294** *Style change stressing post decorations as the horse head assumes minor role;* **293,** *dated 1858, was made by J. W. Fiske of New York*

287

286

288   289

290

291

292

293

294

93

295

296

Fire Fighters
& Bucket Brigades

I F PROMETHEUS was worthy of the wrath of Heaven for kindling the first fire upon earth, how ought all the gods to honor the men who make it their professional business to put it out?"

The colorful saga of fire fighting provides us with one of the most exciting and dramatic

295 *Statuette of a fire fighter given as a trophy for heroism in the line of duty* **296** *Fire-engine weather vane used atop a firehouse. Modeled after an Amoskeag engine of the period 1860–80 and made of copper, brass, zinc, and iron* **297** *Wooden fire hydrant, c. 1842. Before cast iron came into use, water was piped underground through wooden conduits*

chapters in the annals of American life. In the three centuries since Boston became the first city to own and operate a "water engine," imported from England, there has been a succession of developments beginning with the primitive bucket brigade and progressing to early wooden washtub pumpers on wheels and, later, to improved "enjines." The growth of volunteer fire departments, the introduction of horse-drawn steam engines, and finally the high-speed automatic equipment of the present day round out a series of eventful episodes.

The early volunteer firemen left behind them a collection of fascinating relics. Along with an assortment of fire engines, there are hose and reel carts, badges, belts, buckets, trumpets,

297

298

uniforms, and fire insurance company marks, as well as bits and pieces of the painted shields and plaques that adorned the more elaborate engines. In some cases, these were the work of noted painters. Today there are only a handful of fire museums and company collections where this regalia may be viewed.

The earliest fire-fighting methods in the Colonies were primitive. Leather buckets, the handiwork of local cobblers, were used to transport water from a well, cistern, or nearby brook to the scene of the fire. This was long before reservoirs, underground pipes, and hydrants or wooden fire plugs existed in the streets of the larger cities.

When church bells rang out the alarm, or an alarm was sounded by hitting a huge iron ring centrally located on the village green, the call "throw out your buckets" was heeded quickly by all within reach of the disaster area. The buckets, which held about three gallons of water, were passed quickly down the line by able-bodied men and returned by another line of women and boys.

In the cities of this country, where crowded streets and two-story dwellings were the rule, improvements in fire-fighting equipment became a necessity. A variety of hand pumpers were produced in the middle years of the eighteenth century. The hand pumper's main function was to suck and pump water as its tanks were filled by buckets, a long and tedious process that could seldom keep pace with the raging flames. These earliest machines were exact replicas of the hand pumpers used by the ancient Egyptians, as depicted on tombs and artifacts. Later developments included longer pumping brake arms, which accommodated up to a dozen men for greater pumping force, rotary or windlass types, and rowing-type engines in which the firemen sat and rowed in

298 *Engraving depicting bucket brigade trying to extinguish a fire in New York, 1733* **299** *Engraving based on a Currier & Ives lithograph entitled* The Ruins—Take Up: Man Your Rope, *published in New York, 1854* **299A** *From a Currier & Ives lithograph.* The Fire—Shake Her Up, Boys, *published in 1854*

299

299A

300

301

302

303

300 *Hand pumper built by Patrick Lyon in 1806 for Pennsylvania Fire Company No. 22, Philadelphia; painted side panels and decorations by an anonymous hand* **301** *Hand-powered pump, solidly constructed of oak with fine hand-wrought iron hose racks. Built in Boston in 1838* **302** *Combination pumper and hose cart of sturdy construction designed to withstand heavy wear, c. 1850* **303** *Hose reel built by George Ruhl in 1851 for the Neptune Hose Company of Philadelphia. Delicate iron scrolls are typical of superb craftsmanship and grace achieved in much fire-fighting equipment*

304

305

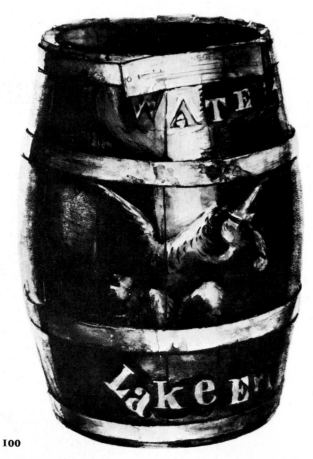

307

306

304 *Painted and gilded shield with eagle, used on fireman's hat* **305** *Hand-painted fireman's hat of bull hide, c. 1850* **306** *Water keg with eagle design* **307** *Carved cowhide fireman's belt* **308** *Painted and decorated helmet with metal ornament* **309** *Presentation silver trumpet with chased ornament, 1853* **310** *Cast-iron hose holder* **311** *Fireman's belt with metal letters*

100

308

309

310

311

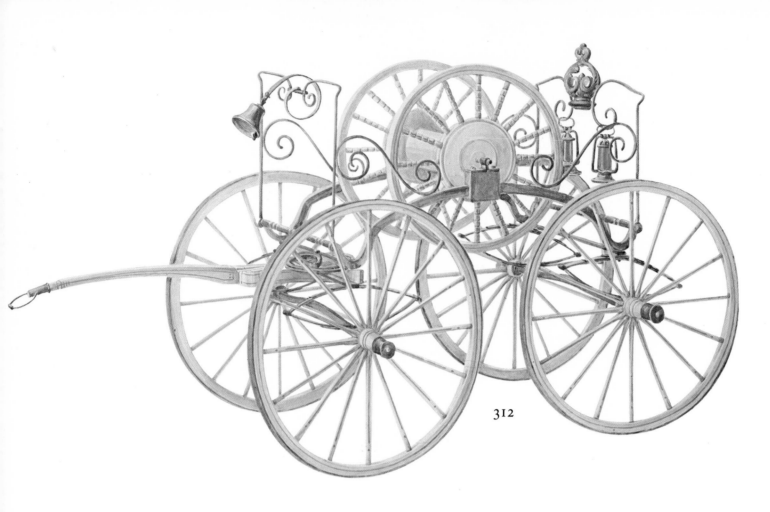

312

312 *Hose reel, the product of wheelwright and blacksmith, with skillfully designed wrought-iron frame and elliptic springs* 313 *Hose holder with phoenix as its central motif* 314 *Engine-company signboard incorporating fire-fighting equipment and fire helmet* 315 *The fabled phoenix rising out of the flames, popular symbol with fire companies* 316, 318 *Leather fire buckets, made by shoemakers, were gaily decorated and identified with company names* 317 *The Green Tree fire mark, originally issued in 1784 by the Mutual Assurance Company of Philadelphia*

313

314

315

316

317

318

319

GUARDIAN

104

320

321

much the same fashion as galley slaves on ancient triremes. For many years gooseneck fire engines, an outgrowth of British Newsham engines, were New York's most popular machines. Goosenecks derived their name from the shape of the pipe that protruded from the top of the air chamber built over the rear wheels and stood about four feet above the deck of the machine. To operate the rotary type, called "coffee mill" or "cider mill," six or eight men would take hold of the long wooden poles and keep circling around until they dropped from exhaustion and were replaced; on some engines a man had to be relieved after two minutes of pumping. No wonder, then, that fire duty was expected of every able man in the community. It took an abundance of manpower to control the simplest of fires.

In many towns, the first person to ring a church bell for a fire received a reward, as did the first volunteer company to arrive on the scene. Often the whole population turned out for the occasion, creating such noise and confusion that the firemen were greatly impeded in their work. The rivalry between volunteer groups was so intense that it was not uncommon for battling and brawling to break out while a building burned. If, as sometimes happened, a fire was extinguished before the building had been destroyed, the event was celebrated with drunkenness and rioting.

A big occasion in the life of a fireman was the annual parade, when all volunteers cavorted in gay dress uniforms, red shirts, capes, helmets, and beribboned regalia. The different fire companies tried to outdo each other with

319 *Eagle fire mark of the Insurance Company of North America, Philadelphia. This sheet-copper version was issued just after 1800* **320** *Guardian Company's mark, issued in 1867* **321** *Old hand pumper, cast-iron emblem of the Firemen's Insurance Company of Baltimore, 1835* **322** *Cast-iron mark of the Fire Association of Philadelphia, c. 1830* **323** *The Green Tree fire mark was first carved in wood, then made of sheet copper, lead, and finally of cast iron. This form, c. 1806*

322

323

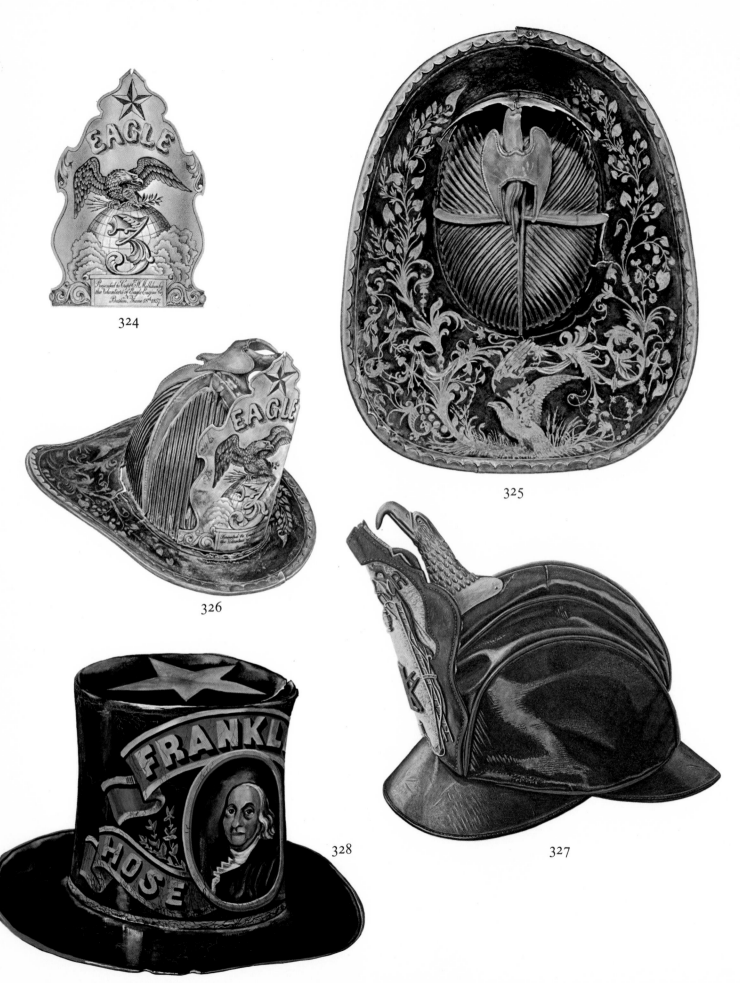

324

325

326

328

327

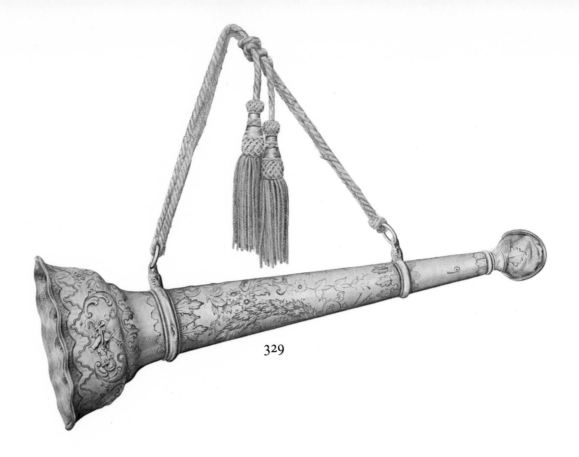

329

lavish costumes and, in the ornamentation of vehicles, with gaudy metal accessories. Celebrated artists were often commissioned to decorate engine panels and trim—among them Thomas Sully, Henry Inman, John Vanderlyn, and David and Joseph Johnson. Many of their commissions hang today in fire museums and company collections.

The colorful nomenclature of the engine companies did much to stimulate the imagination of the painters and gilders. Such engine

324–326 Lavishly decorated fireman's helmet with gilded brim and topped by a brass eagle head that attaches to the badge at the front **327** *This type of helmet offered good protection from falling debris. The eagle badge-holder was generally of sheet brass, c. 1880* **328** *Stovepipe hat, hand-painted and decorated, was worn for dress parades.* **329** *Silver speaking trumpet, an elaborately engraved and embossed presentation piece* **330** *Fire marshal's trumpet of silver-plated nickel, 1877*

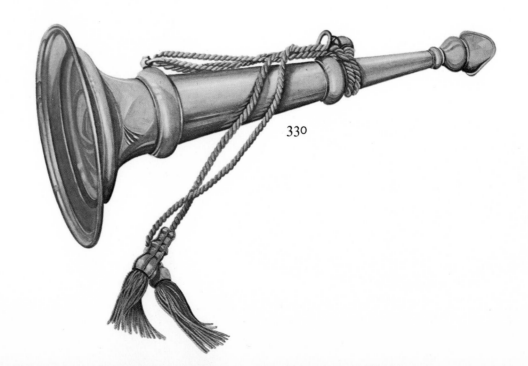

330

331

names as Hayseed, Old Brass Backs, Black Joke, Old Maid, Red Rover, Blue Boys, White Ghost, Mutton Hose, and Mankiller suggested suitable motifs. Paintings showed scenes from mythology or pictured national figures and battle scenes. Plain unadorned surfaces were unacceptable; gold leaf, silver plate, and highly burnished brass were the order of the day.

A fireman regarded his accouterments with affection. Hats, helmets, and presentation shields, always beautifully decorated and highly colored, were the crowning glory of the uniforms. Buckets were hand painted and ornamented with nameplates, ribbons, eagles, and the like. Drinking horns and speaking trumpets used for giving orders or shouting insults at rival companies were elaborately engraved.

Much of the unbecoming behavior of volunteer companies gradually improved after the steam engine was introduced in 1852, and a new order of paid professional fire fighters came into existence.

In retrospect, the competitiveness of the early volunteer companies may be decried, but it must be remembered that their rivalry supplied the incentive for the elaborate trappings of the fireman's art.

332

331 *Iron casting, showing early hand pumper as the fire mark of the Fire Insurance Company of Pittsburgh, c. 1834* **332** *Square iron plate that marked a house insured by the Baltimore Equitable Society, c. 1845* **333** *Fire mark with full name of the insuring company, founded in 1836, running around the edge* **334** *Early pumper identifies a Cincinnati company, c. 1850* **335** *Heavy iron casting of 1860 mark the United Firemen's Insurance Company of Philadelphia*

333

334

335

The Family at Home, *painted in 1836 by H. Knight of Connecticut. National Gallery of Art, Washington, D.C. Gift of Edgar William and Bernice Chrysler Garbisch*

BOOK TWO

In the Home

BOOK TWO: *In the Home*

Gleaming Glassware for Table & Buffet

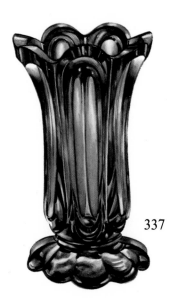

337

GLASSMAKING HAS BEEN a highly honored craft since the days of the ancient Egyptians. During the Middle Ages, the craft guilds emphasized the mysteries surrounding the glassmaking process. To the layman, the making of glass seemed to involve a sorcerer's alchemy, in which a rigid, transparent substance could be created by fusing a composite of opaque inert materials, such as sand, soda, lime, and lead, at high temperatures and then cooling the resulting liquid. Various luminous colors could be produced by adding metallic oxides to this liquid, which could be blown or cast in molds, or drawn or rolled into fine threads of gossamer delicacy.

A few glassmakers came to America from European factories when the Colonies were first established, lured by promises of profit sharing in exchange for assisting in the founding of new factories. Although passage and subsistence were assured, the workers' jobs were often short-lived, and they found themselves lost in an alien environment with meager resources.

In 1608 a small group of Dutch and Polish glassmakers were invited to the colony of Jamestown, Virginia, by John Smith, who had

338

336 *American glass made c. 1770 to 1850. The pattern-molded blue covered sugar bowl with spiral finial, the engraved covered tumbler, and the lily-pad decorated sugar bowl whose cover is topped by a chicken finial are representative of the three major traditions of American glassware which developed in the eighteenth century: the Stiegel, the Amelung, and the South Jersey. The pattern-molded pocket bottles and cruet are characteristic of Midwestern glasshouses of the 1815–40 era, while the mold-blown sugar bowl, decanter, and creamer represent the beginnings of American mass-produced glass. Photograph courtesy Corning Museum of Glass, Corning, New York* **337** *Thick-walled tulip pattern Sandwich glass celery holder with petalous base, c. 1840–50* **338** *Vase with loop pattern bowl, goffered rim, and hexagonal shaft on a square plinth*

observed that there was a plentiful supply of the necessary raw materials in the Virginia countryside. But the enterprise did not prosper and the group soon dispersed.

A second attempt was made at Jamestown in 1621, when Captain William Norton brought over a group of six Venetian glass-blowers. Norton had been employed as a beadmaker, and he probably planned to trade glass beads and trinkets with the Indians for valuable furs and pelts, which he could then export to England. This venture was also short-lived.

Numerous glass-manufacturing efforts followed. Some lasted less than a year, others struggled along for various lengths of time. Glasshouses were set up in Salem, Massachusetts, in 1638, in Dutch New Amsterdam in the mid-seventeenth century, and in Philadelphia, at the behest of William Penn, in 1683. In 1732 two glassmaking factories were established in New York City, and in 1752 four men went into partnership in Orange County, New York. The leader was Lodewyck Bamper, who invited John Greiner of Saxe-Weimar, Germany, to come to the Colonies to teach the "Art & Mystery of Erecting & Building a Glass-House & allso in Blowing & Making of Glass." Two years later, Bamper was operating a factory in Brooklyn, New York.

The first successful glass manufactory was established in 1739 by Caspar Wistar on the banks of Alloway's Creek in southern New Jersey, not far from Philadelphia. Wistar, a German, had come to the Colonies as a young man in 1717. He was a manufacturer of brass buttons, but envisioned an unlimited potential in the glass business. He brought over four "glass experts" from Germany, and thus Early American blown glass was influenced by German styles. Wistar died in 1752, but his son Richard carried on the business until after the Revolutionary War. The Wistarberg works were known principally for window glass, bottles of several types and sizes, snuff and mustard containers, and a variety of chemical wares, such as retorts, globes, and tubes.

Most interesting to collectors, however, are the after-hours pieces made by Wistar's glass-blowers for family and friends. These colorful objects, blown from remelted window or bottle glass in shades of aquamarine, amber, green, and occasionally blue, included small corner pots which, according to craft tradition, were set aside for personal use, sugar bowls, pitchers, vases, and candlesticks. These pieces often reveal the ingenuity of the blower when he strayed from the day's routine. They show a freedom of expression which is highly significant, marking as it does the beginning of what is known as the South Jersey type.

This glassware was for the most part free blown, which means that it was manipulated and shaped in the technique which has been practiced for centuries by Italians, Germans, Swiss, Dutchmen, and Bohemians. The glass gather (a mass of molten glass) is worked at just the right temperature, being blown and rotated at the same time. The blower reheats the glass when necessary, judging the temperature by color and pliability.

Methods of ornamenting blown glass include the following: *crimping*, or the making of dents and flutes, at either the foot or the open neck of an object; *quilling* or *trailing*, the application of glass thread to the surface in wavy ribbons; *rigaree*, the application of bands or ribbons of glass in parallel lines; *prunts* or *seals*, which are applied as hot gathers of glass, then tooled or molded into motifs such as leaves or strawberries; and other superimposed decorations in which the gather of glass is tooled into swirls or draped in the so-called lily-pad type of ornament. The lily pad was the most distinctive ornament of the South Jersey type. It appeared in various forms, including vertical slender stems terminating in a bead and broader stems with oval pads. The handles of pitchers, bowls, and mugs were ornamented, as were finials and footed bases.

In 1781 the Stanger brothers, former Wistar workmen, established in Glassboro, New Jersey, a factory which perpetuated the Wistar tradition and produced many excellent South Jersey pieces.

Henry William Stiegel, like Wistar, came to the Colonies from Germany. He arrived in 1750 at the age of twenty-one and settled near

Lancaster, Pennsylvania. He soon found employment with Jacob Huber, master of a pioneer ironworks, and within two years married Huber's daughter Elizabeth. After several years in the iron business, Stiegel decided to go into glassmaking. In 1763 he built his first glasshouse, near the ironworks. By 1769 he had established two more at Manheim, a town he had founded and where he indulged in a baronial manner of living reminiscent of the German aristocracy. At this point "Baron Stiegel," as·he called himself, employed a hundred and thirty people.

Stiegel's glassware was clear or colored in shades of deep blue and amethyst. It was decorated with engraving, enameling, or pattern-molding, following English and German styles. Pattern-molding involves blowing the molten glass gather into a metal mold, the interior walls of which carry the pattern. After the gather has been impressed with the pattern, it is withdrawn from the mold. The pattern expands as the glass is blown to the desired size and shape. A great quantity of this glassware is known today under the general heading Stiegel-type, since we cannot say with certainty that it was produced in the Stiegel factories.

Patterns used in Stiegel-type glassware include vertical and spiral fluting, paneling, variations of the Venetian diamond, and all-over patterns of diamond-daisy or checkered diamond designs. The daisy patterns are found in perfume bottles, small vases, saltcellars, sugar bowls, creamers, drinking glasses, condiment bottles, and flasks.

Adverse economic conditions and overestimating his market led to Stiegel's bankruptcy in 1774. His plant closed, and many of his former employees migrated to western Pennsylvania and western Virginia.

Another glassmaker of importance was John Frederick Amelung, a native of Bremen, Germany. His New Bremen Glass Manufactory near Frederick, Maryland, operated from 1784 to 1796. He imported highly skilled German workers, and several engraved and inscribed presentation pieces of superior workmanship have come down to us from his enterprise. In addition to window glass and white and green bottles, the New Bremen products included decanters and wine glasses, tumblers of all sizes, and a wide range of tableware. This glass is usually blue, green, or purple, and is characterized by a beautiful smoky hue.

The New Bremen workers engraved devices, ciphers, coats of arms, inscriptions, and other fancy figures on glass. Their copper-wheel engraving was distinguished by a more sophisticated style than that of similar work produced in this country and was considered the equal of any European product. Motifs included wreaths, sprays of flowers, birds—often a dove holding a sprig of flowers—foliated leaves, and daisy-like festoons. Amelung, like Stiegel, overestimated the market for his glassware and had to close his plant. Many of his workmen found employment at the New Geneva Glass Works in Pennsylvania.

As the nation grew, there was a great increase in the number of successful glass factories. By 1820 there were some forty glass factories in operation; by 1830 this number had increased to about ninety, with new firms constantly entering the field.

The industry's new growth centered on Pittsburgh and surrounding areas in what are now Ohio and West Virginia. This section was ideal for glassmaking, having abundant supplies of coal to fuel the furnaces and broad riverways for inexpensive transportation. Of the fifty glasshouses established in Pennsylvania between 1763 and 1850, forty were located in Pittsburgh. All sorts of bottles, flasks, demijohns, and carboys—containers for cider, beer, and whisky—were produced.

As the number of factories in this area increased, glassmaking in the East declined. Wood, its major fuel, became too expensive as forests were depleted, and many glasshouses had to shut down.

In the early nineteenth century, two methods were developed which were to bring attractive and inexpensive glassware within the reach of all. The first, known as the blown-three-mold technique, came into use about 1815. It involved the blowing of molten glass into full-size metal molds, hinged in several parts, which

339

340

341

contained the patterned decoration and were shaped like the final object. Pictorial and historical flasks, decanters, and tableware were produced by this technique. Among the earlier designs in blown-three-mold glass tableware were combinations of vertical ribs and diamond diapers, and fluting and sunbursts classified as *geometric*; elaborate designs of scrolls, palmettes, and hearts in high relief called *baroque*; and patterns with Gothic and Roman arched motifs called *arch*.

The second new development was the invention of the glass-pressing machine in the late 1820s. The first patents for mechanical pressing machines were granted to Bakewell of Pittsburgh and the New England Glass Company.

339 *Open-necked blown amber vase with swirled ribbing* **340** *Stiegel-type blown-glass footed sugar bowl with lid, c. 1770* **341** *Flip glass or runner, with enameled decoration and familiar bird motif used by Stiegel* **342** *Sugar bowl and cover; pattern molded in ogival design with swirl finial* **343** *Footed bowl with folded rim and swirled ribbing, a pattern-molded salt of the late eighteenth century* **344** *Heavy footed eight-sided goblet, with enameled decoration showing strong influence of German and Bohemian styles*

342

343

344

At Sandwich, Massachusetts, Deming Jarves produced the first drinking vessel made by means of a glass-pressing device. As happens with the introduction of many new labor-saving processes, Jarves's workers were infuriated at the prospect of being thrown out of work. They threatened him with bodily harm, and he was obliged to lock himself into his home for six weeks until the furor subsided.

In order to produce pressed glassware of ornamental design, it was necessary to start by cutting a wooden pattern. The skilled pattern-maker incised his design after carefully outlining it on a wooden surface. Then he impressed the pattern into a tray of sand and filled this with molten metal, either iron or brass, producing a reverse replica. This metal mold, hinged in several places, became the matrix and was set into a machine to receive molten glass forced into it by a plunger. Jarves's plant became famous for the production of lacy glass, a term derived from the lacelike patterns which were used to fill in the blank areas so

345

346

347

348

that any imperfections the mold might leave would be covered. These delicate patterns, intricate in design and technique, added a distinctive sparkle of their own.

345 *This Stiegel-type creamer with the diamond pattern (of Venetian origin) and crimped handle appears first in South Jersey and later in Pittsburgh and Ohio* **346** *Enameled barber bottle for bay rum or hair tonic* **347** *Mold-blown toilet bottle with the daisy-in-a-square pattern and fluting below, typical of the inventive genius of Stiegel, c. 1769–74* **348** *Flip glass and cover with engraved decorations similar to those on European peasant glass. Attributed to Stiegel* **349** *Pocket bottle with popular diamond decoration, c. 1810–20* **350** *Stiegel-type "swirl" bottle of handsome proportions, c. 1815* **351** *Early nineteenth-century creamer of ribbed design and goffered rim*

349

350

351

The glass-pressing machine was immediately adopted by a score of factories, and production of glass objects soon developed into a flourishing industry employing thousands of workers in various parts of the country. Because of the speed in manufacturing with the device, and the low unit cost of each article, factories expanded their lines to include just about everything for table and home use, and brought glassware within the means of almost every homeowner. Hundreds of different patterns came into existence, one motif being used for an entire table service of plates, cups, cup plates, goblets, saltcellars, sugar bowls, creamers, compotes, and water pitchers. Today's collectors of patterned glass are challenged to complete a table setting; a complete service, as issued by the factory, represents a collector's dream.

Most manufacturers of table glassware adopted, rather freely, whatever pattern caught the public's fancy. When patternmakers were not busy inventing new designs, they were busy copying those of their competitors. Thus, it is difficult to trace a particular pattern to a specific source.

122

353

Goblets & Tumblers

RINKING GLASSES vary in size, purpose, and color. They can be plain or decorated, footed or stemmed, and so on, and there are many lesser classifications. They fall into two major divisions, tumblers and goblets.

A tumbler is a straight-sided drinking glass without a handle, stem, or foot. Originally, it had a convex or pointed base, and could not stand upright, hence the name tumbler. A tumbler of liquid was served in a tray of sand to keep it in an upright position. The liquid was taken at a single draft and then the tumbler was placed on the table with its bottom up, thus the expression "bottoms up." Most whisky glasses are of the tumbler variety. A large tumbler with a ten-ounce capacity was called a flip glass. Flips were made in plain clear transparent glass, either cut, blown, or pressed, and engraved or enameled.

The term "goblet" applies to a drinking glass of any ovoid or globular bowl shape, supported on a stem. Cocktail glasses are usually tall stemmed; wine glasses or cordial glasses vary greatly in shape. Each major wine calls for its own traditionally shaped glass.

When pressed glass became popular, drinking glasses were produced in hundreds of patterns. Some of the best-known ones include almond thumbprint, argus, blaze, bull's-eye, frosted leaf, gothic, honeycomb, horn of plenty, inverted fern, pineapple, ribbed bellflower, ribbed grape, and waffle.

Some idea of the number of tumblers and goblets produced in this country can be given by examining the output of a single company which specialized in these pieces; A. J. Beatty of Steubenville, Ohio. After acquiring an established factory, Beatty razed the old furnaces

352 *The form and decoration of all pressed-glass pieces starts with the patternmaker's wooden mold. Opposite are a number of these wooden molds with their glass counterparts alongside. At the left of the bottom row is the plaster model made from the wooden mold for the inverted-fern sauce dish; in the center, the wooden and metal mold for the shell pattern. At the right is the three-part plaster model from which metal molds were cast for the inverted-fern egg cup. Photograph by Hugo Poisson, courtesy Sandwich Glass Museum, Sandwich, Massachusetts* **353** *Tumblers were produced in a great variety of designs and were blown, mold-blown, or pressed. This undecorated one with a rounded bottom is from the early 1800s*

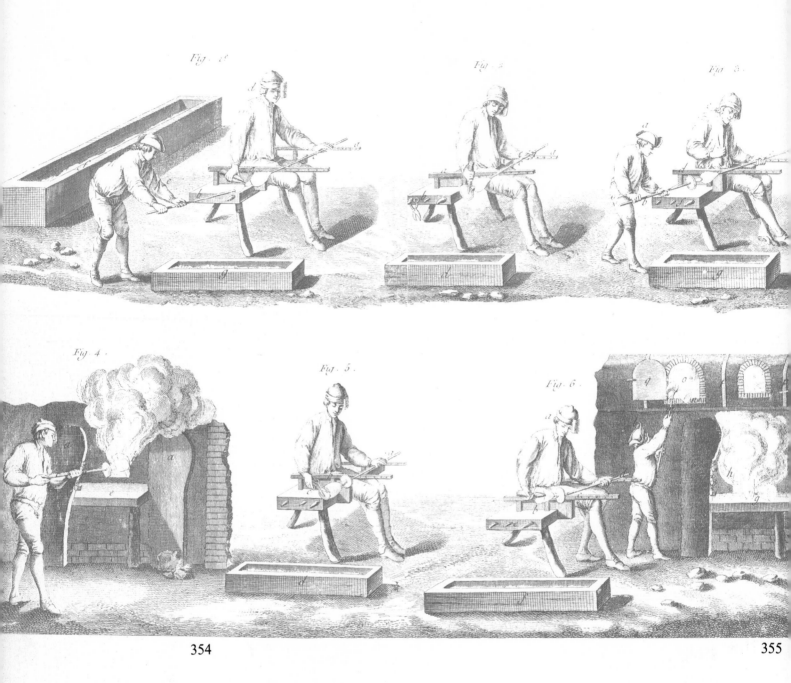

354

355

354 *The blowing of goblets as practiced for centuries by European glassblowers is illustrated step by step in this engraving from Diderot's* Encyclopédie, *published in France in the mid-eighteenth century* **355** *In the array of pattern glass, mostly from the Sandwich glassworks, are shown several goblets. They are decorated with bull's eye and diamond-point designs, two of approximately ninety patterns produced at Sandwich during most of the nineteenth century*

and built new ones large enough to accommodate his production capacity. The factory operated at full blast during the Civil War. Beatty employed 130 men regularly, and turned out an average of 36,000 glasses a day. He became the country's leading producer of glasses, shipping his wares to every port in the world, competing successfully with French, English, and German glass products.

356 *Wide-footed flip glass made by several different glassworks, early nineteenth century* **357** *Tumbler with fluted sides and beading* **358** *Blown-three-mold glass tumbler with varying rows of geometric designs, including swirls, fluting, and all-over diamond-diaper pattern* **359** *Six-sided small whisky glass, early nineteenth century* **360** *Tall-stemmed goblet of pressed glass* **361** *Heavy, footed tumbler, six-sided with arch design* **362** *Thin glass tumbler of expanded diamond-mold design, possibly the most popular early pattern, c. 1810–20* **363** *Stemmed wine goblet with two flanges at the stem*

Overleaf: GALLERY OF GOBLETS AND TUMBLERS. *Mostly clear glass patterns, pressed c. 1840–75 except* **371,** *etched decorations;* **379,** *blown goblet;* **394,** *frosted stem and base. Photographs by the Index of American Design*

360   361

362   363

364

365

366

367

368

369

370

371

372

373

374

375

376

377

379

380

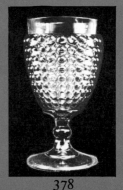

378

128

383

384

385

386

387

389

390

395

388

392

396

391

393

394

Pitchers & Decanters

398

399

400

SOME OF THE MOST distinctive pitchers and creamers were South Jersey pieces. Generally, the South Jersey pitcher had a short neck in proportion to the body, or an applied foot of a short-stemmed form. There were several broad classifications of pitchers: globular body, tapering to a lightly flaring rim, with a stemmed circular foot; globular body with a short cylindrical neck and a tiny pinched lip, sometimes having a petaled foot or solid loop handle; cylindrical body, short shoulder and

397 *Display of blown-three-mold glass, designed in the main by Deming Jarvis (1790–1869) at the Sandwich glassworks. The pitcher on the top shelf at left shows the diamond sunburst alternating with diamond diapering in the wide band; the creamer at the right is light gray-blue with fluted sides. On second shelf, third from left, pint chain with heart-design decanter, blown hollow stopper; at right, deep sapphire blue decanter in shell and ribbing pattern with matching stopper. On third shelf at right, carafe with peacock eye and two bands around neck. On fourth shelf at left, sapphire blue toilet or vinegar bottle in vertical ribbing with band at top. On bottom shelf, from left: quart decanter in arch-and-fern pattern with snake medallion and inscription* RUM; *quart pitcher in pattern mold; quart decanter, double-patterned over diamond-sunburst pattern, with vertical ribbing and matching stopper; quart decanter in diamond-sunburst alternating with diamond-diaper band and famous Sandwich acorn stopper, the rarest of stoppers* **398** *Pitcher with large bird's-eye bowl, straight narrow neck, and ribbed handle* **399** *Ribbed or fluted cruet with matching stopper* **400** *Wine carafe with large stopper in brilliant flint with overlay. Center area of bowl decorated with grape-and-vine motif*

neck, with a slight flare at the rim (larger pitchers usually had a strap handle); slender barrel shape, sometimes called mug shape, with a pinched lip; and a graceful, tapering pear shape, approaching a globular body, but having a slightly longer neck and wider rim, sometimes folded, with a small or deep pinched lip. Most of these vessels were free blown. Decorative effects were achieved by shaping or coloring, or by the application of a layer of glass tooled into a heavy swirl—swagged, ribbed, or threaded—or formed into the lily pad. Other forms of ornamentation, such as prunts, quilling, and rigaree, were also used. In later pieces combinations of colors were applied in swirls, loops, or striations. No matter how graceful the shape and decorative treatment, the thickness of the glass invested the fragile objects with a quality of sturdiness.

The early pitchers in the Stiegel tradition embrace a wide variety of types and decorative techniques. The shapes were more sophisticated and expertly formed than were the South Jersey types and faithfully followed English

and Continental prototypes. Decoration varies: wheel cut, shallow stylized engraving, enameling, and expanded pattern-molded designs, such as paneling, ribbing, fluting, and variations of the Venetian diamond.

Cruets and castor bottles, small variants of the pitcher form which held vinegar, oil, or other condiments, were made in both the Stiegel and the South Jersey types. They are lipped bottles which have either metal tops or glass stoppers and are produced with or without handles. When offered in a set, they were supplied in a cruet or castor frame. They were in general use from about 1750 to the early twentieth century.

The decanter is a vessel which rests on a flat base without footing; the lower portion is usually globular in shape, tapering to a narrow lipped opening. The method of transition from the lower liquid-holding section to the upper narrow neck lends itself to varied interpretation, as does the technique of manufacture and the method of surface decoration. All early decanter forms were of the blown-three-mold

401

402

403

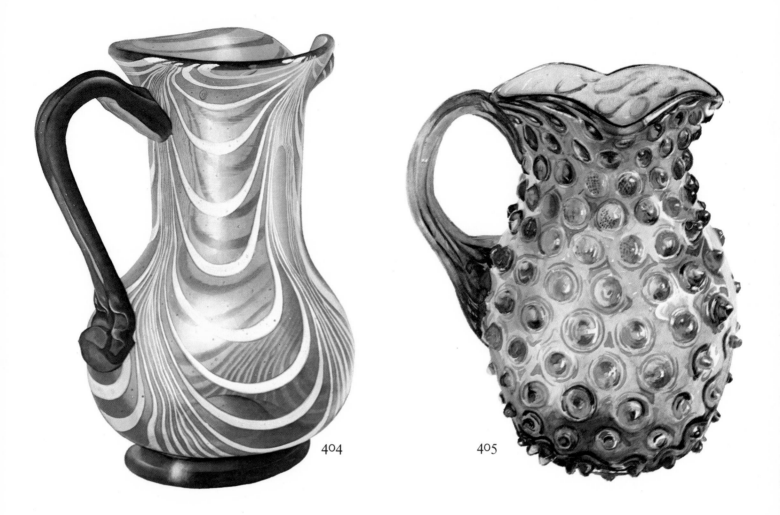

404   405

variety. Many decanters were decorated with sunburst and geometric motifs in imitation of popular English types. The arch and baroque patterns, in various colors, were among the forms used by South Jersey and New England houses. American designers introduced a descriptive panel on the front of the bottle which carried the word "whisky," "gin," or "brandy"; on Continental decanters this information was generally given on a metal label hung from a chain around the neck of the bottle.

401 *Ruby cut-glass creamer with diamond-patterned bowl and pronounced scalloped rim, c. 1870–80* **402** *Cream pitcher of flint glass with Baroque pattern, c. 1825–40* **403** *Hand-blown water pitcher of mottled glass, ribbed, 1850* **404** *Hand-blown pitcher with loopings of opaque white, c. 1825–50* **405** *Hobnail pitcher with ribbed handle, made by Boston and New England Glass Company* **406** *Straight-sided bowl pitcher of Cambridge glass, 1883*

406

407

408

409

410

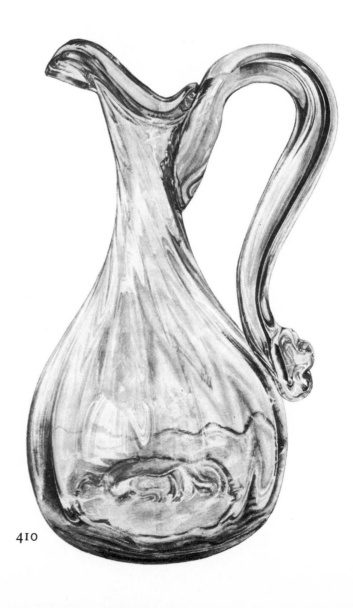

411

412

413

407 *Free-blown South Jersey pitcher with applied lily-pad decoration and crimped footed base* **408** *Lily-pad decorated pitcher with threaded neck. Made in South Jersey* **409** *Cruet of flint glass with threaded neck, 1800–1850* **410** *Flint vinegar cruet with twisted rib design and crimped handle. Attributed to Stiegel, c. 1764–74* **411** *Spiraled rib pitcher made in Zanesville, Ohio; c. 1820–30* **412** *Hand-blown aquamarine pitcher with mulberry loopings, applied foot and handle. Made in New Jersey, c. 1840–50* **413** *Hand-blown South Jersey pitcher with superimposed swagging, c. 1800*

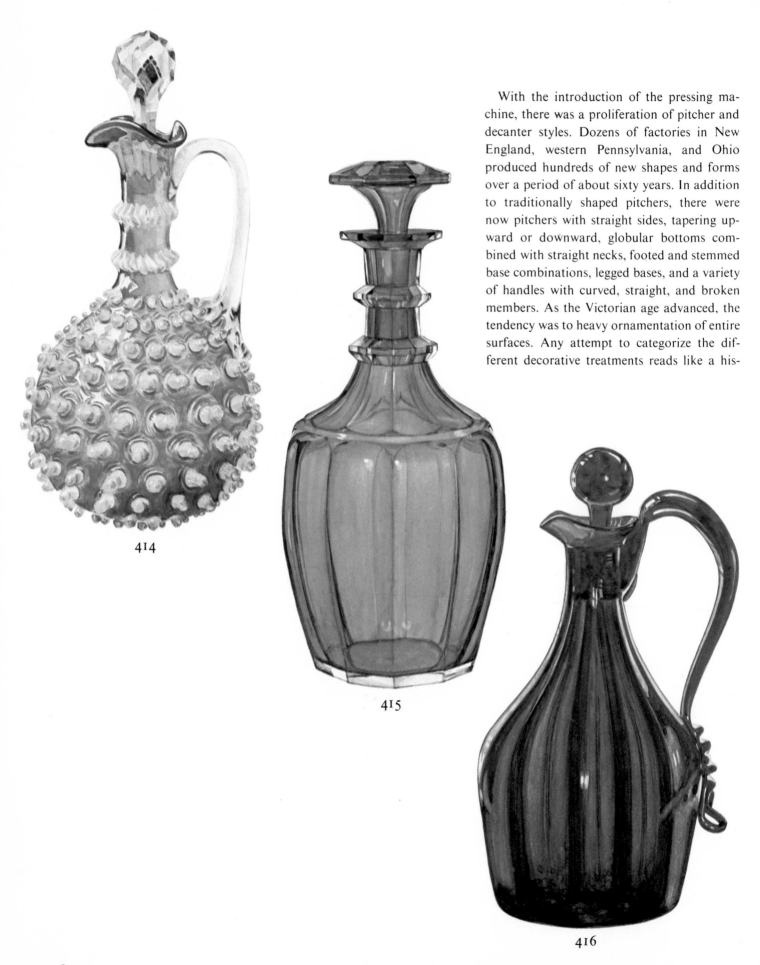

With the introduction of the pressing machine, there was a proliferation of pitcher and decanter styles. Dozens of factories in New England, western Pennsylvania, and Ohio produced hundreds of new shapes and forms over a period of about sixty years. In addition to traditionally shaped pitchers, there were now pitchers with straight sides, tapering upward or downward, globular bottoms combined with straight necks, footed and stemmed base combinations, legged bases, and a variety of handles with curved, straight, and broken members. As the Victorian age advanced, the tendency was to heavy ornamentation of entire surfaces. Any attempt to categorize the different decorative treatments reads like a his-

414

415

416

tory of ornament. Geometric cuts, ribs, flutes, and cross-hatching into diamond and lozenge patterns follow the traditional cut-glass decoration of the Anglo-Irish school. Naturalistic motifs abound, including leaf, flower, bird, and animal forms in a variety of combinations. Panels enclosing Classical figures and cameos were used in contrast with architectonic arrangements, columns, and flutings of many styles. With the public's seemingly endless appetite for more and more decoration, and the patternmakers' efforts to keep up with the entreaties of their sales departments, the elegance and restraint which had characterized earlier pitchers and decanters was lost.

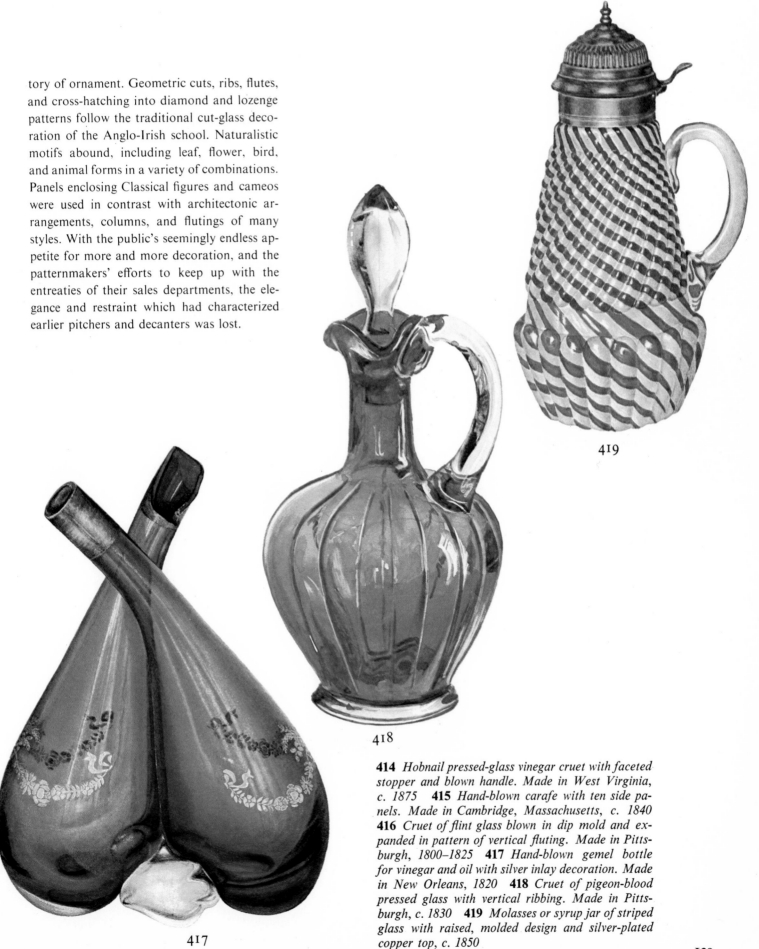

419

418

417

414 Hobnail pressed-glass vinegar cruet with faceted stopper and blown handle. Made in West Virginia, c. 1875 **415** Hand-blown carafe with ten side panels. Made in Cambridge, Massachusetts, c. 1840 **416** Cruet of flint glass blown in dip mold and expanded in pattern of vertical fluting. Made in Pittsburgh, 1800–1825 **417** Hand-blown gemel bottle for vinegar and oil with silver inlay decoration. Made in New Orleans, 1820 **418** Cruet of pigeon-blood pressed glass with vertical ribbing. Made in Pittsburgh, c. 1830 **419** Molasses or syrup jar of striped glass with raised, molded design and silver-plated copper top, c. 1850

420

421

422

424

420 *Decanter with encircled star design and ribbing and matching ball stopper* **421** *Blown-three-mold decanter with Gothic arched ovals, fluting, and beading* **422** *Decanter with baroque pattern of scrolled heart-and-chain design and fluting below* **423** *Decanter with rounded fluting at its base and pineapple stopper* **424** *Blown-three-mold decanter with horn-of-plenty design. Made at Amelung's New Bremen Glass Manufactory, c. 1784–96* **425** *Decanter with spiraling rib design, Wistarberg type made in South Jersey, late eighteenth century*

423

425

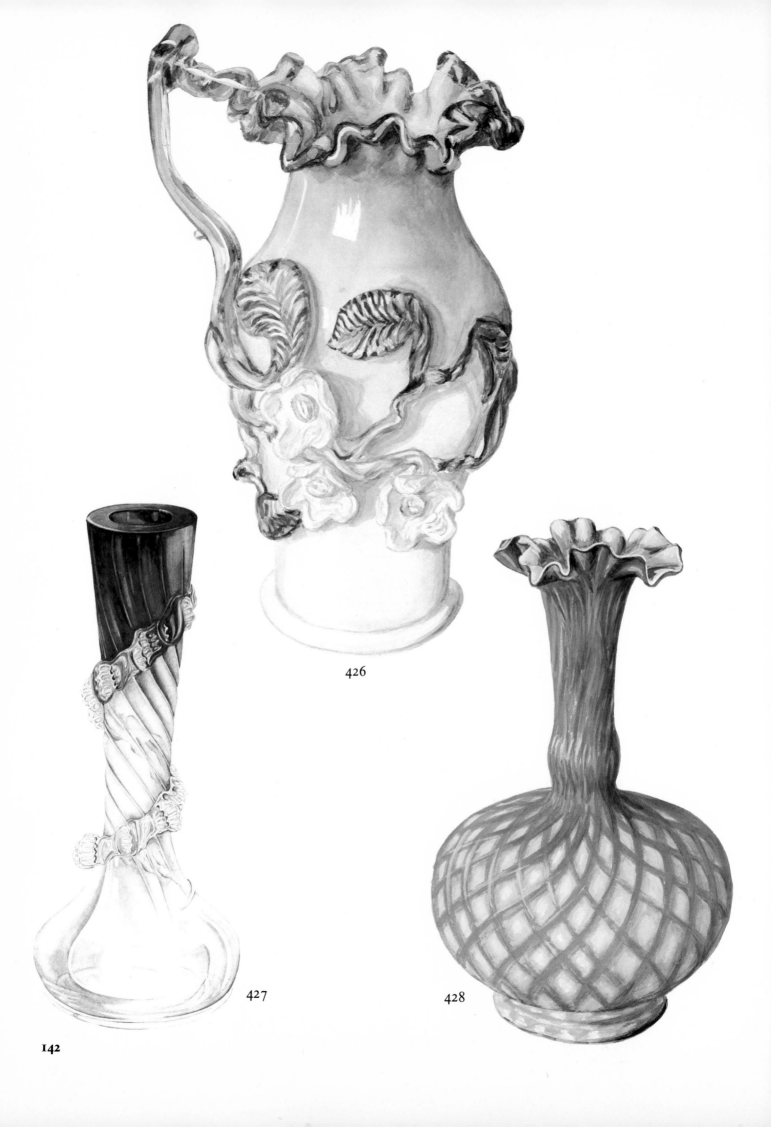

426

427

428

429

426 *Ornamental blue pitcher of overlaid glass with tooled glass deco-*
ration. Exuberant treatment is characteristic of the South Jersey
tradition in which the earlier lily-pod forms developed, by the mid-
nineteenth century, into more naturalistic extravagance 427 *Orna-*
mental vase with spiral spray of crimped forms overlaid on ribbed neck,
c. 1845–55 428 *Ornamental vase of ruby glass called "old satin";*
probably of South Jersey manufacture 429 *Pale blue ornamental*
basket of overlaid glass with naturalistic decorations and crimped
edging. Made in either South Jersey or West Virginia 430 *Blown*
ruby glass vase or ornament with tooled green glass ornamentation,
spiral spray, and petals for footing. Same provenance as 429

Overleaf: GALLERY OF PITCHERS AND DECANTERS. *The examples*
shown are clear glass or frosted, blown-three-mold or pressed, from
factories in New England, New York, New Jersey, Pennsylvania, and
Ohio. Their dates range over the nineteenth century. Photographs
by the Index of American Design

430

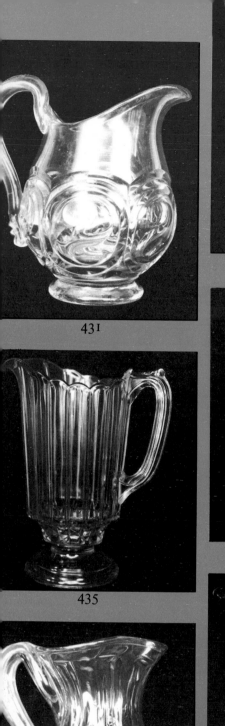

431

432

433

434

435

436

437

438

439

440

441

442

443

444

445

446

447

448

449

450

451

452

453

454

455

456

457

458

459

460

461

462

Candy Jars, Compotes & Cup Plates

464

PRESSED GLASSWARE was found to be ideal for flat or shallow pieces. Service plates, tea plates, cup plates, compotes, trays, spoon and celery holders, candy jars, salts, and covered dishes for butter, cake, and sugar were produced in great numbers. Most of these articles were pressed in clear glass, although a variety of colors, including amethyst, sapphire, green, ruby, amber, canary, and citron, were also used. Exciting designs were created by contrasting large motifs like leaves, palmettes, and bull's-eyes with cross-hatched, beaded, or diamond-cut areas, in imitation of the more expensive cut glass. Characteristic design motifs included acanthus leaves, scrolls, palmettes, peacock feathers, hearts, sunbursts, tulips, fleur-de-lys, roses, thistles, daisies, lyres, cornucopias with fields of diamond point, and strawberry diamonds.

Cup plates became the largest single tableware item produced by the various factories, although they had only an incidental use: to hold a tea cup. It is difficult to determine why the simple little cup plate should have become so popular. Perhaps this popularity stemmed from the widely accepted nineteenth-century custom of sipping tea or coffee from the saucer, or perhaps it was another manifestation of the collector's mania. Whatever the reason, dozens of houses vied with one another in issuing hundreds of new patterns to meet the demands of the market. The design of cup plates falls into three categories: conventional designs,

463 A selection of lacy pressed glass dating from about 1825 to 1850, and pressed pattern glass, about 1840–70. Most of the pieces were produced at the Boston and Sandwich Glass Company and the New England Glass Company. Mechanical pressing of glass, an American invention of about 1825, gave great impetus to glass production and was readily adopted in England and Europe. Photograph courtesy Corning Museum of Glass, Corning, New York 464 Cobalt glass sugar bowl designed by Stiegel. Made in Manheim, Pennsylvania, c. 1770

both geometric and naturalistic; historical; and semihistorical and pictorial. Among the subjects depicted on the flat circular center of the cup plate are portraits, especially of George Washington; eagles in many forms; log cabins; various commemorative subjects, such as the Bunker Hill Monument, the *Constitution*, and the *Clermont*; railroads, stagecoaches, plows, and all types of symbols and figures.

Designs produced by a factory which were especially successful with the public, such as log-cabin and Henry Clay cup plates, were immediately copied by scores of other factories. Sometimes these imitations were exact replicas of the originals; sometimes variations were introduced. Molds were occasionally exchanged between houses on a friendly basis.

Production of other items of tableware, particularly jars, bowls, compotes, and butter and cake dishes, increased with the public's desire for new patterns to accompany each new season. The changing styles in design motifs which occur throughout the field of pressed glassware can be traced in the patterns of these articles. In the late 1830s and early '40s, complicated designs appeared, imitating popular patterns in cut glass. Among these are New England pineapple, horn of plenty, comet, four petal, and Sandwich star. In the 1850s many patterns were characterized by vertical ribbing. Included in this group are ribbed grape, ivy, ribbed acorn, fine rib, ribbed palm, inverted fern, southern ivy, and bellflower. The bellflower pattern is to be found in the greatest number of articles with ribbed designs. By the 1860s and '70s, at the height of the Victorian Age, elaborate designs done in high relief and displaying naturalistic motifs were popular.

465 *Decanter, cake dish, bowl, and vase in blown-three-mold geometric patterns from factories in New England and the Midwest, early nineteenth century. Photograph courtesy the Metropolitan Museum of Art, New York City* **466** *Lacy pressed glass made in the New England area, about 1830–45. The compote and* Constitution *tray are attributed to the Boston and Sandwich Glass Company. The tray was probably made about 1830 after the furor over the proposed scrapping of "Old Ironsides." Photograph courtesy Corning Museum of Glass, Corning, New York*

4
4

149

467

468

469

470

471

467 *Butter dish and cover of red enamel over clear pressed glass. Made in Pittsburgh, c. 1890* **468** *Sapphire blue sugar bowl with octagonal side panels, turned up scalloped rim, and paneled dome with acorn finial. Made in Pittsburgh, c. 1850* **469** *Hand-blown sugar bowl with cover of clear flint glass and loopings of rose and white. Clear glass knob, stem, and circular foot. Made in Cambridge, 1825–50* **470** *Lidded sugar bowl on stem and footing. Probably made in Sandwich, 1830* **471** *Deep blue glass sugar bowl with lid. Made in Pittsburgh, 1830* **472** *Covered butter dish in sawtooth pattern, c. 1855–60*

472

473

474

475

476

473 Clear glass candy jar with paneled sides and dome and circular base. Made in Pittsburgh by Bakewell, c. 1825–40 **474** Pressed-glass candy bowl with pronounced swirl design covering body, base, and top **475** Sugar bowl of clear and frosted glass with stork design on sides and finial, c. 1870 **476** Covered oval dish with sawtooth design and jagged rim which meshes with top. Made by both Cambridge and Sandwich glass companies, c. 1860

477

478

477 Large covered compote dish with clear ribbon pattern. Made by Bakewell, Pears and Company, c. 1887 **478** Covered compote with honeycomb pattern and matching wavy rims. Made in Pittsburgh, c. 1850 **479** Clear pressed-glass lidded fruit bowl with handle **480** Clear glass compote with three-faced motif of frosted glass on base, stem and finial. Manufactured in Pittsburgh. All illustrations on these pages from photographs by the Index of American Design

479

480

153

481

482

483

154

484

481 *Pressed-glass compote without lid. Pattern is a variant of the daisy-and-button design, c. 1890* 482 *Pressed-glass compote or fruit bowl with dewdrop design and stippled panels, c. 1875–80* 483 *Pressed-glass compote, c. 1880* 484 *Pressed-glass compote with paneled sides and stem and circular footing* 485 *Clear pressed-glass fruit bowl on stem with variant of bull's-eye design* 486 *Compote with sultan, or curtain, pattern. Made in Pittsburgh, 1866* 487 *Deep*

485

486

487

488

pressed-glass bowl on stem. Fluted sides with scalloped base and rim **488** *Pressed-glass bowl with bull's-eye pattern and circular footed base*

Overleaf: Gallery of Compotes and Candy Jars. *From the 1850s to about 1890, glass factories from Boston to Pittsburgh and beyond were producing great quantities of pressed glass in an infinite variety of designs. Photographs by the Index of American Design*

155

489

490

491

492

493

494

495

496

497

498

499

500

501

502

503

504

505

506

507

508

509

510

511

512

513

514

515

516

517

518

519

520

521

522

523

524

525

526

527

528

157

529 530

531

529 Clear pressed-glass cup plate with lyre design, c. 1830–40 530 Opalescent pressed-glass cup plate with heart motif in outer rim, c. 1835–50 531 Octagonal plate, c. 1830. Cusped medallion with eagle bordered by stars in circles 532 Clear pressed-glass cup plate with hearts and palmettes, c. 1831 533 Clear cup plate, c. 1830. Large American eagle encircled by stars, border, and scalloped rim 534 Decorative octagonal cup plate with the frigate Constitution in center, c. 1830 All photographs courtesy Corning Museum of Glass, Corning, New York

Overleaf: GALLERY OF CUP PLATES AND DISHES. Development of the glass-pressing machine in the late 1820s led to the perfection of techniques

158

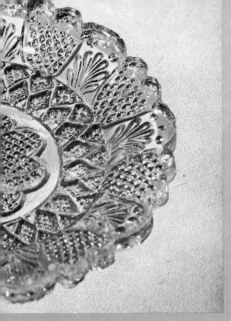

532

533

534

and the production of vast amounts of inexpensive household items, particularly plates and dishes, most of which fall into the category described as lacy glass. Over a hundred factories turned out thousands of patterns, fancifully named, some original, others imitative. In **535–59** are large plates for cakes and cookies. A number of these have footed bases. The motto "Give Us This Day Our Daily Bread," **559**, is the Continental design bread tray. Fig. **560** and **561** show pickle and relish dishes; **562**, a relish dish in the shell-and-tassel pattern. Fig. **565–72** show cup plates mostly made c. 1830–40 at the Sandwich factory. Photographs from the Index of American Design except **560**, a rendering based upon a Currier & Ives print

159

535

536

540

539

545

537

538

544

543

551

542

550

561

41

549

560

558

557

564

546

547

548

553

554

555

556

562

563

564

565

566

567

568

569

571

572

161

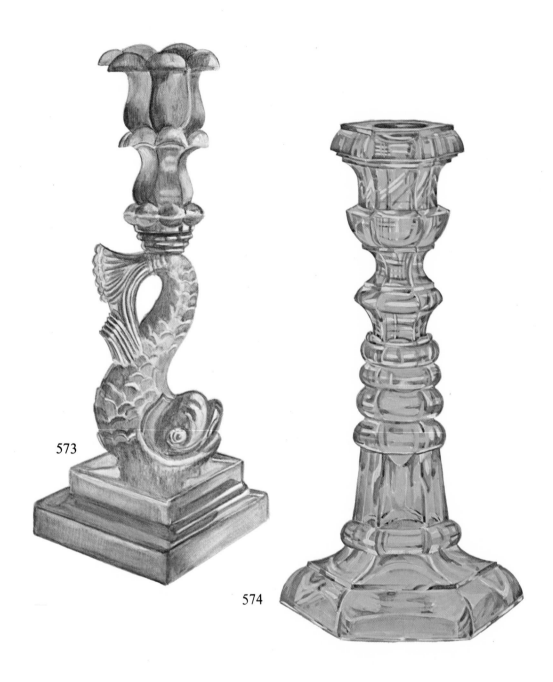

573

574

573 *Dolphin candlestick with petal socket and extension resting on double-square plinth. This very popular glass piece was made in clear glass and in a variety of colors, including canary, light and deep peacock blue, dark sapphire blue, and translucent white. Made by the Sandwich glassworks during the first half of the nineteenth century and copied by other factories* **574** *Hexagonal candlestick with massive socket and multiple deep molding curves forming standard on hexagonal base* **575** *Hexagonal socket and extension; standard composed of large knop, flaring circular pedestal base in loop pattern*

Candlesticks & Lamp Bases

575

Glass objects for home lighting run the gamut of types and styles. In no other area has Yankee ingenuity shown itself to be more prolific than in the making of glass candlesticks and glass lamps.

Before the advent of American commercial glassmaking, Colonial candlesticks were available in a fairly large variety of metals: brass, copper, iron, pewter, and tinware. Glass sticks had been made in Venice and Murano since the sixteenth century, but none found their way to America. A few isolated examples of blown candlesticks were made in this country before 1800, principally by the bottle and window-glass factories, but it was not until glass-pressing operations were in full swing that there was large-scale production of glass candlesticks in many patterns. These candlesticks featured pressed bases, some of which were inverted cup plates, in combination with free-blown stems and nozzles. Above the hollow base, pressed in a variety of designs, the stem was fashioned in a series of hollow

knops, balusters, and wafers. Topping the many separate parts was a rimmed socket, generally upturned to receive dripping wax. Variants of stepped bases in square, quatrefoil, hexagonal, octagonal, or cloverleaf forms were combined with columnar balusters and plain or lacy top sockets to create a number of intriguing designs. Later, when pressed glass ceased to be a novelty and labor costs became a factor, the built-up candlesticks were replaced with simpler molded forms, limited to two or three parts. Designs became standardized and less imaginative except for the introduction of color, which provided elegance. Popular colors were red amber, emerald green, royal purple, sapphire, canary, and translucent white.

By far the most widely imitated design was the famous dolphin design inspired by the Venetians, which made its appearance in the 1850s. Produced in New England factories, principally at Sandwich, and in the Pittsburgh area by McKee and others, the dolphin candlestick became a staple which captured the public's fancy. The dolphin, which did not vary in its basic form, was combined with hexagonal or stepped squares, petal-patterned feet, or scalloped circular bases. This candlestick was available in all colors, translucent, opaque, or alabaster. Estimates indicate that production may have reached a million.

The early glass lamps were simple in design; a graceful, flaring, round or square base held an oval font terminating in a brass or pewter cap. The cover screwed on and contained two wick tubes that permitted the wick ends to reach the font or oil reservoir. Some of these lamps clearly show the pontil mark at the base.

Prior to 1820, lamps were free blown, usually with an applied knop stem and circular foot or base. Some lamps were of table size, about six to ten inches high; most, however, were smaller than this and did not have handles. These smaller lamps were called "sparking lamps," because according to popular legend they were used as timing devices by cautious parents when their daughter entertained a gentleman caller for the evening. The limited oil supply in the lamp determined the duration of his stay, and when the lamp went out, so did he.

In later lamps, the foot or base, standard and socket, and font or bowl were separately pressed. These sections were then joined together with thin wafers of molten glass to form a complete piece.

The different kinds of illuminating fuels had a marked effect on types and styles of lamp bases. Camphine, introduced between 1845 and 1850, was a product of refined turpentine. Because it was extremely explosive, it had to be burned cautiously. It required a longer wick tube than was used for the earlier lamps which burned whale, or sperm, oil.

The sinking of the first oil well in the United States in 1859 and the subsequent production of petroleum, an inexpensive fuel with high lighting efficiency, greatly increased the demand for glass lamps. Lamp bases and lamp chimneys could not be produced fast enough to keep pace with the demand. Staggering quantities were made and new designs proliferated. The entire industry soon adopted the slogan "An oil lamp for every room." The boom, however, was blunted with the outbreak of the Civil War.

576

577

578

579

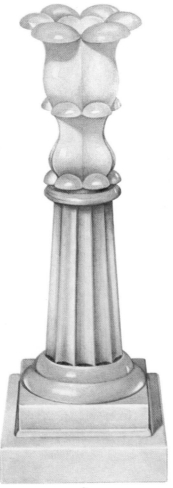

580

581

576 *Lamp base with three-printie-block hexagonal font, ball knop, and hexagonal flaring pedestal base* 577 *Typical of many mid-nineteenth-century lamps which combined glass shades and fonts with metal wick and shade holders* 578 *Lamp base with six-paneled loop font and large round knop; standard consists of octagonal pedestal stem on square plinth base* 579 *Lamp base combining octagonal flared glass font with metal parts and cast figure* 580 *Petal socket and extension joined by wafer to fluted columnar standard on square base* 581 *Hexagonal candlestick socket joined by wafer to columnar standard and base on hexagonal plinth*

Overleaf: GALLERY OF LAMPS, BASES, AND CANDLE-STICKS. *The infinite variety of lamps and lamp bases available from the 1830s to the 1880s is due not only to the interchangeability of glass and metal parts but also to the creative ingenuity of glass-makers and lamp makers. Combinations include blown shades and cylinders, etched and engraved in later years, fonts both blown and pressed in innumerable patterns, stems and standards in glass and metal, and bases of glass, metal, and marble. From photographs by the Index of American Design except* 583, 585, 591, 596, 601, 607, *and* 610, *from renderings*

582

583

588

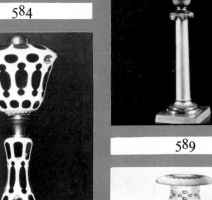

584

589

597

592

598

593

599

607

602

608

603

609

617

612

618

613

619

585

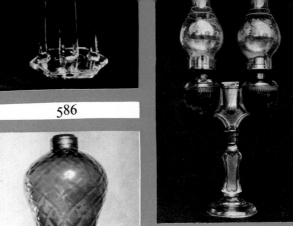

586

587

590

591

594

595

596

600

601

604

605

606

610

611

614

615

616

620

621

Bottles & Flasks
for John Barleycorn

623

ONE WOULD HAVE TO search far and wide to find a single area in which greater inventiveness has been displayed than in the design of nineteenth-century bottles and flasks. The first product of organized glassmakers, bottles were made by about 95 percent of all companies in the industry. There were bottles for bitters, wine, rum, cider, and medicine; bottles for ink, cleaning fluids, kerosene, camphine, rattlesnake oil, bear's grease, and

622 *Figured flasks, some with pictorial and historical subjects, produced in various glasshouses throughout the United States c. 1815–75. They are approximately half-pint, pint, and quart capacity. This type of flask is a peculiarly American phenomenon in glass; only a few pictorial flasks were produced in Europe. Photograph courtesy Corning Museum of Glass, Corning, New York* **623** *Two views of rare eagle flask. On the front, the American eagle with head to the left, shield on breast. On the reverse, eagle in flight carrying a serpent in its beak* **624** *Bitters bottle in the form of an Indian squaw*

624

nostrums of all kinds. Gin, whisky, and cordials were bottled in flasks of all shapes and sizes, from ten-gallon carboys to half-ounce vials. There were squares, ovals, log cabins, fiddles, cornucopias, and calabashes produced in clear glass and in a wide variety of colors, including rose, blue, amethyst, aqua, purple, amber, pale and dark green, and even black. The design treatments were so varied that it has been said that American history can be traced through the subject matter on glass bottles.

Extensive research has failed to establish exactly when the first bottle was blown in full-size piece molds. As early as 1809, a notice in the Baltimore *Daily Advertiser* recommended Dr. Robertson's Family Medicines, in square flint bottles prepared by T. W. Dyott. Before long, decorations appeared on a flask's surfaces. From the time of the War of 1812 to about 1860, dozens of glass manufacturers turned out quantities of bottles, accounting for over five hundred different designs. The advantages of full-size piece molds over the old free-blown techniques were obvious: the assurance of controlled capacities, not to mention labor-saving economies.

The terms "flask" and "pocket bottle" were used interchangeably to describe the majority of bottle types: forms with flat or convex surfaces rising to a shoulder and narrow neck, oval or elliptical in cross section. Usually both sides of the flask or bottle were decorated, sometimes with names and inscriptions. Purely decorative designs were used as well as pictorial representations showing patriotic motifs, portraits of presidents, historical figures and heroes of the day, and social and political events. Sunbursts, urns, cornucopias, wreaths, sheaves of wheat, ears of corn, and geometric

designs decorated one side or were secondary to pictorial themes on the reverse side.

By far the greatest variety of motifs included symbols of patriotic interest such as the eagle, the American flag, Columbia, and the stars and the shield. Over a hundred different flasks used the eagle as the central theme, sometimes as the only decoration, or on the reverse side of flasks featuring portraits of national heroes. The eagle was also paired with Columbia, the Masonic emblem, the American flag, a scroll and floral medallion, sunburst or cornucopia, or the railroad. The constant recurrence of the eagle motif, a symbol of strength and sovereignty, indicates the spirit of unity that marked the first half of the nineteenth century.

The most popular figure for portraits was George Washington. Busts of Washington appeared on more than sixty different types of flask, most of which were molded between 1820 and 1830. Many Washington flasks have the American eagle on the reverse side; others show a ship, a sheaf of wheat, the Baltimore Monument, or portraits of statesmen or generals. Presidents Andrew Jackson, William Henry Harrison, and Zachary Taylor were also popular subjects. Other figures include Benjamin Franklin, General Lafayette, and Louis Kossuth, the patriot of the Hungarian Revolution. DeWitt Clinton, who sponsored the Erie Canal, appears on a few flasks. There are twelve flasks extant which carry the portrait of the Swedish nightingale, Jenny Lind.

Transportation themes on flasks featured horse-drawn carts and steam locomotives with the inscription "Success to the Railroad." These flasks were made in great quantities in factories throughout New York, New Hampshire, Vermont, and Connecticut.

625

626

627

628

630

631

629

625 *Stiegel-type perfume bottle, about half-pint size, with free-blown diamond-daisy design* 626 *Blown-three-mold decanter with diamond-sunburst design and swirled fluting. Madeby Mt. Vernon Glass Company, c. 1820–35* 627 *Stiegel perfume bottle with honeycomb pattern and ribbed neck, fluting in lower half, c. 1770* 628, 629 *Obverse and reverse sides of pint-size flask feature large urn with five vertical bars and cornucopia filled with produce* 630 *Stiegel-type pattern-molded flint toilet bottle with broken swirl fluting, late eighteenth century* 631 *Pint flask with large elliptical sunburst design and horizontally corrugated edging, c. 1815* 632 *Scroll flask with elaborate decoration forming conventionalized acanthus leaves; diamond motif at center. Probably of Pittsburgh manufacture*

632

633

634

635

176

636

633 *Bitters bottle showing realistically modeled Indian maiden. Made in 1868 by Whitney Brothers, South Jersey* **634** *Rectangular bottle with chamfered corners, decorated with graceful urns and floral forms* **635** *Figured bottle features a bearded Rip van Winkle type and is marked with phrase "Poland Water" near base. Made by Kensington Glass Works, Philadelphia* **636** *The American eagle ornaments more than a hundred different flasks made prior to 1850. Often it appears on the reverse side of flasks featuring portraits of Washington or other patriotic figures. Photograph courtesy New York Historical Society, New York City* **637** *Square bottle with twisted neck, marked "McHenry—1812," celebrates the origin of the "Star Spangled Banner." Made in Baltimore, mid-nineteenth century* **638** *Bitters bottle served medicinal purposes. Marked "S.T. Drake 1860 Planttation X Bitters"*

638

637

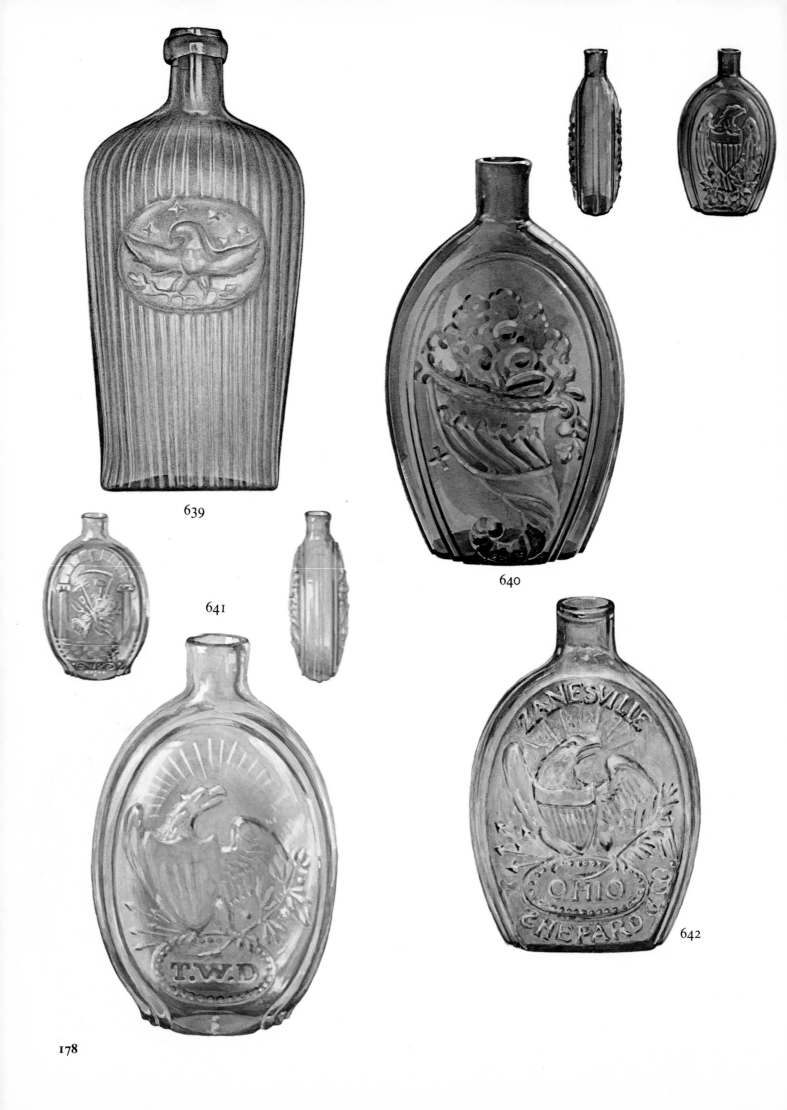

639

640

641

642

639 *Ribbed pint flask with eagle medallion in oval. Made in Louisville, Kentucky, c. 1845–50* 640 *Cornucopia motif, popular with several glass works, was often on the reverse side of an eagle flask* 641 *Eagle with shield and olive branch, over oval with initials "T.W.D."; obverse side displays masonic arch and columns framing "Farmer's Arms." Made by Kensington Glass Works, Philadelphia* 642 *Eagle flask with name and location of maker* 643 *Eagle flask with deep modeling, giving high relief to details. Made by Lancaster Glass Works, c. 1850–60* 644 *Eagle flask with the word "Liberty." Made in Connecticut* 645 *Masonic flask with agricultural implements in archway. Made by Kensington Glass Works, Philadelphia* 646 *Flask featuring General Zachary Taylor and George Washington on opposite sides. Made by Bridgeton Glass Works, New Jersey*

647

648 A

651

652 A

652 B

653

649

650

648 B

657

658

659

655

656

666 A

666 B

663 A

663 B

664

665

675

676 A

673

674

654

660 A

660 B

661

662

667

668

669

670

671

672

676 B

677

678

679

680

681

682

683

684

685

686

687

688

689

690

690 *A typical woodworking shop, illustrated above, belonged to successive generations of the Dominy family of East Hampton, Long Island. It was in operation from the mid-eighteenth century until the 1940s. Displayed here are more than eight hundred tools used in the Dominys' trades as cabinetmakers and clockmakers, craftsmen, builders of gun stocks, boats, and windmills. The "great wheel" lathe in the foreground was manually turned by an apprentice. Hanging from the rafters are documents of the cabinetmaker's craft: templates for cutting cabriole legs, cresting rails, and chair splats. On the work benches are jack and block planes, and the shelf at the rear holds countless molding and shaping planes. A pole lathe operated by foot can be seen in the rear of the shop. Photograph by Gilbert Ask, courtesy the Henry Francis du Pont Winterthur Museum, Winterthur, Delaware*

A Wonderful Way
with Woods

IN THE EARLY years of the Colonies almost everything was made either partly or entirely of wood: houses, ships, bridges, barns, plows, harrows, wagons, carts, sleds, farming and fishing tools, furniture, household utensils, looms, spinning wheels, dishes, and novelties.

To the early settlers, it must have seemed as if the vast forests of timber would last forever. In a letter written by Benjamin Rush to Thomas Jefferson in 1791, Rush stated that six thousand trees had to be cut to clear an average farm in New York or Pennsylvania.

After the trees were felled, the logs had to be sawed into separate boards. This arduous chore was done in a saw pit. The pit was hollowed out and lined with face bricks so that the huge tree trunk, often forty to fifty feet long, could be rolled on transverse rollers as the two sawyers did their backbreaking work. The top sawyer guided a huge pit saw along a snapped-on line, frequently swabbing the blade with linseed oil. The man in the pit pulled the downstroke, for this was the cutting stroke that did the heavy work with the assistance of gravity. This pit method was used until 1816 when Eli Terry, a Yankee clockmaker, invented a "round saw" operated by waterpower.

White pine, a soft pine which grows in the northern regions, supplied most of the settlers' early needs. It is durable, surprisingly free of knots, and easy to work. It was suitable for simple country-type pieces and for furniture wainscoting.

Basswood and whitewood were used in much the same fashion as pine. Basswood is a light wood, soft and tough, that does not show the broad grain of pine. It was often used for chair seats. Whitewood, the market name for tulipwood, is found in the furniture of the southern New England states, particularly Connecticut. It is lighter in weight than basswood. Because whitewood is generally free of knots, it was favored for painted chests. It was also used to line the interiors of chests and bureau drawers and for backboards and other unseen parts of tables. In the nineteenth century, Windsor chair seats were constructed of whitewood.

Soft cedar was used for the interior parts of early furniture, especially drawers.

Another tree which has soft and workable wood is the poplar. It was not used extensively because of the difficulty in seasoning the boards and their tendency to warp.

Oak became popular in certain areas, par-

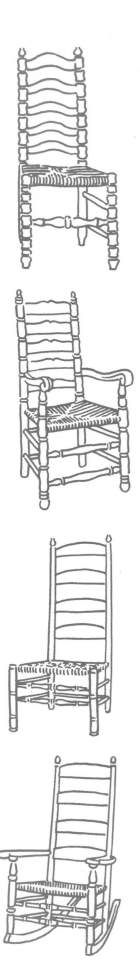

ticularly in Connecticut, for chests, court cupboards, wainscot chairs, Bible boxes, joined stools, and the bases of trestle tables. A small chest, dated 1660, is the earliest known use of oak in the Colonies that can be verified. Furniture pieces in the Pilgrim style of the late seventeenth century were made of oak. Some oak pieces were probably brought over by the English settlers.

Maple played an important role in the construction of medium-quality furniture. It was not as common as pine or as fine as walnut or mahogany. Maple was not generally used for furnishings in the parlor or formal room of a residence, but in less important areas. It could be turned easily, carved well, and with careful staining took on variations of coloring. The most natural maple color is a golden yellow, or amber, in which the grain or flecking provides a rich texture. It is available in three distinct configurations which result from cutting different parts of the sugar maple. These configurations, straight, curly, or bird's-eye maple, can be used to obtain a variety of grains and surface markings. A very hard and close-grained wood with fine pores and fibers, maple calls for very sharp planes, chisels, and saw teeth. It requires the precise workmanship of the professional. The appearance of the curly and bird's-eye grains results from an accidental arrangement of the wood fibers, a condition that also creates the "burl" of walnut and the "crotch" of mahogany. The curly markings of "tiger" maple feature random twists and regular grain alterations. Many maple pieces were made in the William and Mary style (1690–1730).

Other woods, including cherry, apple, and pear, were used to some extent because they were easily obtainable, inexpensive, and preferable for certain pieces. Cherry was used as early as 1680; it has been made into many fine pieces of furniture, particularly tables with broad leaves and turned legs. It is a very hard and close-grained wood and takes on a high reddish-brown color that approaches the look of mahogany. After about 1770, cherry was

often substituted for mahogany in tables, chairs, chests of drawers, highboys, lowboys, chests-on-chests, and mirror frames. In the Connecticut area, tall clock cases were often made of cherry.

Frequently an early piece had a mixture of native woods. A drop-leaf table, for instance, might have had two legs of yellow birch, two of maple, a top of cherry, and possibly one leaf of some other hardwood. The carpenter may have had to use several woods because of a shortage of lumber.

Hickory and ash, both strong and tough, were used where strength was needed. For example, hickory was always used for the spindles of Windsor chairs. Because its fibers are tenacious, hickory was also used for tool handles, particularly axes, hammers, and rakes. It was not favored by cabinetmakers, however, because it cannot withstand heat and moisture. Ash, a heavy wood of great strength, has a grain and texture not unlike oak. Ash bends readily under steam and was used extensively for bows and other curved parts of Windsor chairs and for rockers.

The woods most favored for the more elegant early pieces were walnut and mahogany. These woods came into vogue with the fine classic styles of William and Mary and Queen Anne, and were in fashion through the Chippendale, Hepplewhite, Sheraton, and American Empire periods. In England the "age of walnut" extended from 1660 to 1725. Thereafter, the fashion for this wood faded and finely figured mahogany became a favorite. In America, the same system of dating applies in the major cities, but the use of walnut continued for many years, running concurrently with the use of mahogany.

Walnut trees grow throughout the eastern states. A hard strong wood with a fine texture and a handsome grain, walnut is a moderate reddish brown in color. It was used for many fine pieces in the Queen Anne and Chippendale periods. Later Victorian cabinetmakers treated the wood surface with a stain or acid wash before varnishing, offsetting its natural reddish tinge and creating a darker finish.

Of the many woods used throughout the Colonial and Federal periods, mahogany was the only one to be imported. Although more expensive than native woods, its cost was more than offset by its quality. Mahogany came primarily from Santo Domingo and Haiti in the West Indies, but was also imported from Mexico, Central America, and certain coastal areas of Africa. In the eighteenth century, when Santo Domingo belonged to Spain, the general term "Spanish mahogany" was used. The "age of mahogany" in this country covers the period between about 1730 and 1840. Mahogany has a brilliance that exceeds that of other woods, a fine texture with a variety of grains and figures, and great strength and hardness, which make it capable of taking a high polish. It varies in color from deep reddish brown to red with brown or chocolate undertones. Because mahogany trees sometimes reached a diameter of ten feet, they could furnish wide boards for table tops. A distinctive feature of this wood was its crotch-grain veneer, used for the decorative quality of its markings. This gracious wood was considered the peer of cabinetry woods by cabinetmakers in England and America. The finest and the most elegant pieces of furniture in the Chippendale, Hepplewhite, Sheraton, and American Empire style were made of it.

The first joiners to reach here, among them John Alden, worked as housewrights, barn builders, shingle shapers, carpenters, coopers, and wheelwrights. Before beginning a piece of furniture, the joiner took the irregular boards as they came from the saw pit and by a series of operations reduced the plank to a smooth surface. His most useful tools were a set of planes which he had to make himself. A set of four planes included a seventeen-inch jack plane for the roughest work; a twenty-inch plane called the short jointer for smoothing; a long jointer that measured thirty inches; and a short, seven-inch boat-shaped smoothing plane for surfacing. The planes were made of hardwood, preferably maple, with a wedge-

shaped opening which held the finely formed, razor-sharp cutting blades. The blades were cut by the blacksmith and carefully honed by the joiner on a grindstone or whetstone. In addition to four basic planes, the joiner had a variety of rabbet planes with shaped blades which he used for molding profiles for bead, shiplap, tongue and groove, and wainscot edges. Chisels and gouges, in at least a half-dozen widths, braces, bits, bow drills, augers, squares, saws, clamps, and marking gauges completed his battery of tools for ordinary tasks. His workbench of solid maple—equipped with a fine vise, if he was able to fashion the wooden screws by hand—was most important as a working surface.

No shop for carpentry or cabinetmaking was complete unless it was equipped for wood-turning. Turnings were an integral part of the cabinetmaking process. Certain pieces of furniture, such as bedposts and chair and table legs, called for turned work. On highboys and lowboys in the William and Mary style, the "inverted cup" and the "trumpet" legs formed the base for many pieces. On many tables, especially gateleg types, there are various forms of turnings called spool, ball, sausage, and knob turnings. A spiral turning is one shaped like a corkscrew; bulbous turnings occurred in certain styles which called for a heavy leg. On many chests and cupboards of the late seventeenth century, turned spindles or bosses, cut down the middle and glued to the flat surface, were used as a type of applied decoration. Stretchers on many articles of furniture consisted of straight turned members. The finial that tops many highboys and secretary-bookcases is another familiar turned piece.

Turned work was done on a lathe. In the seventeenth century it was a crude instrument fashioned of hardwoods, consisting of a head and tail stock to hold the wood and a tool rest as a guide for the cutting chisel and gouge. These were mounted on a sturdy wooden frame that could withstand vibration and rotation during the turning process. In order to turn a piece of wood fast enough for efficient cutting,

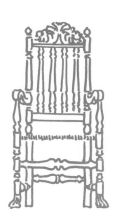

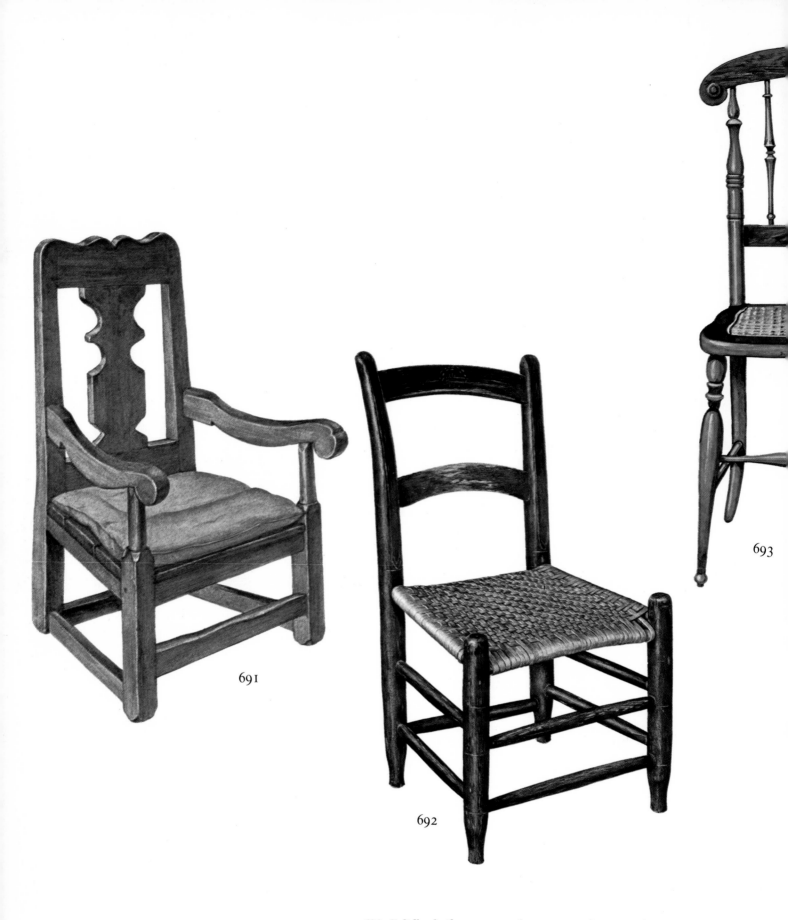

691

692

693

691 *Solidly built seventeenth-century oaken armchair without carving; based on English models* 692 *Simplest type of popular country chair, with double slats and turned forelegs* 693 *Delicately turned spindles, legs, and stretcher distinguish this graceful cane chair* 694 *Victorian side chair with spindle back and carved top rail* 695 *Late Victorian chair with open back, high seat, and splayed, turned forelegs*

694

695

it was necessary to rotate the mandrel holding the wood. This was accomplished by means of a rope which was actuated by the turning of the "great wheel." This wheel, about eight feet in diameter, stood some distance away. As it was turned by hand, it spun the mandrel at speeds of several hundred revolutions per minute while the turner worked the various beads, stops, and subtle curves with a variety of cutting tools. The two-man turning operation was very efficient because the woodturner could devote all his energy to shaping his work. Another type of lathe was called the spring pole, or back-action, lathe. It consisted of a few simple parts that enabled the turner to operate a foot treadle. An up-and-down movement turned the wooden piece in a semicircular motion while the turner shaped his stock with chisel and gouge. The fact that some finely

turned posts and legs were produced with these crude devices is a tribute to the ingenuity and dexterity of the Colonial craftsman.

The entire cabinetmaking process involved a variety of skills, which included design, construction, joinery, molding, shaping, carved ornamentation, inlaying and marquetry, staining, polishing, and gilding. In different periods, some of these operations were omitted, yet the professional craftsman had to be accomplished in a variety of skills in order to produce a complete work.

The quality of carving on a piece of furniture ranged from the crudest to the most elegant, according to prevailing styles and regions. In every style workmanship varied from shoddy to skillful. Carved motifs used during various periods include acanthus leaves, plant and floral forms, cornucopias, wings, bird and

696

697

698

696 *Crude type of peasant chair, generally homemade by a house-wright* 697 *Ladder-back chair with notched ends on uprights suggesting German peasant influence. Rawhide seat indicates cattle-country provenance* 698 *Painted cottage chair with cane seat. Graceful curves of splat and rail combine with turned members* 699 *Ladder-back chair from the Southwest with crudely interwoven seat of leather thongs* 700 *Child's chair from Texas with seat of leather thongs*

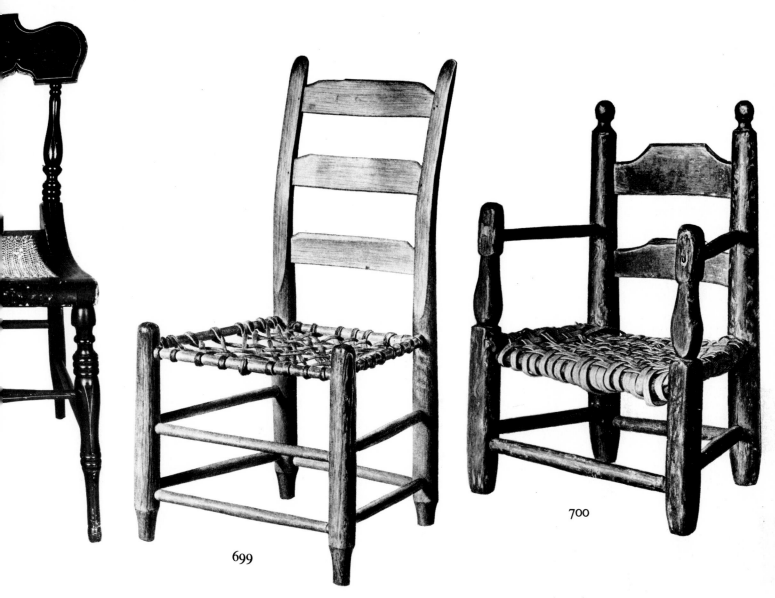

699

700

animal forms, scrolls and volutes, and shells and sunbursts. Variations of these basic forms as well as numerous combinations served as the basis for constantly changing ornamental styles. Mounts (pieces of metal or decorative hardware) were also used. They included knobs, handles, escutcheons, and other hardware pieces, in brass or ormolu.

Some pieces of furniture were decorated with inlays. Ivory and precious metals, often in the form of plaques and medallions, were set into surfaces. In the eighteenth and nineteenth centuries, inlays of wood, shell, or ivory were inserted into thin wooden veneers which were then placed into grooves or sunken areas cut into the furniture. The veneer could be applied in thin lines or stripes as border designs or in overall areas of contrasting grain, textures, and patterns. This process is called marquetry.

After a piece was constructed, carved, and decorated, it was painted, stained, or, in special types of furniture, gilded and stenciled. The early pine, maple, and cherry pieces of the seventeenth century were solidly painted. It was customary to apply one color in several coats. Over the years more coats were added. In the eighteenth century, this practice was discontinued, and natural staining became the vogue. After staining, many coats of varnish were applied and polished.

The work of such master cabinetmakers as William Savery of Philadelphia, John Goddard and the Townsends of Newport, Duncan Phyfe of New York, and many others, is marked by great elegance. Their carvings were executed with fine taste and precision in moldings and details. It is little wonder that their surviving pieces are treasured wherever fine craftsmanship is recognized.

701

702

703

704

705

701–706 *Slat-back or ladder-back chairs were produced in a great variety of styles, ranging from three rungs to as many as seven. They first appeared in the period from 1700 to 1720 and have been a staple item ever since. It is generally agreed that the type with front legs and back posts turned in what is called the sausage-and-ball form is of New England make. Those having plain turned back legs and posts are of the Pennsylvania type, with turned finials of back posts an added feature. The shape of the slats is a distinguishing mark. Slat designs include: (1) curved laterally to conform to the back of the sitter, (2) laterally curved and also shaped in a number of ways: arched, wavy, in double waves, in cyma curves, and in the form of dolphins, head to head. The early slat-back chairs usually had a rush seat or sometimes a rope seat, woven in the same fashion as a rush seat but using good stout cord or rope, either of flax or hemp. When such a seat was badly worn and in need of repair, the thrifty housewife made an upholstered seat, 703, with materials at hand. A typical Pennsylvania armchair with five slats, graduated in size, 705, shows the front stretcher with large bulbous or vase-shaped turnings, c. 1750*

706

707 Ladder-back chair with low cornhusk seat, used in the kitchen **708** Banister-back armchair with high arched rail and bulbous front stretchers. Pennsylvania type, c. 1725 **709** Maple banister chair with turned legs and back posts, c. 1700–1710 **710** Chair with four reeded banisters and scrolled and crested top rail with heart cutout, c. 1860 **711** Painted and decorated curly maple ladder-chair. Made by Shaker craftsmen, 1820 **712** Sturdy, pegged construction, low chair rails, and open wainscot back show strong English influence, c. 1650

707

709

708

710

711

712

193

Please Be *Seated*

714

THE CHAIR, man's simple yet ingenious "machine for comfort," has for over three thousand years been a sign of his civilization, an accepted symbol of status, an indicator of social change, and a yardstick of technological progress. From the *klismos* of ancient Greece, at once graceful and decorative yet strictly functional, to the inflatable plastic forms of the contemporary scene or the form-fitting contour shapes designed for the astronauts, the chair's main purpose has been to rest man's body and relax his system.

From the beginning of the New England settlement there were the Carver chairs with turned members, spindle-backs and also slat-backs, named for John Carver, who was the Colony's first Governor. The earliest examples of this chair were very clumsy, but over the years it was gradually refined. The Brewster chair is generally similar but it is a trifle more ornamental in its many turnings, which number about forty spindles per chair, sometimes even more.

By the last decade of the seventeenth century, joiners and furniture makers in small towns as well as larger cities had expanded their trade into a flourishing industry. While English influences predominated, the Colonial craftsmen were already exhibiting an independence of their own by simplifying forms and eliminating extra embellishments. Banister-back chairs with four or five vertical slats topped by a cresting between stiles were an outgrowth of the more formal William and Mary cane-backed chair. Two flat pieces, temporarily fastened together, were turned on a lathe and then separated; the resulting spindles matched and had flat surfaces. This is just one small example of the ingenuity introduced by native chairmakers within the framework of existing styles imported from abroad.

A most common and popular type of chair is the slat-back that evolved from the heavier form of Puritan chair with turned uprights and three horizontal slats across the back, which was made from 1670 to 1700. Throughout the eighteenth century the slat-back prevailed, with variants in two broad classes: the New England type and that of Pennsylvania. The New England chairs, like their Puritan precursors, are constructed with slats whose

713 *Parlor of the Governor's Palace, Williamsburg, Virginia. The artistry of master cabinetmakers is evident in the upholstered chairs as well as in the other mid-eighteenth-century fine furnishings and architectural detailing of fireplace and mantel. Photograph courtesy Colonial Williamsburg* 714 *Mahogany side chair with eagle splat. Attributed to Duncan Phyfe, c. 1815*

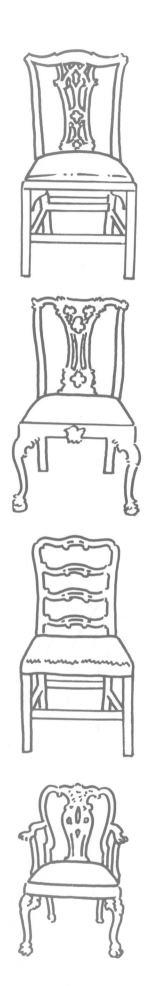

lower edges are straight and whose upper edges are curved. Their uprights are turned with rings and beads corresponding to the spaces between slats. In the Pennsylvania version the slats, as many as six compared to the limit of four in the New England type, are curved, with pronounced arched upswings on both top and bottom edges. Front stretchers show ball or sausage turning, side stretchers are plain. Both types of slat-back chairs use rush seats. Both were made with and without arms, and also in miniature form as a child's chair; their uprights are most frequently of maple or birch, with slats and stretcher parts of oak, ash, beech, or hickory.

The short period of Queen Anne's reign (1702–14) was important in furniture design in England and in the Colonies. In America the style identified as Queen Anne was popular from 1720 to 1750, although its influence lingered on until the close of the century. In the early 1700s the many alien strains that had crept into English designs in the previous generations were more fully assimilated. The Baroque details of Continental origin popular in the reigns of Charles II, James II, and William and Mary, which incorporated intricate patterns, reverse scrolls, and curves, were replaced by a more sober style in keeping with the English dislike for ornamental extravagance. Characteristic of the Queen Anne style was a blending of form and function and the dominance of the curve typified by the graceful, undulating sweep of the cabriole legs on chairs, tables, and other supports. Popular acceptance of the style was widespread in the cities and smaller towns of the main river valleys, where it was identified not only by the curve of the legs but by serpentine stretchers, rounded splats, undulating crests for chair tops, and lower aprons gracefully arched in cyma-curvate shapes.

It has been said that many of the sophisticated amenities of home comfort and utility had their origins in the Queen Anne period. Not only chairs but many other articles designed for comfort and convenience in the home, such as tea, gaming, and dressing tables, mirrors, and frames came into being or were perfected at this time. Earlier Puritan stiffness typified by the hard-seated wainscot chair now melted into grace and classic symmetry as carving gave way to beautifully proportioned flat or contoured surfaces, form-fitting for bodily comfort.

The corner chair, in its many style changes over three centuries, is one of the most comfortable ever devised, ideal for lounging and stretching while seated. Because of its semicircular arm rest one can loll in it, sit sideways or straight to the fore. By the eighteenth century this type had earned the name "roundabout chair." The universal appeal of these chairs is easy to understand. They take up little space and are sturdy in construction, cheerful and inviting in appearance. The diagonally placed seat puts a single leg forward, with the back forming a right-angled corner softened by the rounded arm rest. This curve generally has a low, centered cresting shaped with a backward sweep. A Queen Anne version with vase-shaped splats sometimes has a front cabriole leg ending in a Dutch or drake foot. The square seat is either rushed or upholstered; the fronts may carry deeply valanced skirts. A favorite with fine cabinetmakers, the corner chair can also be a simple country-made piece.

In the period extending from about 1755 to 1785, the greatest foreign influence was that of Thomas Chippendale, whose book *The Gentlemand and Cabinet-Maker's Director*, published in 1754, set forth his elegant designs in some two hundred beautifully engraved plates. Chippendale borrowed freely from his predecessors in the Queen Anne style, and he adapted motifs from the French, the Dutch, the Spanish, and the Italians as well as from the popular and fanciful creations of the Chinese. With these richly engraved plates to guide them, Colonial chairmakers, notably in the large cities, embarked on a period that produced some of the most magnificent examples of the furniture maker's art.

The characteristics of Chippendale-type chairs, while not adhering to any rigidly recognizable formula, have certain features in common. Top rails usually follow the "cupid's bow" curvature, with the two ends or "ears" curved upward. Another top rail variant, not as common as the cupid's bow, carries three curves in a downward design. The back splats are most often pierced, though the solid splat outlined with scrolls occurs in many instances. The open or pierced splats present a great variety of designs, many elaborately formed; some are leaf-carved or interwoven, others carry Gothic details or a lozenge motif. Chippendale's twenty plates of chair styles, displaying over sixty designs, were copied with fidelity, or served as the basis for variations devised by the Colonial chairmakers. Of these, none is more revered than the celebrated Philadelphian, Benjamin Randolph, to whom a few fine chairs now in our major museums have been attributed.

Chairs in the Chippendale style have legs and feet in either of two types: straight legs, which exemplified the taste for design elements in the Chinese style, or cabriole legs terminating in boldly carved claw-and-ball feet. The master in England used the two rather indiscriminately. The front rail of the seat might be plain or scroll-carved, with its lower edge straight or slightly valanced. Chair arms, when present, are outcurved, terminating in voluted scrolls or carved knuckles.

The Chippendale vogue was followed by an era of transition toward Neoclassicism. Furniture made during the first phase of the Classic Revival period is called Federal. It was popular from about 1790–1810 and includes principally the English Hepplewhite and Sheraton styles. *The Cabinet-Maker and Upholsterer's Guide* by George Hepplewhite, published posthumously in London in 1788, did much to popularize the Neoclassical style, which the Adam brothers had already made widespread in Britain. The Hepplewhite style was enthusiastically adopted to replace the elaborate Chippendale, from which it marked a complete departure. The tapered square leg, straight, serpentine, or bow seat fronts, and delicate shield- or heart-shaped backs of Hepplewhite chairs offered emphatic contrasts to the preceding vogue. Mahogany was favored, with inlays of white holly, boxwood, and colored woods.

The popularity of the Hepplewhite chair designs continued throughout the country until about 1800, when it was followed briefly by the style inaugurated in England by Thomas Sheraton. Like his illustrious predecessors, he too issued his designs in book form: *The Cabinet-Maker's and Upholsterer's Drawing-Book,* whose plates were published separately from 1791 to 1793. Again the pendulum swung in an opposite direction, now veering away from Hepplewhite's curvilinear, shield-backed chairs to a style featuring severely square and rigid backs in which vertical members, four or five in number, predominate. This type, called colonette-back because the Classic lines of the uprights suggest a colonnade, was also made as an armchair, with arms curving slightly outward, supported by quarter-round molded arm stumps.

The Sheraton style lasted until about 1820, and in its closing years changes took place within the framework of the square backs. Horizontal bands in varying sizes replaced the strict verticality of previous years. Top rails utilized turned members, and between horizontal crossbars diagonals were introduced. The type was favored by Duncan Phyfe, who made many fine chairs in the general style of Sheraton. A great number of these chairs are made of maple, with rounded seats of cane or rush.

The nomenclature of this era presents a confusing array of terms which does little to clarify the many currents and crosscurrents for the layman. The French Empire style, initiated with Napoleon's ascendancy in 1804, found its counterpart in the American Empire style. This style reflects the continuing interest in Classical motifs and forms, which was expressed in designs intended actually to reproduce ancient furniture models. The most notable American furniture maker of the Classic Revival period was Duncan Phyfe, and the designs produced by him and his contemporaries were many and varied. During the Empire phase of this period Phyfe and others showed a preference for heavier forms, and this merged in the middle of the century with the Victorian style, which then began to turn toward new motifs.

715 *Chair in the Queen Anne style, featuring curved stiles and splat formed by parallel curves and cabriole legs with carved shells at the knees, c. 1730* **716** *Chippendale-style side chair with ornamental pierced splat, carved shells, and claw-and-ball feet, c. 1760–80* **717** *Chair in the Queen Anne style, with four turned stretchers and vase-shaped splat, c. 1730* **718** *Chippendale-style side chair, distinguished by carved cresting and splat* **719** *Armchair with vase-shaped splat and carved shells at top of the crest and on chair front, c. 1760* **720** *Side chair in the American Directoire style with curved top rail and carved crosspiece c. 1810–25*

718

719

The mainstream of emerging styles in furniture, its eddies and currents, sometimes swift and limpid, sometimes sluggish and static, is nowhere as readily studied as in the evolution of the chair. No other single form in the broad area of furniture design has been so variously interpreted throughout the ages. The chair reveals the constantly changing modes and mannerisms of society—its tastes and whimsies, customs and traditions. But the fact that chair forms several centuries old are being reproduced today to serve our needs testifies to the perennial values inherent in certain basic styles. Even in the face of drastic changes in contemporary modes, period pieces and reproductions of them will always find some measure of acceptance, reminding us of the ingenuity and imagination that these masterworks in furniture represent.

720

721 *One of a pair of elaborately carved Chippendale side chairs, characterized by rhythmic curves and floral decoration typical of this style just before the Revolution. Made in Philadelphia, c. 1765* **722** *Popular Hepplewhite-style side chair with interlaced heart-and-shield back and fully covered seat, 1785–1800* **723** *Chippendale-style side chair, with straight legs and stretchers and splat with Gothic details, c. 1780* **724** *Another popular Chippendale variant, featuring turned up "ears" on top rail and pierced rungs, c. 1760* **725** *Hepplewhite-*

725

726

728

727

style mahogany side chair with delicate carved shield back, scrolled and festooned, c. 1790–1810 **726** *Chippendale-style armchair with claw-and-ball feet, c. 1760–80* **727** *Side chair in the Gothic manner of Chippendale, exemplified in the quatrefoils, or four-cusped traceries, c. 1760–80* **728** *Transitional Queen Anne-Chippendale walnut armchair, with elaborately carved, scrolled cabriole legs and claw-and-ball feet, c. 1755*

729

731

730

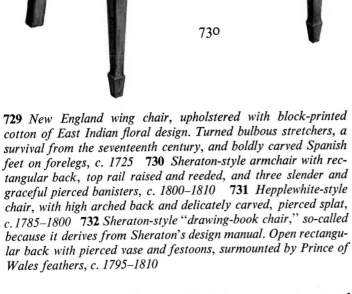

732

729 *New England wing chair, upholstered with block-printed cotton of East Indian floral design. Turned bulbous stretchers, a survival from the seventeenth century, and boldly carved Spanish feet on forelegs, c. 1725* **730** *Sheraton-style armchair with rectangular back, top rail raised and reeded, and three slender and graceful pierced banisters, c. 1800–1810* **731** *Hepplewhite-style chair, with high arched back and delicately carved, pierced splat, c. 1785–1800* **732** *Sheraton-style "drawing-book chair," so-called because it derives from Sheraton's design manual. Open rectangular back with pierced vase and festoons, surmounted by Prince of Wales feathers, c. 1795–1810*

Overleaf: GALLERY OF CHAIRS. *Man's inventiveness is attested to by the infinite variety of forms he has designed throughout the ages for comfortable seating. It has often been noted that no single object or artifact has been a greater challenge to designers or the subject of more interesting variations than the so-called "machine for comfort." The chairs pictured in this gallery range from the plainest cottage types,* **734, 744, 759, 760,** *to formal and often highly ornamented chairs,* **736, 743, 752, 779, 790, 792,** *examples inspired by the great master cabinetmakers of the eighteenth and nineteenth centuries*

733

734

735

736

737

738

739

740

741

742

743

744

745

746

747

748

749

750

751

752

753

754

755

756

757

758

759

760

761

762

763   764   765   766   767   768

769   770   771   772   773   774

775   776   777   778   779   780

781   782   783   784   785   786

787   788   789   790   791   792

793

794

795

796

793–798, 799 *The technique of bronze stenciling Hitchcock-type chairs and Boston rockers was in vogue from 1820 to 1850, although the practice continued beyond this period. The stencil was cut from stiff paper, oiled cardboard, or thin sheet metal; in manufacturing, metal was preferred for durability in mass production. The color was applied through the apertures of the stencil with a stubby brush or dauber. Fruits and flowers, liberally enhanced by leaf forms, were dominant motifs* **797** *"Fancy chairs" were advertised by the "chair manufactories" located in the leading cities of the eastern seaboard. Lambert Hitchcock of Barkhamsted, Connecticut, was the most important maker*

797

Painted & Stencilled

I N THE FIRST QUARTER of the nineteenth century "fancy chairs" became popular. By 1825 every town of any size had a woodworking shop whose sign usually read: "Fancy and Windsor Chairmaker." Leading cities along the coast had many such shops. One of the men who gave impetus to the movement was Lambert Hitchcock of Connecticut.

Hitchcock began by manufacturing chair parts and shipping the unassembled backs, seats, slats, and stretchers, which were assembled on arrival. Since there was no artisan group in the South to supply the furniture needs of the average person, these chairs found

a ready market in Charleston, South Carolina, and other growing southern coastal cities. Hitchcock's simple yet unique procedure was adopted by manufacturers of inexpensive furniture. (The finished chair, painted and decorated, sold for a dollar and a half.)

After a few years, Hitchcock abandoned this method and began to sell the assembled chairs. He was the first to mass-produce these chairs. The different parts were combined on an assembly-line, following the philosophy of enterprising Connecticut clock manufacturers: "Why make one or two when we can turn them out by the hundreds, and then paint and decorate them just as clock dials and tablets are

799

798

painted." Hitchcock employed over a hundred hands in his factory, including many women and children whom he trained in the art of decorating the painted surfaces. The industry became so important that the name of the town was changed from Barkhamsted to Hitchcocksville. The term "Hitchcock chair," as usually employed, was generic rather than specific. It was applied to a wide range of chairs produced roughly between 1825 and 1830 with stencil-decorated surfaces, in gold or other colors.

Stenciling, an ancient handcraft, was a short cut to painting surfaces by hand. Much Early American decoration used stenciled patterns on walls and floors in floral or festoon motifs, and in geometric shapes as borders or all-over diapers. Stenciled ornamentation was widely used on wallpaper, bandboxes, decorated coverlets, trays, and toleware, and on clock dials and the glass panels which were inserted in shelf clocks and banjo clocks. Stenciled forms in countless arrangements were used in creating the charming theorem paintings composed of fruits, flowers, leaves, and baskets.

The typical Hitchcock chair combined the best features of the Sheraton and French Directoire styles. It was of maple. It had a slightly arched top rail, either turned or shaped, leaving a flat middle section for the application of a stenciled design. Front legs

800 *The fruit and floral motifs ornamenting the stiles and rails of this Hitchcock chair create a handsome pattern* **801, 802** *Hand-painted chair and details. Of Pennsylvania German provenance, c. 1842* **803** *Hand-painted pine chair. Made in Pennsylvania, 1855*

800

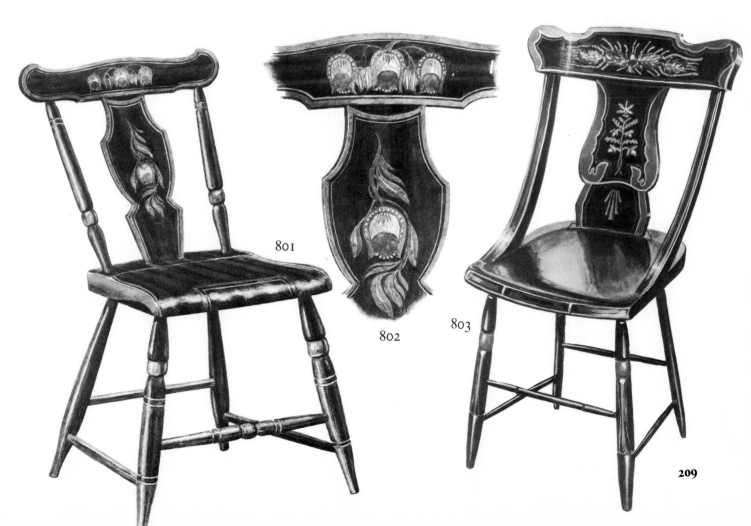

801

802

803

804 *Ladder-back armchair of curly maple with crude and uncertain painted decoration. Made by Shaker craftsmen, c. 1820* **805** *Hand-painted chair with decoration imitating stencil motifs* **806** *Curved top rail and turned spindles and legs add decorative interest to Hitchcock-type chair, c. 1840* **807** *Hitchcock chair has slightly arched concave top rail, turned only at the ends. Across the middle of the open back are a concave wide slat and a narrower one; usually*

807

808

were turned, with shallow ring or bead turnings, and tapered slightly to terminate in small ball feet. A concave slat across the middle of the back received the major decorative stenciling. Favorite motifs included horns of plenty, acanthus scrolls, fruit and leaf patterns, fountains with drinking birds, wreaths, and festoons in blue, red, white, bronze, and gold. The rush or cane seat was rectangular and slightly flaring. When rush was used, it was customary to add a split turning at the front and thin flat strips on the back and sides. These protected the twists of rush which were wrapped around

only the wide one is decorated. Rush seat is protected by a split turning at the front. Made chiefly of maple and copied in a number of shops, c. 1820–50 **808** *Cane-seated Hitchcock chair with wide back slat displaying graceful fruit basket with leaf forms. Flattened portions of back uprights decorated. Turned forelegs splayed with gilding on beading throughout* **809** *All-wooden painted chair, with concave top rail and slat prominent areas of decoration*

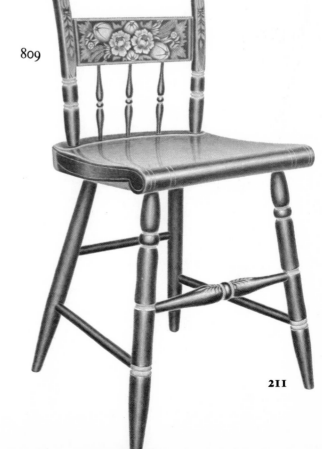

809

810

811

812

the concealed seat rails. The legs were braced at the sides and back by plain turned stretchers and at the front by a ring-turned stretcher with a beaded or bulbous swelling. At first, the chairs were painted a brownish black with irregular veinings to simulate rosewood. Later they were painted black in imitation of ebony.

The painted fancy chairs of Hitchcock and his contemporaries were widely used in pleasure palaces, hotel lobbies, theater boxes, ice-cream parlors, and canal and river steamers. ("Cleopatra's Barge" was another name by which these fancy chairs were known.)

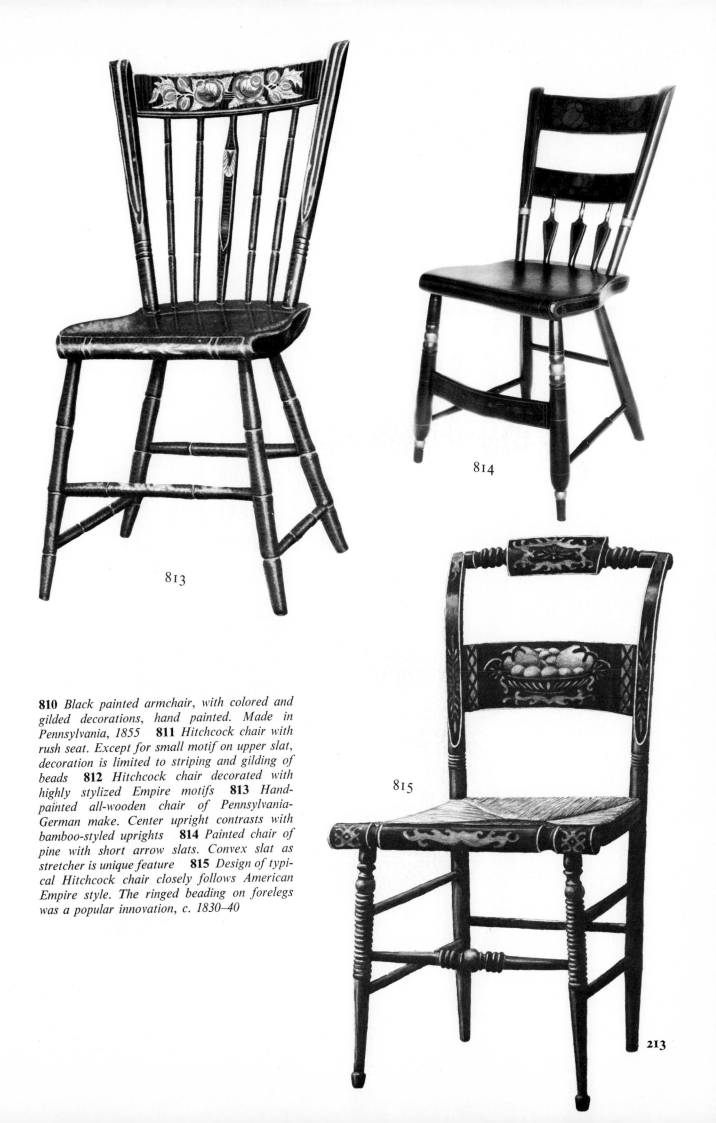

813

814

815

810 *Black painted armchair, with colored and gilded decorations, hand painted. Made in Pennsylvania, 1855* **811** *Hitchcock chair with rush seat. Except for small motif on upper slat, decoration is limited to striping and gilding of beads* **812** *Hitchcock chair decorated with highly stylized Empire motifs* **813** *Hand-painted all-wooden chair of Pennsylvania-German make. Center upright contrasts with bamboo-styled uprights* **814** *Painted chair of pine with short arrow slats. Convex slat as stretcher is unique feature* **815** *Design of typical Hitchcock chair closely follows American Empire style. The ringed beading on forelegs was a popular innovation, c. 1830–40*

816

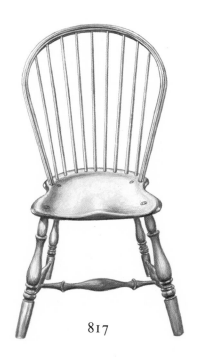

817

The World of Windsors

THE ORIGIN of the Windsor chair has been traced to the English countryside at the time of George II, through a charming anecdote. Tradition says the king sought refuge during a fierce storm in a peasant's cottage near Windsor Castle. He sat in a crudely fashioned chair, made of upright spindles, and remarked on the rare comfort and utter simplicity of its design. The chair impressed him so much that he had it copied by his cabinetmaker. News of this little episode spread, and with it the vogue for the chair, which was marketed from Windsor. Within a

816 *Boston rocker with the grace and sturdiness characteristic of Windsor chairs: the tapered back spindles, scrolled top rail, and shaped seat combine to form a most efficient piece of household furniture. Made by Hitchcock, Alford and Company, c. 1832–40* **817** *Popular hoop-back Windsor, also called "bow-back," first produced by New England makers as a side chair. Raked legs and front and side stretchers, c. 1750–1800*

few years the Windsor chair reached American shores, where it was readily adopted, its popularity lasting from about 1725 to 1860. Although the earlier date is commonly mentioned, the first known documentation points to Governor Patrick Gordon of Pennsylvania, who died in 1736 and whose inventory listed five Windsor chairs. The same year, Hannah Hodge, a Philadelphia widow, included Windsor chairs among her household effects.

It was in Philadelphia that Windsor chairs were first manufactured in the Colonies, possibly as early as 1725. By 1760 the vogue for them was in full swing. They rapidly became fashionable in New York, where they supplanted the rush-bottom, slat-back, and banister-back chairs in popularity. Windsor chairs were not made in Boston in quantity until about 1770, although they had been shipped there from Philadelphia and New York. No single maker of Windsor chairs stands out, but in 1773 Jedediah Snowden advertised domestic Windsors in the Philadelphia *Journal*. In 1785 the *Philadelphia Directory* listed the names of eleven Windsor chairmakers. In the New York *Gazetteer* of February 17, 1774, Thomas Ash of Broadway advertised an extensive line of Windsor chairs. Directories of various cities also listed a growing number of chairmakers who specialized in the making of Windsors. In the *United States Chronicle* of Providence, printed July 19, 1787, an advertisement by David Lawrence read: "Windsor chairs. Neat, elegant and strong, beautifully painted after the Philadelphia mode, warranted of good seasoned materials so firmly put together as not to deceive the Purchaser by an untimely coming to Pieces."

Many advertisements and references indicate the extent to which the industry had grown a few years after the Revolution. The "stick" chair, as the Windsor chair was commonly called, had become the most popular single item of furniture sold on the eastern seaboard. Thomas Jefferson is said to have composed the Declaration of Independence seated in a Windsor chair. Roger Sherman, John Adams, and James Monroe patronized Windsor chairmakers. George Washington bought thirty Windsors for his Mount Vernon portico, where visiting groups gathered on many occasions. Numerous prints, engravings, and paintings feature sitters comfortably ensconced in Windsor chairs of varying designs.

American Windsor chairs have been made in a great number of styles: For purposes of identification, six basic types may be described: low back, comb back, hoop back, New England arm, fan back, and loop back. All types have certain similar characteristics, and the most noticeable are the slender, round, upright spokes or spindles, turned and generally tapering upward. The spindles vary in number but present a graceful outline filled with evenly spaced thin parallel lines. On some types, the spindles at the seat are closer together and fan out as they reach the top rails or loops. The chair backs are slanted backward and are curved laterally to accommodate the back. The arms of the armchair slant outward. As a rule, the spindles taper or bulge slightly on finer examples; in some instances, a bamboo effect is simulated. The seats were made of a single plank, hollowed out in the fashion known as saddle seat.

In the shaping of component parts, the

American Windsors show a delicate balance and harmony, particularly in the contour and slant of the spindles, the splay or rake of the legs, and the vase-form turnings of the legs, which are held securely by well-designed stretcher arrangements.

Though light and airy in appearance, the Windsor chair is exceedingly strong and well braced. The spindles were securely anchored in the solid seat and fitted into holes in the hoop, loop, or arms at the top. For sturdy construction, the legs were driven through the seat and securely fastened by means of fox wedges, the underbraces having first been fitted into position. This resulted in a rigid construction which defied dampness, steam heat, and continual use. The care and skill with which the Windsors were designed and assembled is a tribute to the workmanship of early chair-makers. To those who appreciate pure form and fine craftsmanship, later machine-made replicas are inferior on every score.

Windsor chairs, unlike the other furniture products, were never made of walnut, cherry, or mahogany. They were usually fabricated from several kinds of wood: the hoop or bow of the back from hickory; the spindles and arms from hickory or ash; the legs from oak, hickory, or maple; and the seats from pine, whitewood, or beech. To camouflage this assortment of woods, the chairs, originally intended for garden, tavern, or outdoor use, were painted in a variety of colors. Green, either dark green or apple green, seems to have been the favorite color at first. Then a variety of colors including black, Indian red, yellow, gray, brown, blue, and at times a touch of gold

were used. Although many people felt that white was inappropriate, Benjamin Franklin ordered two dozen in white; Thomas Jefferson ordered four dozen in black and gold, as stated in an invoice dated 1801. The early Windsor chairs were rarely stained.

Another aspect in the making of Windsors is their fabrication, and the interchangeability of component parts, designed to speed the manufacturing process. Templates and gauges, developed early in the nineteenth century, accounted for the large numbers of chairs produced by the more than one hundred makers of Windsors in the eastern states. Sometimes, however, a country gentleman wished to have a personal hand in his finished product; he could purchase separate parts in town and assemble his own chairs.

Wallace Nutting, a noted American furniture expert, admirably sums up the case for Windsors: "The merit and special charm of the Windsor chair are so often overlooked or unknown that we wish here, with almost brutal emphasis, to say that lightness was the chief purpose of the Windsor, to follow the heavy late-Gothic furniture which a woman could not move without a struggle. Hence an American Windsor means a pine seat if it means anything good. Also delicate lines to secure lightness throughout. This includes strongly bulbous legs and a light back. Such chairs well made were durable because they were elastic and bore falls without breaking. In a good Windsor, lightness, strength, grace, durability and quaintness are all found in an irresistible blend."

818 *Low-backed firehouse Windsor with back extension, eight turned spindles, and U-shaped continuous arm ending in scrolls, c. 1840–65* **819** *Low-backed Windsor writing chair with convenient storage drawer. Continuous arm terminates in and is supported by turned spindles; extreme splay of legs produces extra rigidity* **820** *Hoop-back Windsor with intersecting semicircular rail that forms arm ends, supported by turned spindles, c. 1750–1800* **821** *Comb-backed Windsor with thick horizontal rail terminating in scrolls and arm supports of English derivation. Spindles extend upward to support a gracefully shaped comb, c. 1740–80* **822** *Rod-back Windsor with turned spindles and legs; sloping back is supported by uprights with knob finials joined by top rail, c. 1800–1830* **823** *Comb-back Windsor writing chair with six thin spindles forming comb support. Turned legs joined by H-stretcher support seat of unusual front design*

818

819

820

821

822

823

825

826

827

824

824 *Transitional Windsor armchair with straight lines characteristc of the Sheraton period and bamboo turnings throughout; double top rail encloses small panel, c. 1800–1825* **825** *Windsor high chair with bow back and footrest. Made in Philadelphia, c. 1750* **826** *Rodback Windsor with tapered bamboo-style spindles, and heavy uprights and narrow top rail forming back frame* **827** *Loop-back Windsor armchair, with closely spaced spindles turned with swellings at the "bamboo" joints. Made in Maryland, c. 1774* **828** *Loop-back Windsor armchair with hickory spindles and bow. Made in Pennsylvania, c. 1800–1825* **829** *Combback Windsor with horizontal semicircular rail; compare arm supports with those of 821*

828

829

830

831

Made in America...
It Rocked the World

THE ROCKING CHAIR has been with us for many years. When and how it became a part of the family of furniture has long been a subject of controversy. We do know, however, that it is a distinctly American prod-uct, probably originating in the first half of the eighteenth century. Records meticulously kept by Eliakim Smith, a cabinetmaker and repairer who lived in Hadley, Massachusetts, indicate that from 1762 to 1764 he was called on to attach rockers to cottage chairs.

830 *Boston rocker, which in its standardized form was popular from c. 1840–90. A special feature is the "rolling" seat that curves up at the back and down in front, the curved portions originally being separate pieces. Vase-shaped splat and top rail provide sizable areas for decoration by stencil, c. 1875*
831 *Country-style rocker with homespun caning, c. 1870*

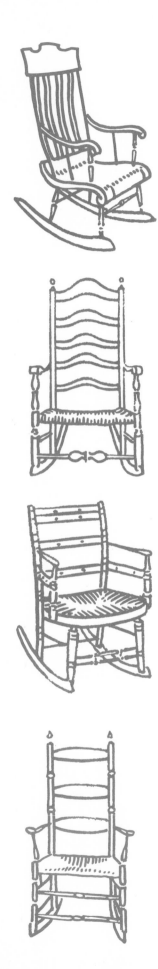

Rocker benches, cribs, and cradles equipped with curved runners were made in abundance during the first half of the century. The earliest rockers, called "carpet cutters," were attached to existing chairs: niches were cut from the inner or outer sides of the chair legs so that the curved runners could be inserted. Windsors, slat-backs, and even banister-back chairs were fitted with rockers.

When a chair was designed as a rocker, however, heavier legs were placed at the terminal points to accommodate the curved pieces, which were inserted into the middle slots. Then a pair of pins or dowels were driven through the legs at the point where the runners were affixed. Later, rockers were broadened to more than double the carpet-cutter dimensions. Hickory, which can be bent easily, was often used for these broader runners. In early examples, the runners generally extend an equal distance beyond the front and rear legs. The makers of later rockers found that greater stability could be achieved by extending the rear runner farther than the front runner.

The rocking chair was affected by the furniture styles of the nineteenth century. The spindle- or rod-back of the Windsor chair served as a prototype for the Boston rocker. From 1840 until the close of the century this sturdy chair was made in many forms, yet the basic type may readily be described. The chair was made chiefly of maple. The seats were of pine in two designs: the solid, rounded saddle form and the "rolling" seat. The graceful cyma curve of the rolling seat echoed the curves of the sweeping arms. It was ingeniously contrived from three separate pieces secured

into a single form. The downward curve at the front provided a smooth, rounded protective rail whose grain, running lengthwise, served to reinforce the construction. The upward swing at the rear of the seat accommodated the body contour. The high, slightly conforming back, consisting of seven or nine tapering spindles, was topped by a wide, concave rail. This surface was ideal for stenciling. The short, turned legs, ring-turned at the front and plain at the rear, straddled the thin rocker blades with a notched joint. Under the Empire influence, the top corners of the rectangular headpiece became rounded, sometimes into a scroll form. The bottom edge of the piece remained straight except for two semicircular indentations which added a bit of grace where the outer spindles were inserted.

Of greatest interest to collectors and art historians are those Boston rockers which have stenciled decorations. In ornamenting the headpiece, the decorator often deviated from his standard templates showing the horn of plenty and baskets of fruits and flowers and instead depicted patriotic figures, landscapes, and houses. If the rocker had a central splat instead of a row of spindles, this, too, was used for ornamentation.

The armed rocker was the favored form. However, a few starkly simple rocking chairs without arms were made in Shaker settlements and typify the severity of Shaker furniture. At the peak of their popularity, Boston rockers were carried by ship captains to remote corners of the globe where they invariably found eager customers.

832

833

834

832 *Scrolled arms and sloping back insure comfort in this cane-backed rocking chair, c. 1870* **833** *Slender, shaped back spindles provide more comfort than straight turnings* **834** *Later models of the rocking chair are heavier, with wide back rails, thickened posts and arms* **835** *Four-slatted ladder-back rocker exhibits turned knobs and finials common to most New England types* **836** *Ladder-back armed rocker with rush-seat, double stretchers, and turnings below arms, c. 1825* **837** *Homely, solidly built household rocker, designed for long service. Midwestern, c. 1860*

835

836

837

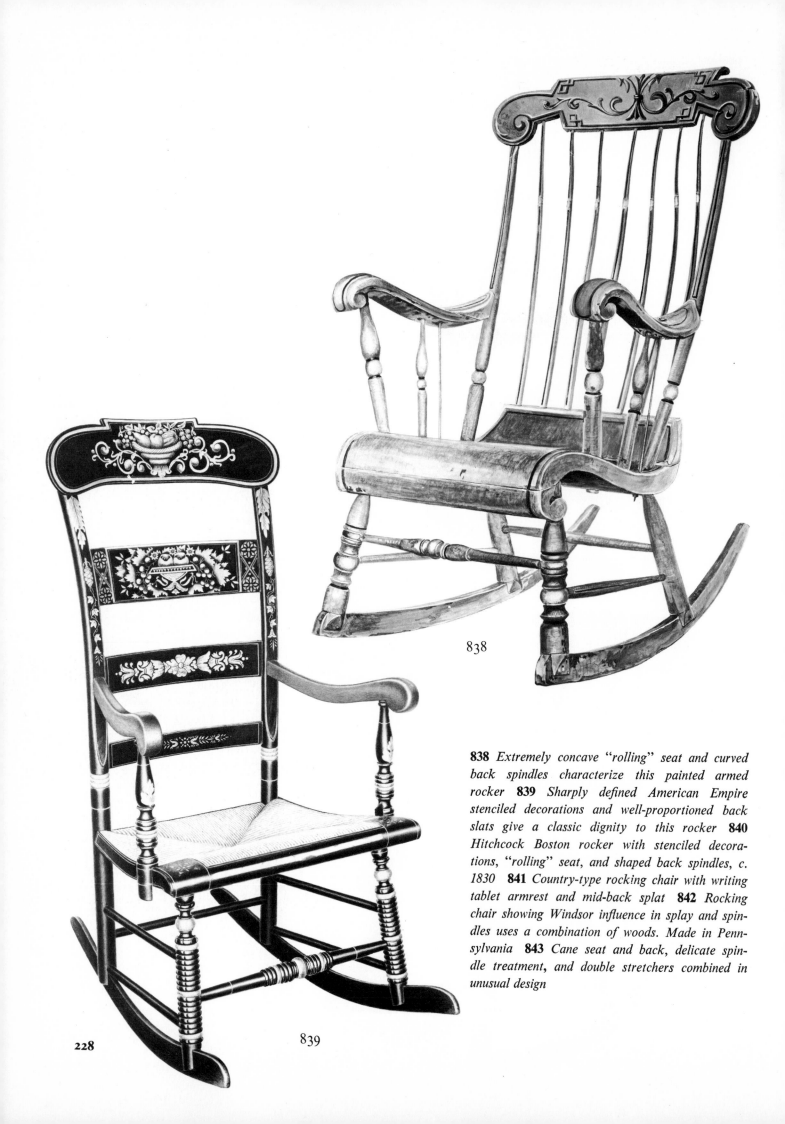

838

839

228

838 *Extremely concave "rolling" seat and curved back spindles characterize this painted armed rocker* **839** *Sharply defined American Empire stenciled decorations and well-proportioned back slats give a classic dignity to this rocker* **840** *Hitchcock Boston rocker with stenciled decorations, "rolling" seat, and shaped back spindles, c. 1830* **841** *Country-type rocking chair with writing tablet armrest and mid-back splat* **842** *Rocking chair showing Windsor influence in splay and spindles uses a combination of woods. Made in Pennsylvania* **843** *Cane seat and back, delicate spindle treatment, and double stretchers combined in unusual design*

840

841

842

843

229

844

844 *The settee and Chippendale armchair in the gracious parlor of the Governor's Palace at Williamsburg are upholstered in antique needlework and are of English origin. An air of quiet magnificence is provided by well-chosen accouterments such as the chandelier of Waterford glass, the carpet of tapestry weave of the Colonial period, the occasional tables, mirror, and handsome mantel and fireplace. Photograph courtesy Colonial Williamsburg*

Sofas for Comfort

DAYBEDS, SOFAS, settees, and lounges, designed for relaxation, were extensions of the chair. The earliest form of the daybed consisted of a banister-back chair with a six-foot extension to the seat. The seat, usually caned, cushioned, rushed, or upholstered, rested on a set of eight legs, turned or cabriole, provided with stretchers to insure greater rigidity. The back of the daybed was often adjustable; chains were attached to the stiles. This type made its appearance in the Colonies about 1700. Later, some noteworthy daybeds in the Queen Anne and Chippendale manner were fashioned by leading New York and Philadelphia cabinetmakers.

The settee may be described as a piece of furniture in which two or three chair backs are blended into a single seat, generally upholstered. Some of the finest examples were executed between 1760 and 1790 in the Chippendale style. The graceful settee of the Hepplewhite period featured the double-shield back with square tapering legs. The square-back Sheraton settees of the period from about 1810 to 1830 had characteristic festoon-draped motifs or caned backs and seats. Robert Fisher, a Baltimore cabinetmaker, produced some very handsome painted settees in the Sheraton style. The top rails of Fisher's settees had painted oval insets showing well-known Baltimore mansions and scenic designs. Parallel to the oval insets were three ornamental spots on the seat rails, each with a bow and arrow and a quiver. Some of these settees had typical Sheraton backs with Gothic arches; others had urn-shaped banisters and plain or bamboo spindles. In most cases, the seats were caned or solid.

In contrast to the formal settee was a country-type seat called the settle. In its crudest form, it was constructed from a wagon seat or the rumble seat of an abandoned carriage. The seat was then attached to the back of a chest or other boxlike structure. The early settle looked like a high-back wainscot chair which had been expanded to twice its normal width to accommodate two people. It was commonly used in Pilgrim households and was usually placed near the fireplace in the kitchen or common room. In the early part of the eighteenth century, large paneled settles were made. They were about ten feet long and were used primarily in meeting places—churches or schools.

The sofa, a term best known in America, refers to an upholstered piece with a back, long seat, and arms. The sofa resembles an upholstered chair whose seat width has been doubled or tripled. It was first used in living rooms in the Chippendale period and may be traced through the Hepplewhite, Sheraton, and American Empire styles. The sofa of the Chippendale period was a stately piece of furniture. Of medium height, it had "roll-over" arms, an enclosed frame above the legs, and a back with a serpentine curve, terminating in a pronounced roll of the out-scrolled ends. The sofa seat was deep, with a straight front, and was supported by six or eight legs. The eight-legged sofa had square legs. The rear ones often slanted and were braced with a box stretcher about three or four inches from the

845

846

floor. The six-legged sofa had cabriole legs at the front, terminating in claw-and-ball feet, with scroll, shell, or foliage motifs at the knees. Some sofas with cabriole legs were made in love-seat size—about four feet long. These were fashioned in leading shops in New York, Philadelphia, Boston, and Baltimore between 1750 and 1775.

The stylistic variations in sofas of the Hepplewhite and Sheraton periods followed the prevailing trends in chair design. Hepplewhite sofas had gently arching backs instead of the serpentine curve of Chippendale pieces. Sheraton backs, a dominant characteristic of the style, are strictly rectangular, either exposed or upholstered. Duncan Phyfe, some of whose sofas are the most distinguished pieces of the nineteenth century, worked in this style. Phyfe, and a notable group of contemporaries inspired by his workmanship, built beautifully proportioned sofas fashioned from the finest mahogany. These pieces had expertly detailed wooden frames featuring reeded or fluted rails, cornucopias, lyres, dolphins, and other Classical motifs, and were upholstered with damask, brocades, and striped fabrics of fine quality and coloring. A notable detail was the graceful shape of the legs, either "saber" (an incurved leg, square in cross section) or horn of plenty, ending in brass cups.

Phyfe unquestionably exerted a restraining and corrective influence on American furniture design. In spite of the fact that he started work at sixteen and lacked academic training, he developed a remarkable knowledge of and feeling for the principles of Classical art forms. It is not unlikely that he owned the books of the leading English cabinetmakers, particularly Sheraton, from which he gleaned ideas in the course of developing his own design philosophy. Phyfe was so successful that he was able to employ a hundred hands to help him serve his wealthy clientele. His reputation rests solidly on the sweeping curves of his pieces and his mastery of line and proportion.

The sofas of the American Empire and Victorian styles suffer by comparison with earlier styles. The workmanship is often very fine, but designs are overwrought and not so tastefully conceived.

845 *Chippendale settee with mahogany legs Three cabriole front legs with knees decorated with boldly stylized leaf carving in low relief. Taloned feet and claws grasp an unusually large ovoid ball. The settee, known today as a love seat, was very popular in its time, c. 1757–60* **846** *Fanciful type of sofa in American Empire style with V-shaped arm frames, highly ornamented with acanthus leaf covering ending in rosettes at the "roll-over" point of the double arms. Elaborately carved legs show lion's claw emerging from a cornucopia with fruit and leaves, c. 1810–30* **847** *Sofa in American Empire style with deep quarter-round concaves on back frame, lyre-curved ends with rosettes. The four legs, on casters, show carved wings of an eagle terminating in a lion's paw. Made of mahogany, c. 1820–40*

847

848 *Settee with rush seat similar in construction to the Hitchcock chair. Top rails of the triple back have graduated splats, with back posts flattened and extending above the top rail. Front legs and arm supports show ringed and beaded turning, c. 1820–50* **849** *Directory-style sofa, sometimes attributed to Duncan Phyfe, c. 1810–25. Top rail is straight with backward roll and quarter-round concave ends conforming to "roll-over" arms. Legs ornamented with acanthus leaves* **850** *Directory-style curve dominates "roll-over" arms of this upholstered sofa, with framing of the arms curving into the seat rail* **851** *Upholstered sofa in the general style of Sheraton. Top rail straight and reeded; delicate tapered front legs on casters, c. 1800–1820* **852** *Sheraton-style settee, c. 1810–25, utilizes the familiar urn-and-flower motif in its triple back, with straight reeded banisters. Front legs are square and tapered; rear legs canted. Decorations painted* **853** *Queen Anne sofa with high stuffed back, seat, and arms similar to wing chair. Back has double cyma curves separated by scallop with "ears" at corners. Supported by five legs, front ones cabriole with shells at knees, c. 1740–50*

848

849

850

851

852

853

235

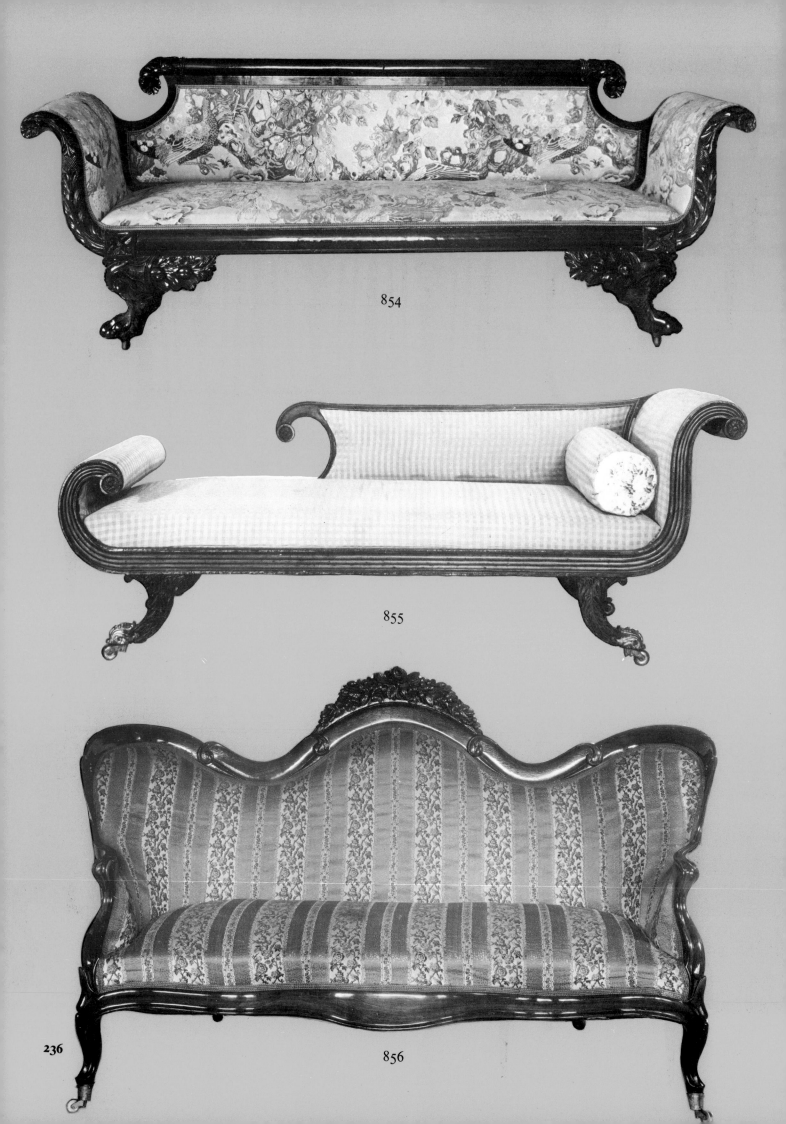

854

855

236

856

857

854 *The sofa in the American Empire style is characterized by a continuous flow of graceful lines. This mahogany one features elaborately carved arm frames ending in a squared rosette at the chair rail. Front legs show cornucopia of fruit blending into lion's paw. Made in Maryland, c. 1820–30* **855** *The "Grecian"-style sofa, which originated in England under the aegis of Robert Adam and was also made by Sheraton, inspired this Classic type, also called "Madam Récamier." The long, continuous front rail sweeps upward into the arms asymmetrically, the sharp reeding terminating in rosettes. Floriated leg designs show brass dolphin heads, c. 1810–25* **856** *Transitional-style sofa with serpentine back and cresting of fruits and flowers at top shows strong rococo, or Louis XV substyle, influence. Top rail continues in unbroken line to enclosed arms. Front of upholstered seat is slightly serpentine, with conforming seat rail and cabriole front legs, c. 1850–70* **857** *Pronounced S-scroll arms are a feature of this American Empire style sofa. Top of back carries a rounded rail with downward scrolls, sometimes called "brackets." Carved legs combine lion's paw with leaf and floral forms, c. 1810–30* **858** *Medallion-back sofa with walnut frame. Top rail molding surmounted by three cresting groups of foliated flowers and fruits. Finger molding of front seat has central group of grapes and leaves. Foliated arm carving supported by cabriole legs, c. 1840–60*

858

859

859 *A long tavern table occupies the center of the Hall family dining room. Made of wide pine boards of generous proportions, it is about twenty feet long, designed to accommodate a large family and many guests. The table is set with "treen" (wooden dishes), horn spoons and cups, some of imposing dimensions. It also holds a collection of kitchen implements, including sharpeners, and a mechanical apple peeler. The room, built in 1760, is typical of an eighteenth-century dining room with its random paneling, hip panels over the fireplace, press cupboard, banister-back chairs with rush seats, kettles, and kitchen equipment at the open hearth. Photograph by Samuel Chamberlain, courtesy Hall Tavern, Old Deerfield, Massachusetts* **860** *Small tavern table whose ball-or knob-style turnings give it its style. Well-shaped brackets under leaves, high stretchers, and medial stretcher, c. 1660–80*

The Table Is Set

860

LEONARDO'S CELEBRATED *Last Supper* pictures a long board resting on trestles of carved shapes, the table prototype which served mankind for centuries. It was not unlike a carpenter's board set on several horses. These were known as trestle-boards throughout the Middle Ages; in America they were called "table board and frame." Early estate inventories indicate that such boards were used in considerable numbers. The oldest Colonial one in existence dates from about the middle of the seventeenth century.

From such plain and practical beginnings the table as a fixed form of furniture evolved through many stages and variations and was adapted to suit many purposes. Thus there are dining tables, tea tables, serving tables, dressing tables, gaming tables, sewing tables, and others. A term used particularly in England to describe many of these is "occasional."

Though the main constructional elements of the table are few, variants are almost endless. Supports may be trestles, pedestals, sawbuck or crossed legs at the ends, hinged legs (including gatelegs and swinging bracket types), three legs (tripod), and quadruped, the last type accounting for the great majority of tables. Stretchers insure rigidity between supports in trestle and sawbuck types, while square or turned rungs brace the legs of smaller tables.

As period styles developed, the changing form of the leg became the table's most distinctive characteristic. The cabriole leg distinguishes tables of the Queen Anne style. Chippendale tables were made with straight as well as cabriole legs. Straight, squared legs of slender proportion mark the Chinese Chippendale style, and the slender, tapered leg is characteristic of the Neoclassical style of the Federal period.

With the emergence of the Colonists from

239

861

862

863

the rigorous restraints of early settlement days, the table took on new forms for specialized uses, each expressive of an advance in the social life of the time. The pioneer character was represented in the trestle and sawbuck types; tavern and taproom forms followed, evolving slowly from the heavy Jacobean shapes to the lighter forms of the eighteenth century. Gatelegs were favored from about 1650 to 1720. The gateleg's popularity was associated with the development of more gracious living in which a room was set aside specifically for dining. These tables were made by country craftsmen as well as by the more sophisticated cabinetmakers in urban areas and could be built in large sizes with as many as eight legs swinging into position to support the circular top leaves. Such a table could seat up to ten people because of the wide overhang of the table top above the leg structure. The single-gate or tuckaway table, simplest of the gateleg type, was popular throughout the Colonies.

In the butterfly table, a new type created in America, a swinging bracket was substituted for the gateleg. This bracket was wing-shaped, hence the name "butterfly." Butterfly tables

861 *Trestle table of the early type referred to in estate inventories as "table board and frame." The three supports, on trestle feet, are held firmly in position by a long stretcher secured by pegs, c. 1650–70* **862** *Oaken hutch table, sometimes referred to as a chair table. The cleats, or battens, have two holes to receive the belaying pins. Seat is hinged, covering lower compartment used for storage; eighteenth century* **863** *Circular hutch table built upon trestle ends, each on a trestle foot; eighteenth century*

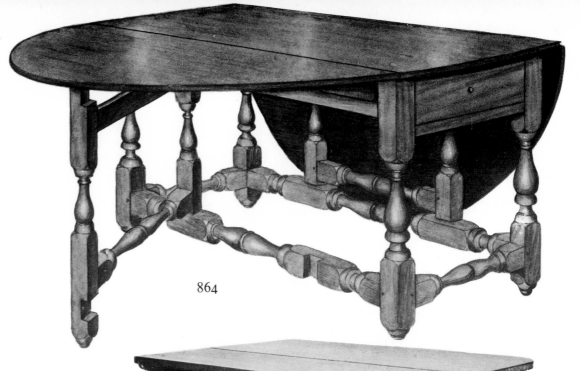

864

were made in many sizes and shapes, including round, square, and oblong. An unusually fine cherry specimen of the oblong butterfly table has four wing brackets to support its long drop leaves.

As the dining room grew to accommodate larger numbers of people, the dining table developed further. Some tables could be extended by the insertion of extra leaves at the mid-section. In long tables the pedestal which supported the center section divided so that extra leaves could be inserted. Dining tables in the Sheraton style, popular in America in the early 1800s, had either tripod or quadruped pedestals, allowing free play to the sitter's knees, an advantage not possessed by many tables of earlier periods.

Over fifty distinct varieties of table were produced by American cabinetmakers in the two centuries ending with the Victorian era. For the most part these were derived from English prototypes depicted in patternbooks published by English masters. However, a distinctively American approach to furniture making inevitably emerged, so that the connoisseur can readily distinguish tables produced in England from those made in America.

865

866

864 *Oval gateleg table with bulbous turned legs and stretchers; drawers at both ends, c. 1700* **865** *Small William and Mary type tavern table. Turned legs, plain stretchers, c. 1725. Photograph* **866** *Maple butterfly table with drawers in frame. Turnings of raked legs symmetrical on a bead; stretchers plain, c. 1700*

867

870

867 *Drop-leaf table with rounded corners. On heavy turned pedestal with fluted legs ending in brass claw feet* **868** *Drop-leaf table with indented, rounded corners. On four turned columns above platform, shaped with concave indentations supported by four animal legs with acanthus carving, c. 1820–40* **869** *Sheraton-style card table with serpentine top and skirt, rounded corners, and delicately tapering legs. In the center, a dark veneered panel with oval insert; c. 1800–1815* **870** *American Empire card table with fold-over top and canted corners. Pedestal in the form of an acanthus carved vase supported by decorated cyma-curved legs, c. 1820–40* **871** *Card table with rounded front corners and two pedestal columns decorated with pineapple sawtooth carving. The narrow rounded platform is supported by cyma-curved legs on casters, c. 1820–40* **872** *Oval Pembroke table of mahogany with satinwood inlays; ends bowed to conform to top. Four slender tapering legs inlaid with bellflowers, c. 1790–1800*

868

869

871

872

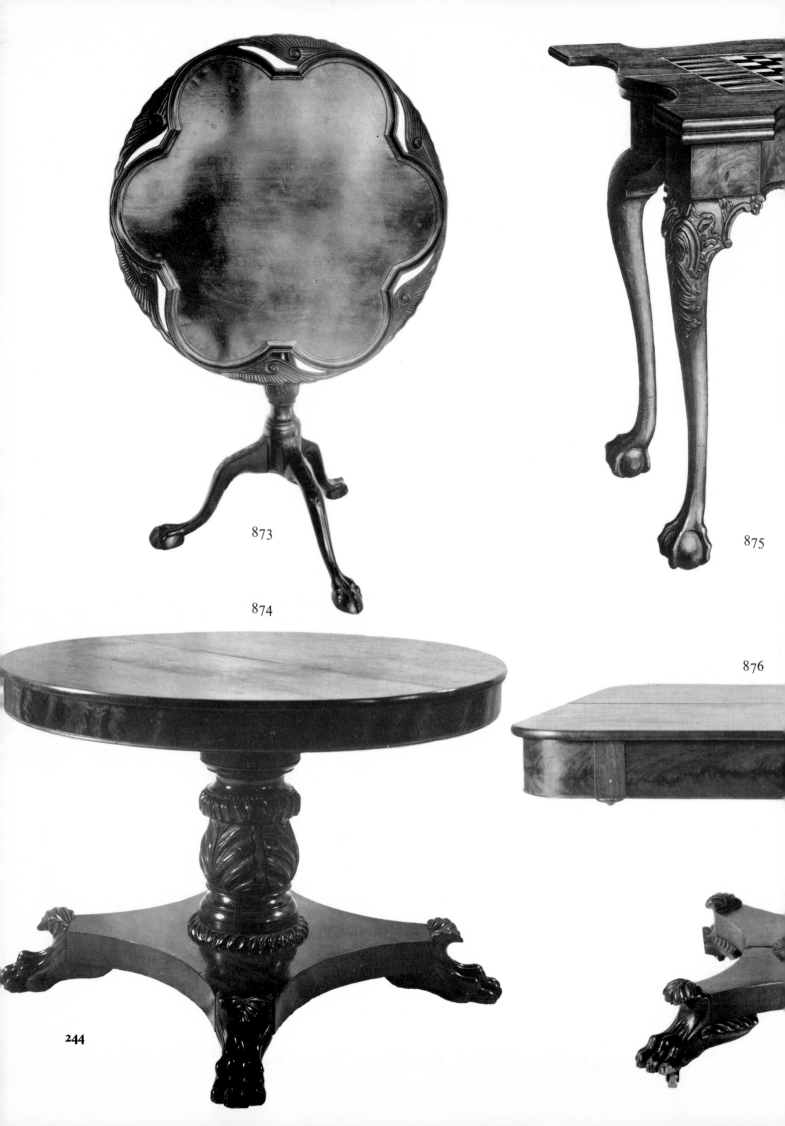

873

874

875

876

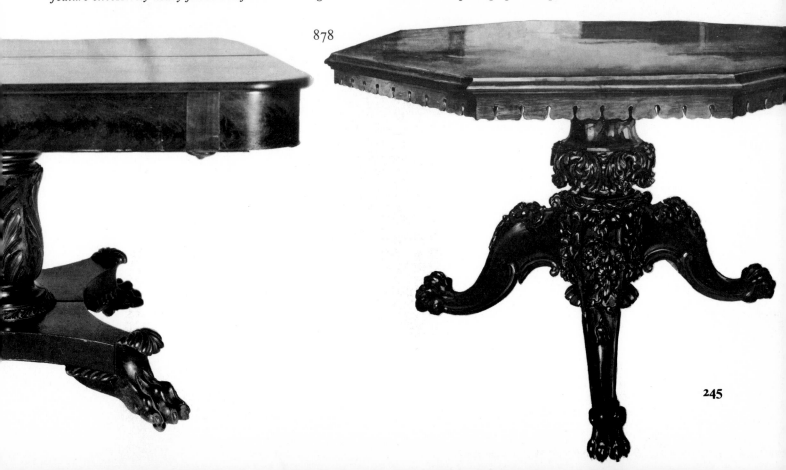

873 *Mahogany tilt-top tripod table of unusual design. The "pie-crust" scallop edging is decorated with a half shell and pierced. Three wide-spreading cabriole legs, ornamented above, end in birds' claws. Possibly of Philadelphia make, c. 1760–80* **874** *Empire dining table with elaborately ornamented pedestal under which is a heavy platform supported by four lion's paw feet, with characteristic acanthus upturn, c. 1820–30* **875** *Five-legged gaming table of beech with mahogany veneer. The bold, graceful curves of the top and finely carved cabriole legs represent exquisite workmanship of the Chippendale period* **876** *Square dining table with unusually massive carved pedestal on platform, split for extension. Lion's paw feet similar to 874, c. 1820–30* **877** *Drop-leaf sewing table of late Empire period. Heavy base platform forms four scrolled feet, c. 1840* **878** *Octagonal table with decorative apron under molding. Pedestal and legs feature excessively heavy floral and foliated carving and rococo curves. From photographs except 875 and 878*

879

879 *The master cabinetmaker, working with walnut, maple, cherry, and mahogany, fashioned his moldings and carved detailing with tools which he often made and ground himself. His chisels, gouges, V-shaped tools, and the cutting blades of his shaping planes had to be razor-sharp for best results. Large case pieces like highboys, desks, and secretaries required many months of labor. After the Revolution, fine pieces were no longer imported from England and cabinetmakers of repute were booked for years ahead. Photograph courtesy Colonial Williamsburg* **879A** *Hadley chest of the Hartford type, made of oak with pine top, c. 1675*

Chests & Drawers
for
Clothes & Linens

879A

THE FIRST COLONISTS had no closets in which to store their clothing, blankets, and household linens. Attics were not readily accessible, and cellars were apt to be damp. Thus, the chest came into use.

In its simplest form, the chest was a large box of wood with a hinged lid. Although it functioned primarily as a receptacle for clothes and valuables, it also served as an additional seating place, for chairs were a luxury in most homes. Frequently chests were used for the storage of linens, especially those a bride brought to her husband.

Early ships' records show the chest to have been the sole item of furniture accompanying the earlier settlers. It is not surprising, therefore, that the chests built by seventeenth-century joiners in this country were copied from English pieces designed in the prevailing Jacobean style. As early as 1660, such craftsmen as Thomas Dennis of Ipswich, Massachu-

setts, and Nicholas Disbrowe of Hartford, Connecticut, were fashioning paneled and carved oak chests, constructed of wide stiles and rails. These had slightly sunken panels with elaborately carved intaglio decorations. Instead of a paneled top in the English fashion, the Colonial chest had a plain pine board top. This unadorned top surface was ideal for seating and did not need cushions.

In their crude fashion, these chests were the counterpart of the elaborate coffers, caskets, and *cassoni* (large Italian chests with fine carvings and paintings) owned throughout Europe by wealthy families.

The Bible box, a smaller version of the chest, was designed to protect treasured volumes and documents. It also held coins, jewelry, and sundries. These small chests were usually made of oak and were decorated with incised linear patterns composed of lunettes, foliage, and floral motifs. The carving of this period is rarely executed in the round to produce bas-relief modeling. To understand the vast difference between the crudeness of these early decorative forms and the sophisticated handiwork of the master European woodcarvers, one must consider what the Colonial carpenter-builder had to work with. His tools were few in number and wrought by the local blacksmith. Also, his time was always limited, and he had no books to guide him.

The typical blanket chest, made from about 1650–1750, stood about thirty inches high and was usually four to five feet long. It had a deep well, bracketed legs, and a top lid, with three sunken panels in front, separated by stiles and rails varying from three to four inches in width. The rails were decorated with running patterns, such as the guilloche, scale, or a double scroll enclosing leaf or rosette forms. The front panels, and sometimes the end panels, were designed symmetrically in the form of tulips, sunflowers, or other floral groups, often arranged in an arched or lozenge shape. Stylized foliage filled the areas; animal or human forms never appeared. The carving, generally flat and crude, cannot be used to date pieces, since many copied previous styles. Over the years, drawers were added to the basic form, increasing the height, and gradu-

ally a different piece of furniture evolved.

An important development in the decorative treatment of chests is attributed to Nicholas Disbrowe, who followed the Jacobean style of using split balusters. These turnings were applied to the flat surfaces of the stiles in place of carved relief. They were usually painted black to simulate ebony and were supplemented with small knobs, diamonds, and lozenges formed from the raised moldings. The so-called Hartford chest, also known as the sunflower chest because of a grouping of three sunflowers on the front center panel, was made by Disbrowe between 1660 and 1680. The flanking panels were ornamented with carved tulips and leafage scrolls. Two full-width drawers under the paneled well had octagon-shaped molded panels with applied bosses and were fitted with elongated turned wooden knobs. This chest was made from oak and had a pine top.

The Hadley chest was named for the town in Massachusetts where it was produced between 1675 and 1740. It was decorated with rather crude and shallow carving of simple designs, usually tulips, vines, and leaf forms, which covered the entire front. It had three rectangular upper panels, one, two, or three drawers, and was made of oak with pine parts. These chests were painted red, black, brown, and sometimes green, and generally bore the initials or the name of the person for whom the chest had been made. About one hundred and twenty examples are known, proving they were very popular in their day.

The town of Guilford, Connecticut, is identified with another type of chest. It had a stile-and-rail construction, with a wide front panel instead of several smaller panels, a single drawer, and a large upright panel at each end. Unlike most other New England chests whose decorations were carved, the Guilford chest featured an all-over polychrome treatment of flowers, foliage, and running bands of scrolls and leaves. Often the end panel carried a large bird rendered in silhouette. The painted designs show strong evidence of Tudor and Dutch derivation and formal patterns of inlay like those used throughout Europe at the time.

880

881

882

880 *Huge secretary desk, elaborately inlaid both outside and inside, exhibits strong Dutch influence, with its large overhanging cornice molding, ball feet, and ornamental style. Inside compartments contain fourteen pigeonholes and fifteen drawers. Made in New York, c. 1690–1710* **881** *Massive molding treatment on cornice and door details reflect Dutch traditions. Made of walnut, c. 1700–1750* **882** *Nowhere is the Dutch influence as marked as in this highly ornamental* kas *made of oak and gumwood. Monochrome painting of fruits and flowers is characteristic of still lifes of the time. Late seventeenth century*

885

883

884

883 The court cupboard was a massive piece of furniture. Of English origin, it was used to store household linens, fine silverware, and articles of value. Ownership was a mark of distinction. Most court cupboards were made in lower New England, especially the Connecticut valley **884** Oak cupboard of sturdy construction features recessed compartments and freestanding pillars of heavy turning. The great torus molding at the midsection is covered with a double band of foliated scrolls, forming a huge drawer which opens at the miter of the corners, c. 1660–80 **885** Three pine drawers ornamented with foliated carving in the manner of the Connecticut valley create a striking effect in this straight-front press cupboard, c. 1670–80 **886** Notable example of the Hartford-type chest with drawers, attributed to Nicholas Disbrowe. It features panels with carved sunflowers and tulips. Split turned spindles and bosses, painted black in imitation of ebony, c. 1660–80 **887** Combination cupboard and chest of drawers whose design shows variations in molding treatments. Upper panels are crossetted; upper drawer shows sharply raked spurs; lower drawer is plain, c. 1670–90

886

887

253

888

888 *Completely ornamented chest. Drawer*
feature a running wave. Tulip scrolls ornamen
stiles and rails. Sunflower motifs are the center.
of main panel and drawer faces, c. 1700 **88***
Two-drawer Hadley chest, c. 1700–1710, with all
over decoration of abstract floral motifs chipped
out in flat relief. The persistence of the tulip
forms is of Lowlands derivation, blending with
an exotic note from the Near East introduced
in the seventeenth century. It was customary for
the carver to include the initials of the owner
prominently displayed on the center pane
890 *It is now known that the Hadley chests were*
the work of Captain John Allis of Hadley, Mas-
sachusetts, grandnephew of master joiner Dis-
browe. Either Allis trained a number of appren-
tices or his style was meticulously copied by
others since over a hundred such chests are

889

890

Hadley Style

891

known to exist. Characteristic of the Allis style is a precise handling of floral forms, with incised lines for detailing; a two-level contrast between surface decoration and sunken portions; all-over treatment of the entire front; and plain paneled construction of both ends. The initials "S S" are visible on center panel of this chest, c. 1700–1710. Handles are a later addition, replacing original wooden knob drawer-pulls **891** The "Mary Pease" chest has been widely publicized because of the prominence of its owner. The chest is attributed to her father, John Pease, a joiner who lived in Enfield, Connecticut. Some sunken portions of the chest are painted black, thus emphasizing the relief designs, c. 1714 **892** Two-drawer chest with stiles and rails carved in running wave with tulip forms throughout

892

893

895

893 *Oak chest with three carved panels showing foliated scrolls with highly conventionalized leaf forms. Stiles and rails of pegged construction, c. 1660–80* **894** *Oak Ipswich chest with pine top. Stiles and rail carry foliated running design. Three insert panels, slightly sunken, are ornamented with formal foliage palmettes; center panel features lozenge design. Brackets under lower rail bear initials "M I." Made primarily at Ipswich, c. 1660–80* **895** *Paneled chest with lower drawers, Jacobean moldings, and split spindles, ebonized. This type survived because it could be built by any fine joiner and did not require special carving skills, c. 1680–1700* **896** *Oak chest of pegged construction. Upper rail features a continuous S-scroll decoration in running band; main panels employ same scroll motif surrounding central "I" shape, c. 1660–80* **897** *Ipswich chest with a wide variety of decorative details: upper rail, the guilloche with rosettes; lower rail, characteristic Jacobean designs. The stiles display conventionalized leafage broken with an interlacement and central rosette. Three main panels show some freedom from conventional palmette treatment. Made by Thomas Dennis, c. 1660–80*

897

896

894

257

898

899

900

Chests of

Drawers

901

898 *Bow-front chest of drawers of the Hepplewhite period. Carcase has four drawers of mahogany veneer with satinwood inlay. Skirt features cyma reverse curve. Made in New York, c. 1793–1803* 899 *Chest of four drawers on a low frame with five legs showing "inverted cup" design and ball feet. Stretchers at front and sides are in the form of cyma reverse curves; rear stretcher is straight, c. 1690–1710* 900 *Bureau or chest of drawers featuring spirally carved three-quarter pilasters and tapered legs at the corners* 901 *Oak chest of four drawers with interesting variations: first and third drawers are similar; second and fourth drawers are similar, with minor changes. Ball-type feet, c. 1670–90* 902 *Serpentine-front chest of drawers richly ornamented with fine grain veneer and striping. Central rectangular panel on skirt interrupts the curves between French bracket feet. Hepplewhite, c. 1785–1800*

902

903

905

903 *Bureau with four drawers of graduated widths, in the "reversed serpentine" form. Bracket legs with claw-and-ball feet, c. 1765–85* **904** *Chest of drawers with bow or swell front. Of mahogany with satinwood veneer on drawer fronts. Quarter-round fluted columns, squared at top and bottom; stamped brass es-*

cutcheons, c. 1790–1800 **905** *Straight-front bureau in the Hepplewhite style, with bracket feet in the transitional form; bail-type handles, c. 1785–1800* **906** *Curly maple chest of drawers on ball feet with full columns at the corners. Drawer pulls of milk glass, c. 1800* **907** *High chest in the William and*

906

904

260

Mary style, with five rope-twist turned legs and ball feet. Front and side stretchers are shaped in curves; rear stretcher is straight, c. 1690–1700 **908** *Bow-front chest of drawers with oval medallion inlays on each drawer. Skirt with cyma reverse curves interrupted by scallop with inlay, c. 1785–1800*

907

908

261

Joiner & Decorator Join Hands

Toward the closing years of the seventeenth century, the art of japanning was introduced into this country from England, where it had caught the fancy of many cabinetmakers. The increasing British trade with the Orient had resulted in the importation of assorted goods from China, Japan, India, and Indochina. In Holland, an influx of Huguenot refugees learned the art, and the mania for everything Oriental was further stimulated and brought from Holland by William and Mary. An important volume written in 1688 by John Stalker and George Parker called A Treatise of Japanning fanned a raging controversy between the Classicists, on the one hand, and the proponents of Orientalism. The English furniture makers and their followers on Colonial shores plunged into an orgy of Oriental fantasies, covering surfaces of cabinets and highboys with chinoiserie that invoked a colorful realm of costumed

909

figures, pagodas, toriis, temples and gardens, birds and beasts. The skillful practitioners of the art of japanning produced raised designs, built up with chalk compounds for relief. Surfaces were highly polished, sized, and metal leaf was then affixed. "Lay on your gold," the Treatise *advised, "if your work be sufficiently moist, you'll perceive how lovingly the gold will embrace it, hugging, and clinging it. . . ."*

Colonial japanners used maple as a ground for their principal surfaces and pine for less important areas. After building up, polishing, and painting, several coats of varnish were applied to give permanence and luster to their painted efforts.

For their source material, the decorators and japanners turned to imported goods—principally the Oriental porcelains, and Delft pottery, using motifs from the Far East and Indian calicoes. Various pattern books published by the leading British cabinetmakers contained plates of value as exemplars. In Chippendale's The Gentleman & Cabinet Maker's Director *many Oriental motifs are shown, particularly on fire screens, tea chests, chemney pieces, and picture frames.*

910

911

909 *Painted chest of drawers ornamented with long, graceful stems, buds, blossoms, and stylized foliage is typical of a style that developed about 1700 in the area of Guilford, Connecticut. Tudor and Dutch design sources supplied the inspiration* **910** *Five-drawer highboy in the Queen Anne style with flat top, slender cabriole legs, and triple-arch base, c. 1720–50* **911** *Painted highboy in the William and Mary style with six trumpet legs, well-designed stretcher, and triple-arch skirt. Each drawer displays a playful chinoiserie composition. All side panels and lower skirt are painted. c. 1700–1710*

263

912

913

912 *Guilford chest on six trumpet legs, indented stretcher on bun feet. Triple arch on front skirt, double arches on side skirts. All decorating, done in a low key, flows from a central vase or urn; a variety of leaf and floral forms display originality, c. 1710* **913** *Painted chest, with four graduated drawers. Stiles and rails show unusual design treatment. Central painted motifs use varying bird forms, with figures on bottom drawer where height permits* **914** *Decorative interest is achieved in this Pennsylvania chest with tiny painted stripes, curves at the corners, and little floral dots as a running border. Dated 1810* **915** *Chest of drawers appears, from drawer and molding construction, to be homemade. Black painted striping around escutcheon plate and corner treatment provide interest by breaking up long areas, c. 1700–1710*

914

915

265

916

917

266

918

919

916 *Painted chest with wide upper panel enclosing desk compartments. Lower frame has double inverted cup legs, scalloped stretcher on ball or bun feet. Three front panels display related compositions in floral designs* **917** *The decorator utilized the three drawer-faces as an entire facade starting at the bottom and building upward with curving scrolls and tulip forms. Introduction of bird forms adds life and gaiety. Made in Guilford, c. 1710* **918** *Painted chest rendered in more vigorous strokes than usual. Drawer panels look similar, but there are minor variations* **919** *Guilford chest of pine and white wood. Decoration shows playful originality. Introduction of faces on upper drawers is an unusual conceit. The flower-pot motif in the center, derived from Moravian sources, often appears in peasant art forms, particularly in Pennsylvania German decoration. Thistle blossom surmounted by a crown, rose, and fleur-de-lys are combined in a distinctively American way. End panel shows a boldly done tulip stem and opened blossom, c. 1690–1700*

920

921

922

923

920 *Guilford painted chest with highly conventionalized treatment of design motifs. Running wave scroll with leaf forms covers stiles and rails with rare precision and sureness of hand, c. 1700–1715* **921** *Front view of Guilford chest seen in 919. The rail moldings separating drawers extend across stiles, making it possible for these areas to be handled as four smaller units with variations* **922** *In contrast to the accepted Guilford style, this chest depends upon diagonal striping and checkerboard in central areas* **923** *Detail of end panel of Guilford chest seen in 919, 921*

924

925

926

Small Chests
& Desk Boxes

924 *Painted Guilford chest with finely conceived decorative composition balanced on central stem. Branching out and upward, wavy scrolls show a strong calligraphic feeling with tulip and leaf forms highly conventionalized* **925** *Small chest with overhanging molding shows strong influence of printed wallpaper designs used extensively on bandboxes. Nineteenth century* **926** *Painted chest with molding grip under lid at the ends. Design in a series of borders; inner panel is handled ineptly; scrolls lack grace and flowing lines* **927** *End panel of 924. Totally linear treatment of naturalistic scroll forms displays originality. Similar to front panel, with variations* **928** *Gumwood bandbox with arched top hinged on leather straps and metal fastener. Box is covered in block-print paper, with hand-painted flowers* **929** *Small chest, about twenty inches long, with gadroon beaded molding top and bottom and skirt of scallop design. Tulip forms appear in original compositions: arboreal arrangement on each side and a ringlet at the center*

927

928

929

930

931

932

933

930 Small pine desk box, chip-carved with an ingenious variety of geometric motifs based upon rosettes, stars, and tulips. Dutch craftsmen, especially in the New York area, practiced this "Friesland Carving," c. 1675 **931** Pine desk box with prominent lunettes forming a triple-arch design; tulips are incised in the spandrels. Dated 1686 **932** Small, beautifully carved box with unusual combination of tulip and leaf forms. Instead of incising or intaglio cutting, decorative forms are outlined and background is cut away, c. 1670–90 **933** Pine box initialed "HS" has clearly defined tulip forms in symmetrical arrangement, c. 1670–90 **934** Decorator of this carved box has sought to follow a pictorial theme with hunters, deer, and birds in a charming group. Made and painted in 1660 **935** Wooden box covered and decorated in tin. Motifs include stars, leaves, dove, and pierced heart with arrow cut-out and applied; moldings and reinforced corners of tin **936** Trinket casket combines painted wooden sides and panels, brass edging, and beading formed of rows of brass tacks. Brass hardware includes escutcheon plate and hinged lifts at sides

934

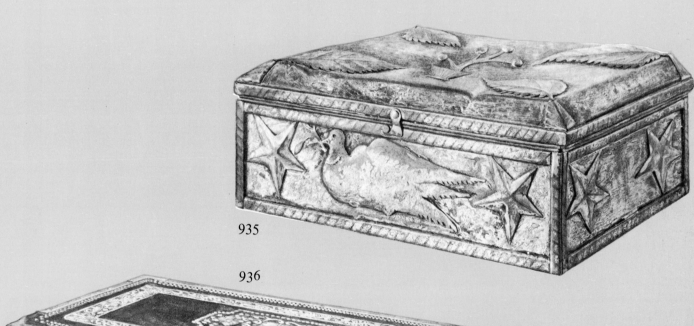

935

936

The Cult of
Fine Cabinetry

DURING THE EARLY Colonial period, the carpenter and joiner provided whatever furniture was needed in the home. All furniture was constructed along rather elementary lines of rectangular joinery. This simple method of structural design depended on the mortise and tenon and the dovetail joint for drawer construction. Chair and table stretchers, following the technique of timber framework, were inserted into vertical legs and stiles by the use of the tenon which fitted into the corresponding mortise.

As a new order of skilled artisans developed in the Colonies, the making of fine case furniture became a highly respected craft. The increased demand for larger and more important pieces and the wish of some to display their newly acquired affluence encouraged cabinetmakers to construct many fine pieces. Two other factors were also important: the introduction of mahogany and the availability of pattern books showing designs by leading English craftsmen.

The more complicated mobiliary forms set forth in the pattern books called for more sophisticated structural devices to accommodate special designs. The accent on curved members, like the cabriole leg and other rococo shapes, encouraged new fastening methods. Although more pronounced carving and the use of inlays, veneers, and japanning came with the increased emphasis on ornamental surface treatment, the achievement of beauty by construction rather than by decoration was of paramount importance.

The art and craft of cabinetmaking required highly developed technical skills. It called for considerable training, at least some knowledge of plane geometry, and a familiarity with the design books of the day. By the middle of the eighteenth century, the Colonists were enjoying a degree of prosperity that made cabinetmaking highly remunerative.

The cabinetmaker's greatest opportunity to become well known was to design unusual and distinctive pieces of furniture. Tables, chairs, and bedsteads followed traditional lines, while the requirements of highboys, lowboys, bookcases, secretaries, bureaus, and

937 Handsome mahogany china cabinet executed in Chippendale's Chinese style during the latter half of the eighteenth century. This piece achieves a classic solidity because of well-ordered rectangulation and notable fretted legs and apron of the supporting member

chests of drawers offered new challenges.

The word *highboy* is said to be of American origin; it is really a high chest of drawers. The highboy developed from the practical need to make the low chest of drawers, or lowboy, more accessible. When the upper part of the stand was fitted with one or more drawers, a new piece of furniture resulted.

The highboy, because of the commodious space afforded by its large number of drawers, became the most important household item for the storage of linens and bedding. The lowboy served as a dressing table and decorative accessory on which to place bric-a-brac and flower arrangements. The highboy, because of its excessive bulk, had to be placed in the bedroom; the lowboy could be placed in hallways, foyers, and parlors. Sometimes, the two pieces were made as a matched set; but, since a greater number of lowboys are found, we may assume that the lowboy survived because of its adaptability to multiple needs.

The first highboys were probably imported from England during the closing years of the seventeenth century and were then copied by Colonial cabinetmakers. By about 1725, however, the use of the highboy had declined in England, either because the upper drawers proved to be inconvenient or because the piece was no longer fashionable.

In this country, highboys developed along two lines: those with flat tops and those with scroll tops. From 1690 to about 1720, the flat-top highboy in the William and Mary style was used. The stands, or lower portions, generally had six turned legs of the "inverted cup" type, connected by flat curved stretchers in front and by one straight stretcher in the rear. The lower stand on which the set of drawers rested had three small drawers, sometimes topped with a single wide drawer. Immediately above the turned legs was a skirt or apron, with an arched central portion as a focal point.

Following the vogue for the flat-top highboy with six legs, the flat-top highboy in the Queen Anne style with four cabriole-type legs came into use. The terminals varied considerably: there were the "three-toed," or drake, feet; the Spanish foot; and one called "cushioned," which had a wooden pad or shoe, giving the foot some protection. An important decorative device called the "rising sun" made its appearance at about this time. It was carved below the surface on the small central lower drawer, or sometimes on the uppermost portion. The drawers displaying this ornament were sometimes called the "sunrise" drawers.

An important change occurred about 1730, when the scroll-top highboy replaced the flat-top one. Starting from the top corners of the piece, a gracefully shaped molding curved sharply upward and broke into a double opening. A carved ornament, such as a flame or urn, was placed in this open space. This same ornament was often placed at the corners and formed a triumvirate of finials.

Differences in detailing developed in New England and in Philadelphia. The New England pieces had less carving but were often ornamented with one or two "rising-sun" motifs. The Philadelphia scroll-top highboy, a magnificent piece of furniture, was developed between 1760 and 1775. Some of the finest Philadelphia highboys were produced by William Savery and Benjamin Randolph, who worked entirely in mahogany, in the manner set by Chippendale. The notable characteristics of the so-called Philadelphia style of Chippendale are the fanciful carvings and applied designs in the rococo style of ornamentation. At its height, this style included a rich assemblage of fantastic scrolls and conventional shell work,.

Herbert Cescinsky, in *English and American Furniture*, states that there is little or no kinship between Philadelphia highboys and those made in England. The principal feature of the Philadelphia highboy is the skillful handling of all architectural and decorative characteristics. The central drawer of the lower portion—the stand—was carved with a shell design, generally fully rounded, from which streamers extend in graceful curves. The apron, or skirt, was cut in cyma curves (a double curve formed by the union of a concave line and a convex line), and in other curves, and had a carved design in the center. The balls in the claw feet were almost round. The inner ends of the scrolls terminated in beautifully carved rosettes. Under and between the scrolls was an elaborate design of flowers and leaves, separately carved and applied. Very creditable pieces in the Philadelphia style were also made by several cabinetmakers in Baltimore.

During this period the Colonies produced some of their most distinguished cabinetmakers. Besides Savery and Rabdolph, these artisans whose masterpieces are found in museums and noted collections, were Jonathan Gostelowe of Philadelphia; Colonel Marius Willet of New York City; John Goddard and his relatives Job, Christopher, and John Townsend of Newport, Rhode Island; Aaron Chapin of Hartford, Connecticut: and Major Benjamin Frothingham of Charlestown, Massachusetts.

938 *Secretary with bonnet top and bust, made entirely of mahogany. Upper doors and rails feature applied fretwork bands; lower panel has shells with rococo moldings applied. A Philadelphia-made Chippendale case, c. 1760-75*

938

939

940

941

Highboys &

Chests-on-chests

939 *Bonnet-top highboy with tiers of graduated drawers. Deep central drawer decorated with fylfot; sunburst or shell motif below. Triple arch skirt is broken by two pendants. Brass bat's-with plates with bail handles and matching keyhole escutcheons. In the Queen Anne manner, c. 1730–60* **940** *Elaborately carved mahogany highboy in the Chippendale style, probably by Benjamin Randolph of Philadelphia. Highly ornamental bonnet with bust and corner urns, dentil molding, and open scrollwork.*

942

943

944

Intricate detailing in lower center panel, rococo skirt, and carving on knees of cabriole legs characteristic of this type, c. 1770 **941** Mahogany chest-on-chest with Chippendale details. Overhanging cornice with band of fretwork · below; corners of upper case chamfered and reeded. Short, stubby claw-and-ball feet, c. 1765. **942** Scroll-top "hooded" highboy, in which front scroll is extended to the back, with flame and urn finials. The sunburst or shell motif appears at top and bottom. Skirt valance is ornamented and leads to slender legs. Queen Ann style, c. 1730–60 **943** Curly maple chest-on-chest with bonnet and double scallop topped by carved bird; flame finials at corners. Corner columns spirally reeded on both upper and lower chests; bracketed feet **944** Curly maple highboy with five tiers of graduated drawers on upper chest. Unornamented except for scalloped skirt valance. Made in Pennsylvania, c. 1750.

945 *Bonnet-top mahogany highboy surmounted by pierced cartouche and two flaming vase finials. Frieze above top drawers decorated with applied rococo scrolls; upper chest has five small drawers above three large ones, with fluted pilasters at corners. On lower stand are four drawers, center one with shell carving and scrolls. Decorative skirt; cabriole legs with carved acanthus leaf, terminating in claw-and-ball feet. Made in Philadelphia, c. 1760–80* **946** *Mahogany bonnet-top highboy, topped by scrolls ending in rosettes, has twelve drawers. Top drawer at center has deeply carved shell topped by applied foliations on the frieze. Skirt at bottom has centered shell and cabriole legs terminating in claw-and-ball feet. Hardware includes open, pierced willow mounts with bail*

947

948

handles; matching escutcheon plates, c. 1760. **947** *Queen Anne highboy of curly maple. Extremely high bonnet-top is closed in at the break, with three vase and flame finials delicately proportioned. The "rising sun" or shell designs on top and bottom center drawers are the only carved elements. Skirt is triple-arched with pendants between; cabriole legs, plain at the knees, terminate in Dutch feet, c. 1750* **948** *Bonnet-top highboy of walnut and satinwood, in the Queen Anne manner. Scrolls at top end in rosette inlays. Contrasting woods and striping supply the decorative interest; skirt has valance of three arches, high in center. Made in Baltimore, c. 1720–40. Figures 946–48 from photographs*

949

951

Lowboys & Dressing Tables

950

952

953

949, 950, 954 *Mahogany lowboys, handsomely carved with quarter-fluted corner columns. Cabriole legs with acanthus detailing on knees and claw-and-ball feet. Middle lower drawer with concave shell or foliations. Shaped skirting with rocaille carving, varying in details. Made by William Savery of Philadelphia, c. 1760–75* **951** *Japanned lowboy from New England. Concave shell flanked by two cupids, chinoiserie on the drawers, and floral decoration suggest the work of Thomas Johnston of Boston, c. 1750–65* **952** *Trumpet-leg lowboy with skirt valanced, the center a deep arch. Cross stretcher and ball, four bun feet, c. 1700–1720* **953** *Block-front cherry lowboy with carved shells, both concave and convex, short cabriole legs with claw-and-ball feet, c. 1750*

954

955

The changing styles of the lowboy generally followed those of the highboy. First came the six-legged type in the William and Mary style with turned, inverted cup legs and ball feet, joined by straight, curved, or X-stretchers. This type was followed by the lowboy in the Queen Anne style, which survived in the Colonies until 1755 or 1760. It featured four cabriole legs with knees, plain or carved in a foliage or scroll motif, terminating in boldly carved claw-and-ball feet. The drawer arrangements varied: four equal half-width drawers, a full-width upper drawer combined with three lower ones, or three equal-sized small drawers. The lowboy of the Chippendale era followed with its rich and elegant ornamentation. The familiar "rising sun," or fan design, carved on the lower central drawer, was an outstanding feature. The apron usually featured the graceful cyma curve—the undulating twist that William Hogarth named "the line of beauty." In his book *The Analysis of Beauty* (1753) Hogarth said: "There is scarce a room

956

957

284

in any house whatever where one does not see the waving line employed in some way or other. Though all sorts of waving lines are ornamental when properly applied, . . . yet, strictly speaking, there is but one precise line properly called the line of beauty."

955 *Cherry lowboy or dressing table with three drawers, graceful skirt of triple cyma curves, and cabriole legs with Dutch feet. Queen Anne style, c. 1720–50* **956** *Dressing table featuring a variety of woods inlaid in bold geometric circles and arches. Pronounced circles on skirt are echoed in the apron curves* **957** *Walnut lowboy with quarter-fluted corner columns, handsome skirt valance with center shell. Cabriole legs decorated with shells on knees. Made in Philadelphia, c. 1760. Photograph* **958** *Curly maple lowboy in the Queen Anne style. Skirt features deep arches of unequal proportions, acorn pendants and cabriole legs with Dutch feet, c. 1720–50* **959** *Queen Anne lowboy of walnut veneer with inlay of lighter wood forming border around drawer fronts. Shell form in the center drawer is a Baroque variant, c. 1750*

958

959

285

960

Secretaries & Desks

961

962

IN THE AVERAGE COLONIAL home of the early days, books were a rare and precious commodity. As the supply increased, however, because of the growing import trade and publishing of books in America, a demand arose for fine furniture cases in which to keep them. This resulted in a variety of pieces, including writing desks, escritoires, bureaus, and secretary-bookcases. Most of these originated in the early part of the eighteenth century and continued to evolve over the next hundred years in the Chippendale, Hepplewhite, and Sheraton styles. In its broadest sense, "desk" applied to any article of furniture intended for writing purposes, but the word was first used to designate a chest of drawers topped by a slanted writing surface which was hinged for lifting.

Of Dutch Colonial origins, the slant-top desk with turned legs and X-stretchers developed in stages into flattops and kneehole desks, with a battery of drawers usually arranged in two tiers. The most popular form of writing desk evolved after the high-legged cabriole type, using slender legs to provide maximum seating space under the desk drawers. As three and four drawers became fashionable, the space below disappeared, and short bracket legs or stubby claw-and-ball types were sufficient. This bureau desk, first made about 1720, was in vogue for perhaps a hundred years. It was made of walnut, plain or curly maple, cherry, or mahogany.

960 *Sheraton-style secretary with tambour roll-top desk. The "pediment" or top valance and case doors feature oval medallions with female figures in the Classical manner. The exquisite artistry of details and proportions depends upon contrast between satinwood and mahogany veneers, c. 1800* **961** *Sheraton-style writing desk of figured mahogany veneer with satinwood inlays, c. 1795–1800* **962** *Mixing table of mahogany and satinwood, with slab of white marble and tambour top, c. 1800*

962 *Mixing table of mahogany and satinwood, with slab of white marble and tambour top, c. 1800*

963

964

The four-drawered bureau desks differed outwardly in minor detail. Drawer fronts were either straight or serpentine, and escutcheon hardware varied in decorative treatment. In the interior compartments, however, there was a great diversity of pigeonhole arrangements, scrolled dividers, and tiers of smaller drawers. A notable feature was the central locker, or document box, sometimes flanked by pilasters and often showing a sunburst or shell motif.

In the hands of John Goddard and John Townsend, from 1760 to 1775, the intricately curved drawer fronts developed into the American blockfront type. Many of the masterpieces of these two superb craftsmen exhibit a characteristic shell design topping the block of drawers and a special style of beading on the bracket feet. Their kneehole desks show an architectonic unity and solidity. On some of these the top drawers feature a triple-shell motif, the outer two in relief and the central one in intaglio. Occasionally, at the rear of the kneehole opening there is a recessed cupboard door with an additional shallow compartment. Such features, charming in themselves, combine into elegant decorative elements.

In the construction of case pieces there were interesting regional differences between the styles of New York and New England. New York cabinetmakers favored straight fronts and sides. New Englanders, on the other hand, preferred the bombé, blockfront, and serpentine drawer fronts. Huge secretaries featuring magnificent rococo carving are characteristic of the Chippendale era. The open doors of these secretaries reveal a wealth of finely executed detailing, rich in decorative design and well arranged to receive ample miscellany. Rich Bostonians patronized such outstanding cabinetmakers as Benjamin Frothingham, John Cogswell, and George Bright.

The Hepplewhite bureau desks, in the closing years of the eighteenth century and a few years beyond the century's turn, featured inlaid oval designs centrally placed on the slant tops. Most popular of these was the American eagle, with wings and legs outspread and with talons clutching an olive branch and arrows. Sometimes a streamer in the eagle's beak displayed stars indicating the number of states in the Union, a great help—as small details often are—in dating the furniture.

965

966

963 *Tambour roll-type desk with knee-hole arch, one large drawer, and two smaller ones. Desk compartment has eight pigeonholes and eight drawers with satinwood facings. Of mahogany veneer with satinwood inlaid stripings. Made chiefly in Philadelphia and Baltimore, c. 1790–1800* **964** *Desk with fold-over writing flap and pulls for support. Four large pigeonholes feature pointed arches; center door panel has oval inlay. Outer surface of mahogany veneer with narrow bands of satinwood inlay Probably made in Maryland, c. 1800* **965** *Maryland-made mahogany secretary, with doors of sunken panels, cut in a series of cyma curves. Slant-top of desk rests on pulls; reeded quarter columns grace corners of lower case, with drawers in graduated depths, c. 1797* **966** *Victorian walnut desk made in Baltimore. The door with double sunken panel hinges down and rests on wide ledge. Legs are spool-turned; handles are wood with slight carving, c. 1850*

967

968

967 *Blockfront kneehole dressing table of solid mahogany. Top drawer features handsomely carved shell motifs characteristic of the work of cabinetmakers Goddard and Townsend, of Newport, Rhode Island. Kneehole niche has a door topped with another shell, barely visible. Late eighteenth century* **968** *Slant-top "bombe" or "kettle" type of desk which swells outward in front and at sides. Made of mahogany, c. 1760–80* **969** *Maple slant-top desk with graduated drawers; straight feet bracketed. Handsome drawer pulls of brass, called willow plates, supply the only decorative note on the severe, well-designed front* **970** *Blockfront slant-top bureau desk of solid mahogany. There is no blocking on the flat lid, but on the front blocking extends down through the molding into the brackets of the legs. A center shell appears below; feet are of the claw-and-ball type, c. 1760–75* **971** *Slant-top mahogany desk with reverse serpentine front, bracketed legs, and claw-and-ball feet, c. 1755–85*

969

970

971

972

973

974

972 Slant-top block-front desk of cherry, in the Chippendale style. Interior displays an ingenious arrangement of twenty-eight drawers. Pigeonholes are topped by tiny drawers of shell design. Front facade, vigorously designed in block tiers, is flanked on either side by delicately fluted stiles. Piece signed by Benjamin Burnam. Probably made in Connecticut, 1769 **973** Slant-top desk with quarter columns fluted at corners. Feet are bracketed and solid **974** Cylinder-fall desk bureau with graduated drawers. Mahogany veneer with inlaid bands. Curved top has large oval set into mitered veneer, with central oval medallion of eagle inlay. In the Hepplewhite style, c. 1800–1810 **975**

975

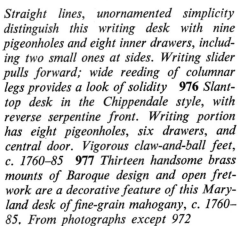

Straight lines, unornamented simplicity distinguish this writing desk with nine pigeonholes and eight inner drawers, including two small ones at sides. Writing slider pulls forward; wide reeding of columnar legs provides a look of solidity **976** Slant-top desk in the Chippendale style, with reverse serpentine front. Writing portion has eight pigeonholes, six drawers, and central door. Vigorous claw-and-ball feet, c. 1760–85 **977** Thirteen handsome brass mounts of Baroque design and open fretwork are a decorative feature of this Maryland desk of fine-grain mahogany, c. 1760–85. From photographs except 972

976

977

978

979

Through the Looking Glass

978, 979 *This general type of looking glass was popular, with many variations in detail, in the period from 1750 to 1800, a time that included many styles: Chippendale, Adam, and Hepplewhite, and a part of the Sheraton period. Decoration is limited to the upper and lower portions, characterized with elaborate fretwork; sides were left plain. Moldings nearest the mirror surface were usually square at the bottom and rounded at the top corners. A popular ornamental feature was a carved bird at the top—an eagle or a pheasant that seemed to be flying. The gilding of this bird contrasted with the walnut or mahogany frame, often veneered upon pine or another suitable base. These two examples, c. 1780–1800* **980** *Gilded mirror in the general period of Sheraton, called a pier glass. Half-colonnettes at the sides are topped with a plaster cresting; the acanthus is stylized in a Classic mold, surmounted by lions' heads. Upper decorative panel of musical instruments painted and gilded on glass, c. 1790–95* **981** *Architectural cornice molding, broken to form a cap for the side pilasters of ringed turning, is characteristic of many American Empire mirrors. All-over gilding, the use of balls as a decorative motif, and carved fruit-basket panel combine to create a dignified looking glass, c. 1820* **982** *Late Empire mirror with symmetrical swan necks forming a lyre shape of striking grace. Acanthus leafage and inverted anthemion at bottom are strong Classical reminders, c. 1840-50* **983** *Oval mirror with molding of wood; ornamental details of composition; entirely gilded, c. 1850. From photographs*

Overleaf: GALLERY OF LOOKING GLASSES. *William and Mary style:* **995** *(1710); fretwork mirrors* **985, 987, 989, 991, 993, 994, 999** *(c. 1770–1800 girandole mirror:* **1000** *(c. 1800–1820): mirror with pineapple pilasters, c. 1810* **988;** *cast-iron mirror frames:* **984, 992, 996, 1001** *(c. 1865–80). From photo graphs except 984, 992, 998, 1000,1100*

980

981

982

983

984

985

986

987

988

989

990

991

992

993

994

995

996

997

998

999

I000

I00I

1002

1003

Of Time & Timepieces

TIME HAS obliterated all trace of the first clockmakers in America, with the possible exception of one Thomas Nash, an early settler in New Haven, whose estate inventory, posted in 1658, listed a number of tools, among them "one round plate for making clocks." None of his work is known today, but the fact that he owned clockmaking tools is a strong indication that he was indeed a clockmaker. In those early days clocks were imported mainly from England and the Netherlands, and in such quantity that the potential of the American market soon became apparent

1002 *In the corner of the Kershner parlor, in Berks County, Pennsylvania, stands the stately grandfather clock made by Jacob Graff, of Lebanon. It is in perfect harmony with its surroundings—the recessed twenty-light window, the imposing armchair, a country version of the Philadelphia Chippendale form, and the dower chest, only partly seen. The tall clock was easily the most important single piece of household furniture, designed and built with care and destined to become a treasured heirloom. Its dial is handsomely engraved and has the moon attachment to foretell the rise and fall of the tides. The case echoes the curvature of the upper dial, above which there is an arched opening and a hooded top with five finals. Photograph courtesy the Henry Francis du Pont Winterthur Museum, Winterthur, Delaware* **1003** *Hand-painted clock face with floral decorations in the spandrels and center circle* **1004** *Tall clock with panels of crotch mahogany and satinwood inlays. Made by Simon Willard, c. 1800*

1004

to European clockmakers. Many of them emigrated, settling in Boston, New York, New Haven, Philadelphia, and other large towns, and immediately started training apprentices, since fine workmen were needed to make and repair not only clocks but also precision instruments.

A few extant clocks from the period of about 1715 are attributable to known makers, who were among the earliest immigrants. These men and their apprentices included such names as Benjamin Chandlee (Maryland), Samuel Bispham (Philadelphia), Benjamin and Timothy Cheney (East Hartford), Gawen Brown (Boston), David Rittenhouse (Philadelphia), Benjamin Bagnall (Boston), David Blaisdell (Amesbury, Massachusetts), and Seth Youngs (Hartford), as well as many others. During the first half of the eighteenth century they produced some of the earliest classic, so-called grandfather clocks. One of our finest examples was made in 1791 by David Rittenhouse, who was also a noted scientist, astronomer, mathematician, and a president of the American Philosophical Society.

The grandfather clocks had fine cabinets and brass eight-day movements. The dials were also usually of brass, with Roman numerals and decorations either engraved or etched; the corner spandrels, outside the circle of the face, sometimes carried an applied cast-brass decoration. The more elaborate dial faces had a lunette on which the lunar phases appeared. The hands were delicately made of pierced steel with thin traceries, necessarily hairlike to keep the weight and resistance to a minimum. For those who could not afford the tall, handsome cabinets a popular version of the bare mechanical clock was available in what was called the "wag on the wall," a number of which were made by the Blaisdell family.

The early clockmakers were craftsmen in the fullest sense of the word. Starting with rough steel or brass blanks, they fashioned every piece from start to finish. Brass was cast in sand molds and then hardened by hammering. Wheels were turned and teeth cut and shaped with the crudest of tools. Working alone or with an apprentice or two, the clockmaker assembled the complete mechanism and built the cabinet as well. If this did not keep him sufficiently employed he turned to gold- and

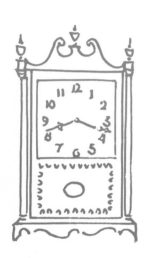

silversmithing, plate and tankard engraving, and the making of fine optical or ships' instruments. Some of the clockmakers are also known to have been locksmiths and gunsmiths.

In 1745 or thereabouts, the clockmaking industry, then centered in Connecticut, was affected by a revolutionary development—the replacement of brass works by hardwood works. This has been credited to Benjamin and Timothy Cheney of East Hartford. Many others in that vicinity began to use wood at that time, but the Cheney brothers were most successful and their influence seems to have been mainly responsible for the growth of the idea. The wooden works made by the Cheney brothers, Gideon Roberts, John Rich, and others were then installed in cases for grandfather clocks. Although the mechanisms were crude, they were able to keep time accurately for thirty hours.

One of the young men traveling to Connecticut for apprenticeship was the noted Benjamin Willard, who came down from Grafton, Massachusetts. When he returned home in 1765, he set up a clock shop in his house and taught the craft to his three younger brothers, Simon, Ephraim, and Aaron, thus starting a family line of clockmakers that would spread to Boston, Roxbury, and Lexington. The Willard, or Boston, school of clockmakers was noted for the fine quality of its clocks as well as for its production methods. It was Benjamin Willard who advertised clocks that "played a new tune every day of the week and on Sunday a psalm tune." The many types, some of which were entirely new in concept and design, included grandfather, tower, banjo, lyre, lighthouse, girandole, and shelf clocks. The Willards used brass movements and made no effort to produce the kind of inexpensive clock being made in nearby Connecticut. In 1802 Simon, the most famous of the Willard brothers, patented the banjo clock, which became one of the most popular of its day. Ephraim made only grandfather clocks, but did not continue for very long. Aaron was a prolific clockmaker and is noted for developing the Massachusetts shelf clock. His sons, Aaron, Jr., and Henry, continued in the business and are credited with originating the lyre clock, which had a circular dial and a mahogany case in the graceful shape of a double scroll.

Two other Connecticut clockmakers deserving special mention are Thomas Harland, who settled in Norwich in 1773, and Daniel Burnap, who opened a shop in East Windsor about 1780. Both Harland and Burnap made a great number and variety of fine timepieces, using brass movements; some had musical attachments. These men trained many apprentices. Most important among those taught by Burnap was Eli Terry, born in 1772, the son of a neighboring farmer. After completing his training, Terry opened a shop in Plymouth in 1793. His first clocks contained brass movement, but he soon experimented with hardwoods, using his previous experience at woodworking to perfect a method of making wooden movements in quantity. In 1803 Terry erected a small building on the banks of a nearby stream, the current of which he harnessed to turn the power machinery he had designed and built. By 1806 his production was so successful that he was able to accept an order for four thousand clocks, and this proved to be the turning point not only in his personal affairs but also for the industry. The mass-production methods he adopted, using an assembly-line approach and interchangeable parts, turned a craft into a leading industry in Connecticut. The great names of this golden age of clockmaking in America include, besides Terry, Ingraham, Thomas, Boardman, and Jerome. These men were more than clockmakers: they were inventors, mechanics, and entrepreneurs.

In 1816 Terry added a shelf clock to the seven or eight models he had been making. This was so well received by the public that Terry and his sons produced it in great numbers until 1840, when the introduction of an inexpensive brass movement by Noble Jerome put an end to wooden works. Since brass movements were not affected by damp weather and were more rugged than the wooden ones, the demise of wooden works was inevitable. The simple ogree molding case, which eliminated the more elaborate scroll top, catered to an ever widening market for reasonably priced wares. The mass production of clockworks caused prices to be lowered so much that inexpensive clocks could be exported to England and other countries.

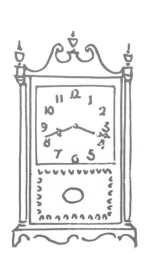

1005

1006

1007

1008

1009

1010

1005 *Mantel clock with flat pediment, lathe-turned and stenciled pillars* 1006 *Eli Terry transitional clock, c. 1825–35* 1007 *Three-tier mantel clock with columns and eagle, c. 1835* 1008 *Clock of mahogany veneer; fine pilasters and carving* 1009, 1010 *Detail showing wooden works and exterior of typical Seth Thomas clock. Photographs courtesy Shelburne Museum, Shelburne, Vermont* 1011 *Terry clock, crotched veneer, hand-stenciled, c. 1830* 1012 *Connecticut clock with scroll and colonnettes, c. 1830*

1011

1012

1013

1014

1015

1016

1013 *Empire mahogany clock with carved eagle and columns. Open face shows label of maker, Jerome & Darrow, Bristol, Connecticut, c. 1824* **1014** *Empire mahogany clock with finely carved decorations. Painted glass panels include eagle and country home set into floral border. Made by Marsh and Gilbert, 1820* **1015** *Mahogany clock of well-proportioned architectural details. Architrave and three-quarter columns above brackets enhance painted glass panels and face, c. 1840–50* **1016** *Mahohany veneer case with glass panel decoration below face. Made by Seth Thomas, c. 1840* **1017** *Highly ornamented clock case with painted floral designs and mother-of-pearl inlays, c. 1830–39* **1018** *Mahogany clock in the distinctive acorn style. Made at Forestville and Bristol, Connecticut, 1830* **1919** *Banjo clock in the Simon Willard style, probably from the shop of Aaron Willard, Jr., in Boston. Mahogany case with pierced side arms, carved and gilded console, and wooden eagle finial, c. 1815* **1020** *Small clock with rounded top and two round doors. Made by the New Haven Clock Company, c. 1860–70. Figures 1013–16 and 1018 from photographs*

1017

1018

1019

1020

1021

1022

1023

1024   1025

1021 *Tall clock by Benjamin Youngs, of Watervliet, New York. Severity of line suggests Shaker influence, 1806* **1022** *Mahogany shelf clock called lyre clock, dominated by handsome pair of cyma scrolls, acanthus covered. Made by Aaron Willard and others, c. 1820* **1023** *Tall clock with rounded hood, open fretwork, tall finials, decorated dial, and fine mahogany case. Possibly made by Ephraim Willard, c. 1780–95* **1024** *Mahogany shelf clock, Gothic type. Decalcomania decorations on glass panels. Made by Birge and Fuller, c. 1845* **1025** *Willard type of shelf clock with two distinct sections; also called Massachusetts shelf clock. Glass panels carry all-over decorations up to outer case, c. 1800–1820*

Overleaf: GALLERY OF CLOCKS. *Veneered frame, rectangular case clocks (Ogee):* **1026, 1054, 1058;** *banjo clocks:* **1038, 1049;** *Gothic or steeple clocks:* **1032, 1044;** *acorn clock:* **1041;** *pillar-and-scroll clocks:* **1030, 1033, 1035, 1046, 1059;** *carved or painted case clocks with side columns:* **1027, 1029, 1039, 1042, 1052, 1057;** *Massachusetts shelf clock:* **1048;** *grandfather clocks:* **1037, 1051, 1055;** *mother-of-pearl, iron-front clock:* **1047;** *looking-glass clock with turned columns:* **1028;** *bracket clock:* **1036;** *column clock:* **1034, 1043, 1045;** *girandole clock:* **1031;** *Empire case clock:* **1050, 1053;** *wall regulator clock:* **1060;** *roundtop "Venetian style" shelf clock:* **1040, 1056.** *Figures* **1026, 1035, 1037, 1038, 1044, 1046, 1055, 1057, 1058 1060** *from photographs*

1026

1031

1027

1028

1029

1030

1034

1032

1036

1033

1035

1037

1038

1039

1040

1041

1043

1044

1045

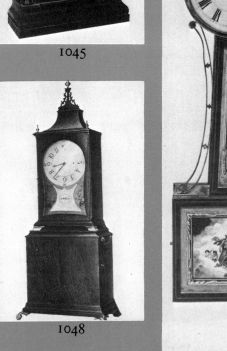

1046

1047

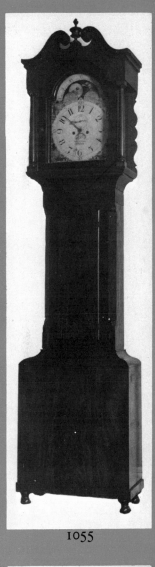

1048

1049

1050

1051

1052

1053

1054

1055

1056

1057

1058

1059

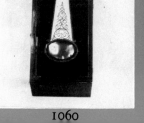

1060

Mahantango Valley Farm *was painted c. 1860
by an unknown artist in Pennsylvania. National
Gallery of Art, Washington, D.C. Gift of Edgar
William and Bernice Chrysler Garbisch*

BOOK THREE

Around House & Garden

BOOK THREE: *Around House & Garden*

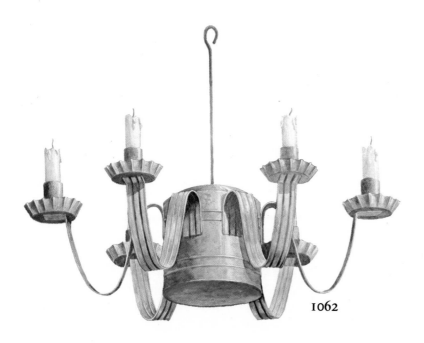

1062

Light After Dark

1063

"RING COTTON YARN for your lamps," Edward Winslow instructed new Colonists. The yarn was a necessity, for crude, oil-burning Betty lamps were the only ones available.

Oil-burning lamps had not changed in essential form since the days of the ancient Assyrians. The lamp body was usually cast or wrought in one solid piece of iron, with a nose or spout at one end and a short, curved upright handle or hanging device at the opposite end. A short link chain and a slender iron pick, used to free the wick when it became encrusted with soot or carbon, were often attached to the handle. These lamps burned fish oil, which was in abundant supply along the coastal waters, but the light produced by this fuel was feeble and the odor anything but agreeable.

Another common type of illumination used by the first settlers was called candlewood. Pieces of resinous pitch pine, common throughout the New England area, were cut into candle lengths and stuck between the rough stones of the fireplace or into holders. They burned freely and, according to Francis Hig-

1061 *In the intimate small dining room of the Governor's Palace in Williamsburg, Governor Spotswood looks down upon a gracious setting, warmed by the soft glow of candles from the silver chandelier and the sticks on the table. The chandelier, c. 1691–97, typical of the elegant fixtures imported to grace the stately mansion, is the work of England's Daniel Garnier. Photograph courtesy Colonial Williamsburg* **1062** *The work of a local tinsmith, this hanging fixture has a simple, honest artistry. Six arms radiate from its central drum* **1063** *Cast-brass candle holder with adjustable feature. Its body imitates early oil-lamp forms*

1604

1605

1606

1607

1608

ginson, "clear as a torch," producing much "fuliginous smoak" and dripping "a pitchy kind of substance" around the hearth. By this uncertain light a man read his Bible while his wife spun her flax or wool and the children studied their primers or did needlework. The family laid in large supplies of candlewood each winter; the Colonists also used rushes, which were stripped, bleached, dipped into fat or grease, and then placed between the pincer-like jaws of a simple, wrought-iron rush holder. The Reverend Nathan Perkins, of Hartford, in his account of a tour through Vermont in 1789, wrote complainingly of his lodging, which "had no comfortable refreshment. . . . I was almost starved because I could not eat ye coarse fare provided for me. . . . No candles, pine splinters used in lieu of them . . . bed poor and full of flees." At best, candlewood, splints, and rush lights served only as inexpensive and inferior supplements to the tallow candle, whose steady light was the standard illuminant in New England farmhouses.

At the same time, Betty lamps were undergoing minor improvements and already were better than the simple one Captain John Carver, first governor of Plymouth Colony, had brought over with him on the *Mayflower*. Tinplate was imported from England, and soon tinkers fashioned oil receptacles that were lightweight and inexpensive. The Ipswich Betty and the Newburyport Betty, named for the settlements where they were made, closely followed the lines of the iron lamps. More significant, however, were the changes in the types of fuel. It was discovered that whale oil made an excellent illuminant and certainly smelled much better than the fish oil in common use.

The coastal waters of New England became the scene of extensive whaling as early as 1680.

This continued well into the 1800s, by which time it had often become necessary for whalers to travel around the world to find whale oil. The great demand for this fuel resulted in a booming industry, centered primarily in seaports like Nantucket and New Bedford. The latter port held its supremacy in this industry for many years, until the discovery and introduction of kerosene.

Of the several types of lighting in use during Colonial times the most common was the candle—hardened tallow, or animal fat, with a central wick. Before the Christian era, candles had been in general use in civilized countries quite distant from one another. They were depicted on the Arch of Titus in Rome and were obviously used long ago in the golden, seven-branched menorah which is described in chapter 25 of Exodus. Candles were commonplace throughout Europe, but few, if any, were brought over to America in the early days; they represented an extravagance.

The first cattle arrived in the Colonies in 1630, but it was not until several generations of cattle had been bred that animal fat became available for the production of candles, which were soon preferred over other forms of fuel. They could easily be made, stored, and carried about from place to place. They could be adapted to simple holders of wood, metal, porcelain, pottery, or glass. They could be supported by wall brackets or sconces, mounted on mirrors, pikes, and outdoor posts, placed in covered lanterns for store windows, or used as streetlamps. Elaborate chandeliers were designed for use in churches, ballrooms, and taverns.

Candles placed in the windows took care of street lighting in Colonial days, although in 1679 a law was passed in New York requiring every seventh house to display a light at the

1069

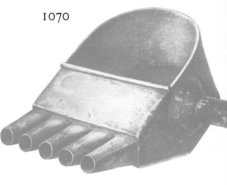

1070

end of a pole. An account of a birthday party given by George Washington, at which two thousand candles were burned, states that the room was brilliantly lighted, yet had a soft and agreeable quality. But even Washington, a planter and landowner of means and a generous host, complained of the cost of candles and retired "soon after candlelight." Benjamin Franklin's axiom "Early to bed and early to rise" was a common-sense application of the principle of frugality: the only sensible way to solve the lighting problem was to retire when the sun set.

Chandler shops sprang up in the smaller towns, but the industrious housewife dipped her own candles and made a supply for months ahead. Tin and pewter molds ranged from single-candle size to molds for two, four, six, or eight candles; commercial molds held as many as eight dozen candles at a time. Home-made tallow candles were produced in quantity when animal fat was available. Wax was also collected from silvery bayberries growing in thick clusters along the seashore; bayberry candles give off a very pleasant fragrance and were greatly favored. Another improvement resulted from the discovery of a crystalline substance in the cavity of the sperm whale. This was used to produce spermaceti candles, which lasted longer and had a less disagreeable odor than tallow ones. The United Company of Spermaceti Chandlers, formed in 1761 in and around Boston Harbor, for a time held a monopoly on their production.

New England excelled in the making of handsome candle holders. Chandeliers for village meetinghouses and large ballrooms were masterpieces of wood, wire, and tin. The wood-turner and the wood-carver had a hand in the construction of chandeliers, but the tinsmith's contribution was notable. He fash-

ioned graceful arms in double and triple tiers holding as many as twenty to thirty separate branches, each with a socket for a candle. The illuminated candles, turned wooden shafts, candle cups, and the elegant curved brackets combined to produce a brilliant effect. These masterpieces were found throughout New England, New York, and Pennsylvania.

Streetlamps and other outdoor lanterns in varying designs were constructed of tin or sheet copper, with open windowpanes of mica or thin horn. Night watchmen patrolling the streets carried small square or triangular lanterns, some with bull's-eye reflectors for illuminating dark corners. Most familiar were the pierced-tin lanterns with conical tops, which emitted a dim glow from the candle within. These so-called Paul Revere lanterns were made in a variety of pierced designs, their intricacy creating a lacelike effect. Lanterns assumed other forms when the candle was replaced by whale oil or fuels such as kerosene and camphine. The lamp base contained a receptacle surmounted by a wick-carrying device to regulate the flow of fuel. Such lanterns

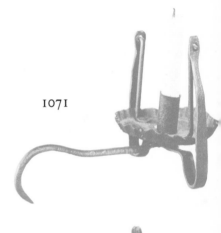

1071

1064 *Iron grease lamp, eighteenth century* **1065** *Slut lamp of wrought iron, used on the early frontier, fed by bear or animal fat* **1066** *Hanging Betty lamp of iron, eighteenth century* **1067** *Slut lamp with cover and standard. At the end of the chain is a wick pick for removing charred mass and lifting it from the oil. Eighteenth century* **1068** *Betty lamp of brass, whose shape follows traditional classic forms. Wick duct is separated from oil font* **1069** *Every farm and cottage burning candles had this type of candle box, made of tin* **1070** *Tin receptacle was used for pouring tallow into the barrels of the candle mold* **1071** *Wrought-iron candle holder with swinging nozzle and drip pan, c. 1830–50* **1072** *Wrought-iron rush holder and candle socket* **1073** *Hanging fixture of four candle holders, with graceful wrought-iron scrolls*

1072

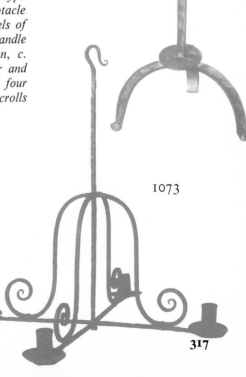

1073

317

1074   1075   1076

1077

were usually designed with a globular glass part that could be raised. This type was a marked improvement over its candle-bearing predecessor and gave more light.

There were candlesticks in every room of a Colonial home. The earliest settlers used wooden candle holders with an adjustable stand. This had a top crossbar which could be lowered by a trammel arrangement as the candle burned. A later development of this candlestand was a central threaded stem for turning and lowering the double-armed bracket. Later candlesticks were made in every possible design of wood, iron, tin, pewter, brass, silver, glass, stoneware, and porcelain. Hundreds of examples exist today.

1079

1078

1080

1081

1082

1083

1074 *Turned wooden candle stand* 1075 *Prim-itive wooden trammel to hold two candles* 1076 *Candle holder with spiral elevating device* 1077 *Pottery grease lamp with handle and base* 1078, 1079, 1081 *A few of the innumerable brass candlestick forms* 1080 *Very decorative vari-ation of candlestick* 1082, 1083 *Brass candle holder, snuffer, and wick trimmer, c. 1840*

1084

1085

1086

320

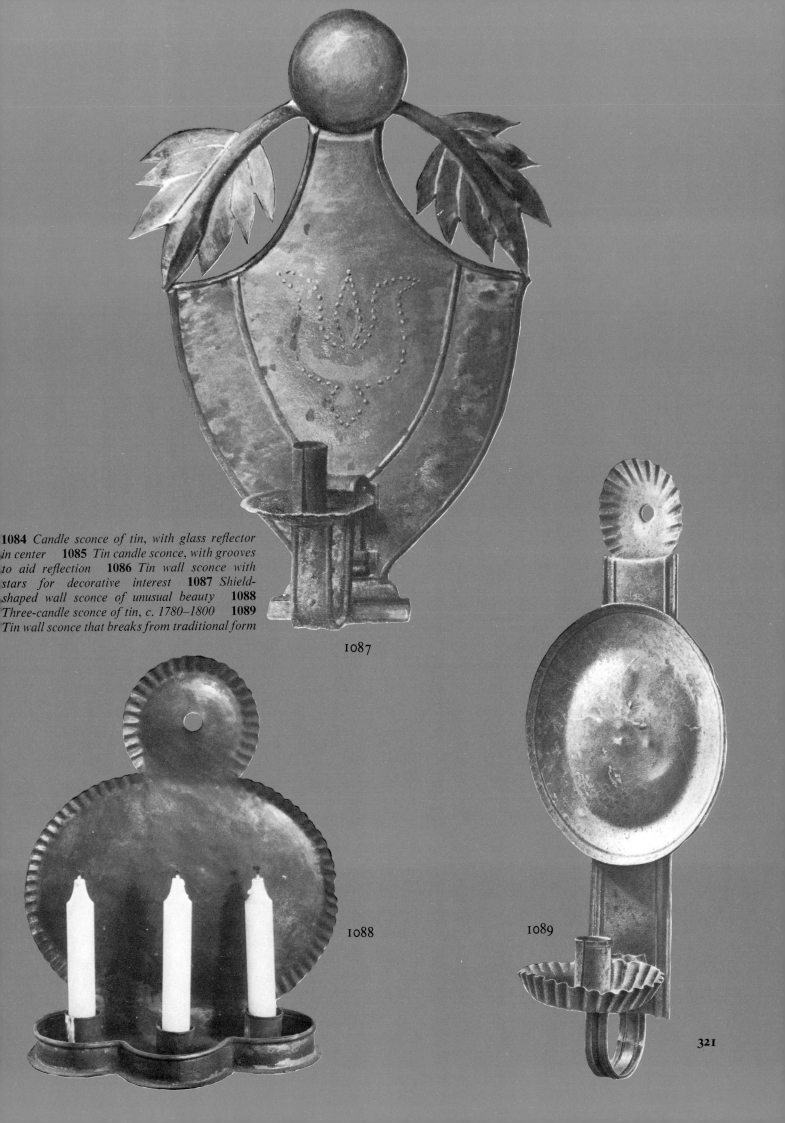

1084 *Candle sconce of tin, with glass reflector in center* **1085** *Tin candle sconce, with grooves to aid reflection* **1086** *Tin wall sconce with stars for decorative interest* **1087** *Shield-shaped wall sconce of unusual beauty* **1088** *Three-candle sconce of tin, c. 1780–1800* **1089** *Tin wall sconce that breaks from traditional form*

1087

1088

1089

1090

1091

1094

1093

1090, 1092 *Brass grease lamps with lower trough to catch drippings, c. 1830* **1091** *Whale-oil lamp with twin wicks, base, and holder* **1093** *Large font and attached snuffer are features of this lamp* **1094** *Scissors-type snuffers on trivet base* **1095** *Twin-wick oil lamp, said to be one of Ben Franklin's inventions, came in a great variety of styles* **1096, 1097** *Glass fonts had larger capacity; decorations were pressed, molded, or engraved, c. 1820–60* **1098** *Lard-oil tin lamp, unusual shape but sturdy*

Brass candlesticks, practically indestructible, were in great favor as they could be produced in a variety of designs from turnings and by the assembly of separate parts. Some, properly called candle holders, had saucer bases and handles. Others had a device by which the candle could be raised as it burned. The elegance of brass candlesticks was not within the reach of the average family; tin and pewter offered less costly substitutes. Glass candlesticks in a wide assortment of styles appeared throughout the middle and latter part of the nineteenth century. Along with brass and pewter candle holders, there were a number of

1095

1096

1097

1098

1099

1100

1101

1102

324

1103

1099 *Lard-oil hanging fixture with eight tin spouts and large receptacle for ample oil supply. Of Pennsylvania German make, early nineteenth century* 1100 *Whale-oil lamp of tin with brass cup, 1840* 1101 *Pewter whale-oil lamp showing snuffers on chain* 1102 *Lard-oil lamp of tin, with broad wick* 1103 *Pewter lamp with swivel for hanging or standing* 1104 *Swinging Betty lamp of tin could be hung on wall* 1105 *Japanned tin lamp for marine use, c. 1850* 1106 *Brass candlestick base with glass font, 1820–40* 1107 *Brass whale-oil lamp with copper spout, c. 1820–40*

1105

1104

1106

1107

1110

1108

1109

accessories, such as snuffer scissors and conical cups for extinguishing candles.

But the candle was destined to be replaced by new lighting fixtures. One of the most prominent of these was the invention of the Swiss scientist Aimé Argand. In 1784 he developed the Argand lamp, the first radical improvement in illumination. Instead of the flat wick used in Betty lamps, this lamp used a hollow, circular wick; the draft thus allowed within the flame caused it to burn more brightly. The addition of a glass chimney at a later date provided extra brilliance equivalent to at least six candles. Both Benjamin Franklin and Thomas Jefferson were so intrigued by the Argand lamps that they brought some back from France; George Washington used a silver-plated Argand lamp in his home at Mount Vernon.

1111

1112

1113

Annular lamps of the Argand type had an oil reservoir in the form of a large ring, which surrounded the lamp and served as a base for the glass shade. The Albion lamp had a reservoir high above the arms of the burners. Following these, a succession of lamps appeared: the Parker lamp, which preheated the oil; the fountain lamp, with a large oil reservoir; the Carcel lamp, with a clockwork mechanism to pump the oil and keep the wick drenched; and the Vesta lamp, which burned camphine. In 1802 Sir Humphry Davy in-

1108, 1109 *Pierced tin "Paul Revere" lanterns shed little light from a single candle; common in New England, late eighteenth century* **1110, 1111** *Sheet brass and copper were used to fashion a variety of oil lamps, c. 1820–50* **1112** *Finely ornamented lamp from fireman's hose reel, with chased silver decoration and engraved glass* **1113** *Wooden frame lantern with candle*

1114

1115

1116

1117

328

1114 *Whale-oil lamp with glass globe and guard, c. 1845* 1115 *Whale-oil lantern with handle for carrying* 1116 *Railroad lantern fitted with red globe* 1117 *Tin lantern with candle holder* 1118 *Fireman's hand lamp; globe has engine number* 1119, 1121 *Pierced tin lanterns, c. 1800–1820* 1120 *Homemade candle lantern, c. 1800. From photographs except 1115, 1119, and 1120*

1118

1119

1121

1120

1122

1123

1124

1125

vented a flameless night lamp. This had a coil of platinum wire over a reservoir of alcohol. The wire was preheated by the flame from a wick which, when blown out, served to supply alcohol vapor to keep the wire hot.

Illuminating gas was first used in England as early as 1798, but it was not until 1847, during the administration of President Polk, that the White House converted from candle-lighting to gas. The popular use of gas was delayed until the latter half of the nineteenth century because of purification problems, but then it brought about a revolution in lighting. Although the fixtures were still of the type used with candles and oil lamps, mantles, like the Welsbach type and others, provided a practical means of regulating the flow of gas from very dim to very bright.

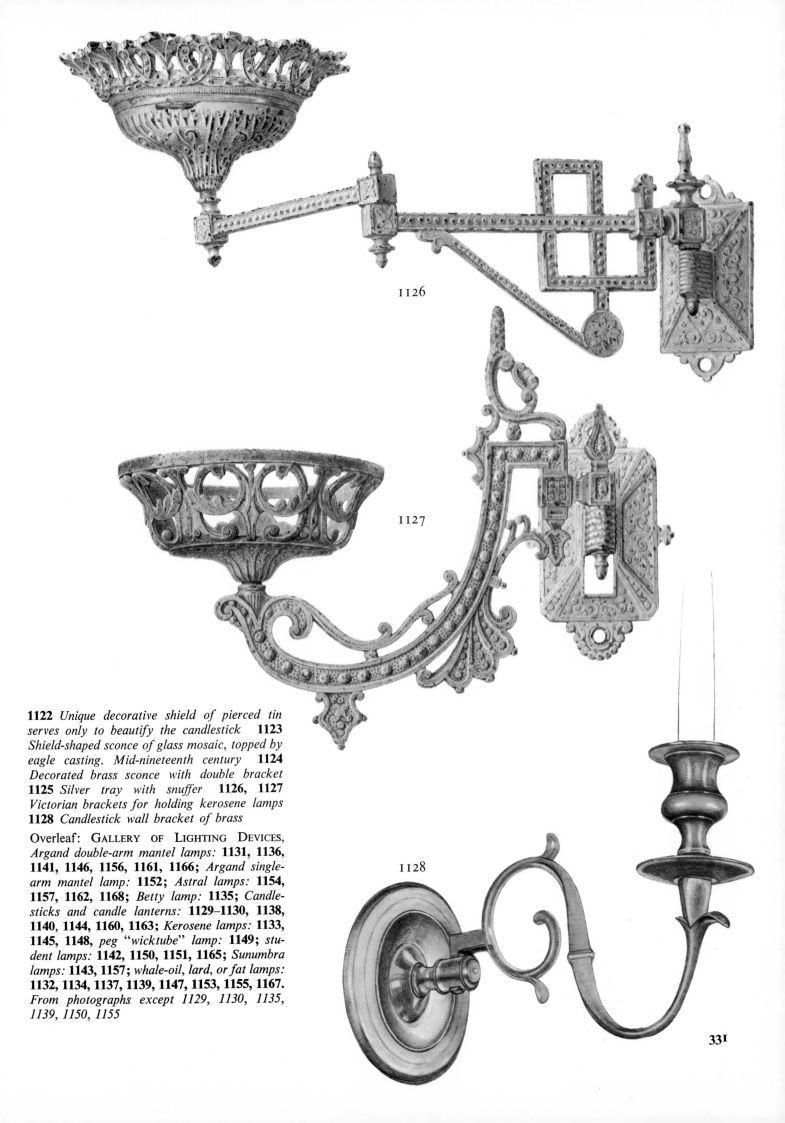

1126

1127

1122 *Unique decorative shield of pierced tin serves only to beautify the candlestick* 1123 *Shield-shaped sconce of glass mosaic, topped by eagle casting. Mid-nineteenth century* 1124 *Decorated brass sconce with double bracket* 1125 *Silver tray with snuffer* 1126, 1127 *Victorian brackets for holding kerosene lamps* 1128 *Candlestick wall bracket of brass*

Overleaf: GALLERY OF LIGHTING DEVICES, *Argand double-arm mantel lamps:* 1131, 1136, 1141, 1146, 1156, 1161, 1166; *Argand single-arm mantel lamp:* 1152; *Astral lamps:* 1154, 1157, 1162, 1168; *Betty lamp:* 1135; *Candlesticks and candle lanterns:* 1129–1130, 1138, 1140, 1144, 1160, 1163; *Kerosene lamps:* 1133, 1145, 1148, *peg "wicktube" lamp:* 1149; *student lamps:* 1142, 1150, 1151, 1165; *Sunumbra lamps:* 1143, 1157; *whale-oil, lard, or fat lamps:* 1132, 1134, 1137, 1139, 1147, 1153, 1155, 1167. *From photographs except* 1129, 1130, 1135, 1139, 1150, 1155

1128

1129

1130

1131

1132

1133

1139

1140

1141

1142

1143

1149

1150

1151

1152

1153

1159

1160

1161

1162

1163

1134

1135

1136

1137

1138

1144

1145

1146

1147

1148

1154

1155

1156

1157

1158

1165

1166

1167

1168

1169

1169 *The feeble glow of candles shed hardly enough light for reading a book or newspaper. It became necessary to move close to the fireplace for that extra light needed to scan a line of small type in the* Virginia Gazette *lying on the table of the Apollo Room, at the Raleigh Tavern. Photograph courtesy Colonial Williamsburg* **1170** *"Dunce-cap" stove was patented by Poughkeepsie man in 1816. Conical cap helped spread heat* **1171** *Fireplace set includes brass kettle and support*

1170

1171

Hearth & Fireside

IN THE COLONIAL ERA the fireplace was the focal point of family life and social activity. The fire radiated warmth, gave off light, and provided the means for cooking and baking. New England's bitter winters, marked by long periods when the settlers dared not venture out into high snowdrifts, meant keeping up the fire, a full-time detail. Fortunately, the nearby forests held a generous supply of fuel, and the strong Pilgrims spent many long, hard weeks cutting and stacking cordwood in piles for the winter. In those first days of the young settlement, when wintry blasts howled, as Governor Winthrop related in his *Journal*, "snowflakes great as shillings" fell and Colonists "starved to death with the cold."

About a hundred years passed before the progressive economy of the Colonies began to affect the ways of middle-class living. The most noticeable change took place in construction of the home with the separation of sleeping quarters from the "common room"—the kitchen. Bedrooms and children's rooms were moved upstairs and families began to have parlors, or sitting rooms. Here the central feature was the fireplace, and all other built-in units, such as corner cabinets, wainscoting, and shelves were integrated accordingly. There were also marked changes in the fireplace opening, chimney breast, and mantel. As cooking moved into the kitchen, the sitting-room fireplace had no need of the spacious proportions that had accommodated an oven and other cooking apparatus. The more compact opening which resulted was formalized and symmetrical, sometimes bricked in or, in later designs, framed in marble or tile. More and more, while retaining their essential function of providing warmth, both literally and figuratively, fireplaces demonstrated architectural creativity and inspiration.

1172

1173

Generally speaking, the domestic architecture of the North and South showed differences in matters of conception and composition, but there was much similarity in interior detailing. The development of mantels and chimney-pieces followed the prevailing English style, gleaned from books and fashion plates. Southern plantations, with their deeply rooted aristocratic traditions, were not as affected by the development of eighteenth-century trade as were the New England seaports and the mercantile centers of New York and Philadelphia. In the manorial plantations along the James, Potomac, York, and Rappahannock rivers, culture was conservative. More than one family of the Virginia, Maryland, and Carolina plantations sent its sons to English schools and universities. This younger generation, steeped at an impressionable age in English customs, traditions, and tastes, brought them back to the Colonies. Thus, the Classicism developing in England, due to the influence of Inigo Jones and others affected by the Classical Renaissance in Italy, was soon evidenced in the Colonies in many ways. Pronounced cornices and crenellated moldings adorned the heavily paneled rooms. Fireplaces acquired an architrave around the opening and

1174

1172 Brass andirons with claw feet, c. 1825 **1173** *Cast-iron fireplace frame in severe architectural style, with columns and central motif of fruit basket, early nineteenth century* **1174** *Franklin stove and grate, with cast-iron detailing in highly foliated treatment, c. 1800–1820* **1175** *George Washington andiron, mid-nineteenth century* **1176** *Fireplace setting with cast-iron fireback, brass andirons, and pierced brass fender showing eagle motif, c. 1800. From photographs except 1175*

1175

mantelpieces became highly ornamental. These reached their apogee under Grinling Gibbons, whose influence can be seen in the buildings of Georgian Williamsburg and in other architecture of Virginia.

Guiding principles of English taste and tradition also operated in the North but with some major differences. By the mid-eighteenth century the rigid Puritan codes originally imposed could no longer be enforced. Social points of view expanded with the growing sea trade and intercourse with the world. The New England aristocracy was one of ship captain, shipowner, and merchant. This wealthy new breed built impressive homes of stone and brick, churches and meetinghouses reminiscent of the work of Sir Christopher Wren and James Gibbs. Some of the most skillful joiners and cabinetmakers in Boston, Newport, New York, and Philadelphia were employed to execute mantelpieces and wainscoted paneling, with fine detailing characterized by a quiet beauty of composition and a delicacy of ornament. An outstanding Colonial home had two features: a finely detailed entrance doorway to

1176

1177 "Hessian soldier" andiron cast after the close of the Revolution. Putting this motif to such menial use was said to represent the Americans' hatred for the role of the Hessians as mercenaries in the war   **1178** Brass andiron made of several swirled parts, with claw-and-ball feet. "Revere Son, Boston"   **1179** Andiron with beaded shank, ball, and finial   **1180** Cast-iron firedog with simple, solid forms   **1181** Andiron of brass compo-

1180

1177

1179

1178

338

1181

1182

nents; short pierced fender with eagle design **1182** *Brass units with beads, balls, octagonal knobs* **1183** *Wrought-iron firedog* **1184** *Urn-shaped body and small knobs combine with original base, footed with balls* **1185** *Brass turnings similar to candlesticks* **1186** *Cast-iron andiron shows the popular Father of Our Country as a squatty figure. Photograph* **1187** *Classical simplicity describes this brass andiron* **1188** *Heavy shank turnings with Baroque foot volutes.*

1183

1184

1186

1185

1187

1188

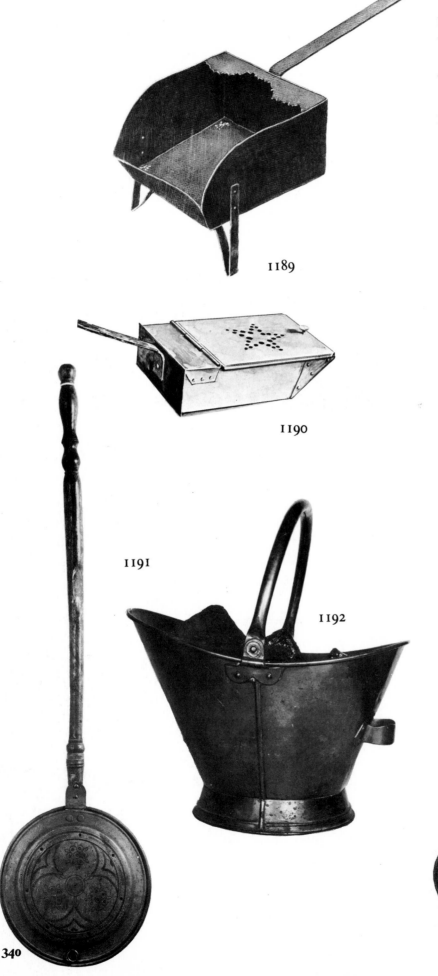

1189

1190

1191

1192

bid one welcome, and a fireplace to provide warmth and hospitality.

Although stylistic attention was given to the decoration of the mantel, the Colonists directed their attention to the practical needs of getting greater efficiency from the open fire. The cast-iron fireback, a plate that covered the rear of the fireplace, was in use in Europe and was designed to reflect more heat into the room. Sometimes andirons, popularly referred to as firedogs, were welded to the fireback. Generally, however, these were separate so that they could be moved about for cleaning and adjusted to accommodate logs of varying lengths. The iron fireback was usually rectangular, higher than wide, and sometimes crested at the top like a gravestone. By the middle of the eighteenth century, especially throughout the Pennsylvania regions, these iron plates were being cast by a number of foundries.

When the formal fireplace became the focal point of a drawing room or tavern, accessories and some housekeeping equipment were added at the hearth. There were andirons, screens, fenders, grates, dustpans, coal scuttles, and wood bins. Sets of fire tools included tongs, poker, shovel, brush, irons, and tool holder.

1193

1194

In addition to these utensils there were ember carriers of tin or brass to transport hot coals. The Cape Cod lighter—a brass tankard containing an oil-soaked stone on a handle—was used to ignite other fires. Portable foot warmers were square metal containers with pierced openings, set into a wooden frame with a handle. These could be taken along in coach or carriage to chilly Sunday services. Samuel Sewall, eminent American diarist, commented upon this exigency: "This day was so cold that the sacramental bread is frozen pretty hard, and rattles sadly." Most Colonial homes were equipped with brass or copper warming pans which stood near the fireplace. Glowing embers placed in this long-handled covered pan served to warm icy bedclothes.

The earliest andirons were of wrought iron, with simple curved feet, a straight flattened shaft, and an enlarged head, which might be looped to hold a roasting spit. It might have been in the shape of a flattened scroll, a Colonial pigtail, a heart, or an ogee. At times the blacksmith varied his design by twisting the square shank of the shaft and then topping it with a goosehead, a flame, a solid ball, or a scroll holding a ring. About the middle of the

eighteenth century, cast-iron andirons were made by a number of foundries. The earliest designs were rather primitive, showing the head of a dog, an owl, or an eagle. Others displayed Adam and Eve. The Hessian soldier proved a favorite about 1780 and the figure of George Washington appeared in several versions. Designs of smokers, ships, and houses were also available. Toward the end of the eighteenth century, as an attractive variant, andirons were made with brass parts, such as knobs, flames, and facets, to supply a touch of luster and sparkle. The Classical influence of the Adam period helped shape brass andirons, which complemented the Georgian homes. At first the bowls and vase forms were large and a part of the shaft proper, but later the vase became the finial, or capping ornament, as the shaft assumed more delicate and slender lines. Various combinations of turned parts accounted for an infinity of forms in the main shaft. The legs and feet were padded or featured the popular claw-and-ball on a cabriole leg. One of the most extravagant brass andirons had a twisted baluster with a diamond-and-flame finial; this was known to be the work of Paul Revere.

1195

1189 *Ember carrier of tin with iron handle*   **1190** *Ember carrier with closed lid, early nineteenth century*   **1191** *Warming pan of sheet copper with wooden handle*   **1192** *Coal scuttle of brass* **1193** *Cape Cod lighter of brass. The rottenstone was dipped into oil and ignited, then used to set other fires where needed. Early nineteenth century*   **1194** *Tin receptacle for carrying glowing embers*   **1195** *Coal scuttle of japanned tin, hand decorated, with cast-iron base frame*   **1196** *Foot warmer of perforated tin set in wooden frame. Smoldering coals or hot stones were placed inside* **1197** *Japanned tin coal scuttle with lid for opening at top, equipped with fireplace set. Decalcomania decoration   Figures 1191, 1192, 1195, and 1197 from photographs*

1196

1197

341

1198

1199

1200

1198 *Iron stove made by the Shakers used only the simplest design to produce a beautiful and efficient heating unit* **1199** *Copper kettle, or hotwater goose, with metal receptacle for coal or embers* **1200** *Charcoal broiler with removable grate* **1201** *Six-plate iron stove with Gothic decorations. Made in Albany, New York, c. 1840–50. Photograph* **1202** *Patented iron stove with inner compartment for pots and kettles; leg supports differ from customary four legs. This tailor's stove belonged to Andrew Johnson, Lincoln's successor to the presidency* **1203** *Highly ornamental surface treatment appealed to the Victorian taste, c. 1849*

1201

1202

1203

343

1204

1205

1206

344

1207

1208

1204 *Parlor stove assumes monumental size and impressiveness with added mirror and iron scrolls, c. 1850–60* **1205** *Filigree scrolls and foliations designed to make this "a thing of beauty," as the manufacturer's catalogue boasted* **1206** *Late nineteenth-century stove whose decorative whorls and twists approach Art Nouveau styling* **1207** *Rococo fireplace setting for the built-in stove expresses unbounded exuberance in iron* **1208** *Patented parlor stove with built-in Stanley columned heaters. Gothic arches and decorations, c. 1850–60. From photographs*

345

1209

Jars & Jugs

1210

Crocks & Churns

LMOST ALL AMERICAN CERAMIC wares may be classified as pottery. Types are designated according to the clay used—red, yellow, gray, tan or white (common crockery). These various earthenwares and stonewares are opaque, whereas porcelain, or china, is translucent.

Common red clay, used for redware, is found along most of the eastern seaboard. It is easy to work, and as early as 1630 American potters were fashioning it into ordinary household plates, platters, pitchers, pots, jars, jugs, and crocks, as well as flowerpots, pipes, and roofing tiles. The potter dug his own clay—red clay lies close to the surface—and then, to

eliminate impurities, ground it with a mill, or quern, a hand-operated device in which a millstone was turned inside of a larger stone. When larger amounts of clay were needed, the potter built a pug mill operated by horsepower. After the clay was cleaned, he then "wedged" or worked it further by hand, a process similar to the kneading of dough. When the wedged clay was ready to be turned, it was placed on the potter's wheel, a simple table with a rotating stand operated by foot. The potter then allowed his product to dry in the sun. This dried, unfired clay was called greenware. When there were enough pieces to fill the kiln and the fire was ready, the potter proceeded with the glazing and firing. Glazing helped

1211

1212

1209 *Upper shelf, left to right: small jar covered in Albany slip, 1861–81; salt-glazed jar, applied "ear" handles, with rich cobalt blue decoration; earliest known piece of Norton stoneware, c. 1800; salt-glazed stoneware water cooler with cobalt blue flying-eagle motif, lined with Albany slip, c. 1861–81; miniature crock, with applied handles, decorated in cobalt. Lower shelf: small tan single-handled jug; two-handled jug probably for cider, marked "I. Judd, Jr. Bennington," c. 1830; earliest known piece of Bennington Pottery, made in 1798; two-handled jug with unusual eagle bas-relief and bands of incised decoration, made for A. Hathaway, 1838–45; Albany slip bank made for Edward Norton. Photograph by Frank L. Forward, courtesy the Bennington Museum, Bennington, Vermont*
1210 *Glazed stoneware wine jug with applied and incised decoration, made by Harris factory in Ohio, c. 1858* **1211, 1212** *Two bird motifs by early potters. These were blue slip designs from New York stoneware*

seal the extremely porous red-clay earthenware and lent a protective coating of brilliance and sparkle to an otherwise dull surface. The firing was done in a kiln by a wood fire that lasted from thirty to thirty-six hours, after which the kiln was allowed to cool before the pottery was removed.

The glaze, a compound of powdered red lead mixed with clay, fine sand, and water, produced an orange-red, dark-red, or brownish color. By adding manganese to the glaze, a brown or black resulted; similarly, by adding oxidized copper filings, a greenish color was produced. The charm of redware lies in the coloration and mottling of the glaze, and the brushings and dribblings of the green or brown as they flow down the surface. The earliest redware was decorated with slip, a liquid clay that was usually trailed on the surface of the unfired ware by being poured through a quill inserted in a clay slip cup.

Yellow earthenware was produced from a yellow or buff clay found in the regions of Ohio. This clay was primarily used for kitchen articles of Bennington flint enamel and Rockingham wares. Rockingham ware is dappled, streaked, or mottled to resemble a rich tortoise shell, with the application of a lustrous manganese brown glaze. From about the 1840s to 1900, it was used extensively in a great variety of household articles.

Stoneware, made of gray and tan clays, had certain qualities that were lacking in the porous redware. It was vitrified at high temperatures to form a hard, glassy body of nonporous base. A pitted glazed finish was produced by throwing handfuls of salt into the kiln at the time of the greatest heat, which produced a surface texture similar to that of an orange peel. The earliest stoneware was unglazed on the inside. After about 1800, the interiors were treated with a dark brown glaze that acted as a sealer. This glaze was named Albany slip, after the place along the banks of the Hudson River where it was found in quantity.

Stoneware pots and jugs can be identified by their method of manufacture and style of decoration. Rings and bands, turned on the potter's wheel, were favorite motifs. Figures and animal forms were molded freely by hand

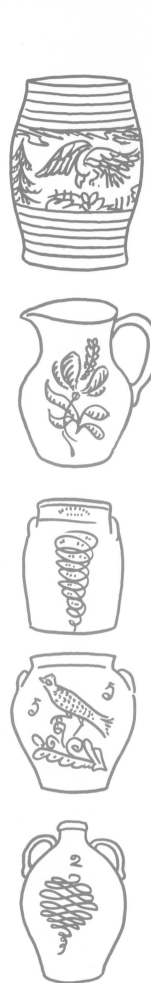

and included Toby pitchers, heads, toys, bird and animal whistles, and coin banks. After 1825 applied leaves and fruit and gadrooned (fluted) borders appear. Relief decoration was applied on borders and especially on handles.

Surface decoration took several forms: sharp linear patterns traced by a quill from the slip cup; broad strokes and blobs from a soft brush, showing gradations in color; or painting of the piece with cobalt blue decorations (which became important about 1825). In addition to hand painting, beginning about 1790 some pieces were stenciled, incised, or scratched. Decorations included flowers, insects, trees, animals, patriotic symbols, and birds, which were most popular. Other forms occasionally represented included houses, sunbursts, stars, compasses, and ships. A group of designs expressing a great degree of originality are those with calligraphic scrolls and curlicues—freehand flourishes closely related to handwriting. These charming motifs twisted and turned in unpredictable directions but were always expressive of the individual who produced them. Many designs can be traced to known potters, and thus the origin of such pieces can be traced as if they had been signed.

The custom of stamping the potter's name on a piece became a common practice at the start of the nineteenth century. Nameplates were made from metal dies and impressed into the clay before firing. These were trademarks rather than a declaration of the potter's pride in his creation, for there was rarely much personal feeling about these common household objects which were destined for sale in the marketplace.

Stoneware jars, crocks, and jugs came in varying sizes—some had a capacity as great as thirty gallons—and shapes. Because they were functional rather than ornamental, emphasis was on simple, straightforward designs. Crocks and preserve jars usually had straight sides, but some bellied out at the middle of the body. Jugs were single-handled vessels with a swelling body and a small mouth for corking and sealing. Although pottery usually kept to these basic forms, the manner of decoration provided an outlet for artistic self-expression.

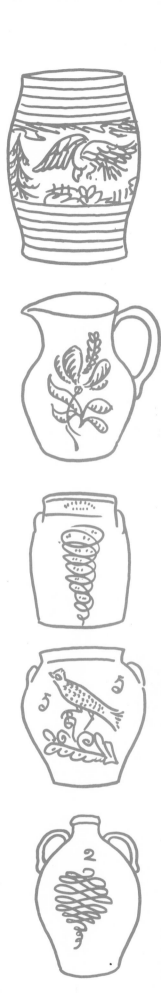

1213

1214

1215

1216

1217   1218

The larger crocks and ovoidal shapes that bellied out particularly invited the hand of the decorator, and thus the area of decoration is often the upper third of the piece's surface. Glaze, texture, color, and brushwork combined to produce sparkle and brilliance, simultaneously revealing the personal taste of the craftsman and pointing up regional differences.

1213–1219 *Earthenware jugs and pitchers are not always dated, but the following information is well documented: figure* **1213**, *Philadelphia, c. 1865–70;* **1214**, *c. 1875–90;* **1215**, *1868;* **1216**, *c. 1850;* **1217**, *Greensboro, Pennsylvania, 1797;* **1218**, *Waynesboro, Pennsylvania, c. 1830;* **1219**, *New York City, 1798. Most of these stoneware vessels are decorated with varying floral and foliated forms. The single-handled jug generally shows some ribbing at the neck, above which is a separate piece of decoration (as in* **1213**, **1217**, *and* **1218**). *The ovoid vessel form presents the greatest opportunity for decorative treatment at the wide portion of the belly. Some patterns employ symmetrical plant forms, while in others the forms move around the body of the vessel*

1219

351

1220

1221

1222

1223

1224

1220, 1221, 1223, 1224 *Wide-mouthed earthenware crocks used for food storage. Generally gray with slightly brownish tinge, lined with Albany slip and featuring a variety of decorative motifs and techniques. Mid-nineteenth-century* **1222** *Glazed earthenware jug, with brownish stain, used for food storage. The freely rendered floral and leaf forms feature a heart in which is inscribed "W. K. 1788 N.Y." Made in Pennsylvania*

1225

1226

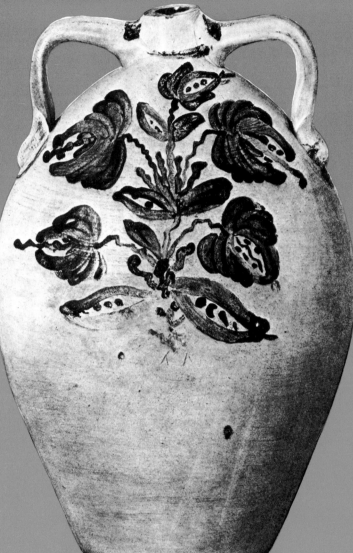

1227

1228

1225 *Wide-mouthed jar with applied "ears" and a simple, gracefully executed floral decoration* **1226** *Two-handled water cooler or cider jug with spout opening at bottom. Ingenious and original design features floral forms* **1227** *Stoneware jug with cobalt blue flower design rendered as a finger decoration. Made in Ohio, c. 1840* **1228** *Four-gallon crock with handles. Bird and floral design were first incised in soft clay and later painted, c. 1857–72* **1229** *Two-gallon crock made in Albany. Graceful floral form applied with thick, superior blue impasto in relief, emphasizing the crock's broadest part*

1229

353

1230 Jug decorated with vigorous floral and leaf forms, 1850 **1231** Water jug with pouring spout, decorated in the "sgraffito" manner of the Pennsylvania Germans, 1798 **1232** Stoneware wine keg with outstanding relief treatment of the ribbing, stars, and the especially competently modeled eagle **1233** Crock with freely rendered eagle and shield c. 1790–1820 **1234** Two-handled jug with incised and slip-decorated birds and flowers. Probably Pennsylvania German, 1844 **1235** Wine or water jar with spigot hole. Plant and flower forms in a charming, fluid design **1236** Crock with lid and "ears." The slight neck and tapering body that swells at the base create a pleasant shape to which decoration has been tastefully applied

1230

1232

1231

354

1233   1234

1235   1236

1237

1238

1239

356   1240

1241

1242

1244

1243

1245

1237 *Glazed stoneware crock with decorated panel for the owner's name* 1238 *Graceful vessel with scalloped decoration and loose flower design* 1239 *Nineteenth-century water cooler or wine keg, similar in shape to 1232* 1240 *Gray stoneware crock with small, free standing handles, bird on other side* 1241 *Gray crock with floral bouquet in blue slip, c. 1850–60* 1242 *Pitcher featuring American eagle in low relief, 1864–70* 1243 *Straight-sided, three-gallon gray stoneware crock with stenciled eagle, applied in blue. Made in Greensboro, Pennsylvania, c. 1860* 1244 *Stoneware water cooler, adorned with finely modeled eagle, flanked by sprays of grape leaves. Made by Sidney Risley, Norwich, Connecticut, c. 1840.* 1245 *Deep butter churn with blue decorations painted with broad strokes, running around the body, c. 1850–60* 1246 *Distinctive New York pitcher with realistically modeled floral and leaf forms, including oak sprays and acorns. Lid topped with a squirrel*

1246

357

1247

1248

1249

1250

1251

Overleaf: GALLERY OF CERAMIC VESSELS. *Churn:* **1302**; *crocks:* **1257, 1258, 1260, 1264, 1265** *(1802),* **1271** *(1791),* **1272, 1275, 1276, 1279, 1281, 1287** *(1842); jars with lids:* **1261, 1277, 1280, 1293, 1295** *jugs:* **1256** *(1788),* **1259, 1262, 1263, 1267, 1269** *(1798);* **1273, 1282, 1294, 1297, 1303** *open jars:* **1284, 1285, 1289, 1292, 1298, 1301** *pitchers:* **1268, 1270, 1274, 1283** *(1862),* **1286, 1291** *(1796),* **1296, 1300** *vase:* **1266** *wine bottles:* **1255, 1299**

1252
1253

1254   1254A

1247 *Pottery flower pot, with ruffled flange and drip pan. Laurel wreath encloses manufacturer's name* **1248** *Whisky or water jug with serpent entwined around the body to form a handle, a jug type usually produced by individual potters rather than potteryworks* **1249, 1250** *Octagonal fluted cake or pudding mold with fruit motif* **1251** *Whimsical glazed pottery duck with handle and beak, which functions as the spout* **1252, 1253** *Two views of unique grotesque jug in a greenish glaze for storing whisky or apple juice, c. 1800* **1254** *Grotesque jug of gray stoneware covered with olive green glaze. Probably made in Connecticut in the early nineteenth century* **1254A** *Jug. Photograph courtesy Abby Aldrich Rockefeller Folk Art Collection, Williamsburg, Virginia*

1255

1256

1257

1258

1259

1265

1266

1268

1267

1269

1275

1276

1277

1278

1279

1285

1286

1287

1288

1289

1295

1296

1297

1298

1299

1260

1262

1264

1261

1263

1270

1272

1274

1271

1280

1282

1273

1284

1281

1283

1290

1292

1294

1291

1293

1300

1302

1301

1303

1304

361

1305

1305 *In the Harvest Room of the Dutton House, a modest cottage built in 1782, the dishes are placed on the broad-planked, pine dining table. From nearby Bennington, where Captain John Norton started making stoneware pottery in 1793, came pieces used for table service, including mottled ware plates, hound-handled pitchers, butter dishes, and the attractive center piece. Standing on the rear side bureau is a large Bennington octagonal water cooler and brown pitcher. The open dresser shelves display porcelain pitchers in various patterns and colors as well as a number of jugs and crocks. Photograph by Einmars J. Mengis, courtesy Shelburne Museum, Shelburne, Vermont* **1306** *Small milk pitcher made at Bennington, c. 1850–60* **1307** *Toby pitcher, a name derived from the popular English character Sir Toby Belch and designating a pitcher type first made by Staffordshire potters*

Rockingham & Bennington

1306

AMERICAN ROCKINGHAM, THE ware for which Bennington, Vermont, became famous in the mid-nineteenth century, is English in origin and is named for the Marquis of Rockingham, whose works at Swinton produced a ware of a similar brownish color. The pottery itself is a cream-colored or yellow ware that is dipped or spattered with a brown glaze before firing. The mottled-brown glaze achieves an overall effect which is dependent upon the amount of oxide, the viscosity of the glaze, where it is placed, how it is applied, and the number of times it is fired.

Captain John Norton, whose pottery works was founded in 1793, was the pioneer of Bennington pottery. His works, operated by his descendants after he died, produced a great variety of wares for over a century until they closed in 1894. Christopher Webber Fenton, who married Norton's granddaughter, was the other key figure in the development of Bennington pottery. The Norton Company and the company with which Fenton was chiefly associated—the United States Pottery Company, which lasted from 1847 to 1858— are responsible for many innovations as well as for a prolific and varied output including

1307

not only the mottled-brown Rockingham type but Parian ware, flint enamel, graniteware, and yellowware, as well as porcelain and china.

Christopher Fenton wished to make Bennington the Staffordshire of America, and he succeeded in no small measure. The little Vermont hamlet became the center of experimentation with new clays and techniques. The great variety of items manufactured at the United States Pottery Company were featured in a special exhibit at the Crystal Palace Exhibition in London in 1851 and were seen at New York's Crystal Palace Exhibition in 1853. This display of Rockingham ware included pitchers, bowls, toilet sets, urns, vases, cuspidors, pedestals for flowerpots and statuary, columns, figures, lions, cows, and Toby mugs. Rockingham ware became so popular, especially after the impressive showing at the New York exhibit, that more than sixty American potteries manufactured it up until 1900.

Among the outstanding items in Rockingham ware were pitchers, Tobies, coachman bottles, lions, and poodle dogs. These objects were of English design, to which American potters added their own glazes and color. Daniel Greatbach, the master potter of Staffordshire, England, was brought over to work at the Henderson pottery works in Jersey City. In about 1843 he modeled a hound-

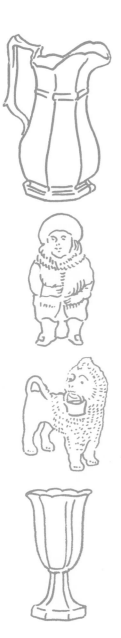

handled pitcher that was then copied by most of the other potteries. Another pitcher modeled by this craftsman had a mask on the front of the spout, a hunting scene, and an American eagle pulling the tail of a British lion. He also made the "Apostle pitcher" displaying embossed figures of the Apostles within Gothic arches. Also of special interest to collectors of Rockingham is the "Rebekah at the Well" teapot modeled by Charles Coxon for the Baltimore pottery of Bennett and Brothers. It was copied from the design of an English porcelain jug. This, too, became a popular item that was produced by a number of factories. Household articles of Rockingham ware include baking dishes, pudding and jelly molds, pie plates, picture frames, soap dishes, bedpans, flasks, foot warmers, cuspidors, doorknobs, and tiebacks for curtains. However, these common, everyday items are not considered of prime importance when compared with the highly prized pitchers and statuary pieces.

The Rockingham ware produced in Bennington was among the finest, but good ware was also made by the other potteries. Whether it was made in Bennington, East Liverpool (Ohio), Pittsburgh, or Baltimore, this brown-flecked and mottled ware was a distinctive, highly popular addition to American ceramics.

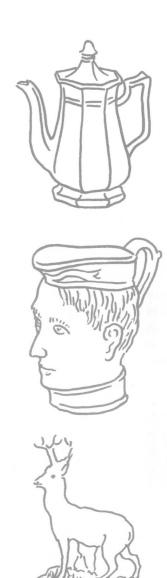

1308 *Toby pitchers. Top shelf, left to right: dark Rockingham bank; flint enamel snuff jar; yellowware snuff jar; rare jar with tricorne hat; Rockingham snuff jar; green flint enamel snuff jar; Albany slip snuff jar. Middle shelf: Albany slip Toby bottle, also called Coachman bottle; two Rockingham bottles; rare stoneware bottle with cobalt blue decoration, dated 1849; three flint enamel bottles. Bottom shelf: two large and rare Zachary Taylor "Rough and Ready" pieces in Rockingham glaze, 1849; flint enamel jar with "I'm a Brick" inscription on hat. Photograph by Frank L. Forward, courtesy the Bennington Museum, Bennington, Vermont*

1309 *Many hundreds of different pitcher designs, shapes, and colors were produced in Bennington. Illustrated here are some of the most popular pieces. Top shelf, three pitchers marked "Norton and Fenton" and dated 1845 to 1847; from left to right: six-sided Rockingham pitcher called "Dark Lustre," yellowware pitcher, pitcher with lead glaze. Middle shelf, three variations of the hound-handled pitcher with grapevine on neck and collar and stag hunting scene on the body; middle pitcher is lead glazed. Bottom shelf: tulip and heart pattern flint enamel pitcher, c. 1849–58; diamond pattern with brilliant green oxide streaks; flint enamel pitcher with alternate rib pattern. Photograph by Frank L. Forward, courtesy the Bennington Museum, Bennington, Vermont*

1310

1311

1312

1313

1314

1310 *Dog of glazed and mottled yellowware. The popular poodle was made in Bennington in a great variety of glazes and colors. Mid-nineteenth century* **1311** *Open-mouthed fish vase, a graceful shape that caught the Victorian fancy* **1312** *Eight-sided hound-handled pitcher, with eagle under spout and animals of the hunt decorating each side* **1313** *Small hound-handled pitcher with decorations on neck and shoulder, and hunting scene on body*

1314 *The large molded animals in Rockingham or flint enamel glazes are perhaps the rarest and most sought after Bennington pieces. Most of the animals were made as facing pairs, and all the lions have a front paw raised, resting on a ball. Top shelf, left to right: Rockingham lion with "cole-slaw" mane; flint enamel lion on rectangular base; dark Rockingham lion with smooth mane. Middle shelf: pair of facing lions with "cole-slaw" manes. Bottom shelf: deer, the rarest Rockingham animals, were originally made in pairs of a doe and stag. The recumbent deer rest near hollow tree trunks; the center figure is the only known example of the standing stag, made in flint enamel glaze for the Crystal Palace Exhibition, New York, 1853; recumbent deer. Photograph by Frank L. Forward, courtesy the Bennington Museum, Bennington, Vermont.*

369

1315

1316

1317

1318

370

1319

1320

1321

1322

1315 *Ewer with Robert Fulton steamboat, c. 1830–40* **1316** *Rockingham pitcher probably made in Zanesville, Ohio, c.*
1850–75 **1317** *Rockingham pitcher made at the Salamander Works, New York, 1848* **1318** *Rockingham pitcher, c.*
1850 **1319** *Pitcher made by J.E. Caire & Company, Poughkeepsie, New York, c. 1849* **1320** *Rockingham pitcher made*
in Bennington, 1844 **1321** *Pitcher made by Solomon Bell, Strasburg, Virginia, c. 1850* **1322** *Pitcher made by Fenton at*
Bennington, 1849

1323

1324

1325

1326

372

1327

1323 *Rockingham pitcher made in Bennington, 1844* **1324** *Tall porcelain pitcher with all-over diamond pattern on side panels. Made in Bennington, c. 1853–58* **1325** *White china pitcher with floral body decorations, gilded bands, and fluted base* **1326** *White glazed stone china pitcher, c. 1843, depicting the landing of General Lafayette at Castle Garden* **1327** *Mid-nineteenth century vases produced by Fenton's potteryworks in Bennington. Top shelf, left to right: vase with shell motif; imitation Belleek glaze, with applied bunches of grapes and leaves; blue and white porcelain in fern pattern with roses and buds; rare eagle design with Belleek-type glaze; vase with applied bunches of grapes and leaves. Middle shelf: tulip vase in flint enamel glaze; graniteware tulip vase; Rockingham vase on yellow body; scroddled-ware tulip vase; dark gray tulip vase. Bottom shelf: elaborately decorated blue and white porcelain ewer; blue and white porcelain vase in poppy* 373 *pattern; Parian ewer with pierced edge and applied grapes; blue and white porcelain vase, with grape decorations and handles; Parian porcelain ewer. Photograph by Frank L. Forward, courtesy the Bennington Museum, Bennington, Vermont*

1329

1330

1328 *Upper shelf: tan and white porcelain pitcher with palm tree pattern; glazed porcelain syrup pitcher with dark blue-green background to spinning wheel pattern; snow-drop pattern pitcher in Parian porcelain; sheaf-of-wheat pattern in glazed blue pottery; sheaf-of-wheat pattern in putty color. Middle shelf: blue and white porcelain pitcher in tulip-and-sunflower pattern; charter-oak pattern pitcher in glazed white porcelain; Cupid and Psyche pattern, pink and white pitcher; fern-pattern pottery pitcher in white; fern pattern in light green pottery. Bottom shelf: varicolored decorations on Parian porcelain body; light blue pottery pitcher in paneled grapevine pattern. banded pottery pitcher; glazed pottery pitcher in cascade pattern. Photograph by Frank L. Forward, courtesy the Bennington Museum, Bennington, Vermont* **1329** *Pottery mug modeled after German steins* **1330** *Gray earthenware beer pitcher with cobalt blue decorations and pewter lid* **1331** *Six-sided William Henry Harrison commemorative jug, with portrait, log cabin vignette, and eagle motif each repeated on sides, 1841*

Overleaf: GALLERY OF POTTERY AND PORCELAIN PITCHERS. *Rockingham pitcher with corn motif:* **1332** *glazed earthenware Toby portraying Napoleon (1876),* **1333**; *decorated earthenware pitchers:* **1334** *and* **1335** *glazed white pottery jug with corn and shell pattern:* **1336** *graniteware pitcher with transfer decoration:* **1337** *teapot with lid:* **1338** *pitcher with buff body and mottled brown glaze, with hunting scene:* **1339**; *decorated drinking mug:* **1340** *lustre shaving mug:* **1341** *white glazed porcelain pitcher (1828):* **1342** *decorated brown earthenware jug:*

1331

375

1332

1333

1334

1338

1339

1340

1335

1336

1337

1341

1342

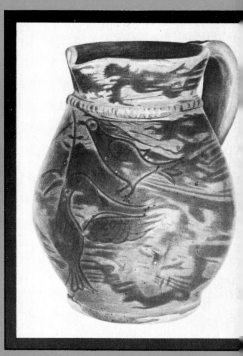

1343

1344

Painted Images
in Plaster of Paris

1345

THE SLOW TRANSITION from the early settler's way of life to a more cultivated style of living during the nineteenth century brought many changes in comfort, convenience, and decorative accessories. These changes were noticeable in household furnishings: crude treenware (woodenware) was replaced by stoneware and china, the open hearth by the cookstove, and candlelighting by kerosene and camphine lamps. Many of these domestic needs were supplied by peddlers and hawkers who traveled from town to town and from house to house, offering wares that could not be found locally.

Carpenters, blacksmiths, tinsmiths, tailors, shoemakers, hatters, and "image makers" were among those whose products were sold door to door. These peddlers were a thorn in the side of the shopkeepers, who had overhead and inventories to worry about. In addition, as roads were bad and travel slow, it was more convenient for the customer to buy from the peddler than to come to the merchant's emporium.

One colorful peddler carried on his head a tray displaying a dozen or more painted chalkware figures. In an 1808 publication called *Cries of New York*, the plaster peddler cries out, "Images, very fine, very pretty." The ac-

1346

1344 *Chalkware cast of peasant couple, typifying the folksy subject matter of popular nineteenth-century household ornaments* **1345** *Pair of lovebirds, a perennial best-seller of itinerant peddlers of images* **1346** *Plaster deer, another favorite, colored in different hues for varying tastes*

companying text explains, "They are made of plaster of Paris, which is a kind of stone that abounds in Nova Scotia." In a Philadelphia volume of 1851, we learn that most of the trade in plaster pieces was carried on by Italians:

> The itinerant seller of plaster casts is a regular street figure in all our great cities. By means of a few worn-out molds which he has brought from Italy, the poor man makes a stock of casts, and mounting them on a board, cries them about the streets. When he has followed this street traffic for a few years, he has amassed enough money to begin business on a larger scale; and accordingly he hires a shop, and commences the making and selling of all sorts of plaster casts. Instead of carrying a small shop on his head through the streets, he now sends forth a little army of his compatriots, poor expatriated Romans or Tuscans, regretting the glorious skies of Italy, while they are selling busts of the glorious heroes of America.

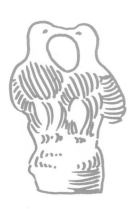

Although the making of plaster figures has been described as a folk art, because all images were hand painted and each piece varied, this was actually a commercial operation of a single artisan or a shop employing apprentices. The manufacturing process was simple. The molds were made of plaster of Paris, sometimes called potter's stone; as such, they were fragile and expendable. After the original molds were destroyed, a new pair of molds could be made by using the cast as a matrix. Molds were two-piece affairs held together with string or clamps. Plaster of the consistency of cake batter was poured into the mold and rapidly swirled around until it hardened in a thin layer on the oiled inner surface. Afterward, the halves were cemented together and the rough edges smoothed before painting. The hollow chalkware pieces were extremely light, although some were filled to give them added weight.

The earlier pieces were prepared with sizing and then painted with oil, but the later figures were painted with watercolors and not sized before painting. These pieces were never glazed or fired. The figurines, fruits, and

animals were hand decorated, and it is this personalized treatment that provides the charm and naiveté so universally admired. Subtle colors were not used, but usually pure red, green, yellow, brown, and black; although the pieces looked garish and gaudy when first made, their appearance mellowed with the passage of time.

The familiar Staffordshire figurines and animal forms were often imitated in chalkware. There are cats, dogs, lions, deer, lambs, rabbits, squirrels, and domestic and wild fowl. The eagles resemble the carved wooden eagles of Schimmel, the famed Pennsylvania whittler. Pastoral scenes of shepherds and shepherdesses, quaint bloomer girls, angels, and saints were popular. Portrait busts of national celebrities were molded or executed in basrelief and set into oval plaster frames, which were then painted to simulate walnut frames.

In the treatment of religious figures and cherubs, an Italian influence manifests itself. The ecclesiastical fervor of the predominantly Catholic countries of southern Europe and the Palatinate was transferred to America. Plaster ornaments in the form of niches survive. They provided space for a favorite saint but were often secularized by the insertion of a child, bird, or animal. From the wide array of molded angels, saints, and animals, it was possible to assemble a crèche, complete with Christ Child.

Chalkware figures have been found in many areas of the eastern seaboard. However, more figures have appeared in the Pennsylvania German territory than elsewhere. The first public notice announcing the sale of plaster figures appeared in the *Boston News Letter* of January 25, 1770. Henry Christian Geyer, a stonecutter, advertised "imagemaking of Fuser Simulacrum, Kings and Queens, King George, Queen Charlotte, King and Queen of Sweden etc. . . . animals, parrots, cats, dogs, lions, sheep . . . Country shopkeepers supplied." Since Geyer was German, he developed much of his trade supplying the Pennsylvania German (or Dutch) country. These chalkware pieces have the charm and primitive quality of works created by unsophisticated artists who have a natural love for color.

1347

1348

1349

1350

1347–1352 *Figures of shepherdesses, queens, madonnas, and angels appealed as icons for religious significance or as household ornaments, which were sometimes accumulated in large collections*

1351

1352

1353

1354

1355

384

1356

1357

1358

1359

1360

1353–1361 *Brightly painted chalkware figures at times assumed an air of humor as in the sailor (1354) and the Toby (1353). The ornamental base with figures (1355) reveals an aperture for inserting a clock movement*

1361

1362

1363

1364

386

1365

1362–1369A *The craze for accumulating chalkware figures inspired the frequent creation of new designs. To the line of religious and secular characters, figures of animals, fruit, buildings, churches, and altars were added*

1366

1367

1368

1369

1369 A

1370

1371

1372

1373

1374

388

1375

1376

1377

1378

1370–1379 *Chalkware makers soon found that animals proved ready sellers and thus made available a veritable Noah's Ark of birds and beasts. These later came in all sizes, even larger than life. Colors were more or less realistic but often led to fanciful results*

1379

1380

1380 *The Colonial master silversmith was capable of designing and fashioning jewelry, candlesticks, or a complete silver service to grace the most elegant table. First he cast the metal in sheets and then proceeded to work his pieces from them, rolling or hammering the silver to the requisite thickness, cutting out the pattern with shears, and, finally, in the case of hollow ware, beating it over a mold or form. Engraving or chasing was the principal means of decoration, with some cast or repousse work. Photograph courtesy Colonial Williamsburg* **1381** *Silver teapot, with molded ribs, straight spout, ebony handle, and chased heraldic shield and borders, c. 1800* **1382** *Vase-shaped silver caster with high domed lid and molded finial. Made by Stephen Emery, Boston, c. 1775–1800*

Teapots, Tankards & Plate

1381

B OSTON, NEWPORT, NEW YORK, and Philadelphia were the centers of Colonial silversmithing. In these seaport cities, silversmiths found eager purchasers for their products. Each center developed distinctive craft characteristics. If the term "Early American" is applied to their first pieces, the period indicated must of necessity be flexible. The first Colonial silver was crafted in Boston, and early New England silver covers the period 1650 to 1775. Early New York, or New Amsterdam, silver began to be produced about a generation later than in Boston, while early Pennsylvania silver dates from 1690. The southern colonies of Maryland, Virginia, and the Carolinas, however, with their agricultural economy, lagged behind the North in the development of native silversmithing until the eighteenth century.

Fine silverware was not always acquired solely for reasons of beauty or luxury, but for the eminently practical one of investing in useful objects that could be readily reconverted into currency. This was particularly true in New England, where simple English forms prevailed, although some elaborate work was executed there. The Dutch inhabitants of New Amsterdam early appreciated silver for its beauty, luxury, and value. In Philadelphia a display of silver served as a badge of gentility. In Virginia and most area's of the South, silver became the accepted domestic accouterment for a lady or gentleman. Thus, in Colonial America silver became simultaneously a part of a person's estate and the symbol of a gracious and aesthetic way of life.

The skill and sophistication of Colonial silversmiths were unmatched in any other craft. Each piece started with a sheet thinned from an ingot. The sheets were rolled or hammered to the requisite thickness, cut with shears according to the desired pattern, and

1382

then hammered into shape. In the case of hollow ware, the sheet was hammered over a mold or formed with shaping tools. Handles or ornaments were first cast in pewter, lead, or sand molds and were finished with hand tools. Engraving was the principal form of decoration, although there was some repoussé work. Engraved decorations, which were derived from pattern books, followed the styles prevailing in England and on the Continent, using rococo motifs, acanthus scrolls, cartouches, and ribbons, as well as inscriptional lettering, armorial crests, and heraldic devices.

Early silverware, made from rolled and hammered ingots, has a softer, more pleasing sheen than the harder polish of later silver made in factories from thinner, mechanically rolled sheets. In early ware, simple geometric shapes were preferred by craftsmen; purity of form, sense of proportion, and perfection of line were favored over elaborate ornamentation. For sheer grace and elegance it would be difficult to improve upon the earliest examples of Colonial silver.

Probably the earliest silver was the work of English craftsmen who had emigrated to Massachusetts and their apprentices. Some silver was undoubtedly made before 1650, although none is extant. Between 1650 and 1700, silver was fashioned in quantity in Boston; each piece was well designed and carefully executed, the equal of any produced abroad. Because of the Puritan distaste for ostentation, the silverware of this area consisted chiefly of utilitarian pieces, and most is characterized by austere, Classical lines

The value of a silversmith's work practically insured its survival. Fortunately, a large number of domestic silver pieces have been preserved by descendants of old New England families and by churches, where a number of tankards, caudle cups, beakers, mugs, and communion plates are to be found. In many cases, communion cups were used in the homes of the donors long before they were presented to the church.

As one of the wealthiest and most cultured Colonial cities, Boston was a natural center

where silversmiths could thrive. Highly proficient in their craft, they enjoyed a position superior to that of craftsmen in other fields because of the esteem and demand for their products and because they were respected as men of integrity. The names of many Boston silversmiths have been recorded, the most celebrated of the early ones being John Hull, a successful merchant and respected citizen who became the city mintmaster. Finely modeled standing and caudle cups produced by him and his partner Robert Sanderson still belong to New England churches, and a few are in museum collections. One of Boston's first native silversmiths was Jeremiah Dummer, born of English parents in 1645. A prolific craftsman, he served an eight-year apprenticeship under Hull from 1659 to 1667. He became a man of substance—a selectman, justice of the peace, treasurer of the county, and a member of the Council of Safety of 1689. In 1710 he engraved and printed Connecticut's first paper currency. Other noteworthy apprentices of Hull included Samuel Paddy, Timothy Dwight, and John Coney.

An acknowledged leader in his chosen field during the late seventeenth and early eighteenth centuries, John Coney left a rich legacy of his superior handiwork, which includes many large pieces, such as the Harvard University loving cup, a sweetmeats box belonging to the Boston Museum of Fine Arts, the capacious Parish punchbowl, and elaborately embossed caudle cups. Other celebrated eighteenth-century Boston silversmiths include Edward Winslow, John Edwards, John Dixwell, William Cowell and his son William Cowell, Jr., Andrew Tyler, and Jacob Hurd, who was succeeded by his sons, Nathaniel and Benjamin. The most interesting of these was Winslow, highly respected both for his work and for his many community activities.

Paul Revere was the son of a French Huguenot silversmith, Apollos Rivoire—a name soon Anglicized. Revere became noted for his various activities as a manufacturer of gunpowder, maker of church bells, engraver, and publisher of historical and political car-

1383

1384

1385

1383–1390 *A most important piece in the silver service, the teapot was not common until after 1730. With increasing popularity it came in many shapes, including oval (**1384,** c. 1790); round or globular (**1385,** c. 1698, and **1386,** c. 1775–84); bell-shaped (**1383,** and **1387,** c. 1720); pear-shaped or pyriform (**1389,** c. 1757, **1390,** c. 1700–1722). A heraldic crest, escutcheon, or engraved monogram was sometimes a prominent feature*

1386

1387

1388

1389

1390

1391 Tripod cream pitcher with bulbous body, c. 1775–80   1392 Bowl with Classic anthemion motif, c. 1700–25   1393 Caudle cup with repoussé floral decoration, 1765–70   1394 Oval sugar bowl with Classic lines, c. 1810   1395 Cream pitcher on pedestal base with rococo decoration   1396 Sugar bowl with elaborate acanthus motif, c. 1690   1397 Tankard made by Edward Winslow, Boston, c. 1727–50   1398 Tea caddy by Thauvet Besley, New York, c. 1750   1399 Mug by William Thomson, New York, c. 1810–25.

1391

1392

1393

396

1394

1395

toons. From his father he learned to make silver pitchers, ewers, tankards, teapots, cans, spoons, and porringers. He also learned chasing and engraving, at which he became an expert. With the death of his father in 1754, Revere, at nineteen, took over the shop. His varied patriotic services began in 1756, when he joined the local artillery company and participated in the expedition against the French at Crown Point. After many assignments in the service of his country, including the cele-

1396

1397

1398

1399

1400

1401

brated midnight ride, Revere devoted most of his time to his silverware business. In 1783 he opened a jewelry store (then called a hardware shop) where he sold gold necklaces, bracelets, rings, medals, silver pitchers, teapots, spoons, and knee and shoe buckles.

Throughout his long and varied career Revere made almost every form of silver and gold piece then used. His most famous piece was the bowl commissioned by the fifteen Sons of Liberty to honor the glorious ninety-two members in the Massachusetts House of Representatives who protested the Townshend Acts. Revere's larger pieces, particularly his bowls and pitchers, were often simple and Classic in line and form. However, at other times he employed a whole range of engraved motifs—such as scrolls, garlands, rococo shells, and leaf and floral forms, curved and contorted in the prevailing Georgian style— in his coffee- and teapots, plates, spoons, and casters. Although Revere's ability as an engraver suffered from his having had to hurriedly execute political cartoons for penny newspapers, his skill in silver is demonstrated by numerous pieces. Revere's feeling for engraved line as well as his touch with the hammer uniquely qualified him to serve Boston families, with their mingling of aristocratic and democratic tastes and their fondness for crests, armorial designs, and cartouches encircling initials, names, and inscriptions.

Less than a hundred miles to the south of Boston, Newport was an active commercial metropolis serving Rhode Island, Connecticut, the Long Island Sound region, and the nearby

fishing and whaling center of New Bedford The seaport trade produced many families o wealth there, and during the eighteenth cen tury such proficient silversmiths as Samue Vernon, Arnold Collins, Daniel Russell, and Samuel Casey served these families. However despite the fact that local craftsmen produced exquisite pieces, when a wealthy Newpor resident contemplated an important silve purchase, he usually went to one of the leading Boston smiths.

In New York, Dutch, Huguenot, and Eng lish elements entered into the development of a silver style, whereas in New England the ideal of the Scottish and English designers produced a modified, and usually simplified, Georgian style. During the early New Amsterdam period, silver pieces were definitely inspired by Dutch sources, as seen in the tall, engraved beakers, the sturdy baptismal basins, and the two-handled bowls decorated with formal floral designs. A conservative group, the firs silversmiths of New York persistently drew from Dutch styles. Later smiths combined Dutch and English fashions. The tankards made by these smiths are excellent examples o the blending of these two influences. In shape they resemble tankards of the English Restora tion but they have a massiveness and vigor un mistakably Dutch. In contrast to the plain tankards of New England, those made in New York were usually enriched with engraved embossed, or cast designs of Dutch derivation Common motifs include cherubs, masks, bird: foliated scrolls, garlands of fruit and flowers and ciphers. The engraving of crests and coat

398   1402

1403

of arms is noteworthy for graceful execution.

Noted eighteenth-century New York silversmiths include Jacob Boelen, Peter van Dyck, Jesse Kip, Cornelius Kierstede, and Adrian Bancker, and nearly two hundred silversmiths are known to have plied their trade there prior to 1800. The engraved beakers and chalices used in church communion services, and household plates, mugs, tankards, flagons, and teapots comprise the major portion of early New York silver now extant.

In Philadelphia, the controlling influence was English Quaker, which in silver implied simple English forms. Nearly one hundred silversmiths were at work in Philadelphia prior to 1800. One of the earliest, who immigrated to America with William Penn, was Cesar Ghiselin; he specialized in spoons of English design. The city had three notable families of three generations of craftsmen who almost spanned the eighteenth century: the Syngs, the Richardsons, and the Anthonys. Philip Syng was followed by his son Philip, Jr., who made the famous standish in which the quills were dipped for the signing of the Declaration of Independence. Francis Richardson was followed by his sons Francis, Jr., and Joseph. Joseph Anthony, Jr., was the creator of some exquisite pieces.

The early Philadelphia silversmiths were able and distinguished, but their successors enjoyed greater patronage, for during the middle and later part of the eighteenth century, Philadelphia became the richest Colonial city and the capital of the infant republic. Renowned for her abundant hospitality, she counted among her silver pieces many of the finest tea services.

Although smaller, Hartford, New Haven, Albany, Troy, Trenton, Baltimore, and many other cities also had famous silversmiths. Almost every American town had its silversmith (who might also have been a blacksmith, clockmaker, or innkeeper) who made spoons and silver plate to order, repaired jewelry, and did engraving. As the nineteenth century advanced, these local craftsmen became fewer, and in about the middle of the century, the trade came into the hands of large manufacturers. Until that time the American silversmith had been both designer and craftsman. Every item he produced was made to order, with the customer frequently supplying the material in the form of coins to be melted down. Working with meager tools and equipment but with energy and imagination, he fashioned handsome cups, bowls, and tankards that command respect and admiration today.

1404

1405

1400 *Silver service made by A. DuBois, Philadelphia, c. 1790* **1401** *Coffee urn made in Philadelphia, 1832* **1402** *Cream pitcher made in Philadelphia, 1832* **1403** *Monogrammed silver service, c. 1790* **1404** *Sugar bowl with repoussé decoration, c. 1850* **1405** *Urn-shaped cream pitcher, 1850 From photographs*

Overleaf: GALLERY OF SILVERWARE. *Bowls and fruit baskets:* **1417, 1419, 1422** *(c. 1850–60); coffee pots:* **1414** *(1836); cream pitchers:* **1407** *(1850),* **1412** *(1846),* **1415** *(1815–18); egg boiler:* **1411** *(1780–85); pitcher:* **1420** *(1794–1813); tankard, mug, and porringer:* **1410** *(1750–60); teapots:* **1421** *(1870),* **1423**; *silver service, with creamer, sugar bowl, and waste bowl:* **1409** *(c. 1840–50); whisky flask:* **1416** *(1850). From photographs*

1406

1407

1408

1409

1410

1411

1412

1413

1414

1415

1417

1416

1418

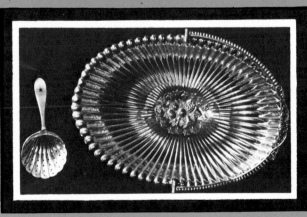

1419

1420

1421

1422

1423

1424

1424 *Arrayed on the shelves of a walnut dresser is an assortment of eighteenth-century pewter, mostly from New York and Philadelphia. On the top shelf are three chargers—the center is the largest known of American make, measuring nineteen inches—creamers, beakers, chalices, a sugar bowl, and a teapot. On the middle shelf are porringers, with variously designed handles, and an assortment of spoons. At the bottom are a number of plates, tankards, and other utensils needed to complete the service for the farm family's best table setting. Photograph by Gilbert Ask, courtesy the Henry Francis du Pont Winterthur Museum, Winterthur, Delaware* **1425** *Pewter tea service, including hot water pot, teapot, creamer, sugar bowl, and waste bowl* **1426** *Tankard with German-style engraving, seventeenth century. This and 1425 from photographs*

1425

Pewter for Many Purposes

EWTER SERVED as the middle-class family's tableware in Europe for at least five centuries. In the Bronze Age, man had succeeded in creating bronze by adding tin to a crucible of molten copper. Later, by reversing the steps and adding copper to tin, he produced another important alloy, pewter. (The term is derived from the French *peutre*, indicating an alloy of tin and antimony with lead or copper.)

A generation after the first Colonists settled in America, pewter ware was gradually replacing crude wooden kitchenware trenchers and plates, and horn and leather cups and tankards. Eating utensils were already fairly common, although the earliest families arrived with only a limited supply. Eating tools were an outgrowth of kitchen utensils: forks evolved from two-pronged skewers; cups and beakers were small pots; plates were merely flat bowls; the knife was a small cleaver; and the spoon was derived from a small bowl with a long handle.

In America the production of pewter ware extended from about 1650 to 1850—the greatest quantity being made between 1750 and 1850—when it was replaced with a harder alloy called Britannia ware. Molds for pewter were generally of brass and therefore expensive. The molds were the pewterer's stock in trade, a valuable asset that could be sold or passed on from one generation to the next. The use of secondhand molds retarded the development of designs, by contrast to the situation

1426

with silver, in which new styles were continually being developed.

During the seventeenth and eighteenth centuries, ordinary pewter was often cast by householders because the process was fairly simple. The first American to be interested in the making of pewter as a vocation was Richard Graves, who opened a shop in Salem, Massachusetts, in 1635. Records about other early craftsmen are scant and none of their works remain, but we do know that about ten Colonial pewterers were working before 1750.

By contrast, in England and Europe this was the great age of pewter. As European mining and transportation methods improved, the price of pewter dropped, making it available for export as well as for domestic use. The absence of tin in the Colonies limited production and spurred its importation. Thus, from 1720 to 1767, the value of pewter imports far exceeded the combined value of furniture, silverware, and tinware. By the time of the Revolution, many pewterers were at work in America's leading cities and small towns. Boston was in the forefront of pewter manufacture, with New York following closely. In the seventeenth century Boston pewterers included Thomas Bumsteed, Thomas Clarke, John Comer, and Henry Shrimpton. In New York reference is made to John Halden, James Liddell, and Robert Boyle, all of whom were active about 1750, and to William Kirby and Henry Will, who were active in the last quarter of the century. Philadelphia's earliest known pewterers were James Everett and Simon Edgell, first mentioned in 1718. Providence, Baltimore, and Cincinnati show early evidence of pewterers, but records are incomplete. Smaller towns also had some fine pewterers; those in Hartford included Thomas Boardman and Samuel Danforth.

For the most part, plates, chargers, platters, spoons, and forks were in common use. Drinking vessels, such as mugs, tankards, and

beakers, were also in demand. Tankards were six or seven inches high, with S-shaped handles, straight, tapering sides, and hinged covers. The cans and mugs were somewhat smaller; flagons were similar to the larger tankards. Pewter was also used for most of the chalices for communion services and for baptismal basins.

On the whole, the pewterers crafted utilitarian wares which were rarely decorated. The engraving of beakers and tankards provides some ornamental examples, but these are exceptions. Pewter pieces on which attempts were made to copy the appearance of silver failed in their purpose and seemed fraudulent. The best American pewterers recognized this, and their work, as represented in plain candlesticks, mugs, plates, and bowls, displays a fine appreciation of form and finish.

Some Colonial pewterers used familiar English devices as touch marks: the rose and crown, the lamb and dove, and the golden fleece. They also used lions in circles and ovals, shields, columns, urns, hallmarks, initials, and many other motifs. This practice, however, was not generally followed, as the pewterer had few illusions about the aesthetic value of his humble product. After the Revolution, of the twenty-three registered craftsmen working between 1790 and 1825, more than half had adopted some form of the eagle as a touch mark, combining this motif with their name or initials. As the nineteenth century advanced and the novelty of the eagle declined, many craftsmen began using plain initials set into a square or oval.

About 1850 the popularity of pewter declined as the vogue in tableware turned to china and porcelain. At this time, much pewter ware was disposed of, which accounts for the scarcity of early pewter in comparison with silver. In humbler homes, however, pewter pieces were used until they wore out.

1427

1428

1429

1430

1431

1427 *Flagon with unique swirled fluting and beaded ribs* **1428** *Tall flagon with long spout by Thomas Boardman, first half of nineteenth century* **1429** *Flagon with several touch marks on lid, 1737* **1430** *Van der Spiegel tankard, mid-eighteenth century* **1431** *Because pewter plates, mugs, and tankards were durable and economical and required little polishing, they were especially popular in public taverns and hostelries such as the Raleigh Tavern, shown above. Displayed are chargers, tankards, and porringers, mostly of the mid-eighteenth century. Photograph courtesy Colonial Williamsburg*

1432 Six-sided cream pitcher with long spout, c. 1835–45 1433 Coffee pot made by Smith & Company, Philadelphia, c. 1830 1434 Coffee pot with S-shaped spout and ebony handle 1435 Popular pear-shaped teapot in simplified form, c. 1850 1436 Conical ribbed coffee pot, with domed lid and unusual handle 1437 Tankard with ribbed design and base 1438 Teapot, battered after years of tavern use 1439 Porringer with eagle touch mark, signed Calder, 1850

1436

1437

1438

1439

1440

1441

410   1442

1443

1444

1445

1440–1445 *The grace and purity of pewter forms can best be seen by comparing details of the varied shapes represented here. The sides of pots and beakers may be straight, tapered, or conical (1441, 1443, and 1444); urn-shaped or pear-shaped (1440, 1442, and 1445). Spouts may be plain, ribbed, or decorated (1440–42 and 1445). Handles vary greatly from C-shape to "double-jointed" types, in wood or solid pewter. Fluting, ribbing, and beading are often introduced to rounded surfaces. When the pewterer imitated the more ornate details of silver, he failed to achieve lasting beauty; but when he recognized the limitations of his material and kept within them he evolved forms and shapes whose linear beauty is perennially admired*

Overleaf: GALLERY OF PEWTERWARE. *Ale mugs, beakers, and tankards:* **1449, 1453, 1456, 1465, 1470, 1473;** *bowls:* **1448, 1468, 1472;** *chalice:* **1446;** *coffee pots:* **1451, 1459, 1467;** *creamers:* **1450, 1455;** *hot water jug:* **1464;** *molasses jugs:* **1447, 1472;** *teapots:* **1452, 1454, 1457, 1458, 1460–63, 1466, 1469, 1471, 1474;** *tea service:* **1475.** *From photographs except 1446, 1447, 1461, 1465, 1468, 1469, 1471–73*

1446

1447

1448

1449

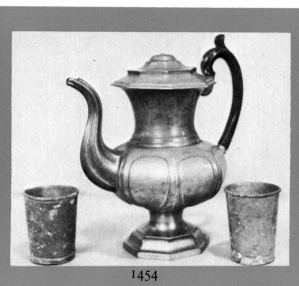

1454

1455

1456

1457

1461

1462

1463

1464

1469

1470

1471

1472

1450

1451

1452

1453

1458

1459

1460

1465

1466

1467

1468

1473

1474

1475

Decorated Tin & Toleware

1477

B Y THE CLOSE of the eighteenth century, several tin centers had been established in New England. Boston, as the chief Colonial seaport, was the place where tinplate imported from England arrived. The plates, generally ten by fourteen inches, arrived in wooden boxes, and were transported by horse or oxen to tin shops throughout the countryside. One of the better known and most prosperous tin shops was established in Berlin, Connecticut, by the Pattison brothers from Ireland. Zachariah Stevens, trained as a blacksmith, abandoned this trade for the more lucrative practice of tinsmithing. He set up a shop at Stevens Plains, near Portland, Maine, and his business eventually prospered to the point where eleven shops were in operation under his direction. Oliver Filley, a former peddler in Vermont, began to manufacture tinware in 1800 and sub-

1478

1476 On the open shelves of this pine dresser is a collection of decorated nineteenth-century tinware including teapots, pitchers, beakers, plates, trays, and other utensils. The vivid coloring of the free-hand brush strokes and the spontaneity of the compositions reveal their rural origins in the Pennsylvania German regions and New England. Photograph courtesy the Henry Francis du Pont Winterthur Museum, Winterthur, Delaware 1477 Can for delivering water to wash basins. Hand painting is further assisted by transfer inserts from decalcomania designs, c. 1870 1478 Slop pail, companion piece to the watering can

sequently opened three branch operations to meet the demand for his products. The Butler family ran a successful shop in Greenville, New York, where various family members made, painted, and decorated a complete line of tinware. In addition to these personally directed ventures, tinware factories were in operation in Albany, New York, and in Litchfield and Clinton, Connecticut.

The tinsmith, or "whitesmith," as he was called to distinguish his trade from that of the blacksmith, required few tools other than hardwood mallets, shears, and molds to pattern his beaten forms. Later, to supplement his crude utensils, he acquired some simple machinery, such as a roller, crimper, edger, and power-operated shears. When extra helpers were needed, they were brought over from England, where the tinware industry had been firmly established, and both makers and decorators had practiced the art for generations. If the tinsmith sought to build up his trade beyond his community, he took to the road in a wagon filled with his wares, which included pans, teapots and coffeepots, colanders, graters, cookie cutters, canisters, trays, candlestick holders, and small toys fashioned out of scraps. Light tinplate was used for decorative articles; wares designed for cooking or baking were made of heavy tinplate. The Yankee peddler soon became a regular visitor to farms at a distance from convenient shopping centers. As early as 1800, consumer preferences dictated the market for goods in all categories, whether plain tinware for cooking utensils or fancier goods—hand painted, stencil decorated, or japanned. Tinware varied considerably in price and fell into three classifications: inexpensive articles with a minimum

of decoration called "painted tin"; moderately priced goods known as "japanned ware"; and the more expensive decorated pieces called "tole," from the French *tôle peinte*, meaning painted tinware.

Generally, decorated toleware had a black background on which the colors were opaquely applied in one of two techniques. One method called for stenciling through cutout areas, the open spaces, cut from stiff cardboard or thin sheet metal, serving as a template for the colors. The other method involved hand painting directly onto the surface, either freehand or following drawn guide lines. The black backgrounds were painted with asphaltum, a brownish-black substance mixed with varnish. It produced a rich, velvety surface that was particularly durable after firing and had a magnetic affinity for gold leaf—one of the reasons it was favored for toleware and furniture painting.

On the dark background, such colors as Chinese vermilion, red-earth rust, old pumpkin yellow, yellow ocher, tan, and green were applied; blue was rarely used on what became known as "country tin." The earthy substances were ground to a fine powder, to which resins were added. Some earth colors were mixed with whisky or other liquors. Varnish, which gave them greater stability, was prepared from the drippings found on the trunks of cherry trees. Many dyes were extracted from herbs and plants, and these were converted into colored pigments. Green was produced from skunk cabbage and wintergreen. Deep red resulted from madder extract. Many kinds of roots, berries, tree barks, and nut shells were boiled to produce various shades and colors.

Hand decorating was done with a choice of

brush strokes which permitted a wide variety of effects and patterns. C-strokes were applied in which the deft touch of the brush produced a big blob that tapered off to a hairline. S-strokes, curlicues, wavy strokes, and spiraling tendril lines appeared, all of which were blended intuitively by the accomplished decorator. Regional characteristics of New England and Pennsylvania were often difficult to distinguish. Pennsylvania coloring was somewhat brighter and bolder, exhibiting traces of European peasant-craft origin. Popular motifs were birds, hearts, tulips, pomegranates, horses, unicorns, angels, and people, woven together with charm and naiveté. In the lexicon of the Pennsylvania Dutch tradition, certain designs acquired special meaning. Turtle doves represented love and beauty; the peacock, spiritual majesty. The tulip, of ancient Persian origin and transplanted into central European culture, was a universal favorite. Since the Pennsylvania Dutch were an isolated group, seldom mingling with outsiders, their artistic proclivities were little influenced by the world around them. However, some patriotic motifs, such as the eagle, were incorporated into their decorations. Hence, their pieces had a decorative character that made them easy to identify.

Country tin, as well as the better decorated toleware, came in a wide variety of household objects. Large trays were important showpieces, designed in a number of shapes and decorated in various styles. The trays were never entirely flat; their outer margins were raised above the central portion. Some were square with rounded corners; others were octagonal with cut corners, called "coffin" because they resembled the coffins of that era. Lace-edged trays had perforated outer borders,

and gallery trays had deeply slanted or perpendicular edges. Circular and oval trays afforded an opportunity for different design treatment. The piecrust, or Chippendale, trays, also termed "Gothic," can be traced to the English Chippendale period (about 1760). These curvaceous trays were heavily decorated. Motifs included pictorial scenes, center cameos fountains, fruits and flowers, and birds and naturalistic designs, with or without bronzing. Whether hand painted or stenciled, a Chippendale tray became an important wall decoration and was either hung or stood on a dresser or sideboard.

Tin boxes were available in a variety of types and sizes. The large ones were used for bread and cake; next in size were document boxes, also used to store the family Bible or precious bibelots. Hinged circular containers with a latch were used for sugar or flour; low, flat circular boxes were used for spices and contained a smaller set of canisters to hold nutmeg, cloves, cinnamon, allspice, and ginger. Canisters ranged in size from small to very large; cups and pails also constituted an extensive line of decorated tin objects. Teapots, tea caddies, and coffeepots were most important. They were used constantly and received lavish decorative treatment. Many household articles were also decorated. These include watering cans, flowerpots, candlestick holders, tubs, wash basins, slop pails, wall sconces, and hanging candelabra. There was hardly an accessory for the home that could not be made by the whitesmith, thus lending itself to the impulse of the folk artist. His touch added color and character to the everyday objects that made the home more livable.

1479

1480

1481

1479–1484 *The large surface of trays presented an opportunity to design, improvise, and otherwise express a love of ornamentation. A particularly pleasing composition is shown in* 1479, *in which fountain, flowers, and leaf forms —further amplified with an abundance of delicate tendrils—combine to produce an inspired garden fantasy, made c. 1850. Totally different in design and feeling is the "coffin tray" for bread or cake, typical of Pennsylvania German motifs, shown in* 1480. *The Chippendale*

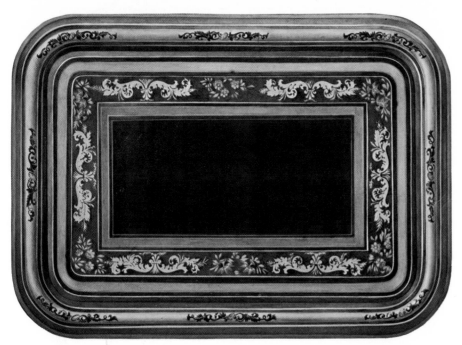

1482

tray with piecrust rolled edge, 1481 and 1484, broke away from traditional rectangular and oval shapes. In **1481** naturalistically represented flower and leaf forms are geometrically positioned, while **1484,** c. 1840, includes a stenciled rendition of one of the first trains. The tin tray in **1482** has a series of striped borders with formalized floral designs repeating around four sides. The deep apple dish, **1483** was painted by Zachariah Stevens, Portland, Maine, c. 1810–20

1483

1484

1485

1485 Oval tray with stenciled center of birds, fruits, and leaves, c. 1830　1486 Japanned tray with turned-up edge, c. 1840　1487 Bread tray with naturalistic floral decorations, Lebanon, Pennsylvania, c. 1840　1488 Still life of fruit surrounded by geometric border on raised edge, c. 1825　1489 Bread tray with painted border, from Stevens Plains, Maine, early nineteenth century　1490 Hand-painted bread or fruit tray, showing two ends seamed together at center, c. 1830–40

1486　　　　1487

1488

1489

1490

1491

1492

1491 *Syrup pitcher with bulbous floral forms and petalous decoration* **1492** *Teapot with petalous forms grouped around a central flower* **1493** *Tea canister with conventional floral design, c. 1840* **1494** *Watering can decorated with the ever-popular circular fruit or tomato, with petalous forms* **1495** *Syrup or molasses can decorated by a graceful spray of the familiar floral motif* **1496, 1497** *Decorated sugar bowls with lids*

1493

1494

1495

1496

1497

1498

1499

1500

1501

424

1502   1503

1498–1501 *Teapots and coffee pots of decorated tinware were common household objects in most mid-nineteenth-century homes. The pots were almost always conical, with S-shaped handles sometimes reinforced for strength; spouts varied from straight to goose-necked. Cheaply made, the pieces were a substitute for the pewter and silver of more comfortable homes. Bulbous fruit and vegetable designs predominate, with graceful stems and petals added. The coffee pot* **1500,** *is of Pennsylvania German origin* **1502–1505** *Document boxes (1502 and 1504) and rounded canisters, 1503 and 1505 demonstrate a variety of floral motifs*

1504   1505

425

1506

1507

1508

1506–1512 *The coloration of various tinware and toleware objects shows a great variety of treatments, although certain colors predominate. Where the background color is not black, crimson, vermilion, and coffee-brown are preferred. A few yellows may also be seen. Floral motifs call for reds and golds, and petal forms for dark emerald greens; blues appear sparingly. White accents occur in bands and elsewhere as chiaroscuro highlights. Aging contributes to the overall effect, as the darkening of leaf forms and the patina acquired by the bright colors, plus the flecking of tin at the corners combine to produce a blend that is altogether pleasing*

Overleaf: GALLERY OF TINWARE AND TOLEWARE. *Bread trays:* **1519, 1520, 1535** *coffeepots and teapots:* **1516, 1517, 1523, 1524, 1525, 1528, 1532** *document boxes:* **1515, 1533** *pitchers:* **1514, 1527, 1536** *sugar bowl:* **1513** *tea caddies and canisters:* **1522, 1531, 1534** *trays:* **1520, 1521, 1526, 1530** *wash basin:* **1518**

1509

1510

1511

1512

427

1513   1514

1515

1518

1519   1520

1524   1525

1526

1531   1532

1516   1517

1521

1522   1523

1527   1528

1529

1533

1534   1535   1536

429

1537

1538

1537, 1538 *Carved wooden* Hope *and* Justice, *attributed to Simeon and John Skillin and said to have been placed in front of the Royal Custom House in Boston, c. 1800. Hope, with her right arm resting on an anchor and her right foot slightly forward, seems solid and compact. The more slender figure of Justice balances a heavy sword on its point with her right hand. Body structure, which in both is obscured by heavy drapery, is characterized by a narrow upper trunk, sloping shoulders, and heavy neck. Each combines academic modeling and folk expression that yield a charming and indi-vidual result* **1539** The Cycle of Life, *an elaborate carving of elmwood by Pierre Landry, Jr., was made in Louisiana in 1834. In it the artist depicts the ages of man from birth to the grave.* **1540** *Voltaire bust by Samuel McIntire of Salem, Massachusetts, one of New England's finest craftsmen in the late eighteenth century*

1539

Carved of Wood or
Cast in Metal

1540

AST FORESTS assured settlers of an abundant supply of building material, and wood, in seemingly endless variety, was everywhere. The Colonial joiners and carvers could choose the wood most suitable for architectural uses and shipbuilding, as well as for furniture and tools. For decorative detailing—such as scrolls over doorways, finials, and posts, as well as for signboards—pine and walnut were ideal. Where a large, massive piece was needed for a garden statue, the trunk of a centuries-old pine was best. It offered less resistance to the cuts of chisel and gouge than oak, with its pronounced grain, or walnut, which was better suited to fine furniture detailing.

In the second quarter of the eighteenth century, a period of growing affluence and peaceful prosperity began; large homes with spacious gardens were built, especially in the thriving commercial centers such as Boston, New York, and Philadelphia, and also in tidewater Virginia. Successful merchants, traders, and shipowners vied with one another in their display of opulence, which was expressed in domestic architecture and in the treatment of their gardens. Often pride was carried to extremes, a notable example being the palatial home of "Lord" Timothy Dexter of Newburyport. A shrewd Yankee trader and self-styled merchant prince, Dexter had a mania for ornamental accessories. His fenced garden was converted into a network of columns and

archways housing more than fifty life-size figures of famous personalities, all in Classical poses. Mounted on columns, these constituted a personal Hall of Fame. Included were presidents George Washington, John Adams, and Thomas Jefferson, and statesmen Benjamin Franklin, John Hancock, and Alexander Hamilton. His choice, however, was not limited to Americans; among the Europeans represented were Lord Nelson, Napoleon, and Louis XVI. Most of these figures were carved by Joseph Wilson, a local ship carver, who with several assistants executed the prodigious amount of sculpture commissioned by this eccentric patron. Unfortunately, with the exception of a figure of William Pitt and several female figures in relief, the elaborate collection of carved statuary has disappeared. The figure of Pitt has a stiff and static quality, and if this statue is representative of the rest of the figures, we may assume that while typical of much of the period's folk art, Wilson's sculptural efforts were mediocre. However, the extent of the Dexter project and the demands on the carvers for prompt delivery may have precluded more studied workmanship.

The large body of eighteenth-century decorative carvings, either of full figures or of decorative accessories, expressed the craftsmen's innate desire to beautify their surroundings. Some outstanding works were produced which show a vigorous and uninhibited sense of design. Ornamental figures were made for public buildings, parks, and fountains. Courthouses might call for a figure of Justice; a post office might require a statue of flying Mercury. The pediment of a building conceived in the Classical style usually called for a group of figures in relief.

Wherever elaborate wood sculpture was necessary, the skilled ship carver, because of his long experience and traditional occupation, dominated the scene. Since ship carvers neces-

sarily inhabited the eastern shipping centers, most architectural carving was also done there, and such work was rarely found inland.

The Skillin brothers, John, Samuel, and Simeon, Jr., were well-known ship carvers who worked in Boston during the latter part of the eighteenth century. When an architect or homeowner desired a finely carved wooden figure, he turned to the ship carvers; thus, the Skillins also had commissions that had little to do with seafaring activities. For example, a garden figure of the Roman goddess Pomona, carved by Simeon Skillin, Jr., depicts a sentimentally posed girl in a draped costume holding a cornucopia overflowing with fruits. The girl wears a brimmed hat and has a piquant smile. Her costume and pose seem related to well-known eighteenth-century engravings and are particularly reminiscent of Boucher and Watteau. A more competently executed statue by this carver is *Justice*, which is said to have been placed before the Royal Custom House in Boston. Here, the blindfolded figure is covered in flowing robes—the sloping shoulders, narrow waist, and stylized drapery all being characteristic of Skillin. The heavy-handed treatment of the folds, so typical of work by ship carvers, and the stilted posture and disproportionate body contribute to the impression of naiveté. In this outstanding work, academic tradition and folk expression combine to produce a charming individuality.

Also attributed to the Skillin shop in the early years of the nineteenth century is a companion figure, *Hope*. A bit more daring, *Hope* reveals a single breast. The figure gives an impression of greater solidity than does *Justice*. Hope's right arm rests on a heavy anchor, while her left is raised with the index finger pointing skyward.

Another *Justice*, made about 1843 by David Woodward, was mounted on the top of the Worcester, Massachusetts, courthouse. The

1541

1542

434

DE LAWREY JUSTIEE

1543

1544

1545

1546

1541 *Eagle as a religious symbol, carved from a log*
1542 *Garden figure of woman holding a dove seems weighed down by excessively heavy drapery covering the lower body, a mannerism common to garden and figurehead carving* 1543 *Delaware Justice, small carved group depicting two convicts in stocks and another being flogged* 1544 *Folk-art carving of lumberjacks sawing, probably whittled by a woodsman in Wisconsin, c. 1885* 1545 *Life-size figure of Andrew Jackson, a fine piece of wood sculpture in a Classical pose, c. 1830–35* 1546 *Mercury, modeled by Simeon Skillin Jr. for the Boston Post Office, c. 1800.* 1547 *Barnyard goose with primitive yet realistic treatment of feathers*

1547

435

1548

sculptor seems to have lost himself in the maze of drapery which so completely envelops the female form that it becomes anatomically meaningless. An extremely narrow pectoral region with pronounced whorls further emphasizes the stiffness of the clothed figure, which holds the symbolic thin sword and scales. An unsuccessful striving for a Classical effect can be detected; yet despite the creative limitations of the artist, he has produced a work of charm and simplicity.

Examples of carved male statues are less numerous than female figures and busts. However, a male portrait was generally commissioned to occupy an architectural niche or other commanding position. Several busts from the chisel of Samuel McIntire, the "master carver" of Salem, have been preserved in museum collections. His well-known bust of John Winthrop, first governor of the Massachusetts Bay Colony, reveals how this craftsman trained in carving architectural details followed his natural instinct to treat hair and collar ruffs with the same meticulous precision. However, his training and experience illprepared him to interpret character. This can be seen from the fact that another bust of similar proportions and styling representing Voltaire reveals only minor differences from that of Winthrop, the essential distinction lying in the treatment of costume and wig.

McIntire also produced a few fine carvings in relief; particularly excellent is one of George Washington in an oval frame. At the time of McIntire's death in 1811, an inventory lists "eight medallions of Washington," a piece for which there was a consistent demand. The best of McIntire's carved work, however, is found in the architectural details of the magnificent houses he designed and built for Salem merchants. Fruit baskets, cornucopias, flowered festoons, shields, urns, and especially fine eagles, which were mounted on gate posts or used as lintel decorations, all attest to his skill. In these details, the proportions are perfect, and the balance between plain and decorated surfaces is carefully studied. His finely modeled cornices, pilasters, wainscot borders, and lintels are never overelaborate; rather his applied ornament is always clean-cut and graceful.

In contrast to McIntire's compositions in the New England tradition were the sculptural works of a self-taught Louisiana carver, Pierre Joseph Landry, Jr., the son of a French immigrant. He carved a fine self-portrait from elmwood and stained it dark brown. Another example of his carving is the *Cycle of Life*. This elaborately carved piece, more than two feet in diameter, is an allegorical composition representing the ages of man, from birth to death. Landry treats this subject with directness and refreshing simplicity in nine sculptural groups arranged in a circle.

Some fine free-standing male statues were modeled by wood-carvers. Popular subjects were Benjamin Franklin, Henry Clay, and George Washington, who remained an object of universal admiration. As late as 1907, A. L. Petersen, of Scandia, Washington, carved an equestrian statue of our first president from a piece of dark-stained mahogany. For a wider range of subjects in male busts, one must examine the many fine examples that appeared under the bowsprits of early vessels. These include national heroes, statesmen, and men of letters, as well as shipowners and captains.

About a century after McIntire and the Skillins, Edbury Hatch, one of the last ship carvers, lived and worked in Newcastle and Damariscotta. He was employed by Colonel Sampson of Bath, for whom he carved figureheads for a number of clippers and schooners. In the 1880s, with the decline of the shipping industry, he turned to carving other than ship carving "for the joy of the work." His home

1548 *Painted pine garden figure of Pomona, in which the fruit basket and symmetrical drapery folds enhance the decorative effect. Attributed to Simeon Skillin, Jr. c. 1793* **1549** *Carved and gilded figure of* Justice *by David Woodward. Made for the dome of the courthouse in Worcester, Massachusetts, 1843*

1549

1550

1551

became a veritable museum filled with ornamental bits of his handiwork that included a portico for the front door and a fantastic gutter spout that was a hybrid derived from a horse's mouth, a shark's teeth, a French gargoyle, and leaf forms. Doorway details included heads of lions and foxes, joined by serpents, and a pediment filled with a rich variety of fruits and vegetables. Another striking creation by Hatch was made for a local fire company and featured a fireman's hat surrounded by ropes, bucket, lantern, ladder, hatchet, hose, and bugle horn. Hatch's wood carvings were characterized by native virtuosity, employing motifs indigenous to Maine. He represented the flowering of a New England folk tradition.

More likely to be handed down from generation to generation than the large wooden figures and busts were the smaller, incidental household carvings that were frequently the product of amateurs. These pieces usually occupied a little niche on the mantelpiece or were

1552

1553

placed in a corner cupboard and thus did not present a space problem. Animals were the most popular whittled statuettes, for in households closely tied to livestock they were logical models for the man with a jackknife. If he were particularly ambitious, the whittler produced a great variety and quantity of animals, finally adding a Noah's Ark to house and complete his menagerie. Hunting scenes were also favorite subjects, as were historic incidents, especially those involving Indians and the frontier. Typical of the best animal carvings, now in great demand by collectors, are those by the Pennsylvania carvers Wilhelm Schimmel and Aaron Mountz.

The number of large wooden sculptures extant is limited compared to the number of smaller ones in existence. The large sculptures were exposed to the elements (whereas the small ones were kept indoors), and decay and breakage took their toll. However, examples of these pieces survive, having been rescued and restored by antique dealers or museums.

1550 *Carved bust of John Winthrop, first governor of the Massachusetts Bay Colony, that displays the approach of a sculptor of architectural details. By Samuel McIntire, 1798* **1551** *Bust of Benjamin Franklin in a posture suggestive of figurehead attitudes. Attributed to William Rush.* **1552** *Vigorously modeled portrait bust of Henry Clay.* **1553** *Self-portrait bust by Pierre Landry, Jr., an entirely self-taught woodcarver, 1883.*

439

1554–1561 *Following the Victorian fashion imported from England in the 1840s and 50s, the makers of cast-iron garden ornaments designed and produced a menagerie of wild and domestic animals. The stag and greyhound were favorites. Many different species of canines were also cast in great numbers as lawn decorations* **1554** *Cast-iron griffin, used as a doorway guardian or fencing support* **1555** *Hollow cast-iron rabbit lawn decoration or doorstop* **1556** *Hollow cast-zinc deer, made by J. W. Fiske, one of the leading producers of cast figures. 1870* **1557** *Hollow cast chamois, with glass eyes inserted for realism, c. 1870* **1558** *Lead rooster, typical of figures of barnyard fowls which were made in a variety of forms and sizes* **1559** *Iron dog doorstop made from split molds and polychromed* **1560** *Recumbent hound was a popular canine guardian on the front lawn* **1561** *Hollow cast bulldog, used as a doorstop. Figures 1554 and 1558–61 from photographs*

1554

1555   1556

1557

1558

1559

1560

1561

441

From Anvil, Forge & Foundry

1563

DECORATIVE IRONWORK, whether wrought by hammer and anvil (from about the middle of the eighteenth century) or cast in the foundries (beginning in the early nineteenth century), may be seen in gateways, grilles, fences, railings, balconies, balustrades, and garden and domestic accessories. Fine examples of this early ironwork are found in quantity in the southern cities of Baltimore, Charleston, Mobile, and, above all, New Orleans. In New Orleans, French and Spanish characteristics are marked. The city was founded in 1718 by French settlers, becoming capital of the French colony of Louisiana four years later. Louisiana was ceded to Spain in 1763 and was under Spanish rule until 1801. A few government buildings such as the Cabildo (destroyed by fire in 1788 and rebuilt in 1795),

and especially the residential stucco dwellings with their iron balconies, represent a pure Latin architectural strain that stands apart from the mainstream of Colonial architecture and has a beauty and quaintness all its own.

The warm climate and the consequent emphasis on outdoor living are probably responsible for the extensive use of ironwork in New Orleans. Houses in the Vieux Carré, the French quarter, laid out by J.-B.-L. de Bienville in 1718, accommodated business quarters on the *banquette* (a raised footway or pavement beside a thoroughfare) and were occupied by merchants, bankers, and doctors. The family quarters above the banquette were reached through an arched entrance and paved passageway. Invariably the entrances were closed by handsome wrought-iron gates. There is a sharp contrast between the severely simple

1562 *Wrought-iron gateway to the Governor's Palace, Official Williamsburg residence of the king's representative to the Virginia colony. The overhead cresting, bearing the gilded cipher of George II flanked by scrolls with floriated ornamentation, and the imposing gates exemplify the finest Colonial designs in iron. Re-created in the twentieth century from original plans found in the Bodleian Library at Oxford. Photograph courtesy Colonial Williamsburg* **1563** *Eagle head with foliations, from a fragment of a cemetery fence, mid-nineteenth century*

ironwork of the lower floor and that of the upper floors where the living quarters are located. Plain iron colonettes rise from the street, but once the family level is reached, the taste for ornamentation is given free rein. The arcaded galleries serve as marquees for pedestrians, affording protection from the hot sun and from sudden showers. Along some of the streets, galleries run continuously across the fronts of adjoining buildings, broken only by guardrails which separate each building from its neighbor. This wrought ironwork dates back to the Spanish period and is reminiscent of the gracefully designed grilles and gates of Spain. The oldest examples of wrought iron in New Orleans are in the Ursuline Convent, erected in 1727. Records indicate that the convent's gates and hardware were wrought by slaves, referred to as "brute Africans."

The old city directories contain listings of *forgerons* (blacksmiths), each of whom had favorite designs which he wrought with particular adeptness. Many of their delicately tapered iron scrolls required up to eight heatings and were bent into patterns whose names were suggestive of popular quilt and coverlet motifs: arrow, leaf, widow's mite, diamond, grape, shell, acorn, and tulip. Some of New Orleans' handsomest balconies and grilles are from the period 1805–15 and have been attributed to Jean and Pierre Lafitte, notorious pirates who also had a blacksmith shop.

The transition from wrought iron to cast iron was a gradual evolution brought about largely by the increased cost of labor and the scarcity of craftsmen who could produce wrought ironwork in quantity. In 1823 Rudolph Ackermann, an Englishman, mentioned in a book on furniture the functional and aesthetic qualities of cast iron: "The rapid improve-ment that has taken place in the manufacture of cast iron, has elevated it from its late uses in ponderous and gross articles merely, to those of ornamental embellishment; not only where strength is required, but where lightness and elegance are purposed to be united, and to which may be superadded, a considerable economy." Many foundries began to issue catalogues in which they offered a variety of cast-iron patterns. In the cities, particularly, evidence of their activity was seen on all sides. Commercial buildings were appearing in which cast-iron elements such as columns, capitals, arches, cornices, and balustrades were readily assembled in innumerable combinations to give facades a new look. Rows of brownstones in residential areas incorporated cast-iron railings, fences, grilles, and other architectural ornaments. Inside as well as outside the home, the enterprising foundries tried to increase their market. Among the cast-iron interior furnishings that appealed to Victorian taste were multi-tiered corner whatnots, hat racks, and umbrella stands, designed elaborately and incorporating scroll and leaf forms. Semicircular and arched fireplace interiors of cast iron, contoured to fit inside the period's marble mantelpieces, were also introduced and widely used. Ornamental doorstops, doorknockers, footscrapers, card trays and ashtrays, lamp bases, candlestick holders, matchboxes, and mantel clocks extended the use and influence of the material until hardly a room lacked an object made from cast iron.

The Greek Revival architecture that predominated in the first half of the nineteenth century also affected New Orleans, where ironwork was so important. It called for cast-iron architectural elements incorporating Classical motifs such as anthemions and frets. In the

1840s, however, long rows of houses with two- and three-storied verandas developed more ornate styles. Cast-iron fences, from five to eight feet high, displayed a great variety of patterns, from those with simple straight lines to others incorporating garlands of flowers and fruits, and such unusual native motifs as sugarcane and corn. The gates of the old courtyards in the Vieux Carré are still in use, although many houses have been converted to apartments and their courts into tearooms. Wrought-iron lamps that hung in these courtyard passages still exist, but some of the balconies and grilles have disappeared, often through purchase by northern antique dealers. (Fortunately, the landmark designation of this charming district has finally halted the dismantling of these period buildings.)

In the 1840s the American ornamental cast-iron industry began to move into high gear as the number of foundries increased. In Pennsylvania, the heartland of iron production, many foundries were manufacturing all kinds of ironware for architectural and household needs. The Philadelphia firm of Wood and Perot was the first to produce castings for decorative purposes on a large scale. Lesser foundries imitated the offerings of the industry's pacemaker, pirating what they considered best for their markets from Wood and Perot's widely circulated catalogue. The ever-widening circle of distribution meant that a leading Philadelphia foundry could sell its products readily in Baltimore, Richmond, Pittsburgh, Cincinnati, or Mobile. By studying patterns found in areas hundreds of miles apart, one can trace the far-reaching effects of this new era of distribution, for patterns were no longer limited to their place of origin. Furthermore,

the American manufacturer did not hesitate to use European patterns instead of inventing designs of his own.

The lacy and filigreed porticoes, like the embroidery on a shirtfront or a crinoline, were enriched and embellished with scroll designs derived from nature. The ease with which cast-iron designs could be multiplied encouraged the followers of the romantic and naturalistic schools to use elaborate floral and arboreal motifs, until a monstrosity resulted from the complicated treillage, which was then grown over with climbing and flowering vines. Cast-iron urns and fountains—often adorned with figures from Classical mythology—appeared in gardens, and a front lawn was considered incomplete unless it displayed one or two cast-iron animal statues, the stag and greyhound being favorites. Cast-iron fountains of various types also made their appearance in city parks and squares. In 1851 the use of cast iron (in combination with glass) in the building of the Crystal Palace that housed the great London exhibition of that year constituted indisputable proof of the material's usefulness, and two years later the New York Crystal Palace Exhibition further contributed to the enthusiasm for cast iron in America. By the time of the American Centennial Exhibition twenty-five years later, the Victorian movement in art had lost all sense of restraint. The cast-iron drolleries that included elaborately wrought verandas and grotesque garden statuary properly represent the Victorian era. Until recently, many of these had for long been considered anathema; however, as we understand them better and because we have recently come to appreciate the Victorian preference for natural forms, we are finding them more sympathetic.

446   **1564** *Iron gates of thinly beribboned scrollwork, St. Michael's Churchyard, Charleston, South Carolina*

1565

1566

1567

1568

1569

1570

1565–1570 *Wrought-iron balustrades, Baltimore, 1800–1825. From photographs*

447

1571

1571–1577 *The art of cast iron seemed to bloom with the opportunities offered by the construction of gates and fencings, particularly notable among which were those of cemeteries. By the 1830s, in the three principal cities of the United States—Boston, New York, and Philadelphia—great cemetery tracts were set aside on sites carefully chosen for accessibility, natural beauty, and picturesqueness. The promoters of these beauty spots for sepulchral quietude engaged the finest landscape architects and designers. The weeping willow—that time-honored arboreal symbol of grief—was planted everywhere and was also a favorite motif in iron, as were the tender lamb and mourning doves. The Philadelphia firm of Wood and Perot made many such designs which were marketed throughout the country by catalogues*

1572

1573

1574

1575

1576

1577

449

1578

1581

1579

1580

1578–1580 *Decorative cast-iron spandrels, featuring the phoenix rising from the flames, the swan, and the heron, designed in open panels set within cusped forms* 1581, 1582 *Cemetery-gate panels with willow and lamb motifs, c. 1845* 1583–1585 *Balcony railings were produced in a variety of patterns and incorporated smaller units of varying lengths. This mode of manufacture was made possible because of the ease of repeating a given pattern in a number of molds, a great advantage over previous methods. From photographs of Baltimore homes, c. 1850*

1582

1583

1584

1585

1586

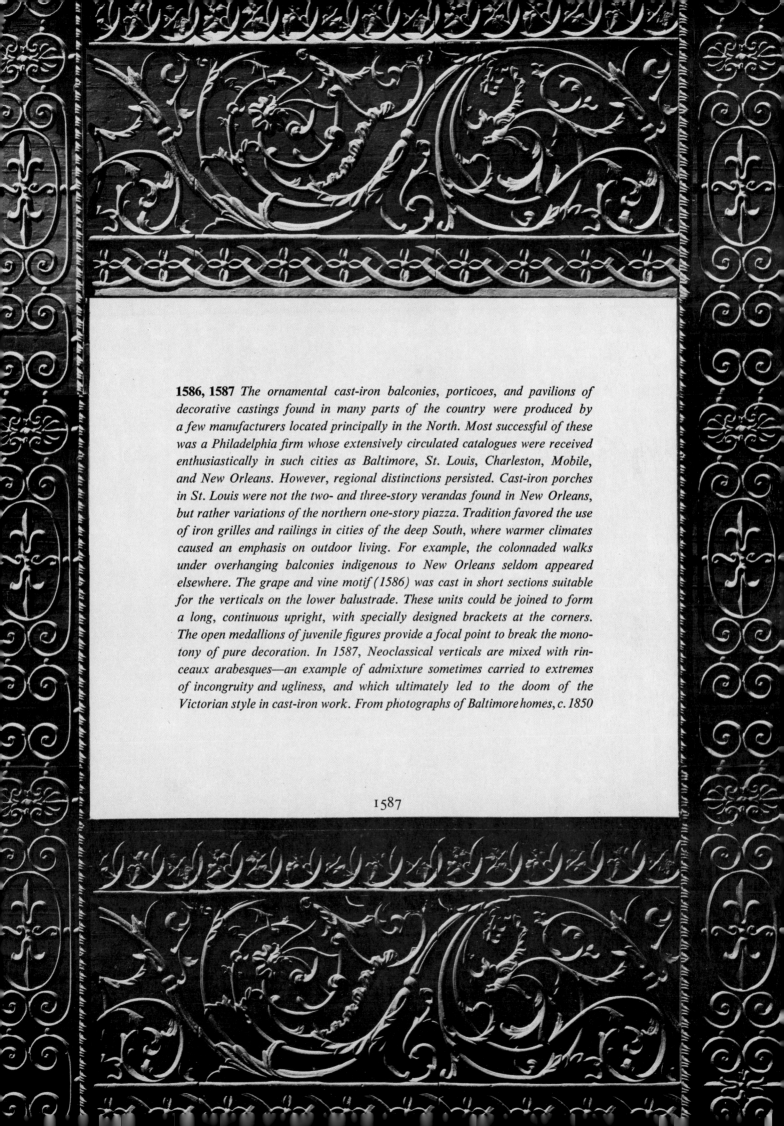

1586, 1587 *The ornamental cast-iron balconies, porticoes, and pavilions of decorative castings found in many parts of the country were produced by a few manufacturers located principally in the North. Most successful of these was a Philadelphia firm whose extensively circulated catalogues were received enthusiastically in such cities as Baltimore, St. Louis, Charleston, Mobile, and New Orleans. However, regional distinctions persisted. Cast-iron porches in St. Louis were not the two- and three-story verandas found in New Orleans, but rather variations of the northern one-story piazza. Tradition favored the use of iron grilles and railings in cities of the deep South, where warmer climates caused an emphasis on outdoor living. For example, the colonnaded walks under overhanging balconies indigenous to New Orleans seldom appeared elsewhere. The grape and vine motif (1586) was cast in short sections suitable for the verticals on the lower balustrade. These units could be joined to form a long, continuous upright, with specially designed brackets at the corners. The open medallions of juvenile figures provide a focal point to break the monotony of pure decoration. In 1587, Neoclassical verticals are mixed with rinceaux arabesques—an example of admixture sometimes carried to extremes of incongruity and ugliness, and which ultimately led to the doom of the Victorian style in cast-iron work. From photographs of Baltimore homes, c. 1850*

1587

1588

North, East, South, West

ANDRONICUS, A GREEK astronomer living about 100 B.C., created the first recorded weather vane when he hoisted a bronze figure of Triton atop his Tower of Winds in Athens. The winds were worshiped as oracles for good or evil, and the adage "An ill wind that blows no good" was scarcely an empty metaphor. Early Scandinavian seafarers used vanes on their ships to help predict the weather. In ninth-century Europe, the pope decreed that the rooster should be placed on top of churches as a religious symbol to ward off evil and as evidence of good faith. The cock that crowed thrice to the apostle Peter prevailed throughout the Middle Ages not only for its religious significance but also for its functional and decorative value. These ideas were inherited by the early Colonists, who followed European examples in their vanes. The rooster, because of its association with traditions in Christendom, became the predominant motif used atop barns and houses. At first the weathercocks were cut from flat wooden boards or sheet iron, but as early as 1656 a handsome copper cockerel graced the Dutch Reformed Church in Albany. An Indian weather vane of hammered copper for the Province House in Boston was the work of "Deacon" Shem Drowne, a craftsman and metalworker noted for his mantelpiece carvings, figureheads, and trade signs. The chanticleer vane taken from the Fitch Tavern at New Bedford,

1588 *Gilded iron weather vane with the angel Gabriel blowing a trumpet presents an unusually handsome silhouette. The figure of Gabriel was a popular subject for weather vanes well into the nineteenth century. Made by Gould and Hazlett, Boston, in 1840* **1589** *Wrought-iron weather vane with gilded banner and finial, one of the oldest extant American vanes. Made by a local smith in 1673 for the first church in Concord, Massachusetts*

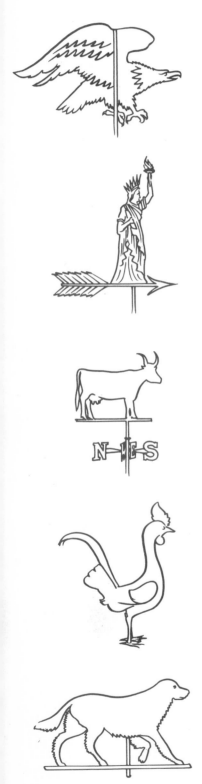

Massachusetts, is an outstanding example of the early wooden, painted board type. Gracefully styled with a long curved neck and a sweep of its back and tail, it is almost four feet tall. (Also from the hand of Drowne is the unusual and celebrated grasshopper vane dated 1742 that still tops the cupola of Faneuil Hall in Boston—a design duplicated a century later by the Cushing Company of Waltham, Massachusetts, whose copies are highly prized by collectors.)

The artistic treatment of the rooster motif in vanes varies greatly with the local craftsman. Without pictorial sources for guidance, each farmer or carpenter fashioned his own weathercock. The outer silhouette, cutout areas, and the arrangement and grouping of tail feathers attest to the creative ability of the folk artists, who exhibited a flair for functional design and a native vitality difficult to match in their purity of line and expression. In later years, however, the weathercock lost much of its grace and originality, becoming chunkier and more realistic; perhaps this was brought about by its changing from a quasi-religious to a secular role. This contrast is particularly noticeable if one studies the catalogues of weather-vane manufacturers issued in the second half of the nineteenth century, for their realistic zinc- and copper-stamped roosters

have lost all traces of the unique design qualities that typified the handiwork of the farmers who had originally fashioned them.

It would be difficult to find an artifact in which design variants outnumber those of the weather vane. Personal tastes, regional economy, and the materials employed account for this variety. In agricultural communities, farmers preferred weather vanes in the form of a cow, horse, sheep, or pig—in addition, of course, to the cockerel—while in seacoast towns, houses and barns are marked with cod, swordfish, seagulls, whales, dolphins, and sailboats. Other occupational designs were also featured: a firehouse displayed a vane with a fireman blowing his trumpet or a fire engine; a train station was surmounted by a vane with a locomotive. Many tradesmen found that the weather vane provided an opportunity to call attention to their wares and services. A butcher, for example, advertised with a pig being dragged to market; a woolen textile factory displayed a sheep or ram; a shipbuilder featured a two-masted schooner; and a racetrack exhibited a horse-drawn sulky and rider. Thus the weather vane, in addition to its functional purpose, took on the character of a trade symbol.

Mythological, Biblical, and historical sources furnished further motifs for weather vanes.

456

Diana, the huntress, with her bow and arrow, was a favorite. The floating figure of Gabriel with his trumpet was deemed an appropriate herald of the four winds and signalized the great religious revival of the nineteenth century. The frequent use of the Indian-archer motif is understandable, as the early Colonists wished to indicate friendship with their New World neighbors; also, the bow and arrow—which, poised for battle, pointed in the direction of the wind—functioned effectively as a design motif.

Almost two centuries separate the crudely wrought iron and scroll-cut wooden figures of the early settlers from those produced by the manufacturers of the 1850s. The lightweight, hollow forms of the coppersmith provided an opportunity for detailing. Carefully modeled relief treatment could be accorded the feathery forms of the rooster, the muscular delineation of horse or cow, and the anatomy of Diana or of an Indian. From a distance only the silhouette was important, but on closer observation, as further features were revealed, function and beauty were blended into a single form.

A preponderance of the later vanes were fabricated of lightweight copper. First a wooden pattern was fashioned by a master patternmaker; then artisans, guided by this pattern, carried out the work. A cast-iron template was made from the original wooden pattern; this then served the coppersmith, who beat out the two sides and then soldered them together. Hence, by this simple yet ingenious method, a three-dimensional effect of full relief was created.

The eagle in many poses and attitudes, crouching or with outstretched wings, appeared in weather vanes of wood or sheet metal and in castings. Although patriotic feelings were asserted following the Revolution and during the early Federal period, it was not until the 1850s that the eagle motif was widely used. In most eagle weather vanes, the native instincts of the individual craftsman, unhampered by rules of heraldry or tradition, resulted in freedom of expression.

Other national emblems appeared in lesser numbers. Miss Columbia and Miss Liberty survive in a few well-preserved examples; Uncle Sam appeared in a few instances. Flags, ribbons, pennants, and bannerets, all useful appendages with decorative potential, were made in wrought iron or copper. One writer, expressing the difference that developed between American and European weather vanes, summarizes the American tradition by calling it "a new and ingratiating heraldry, a heraldry of democracy."

457

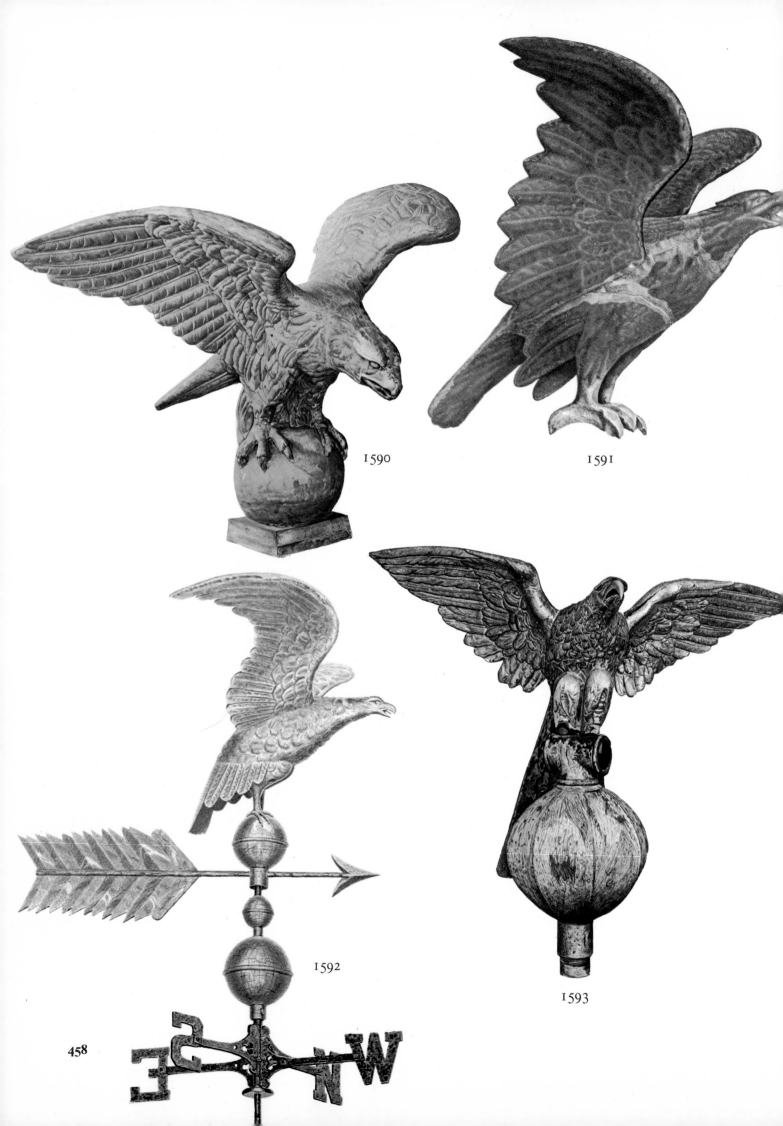

1590

1591

1592

1593

458

1594

1595

1590–1596 *In agricultural communities various types of birds and domestic animals were used, but the most popular motif was the rooster. Details such as the coxcomb, wing, and especially the tail feathers lent themselves to effective design treatment, The eagle's popularity as a patriotic symbol accounts for its continued use throughout most of the nineteenth century, and eagle weather vanes were mass-produced in great numbers between 1850 and 1880*

1596

459

1597

1598

1599

1600

460

1601

1602

1597–1604 *Hollow-formed eagle weather vanes of copper required intricate molds and soldered seams because of extended wingspread. Rooster forms were usually in silhouette, with modeling limited to surface details in comparatively low relief, c. 1850–80*

1603

1604

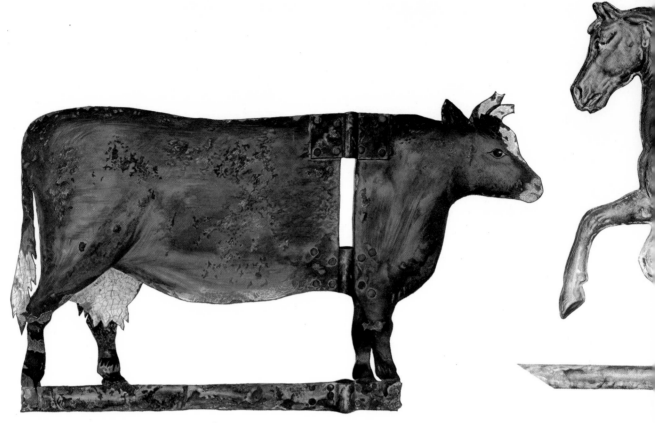

1605

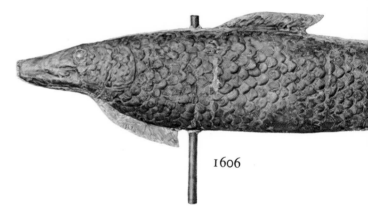

1606

1607

1605 *Cow weather vanes used atop barn cupolas did not appear until the late nineteenth century.* **1606** *Fish weather vane—here with a glass eye—a motif limited to the eastern seaboard and especially New England* **1607** *Indian weather vane, hollow copper, c. 1850* **1608–1610** *Running horse, a highly popular weather vane motif, c. 1870–1900* **1611** *Horse-drawn sulky and driver weather vane, sometimes used to indicate the breed of racing horse housed in a barn, and a more distinctive symbol than the horse alone, c. 1875.*

1608

1609

1610

1611

463

1612

1613

1614

1615

464

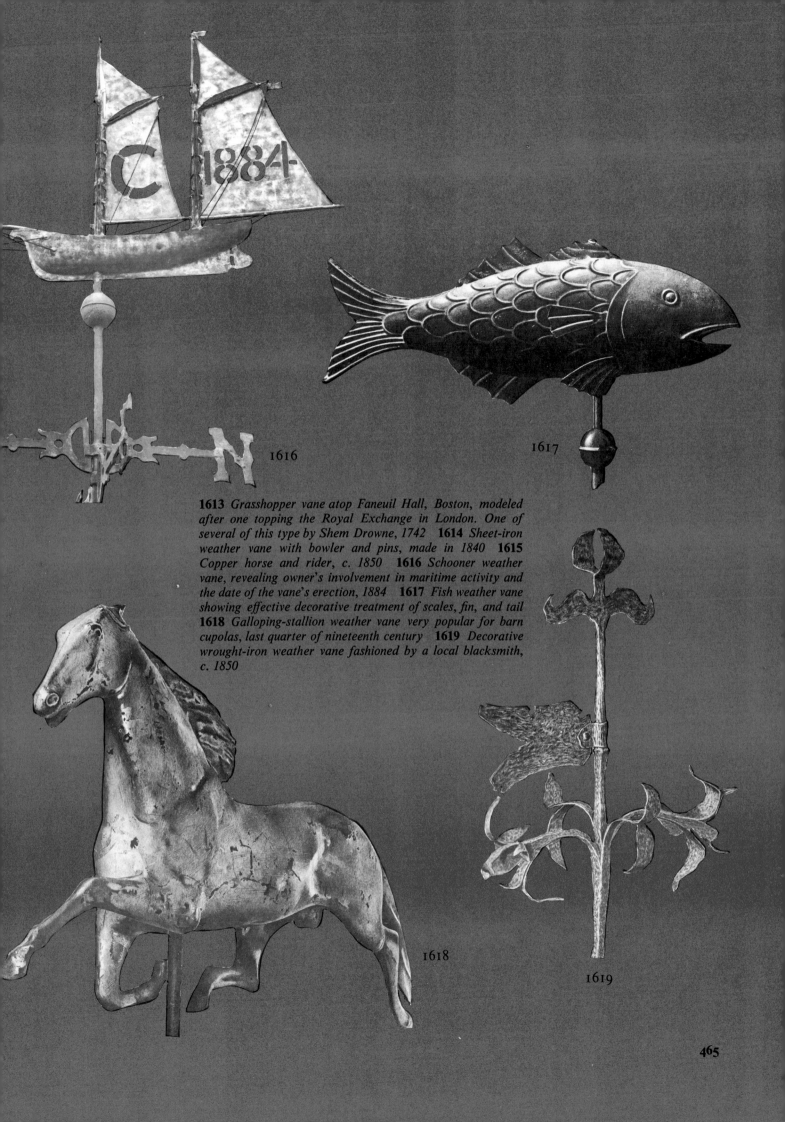

1616

1617

1613 *Grasshopper vane atop Faneuil Hall, Boston, modeled after one topping the Royal Exchange in London. One of several of this type by Shem Drowne, 1742* **1614** *Sheet-iron weather vane with bowler and pins, made in 1840* **1615** *Copper horse and rider, c. 1850* **1616** *Schooner weather vane, revealing owner's involvement in maritime activity and the date of the vane's erection, 1884* **1617** *Fish weather vane showing effective decorative treatment of scales, fin, and tail* **1618** *Galloping-stallion weather vane very popular for barn cupolas, last quarter of nineteenth century* **1619** *Decorative wrought-iron weather vane fashioned by a local blacksmith, c. 1850*

1618

1619

1620

1621

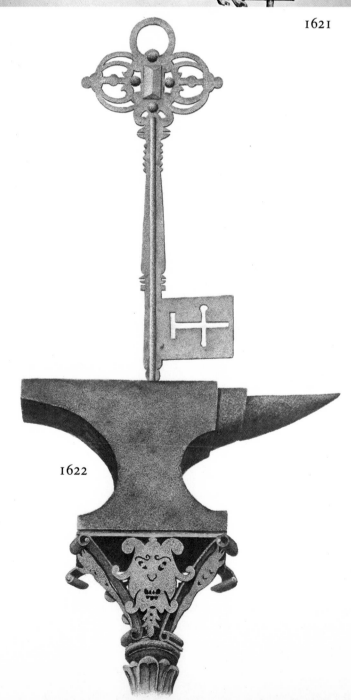

1622

466

1623

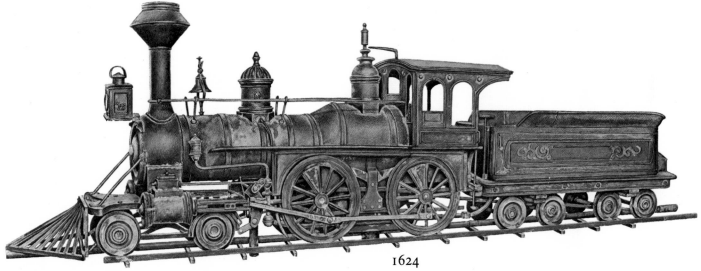

1624

1620 *Pig weather vane over six feet high used to designate an abattoir, late nineteenth century* **1621** *Copper rooster, c. 1870–80. Photograph courtesy The Smithsonian Institution, Washington, D.C.* **1622** *Key weather vane from Louisiana, used by a locksmith as a sign of his craft, 1895* **1623** *Rooster weather vane providing an interesting comparison with pose in 1621* **1624** *Locomotive weather vane, elaborately wrought of copper sheet and cast zinc parts, fashioned and displayed by a true railroad buff, c. 1875*

OVERLEAF: GALLERY OF WEATHER VANES. *Animals:* **1625, 1631, 1653, 1657, 1663, 1678**; *birds:* **1638, 1664**; *cows:* **1639, 1643, 1654, 1669**; *eagle:* **1635**; *figures:* **1641, 1646, 1672**; *horses:* **1627, 1629, 1637, 1645, 1647, 1651, 1655, 1659, 1661, 1665, 1667, 1673, 1676, 1677**; *Indians:* **1640, 1644, 1649, 1650, 1652, 1658, 1674**, *roosters:* **1626, 1628, 1630, 1632–34, 1636, 1642, 1648, 1656, 1660, 1662, 1666, 1668, 1670, 1671, 1675**. *Figures* **1630, 1631, 1638, 1645, 1654, 1665, 1673** *from photographs*

1625

1626

1627

1628

1634

1635

1636

1637

1643

1644

1645

1646

1652

1653

1654

1655

1661

1662

1663

1664

1670

1671

1672

1673

1630

1631

1632

1633

1639

1640

1641

1642

1648

1649

1650

1651

1657

1658

1659

1660

1666

1667

1668

1669

1674

1675

1676

1677

1678

Watercolor of cornucopia with fruit. Painted by an unknown Ohio artist, c. 1800

VOLUME
TWO

472

Portrait of Mrs. Samuel Chandler *by Winthrop Chandler, a relative, painted about 1780. The artist was born in Woodstock, Connecticut, in 1747, and was probably apprenticed to a house painter in Boston, where he eked out a living painting signs and doing odd jobs. National Gallery of Art, Washington, D.C. Gift of Edgar William and Bernice Chrysler Garbisch*

BOOK
FOUR

Woman's World

BOOK FOUR: *Woman's World*

1679

1679 *Tending fire, a full-time chore at the giant kitchen fireplace (six feet high, nine feet wide, and four feet deep) of the Governor's Palace in Williamsburg, Virginia. The fireplace could accommodate a number of different foods cooking at one time, but each required individual care. With family, servants, and a constant stream of guests, the kitchen staff often had to prepare meals for sixty or more. "Fifty-two dined with me yesterday," wrote the governor, Lord Botetourt, in 1769, "and I expect that number here today." Over the fireplace hang a variety of utensils including the clockwork-jack timing device, extreme right. Photograph courtesy Colonial Williamsburg* **1680–1683** *Mortars and pestles for grinding grains and spices, turned of hard woods such as maple, walnut, and ash* **1684** *Larder of the manor house of an eighteenth-century southern plantation, displaying meat hooks suspended from ceiling and a large variety of food storage containers including earthenware jugs and crocks, wooden tubs, casks, kegs, and woven baskets. Photograph courtesy Mount Vernon Ladies Association, Mount Vernon, Virginia* **1685** *Washington's kitchen at Mount Vernon with well-equipped fireplace displaying wrought-iron pothooks, spits, firedogs, and utensils. Also in evidence are a number of pewter, copper, and brass items, including the spiral-wooden handled warming pan on the left wall. Photograph courtesy Mount Vernon Ladies Association, Mount Vernon, Virginia*

What's Cooking

1680 — 1683

F
ROM EARLY WILLS and inventories one gains a significant view of the Colonial household. Such a list as "1 frying pan, 2 skillets, 3 bake pains, iron pothooks, warming pan and trivet" suggests the austerity of existence in the New World. Family life revolved around the common room, which was usually teeming with all sorts of activity. Here the settler huddled to keep warm, mend his tools, and read his Bible, while his wife wove cloth, made the family's clothing, and cooked.

The common room was termed the hall before it was called the kitchen, especially in New England and the Middle Atlantic states, where winters were severe. A huge fireplace, derived in type from that of an English manor house, was the hub of this room, supplying warmth, light, and a source of heat for all cooking and baking. Built of stone and later of

1684

1685

1686

1687

1688

brick, the fireplace was topped by a broad, rough-hewn lintel ten to twelve feet long, made from a solid tree trunk. At first the lintel was set flush with the masonry wall; later it projected from it, providing a shelf for tools, kitchen utensils, and other artifacts.

As more comfortable houses became possible, the common room ceased to be an all-purpose living area for the family's activities. Beds were removed to separate rooms upstairs; a buttery was created for the churning of butter and the making of buttermilk and cheese; a larder was created for the drying and storage of fruit, vegetables, spices and herbs, and for the hanging of meat and dried fish; and a small room or alcove called the pantry accommodated china, glassware, and stoneware on its shelves. Such specialization developed gradually and depended on a family's economic circumstances. However, the evolution toward comfort and convenience was more rapid in urban areas and on the large plantations of the South, where there was an abundance of domestic help.

In the seventeenth century, cooking at the open fireplace was carried on by three distinct methods: boiling, roasting, and baking, each of which required special utensils. Boiling, and the later refinement of steaming, meant cooking in hot water in a pot or kettle. At first, the Colonist used a lug pole, a wooden bar placed across the fireplace at a distance from the intense heat. Later on, this bar was replaced by an iron crane that was fastened into one side

of the chimney and arranged like a supporting bracket. Pots and kettles were hung on this crane by pothooks, also called trammels. The housewife could swing the crane into the room, hang her pots and kettles on it, then return it to the fire. She was kept very busy, having continually to gauge the heat of the fire and tend it. Roasting consisted of cooking chunks of meat, game, or poultry on the open fire. Here the housewife used a spit; this sharp iron rod, supported on two forked uprights in front of the fire, was thrust into one end of the meat. The handle at one end of the spit required turning, usually done by one of the children. (Later, in the eighteenth century, a mechanical clock arrangement was invented to do the laborious job of turning the roast.) Baking was done with dry heat in a closed compartment. The earliest baking utensil was the heavy, covered pan with legs, called a bake kettle, which was usually placed directly on the red-hot embers. These covered pans came in various sizes and shapes. Other necessary iron cooking utensils included long-handled skillets, cooking pots, tea kettles, gravy-drip broilers, rotary broilers of the gridiron type, trivets, toasters, waffle irons, and plate warmers that hung from one of the andirons.

When chimneys came to be built of brick, a separate oven with a built-in flue and an iron door opening into the kitchen was incorporated in the fireplace. For best results, a hot fire of dry wood, called oven wood, was built about once a week and fed until the bricks

1689

1690

1692

were hot. Wood and ashes were then swept out, the iron door closed, and as many foods as the oven could accommodate, such as baked beans, brown bread, and pies, were pushed in by a special long-handled shovel called a peel.

Kitchen utensils since the arrival of the Pilgrims have been fashioned from wood, stoneware, pewter, tin, iron, copper, and brass. Wood was used extensively for plates (called trenchers), platters, bowls, ladles, and tableware. The wooden pitcher, called a noggin, was passed from mouth to mouth. The tankard, staved and hooped, with a cover, was another wooden drinking vessel. Kept near the fireplace, it held warm toddy and was used for guests rather than for ordinary drinking by the family at the table. The use of a wooden table service, which was easily made on the woodturner's lathe, was a matter of economy with most of the early settlers. Families of wealth adopted china and pewter, relegating this treenware to kitchen use and the servants' quarters. The plentiful supply and variety of wood encouraged the handy householder to shape many items that could be made by turning or simple carpentry. Circular boxes for storage were also used extensively in the kitchen. They were made from thin layers of previously moistened softwoods and pliant birch in many sizes—from pill boxes to spice boxes to those large enough to hold a

wheel of cheese. The mortar and pestle for grinding and crushing grains and spices were usually fashioned from maple, walnut burls, or birch.

The majority of kitchen utensils were made from iron. Wrought iron was used to make tools, prongs, forks, skewers, pothooks, spits, gridirons, toasters, steelyards, firedogs, and trivets. Iron was a common, readily available material mined in many areas from the earliest days of the Colonial period. However, despite their extreme industriousness, the Colonial blacksmiths could not keep pace with the increasing demand for service. Such was the smith's usefulness that he was placed under special guard at the time of the Revolution, since he supplied the tools of war. The characteristics of the Colonial blacksmith's handiwork are utilitarian forms and lack of ornamentation. Old World decorative effects and whorls do not appear in Early American ironwork, and only occasionally does a kitchen artifact incorporate an extraneous curve or scroll. Even the Pennsylvania German smiths, known to favor decoration, practiced restraint and stressed utility. Excavations at Williamsburg, in Virginia—one of the most aristocratic and wealthy of the Colonies—have revealed thousands of iron artifacts, among which are carpenters' tools, carriage hardware, kitchen equipment, and door hinges. Almost without

1693

1686–1694 *Kitchen woodenware, or treen, including scoop, 1686; mixing bowl, 1687; butter paddle, 1688; butter scoop or ladle, 1689; spoon,* *1690; cheese board, 1691; bucket, 1692; knife box, 1693; and spoon rack, 1694*

1691

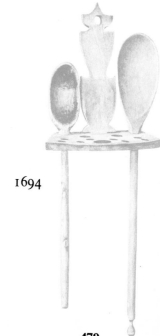

1694

479

1695

1696

1697

1699

1698

exception—including items found at the site of the Governor's Palace—these are simple and utilitarian in design.

Brass and copper, in widespread use for kitchen utensils, continued to be imported from Europe well into the nineteenth century. However, there were braziers in the Colonies as early as 1717, in New York and Philadelphia. Lighter than iron, copper and brass items dented easily and thus had a shorter life. These metals, which could be shaped from sheets and easily brazed at the joints, were used for tea- and coffeepots, urns, skillets, frying pans, saucepans, washbasins, warming pans, skimmers, ladles, scoops, measures, and scales. In the middle of the eighteenth century, braziers and coppersmiths advertised their wares and repair services in Colonial

1695–1704 *Metal kitchen utensils, including iron skillet, 1695; copper kettles, 1696, 1698; flour sifter, 1697; brass starch strainer, 1699; copper pot for candy making, 1700; copper ladle for candy making, 1701; brass tea kettle, 1702; tin tea kettle, 1703; and copper tea kettle, 1704. Except for 1697 and 1701–1703, c. 1830–65, most utensils are of late eighteenth-century make*

1701

1702

1703

1704

journals and, at a later date, in city directories. Frequent references to such services exist in the gazettes of the larger cities. By the end of the century, a number of brass foundries were established, so that cast brass as well as hammered sheet brasswares were available.

Jacob Wilkins, of New York, advertised all manner of brasswork at the "Sign of the Brass Andiron and Candlestick." Peter van Norden operated a brass foundry in Bound Brook, New Jersey, where he manufactured kitchenwares as well as brass andirons, candlesticks, shoe and buckle ornaments, pitchers, measures, pipkins, coal scuttles, and brass kettles "from a barrel to a quart," sold in nests. Brass kettles could be cast, or hammered over a mold with the handles riveted on. A complete kitchen assortment of bright, gleaming brass-

1700

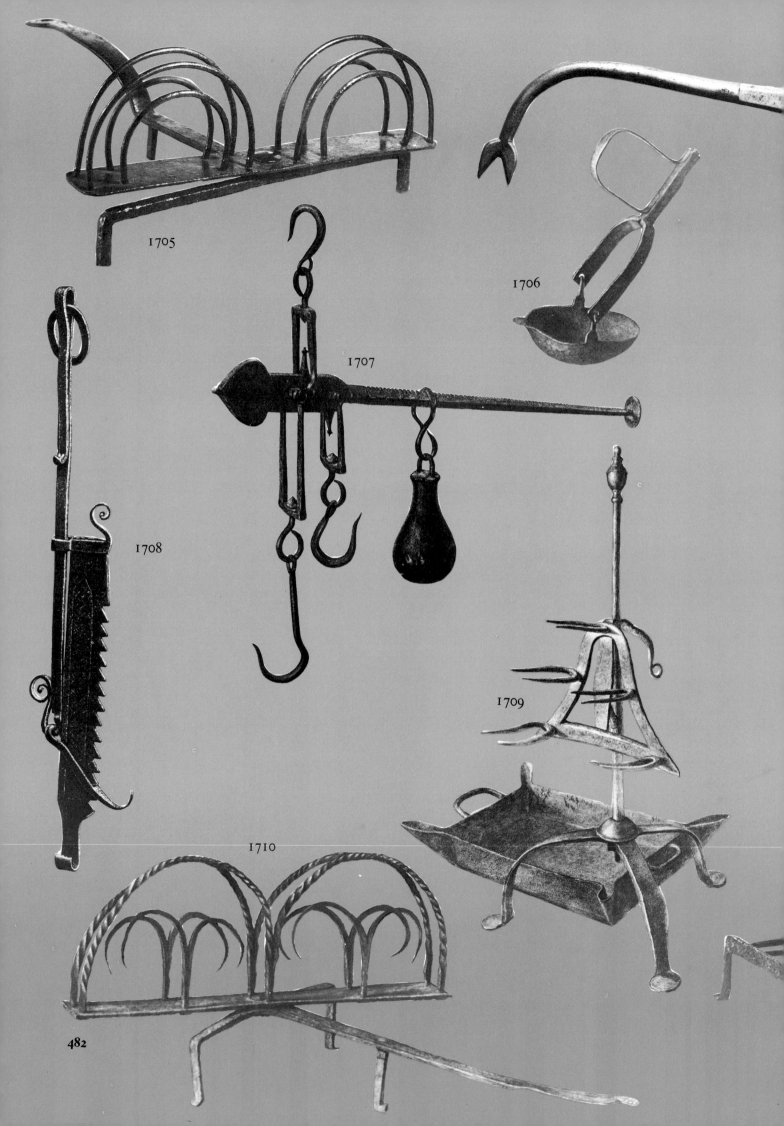

1705

1706

1707

1708

1709

1710

482

1712

1713

1714

1715

1716

ware was rare—indeed, a sure sign of affluence in early days. Today a collection of these wares may be seen in the kitchen of the Governor's Palace in Williamsburg.

By the nineteenth century, the brass industry centered largely in New England. Important foundries were located in Waterbury, Bridgeport, and Torrington, Connecticut. Copper was used for the same kinds of articles as brass and was ideal for warming pans, kettles, and saucepans. A major objection to the use of copper, however, was its disagreeable taste. To overcome this, a thin coating of tin was used to line the inside of most copper culinary vessels. When this coating wore away, the vessel had to be relined. The bottoms of kettles and pots also needed constant repairing. Like brass, copper utensils could be both hammered and cast. The first hammered utensils were beaten on an iron mold with a wooden mallet. Spouts and handles were riveted on by hand and were sometimes made from copper tubing. Surface decoration was rarely applied to brass or copper utensils, with the exception of warming pans and trivets. The warming pan, used for warming cold bedsheets, had a hinged lid with pierced designs and, often, scrolls or foliated engraving, and the brass tops of trivets had similar designs, following English precedent.

1705–1713 *Wrought-iron kitchen utensils, including toasters, 1705, 1710, 1713; grease lamp, 1706; steelyard, 1707; pothook, 1708; roasting stand and drip pan, 1709; trivet, 1711; and piecrust cutter, 1712* **1714–1717** *Cast-iron kitchen utensils, including skillet, 1714; three-legged pot, 1715; mortar, 1716; and muffin pan, 1717. Figures 1705, 1711, 1712, and 1716 from photographs*

1711

1717

483

1718

1719

1720

1721

484

1722

1723

1718–1726 *Variously called match safes, matchboxes, and match holders, these containers were found in every kitchen as well as in other rooms in the period 1860–1900. Most were made of cast iron, as are those illustrated here, but tin boxes, stamped out of sheet metal and decorated, were also available in a variety of designs in this period*

Overleaf: GALLERY OF KITCHEN UTENSILS AND GADGETS. *Buckets:* **1730, 1738** *butter churns:* **1737, 1752** *cake molds:* **1736, 1751, 1756** *charcoal burner:* **1776** *cheese strainer:* **1746** *cherry stoner:* **1765** *coffee mills:* **1728, 1758, 1762** *coffee roaster:* **1731** *dish drainer:* **1774** *dough trough,* **1780** *food choppers:* **1734, 1735, 1742, 1755** *ice cream freezer:* **1777** *copper and tin kettles and pots:* **1727, 1739, 1743, 1750, 1763, 1775** *iron kettles and pans:* **1733, 1741, 1749, 1760, 1769** *knife box:* **1747** *ladle:* **1757** *match holders:* **1744, 1748, 1764, 1773** *mortars and pestles:* **1754, 1759, 1768** *rolling pin:* **1767** *scoops:* **1772, 1779** *spoon rack:* **1766** *water kegs:* **1745, 1771** *wrought-iron utensils:* **1732, 1753, 1761, 1770** *toasters:* **1729, 1778**

1724

1725

1726

485

1727

1728

1729

1730

173

1736

1737

1738

1739

1745

1746

1747

1748

1749

1754

1755

1756

1757

1758

1763

1764

1765

1766

176

1772

1773

1774

1775

1776

1732

1733

1734

1735

1741

1742

1743

1744

1750

1751

1752

1753

1759

1760

1761

1762

1768

1769

1770

1771

1777

1778

1779

1780

1781 *Virginia "shoo-fly" chair, a simple but ingenious device operated by a treadle that activates the cloth strips overhead. Photograph courtesy Colonial Williamsburg* **1782** *Wire beater, operated by rapidly opening and closing the wooden handles*

To Beat a Better Batter

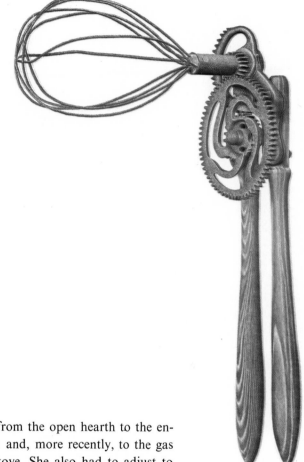

1782

OST DOMESTIC timesaving devices have been invented for use in the kitchen. This was especially true during the Colonial period, when the kitchen was the center of all household activity. The day was never long enough for the housewife, who often had to feed a family of ten or more in addition to farmhands. The day's meals required endless preparation before the actual cooking could begin: cutting, shredding, chopping, beating, grinding, mixing, pitting, and paring. Hence, each new gadget that could afford some relief to the cook was taken up with enthusiasm. As appliances invaded the kitchen in a bewildering variety, the housewife had to adapt to new cooking methods. She had, for example, to adjust to changing heat sources, first from the open hearth to the enclosed firebox and, more recently, to the gas and electric stove. She also had to adjust to copper or brass pots, instead of iron ones.

The steady stream of laborsaving kitchen appliances included eggbeaters, meat grinders, sausage stuffers, kraut cutters, apple parers, cider presses, cherry pitters, and ice-cream freezers. Before these started to appear in the mid-nineteenth century, homemade coffee and spice grinders—miniature imitations of the age-old milling and grinding apparatus—were already found in many kitchens. However, with the popularization of cast iron, coffee grinders with cast-iron wheels and parts began to be manufactured in great numbers.

A distinctly American device was the apple parer, extremely useful since apples were a

1783

household staple for pies, applesauce, apple butter, and cider. The principle of the turning lathe was the basic concept behind every apple-peeling and coring gadget. As early as 1803, a wooden appliance with a fork for holding the apple, a handle and turning device, and a sharp knife edge was the forerunner of similar machines which developed throughout the century. At harvest time, it was not uncommon for a single household to pare three hundred bushels of apples for use throughout the winter months. This need led to the addition of apple-paring bees to the existing quilting bees and barn-raising celebrations, all festive occasions at which gallons of cider, America's most popular drink, were consumed.

Eggbeaters represented a new application of the principle of the hand drill. Through an arrangement of gears that operated revolving wire beaters, the manual beating process was accelerated. Another useful mechanical device was one for chopping and mincing which, by a continuous up-and-down movement of a blade, cut and shredded meats and vegetables in an efficient manner similar to the operation of a guillotine.

The many thousands of patents issued for household devices evidence human ingenuity and confirm the fact that mechanization in the home, as typified by these kitchen aids, is an activity for which Americans have been largely responsible. Some of these early appliances were cumbersome in construction, but many were simple and forthright, possessing an inherent beauty by virtue of honest lines and forms. However, in the mid-nineteenth century, when cast iron became the material commonly used for many household items, manufacturers began to decorate these appliances with elaborate designs. In so doing they expressed the Victorian desire to disguise utilitarian purpose, preferring to create objects which were believed to be aesthetic additions to the home.

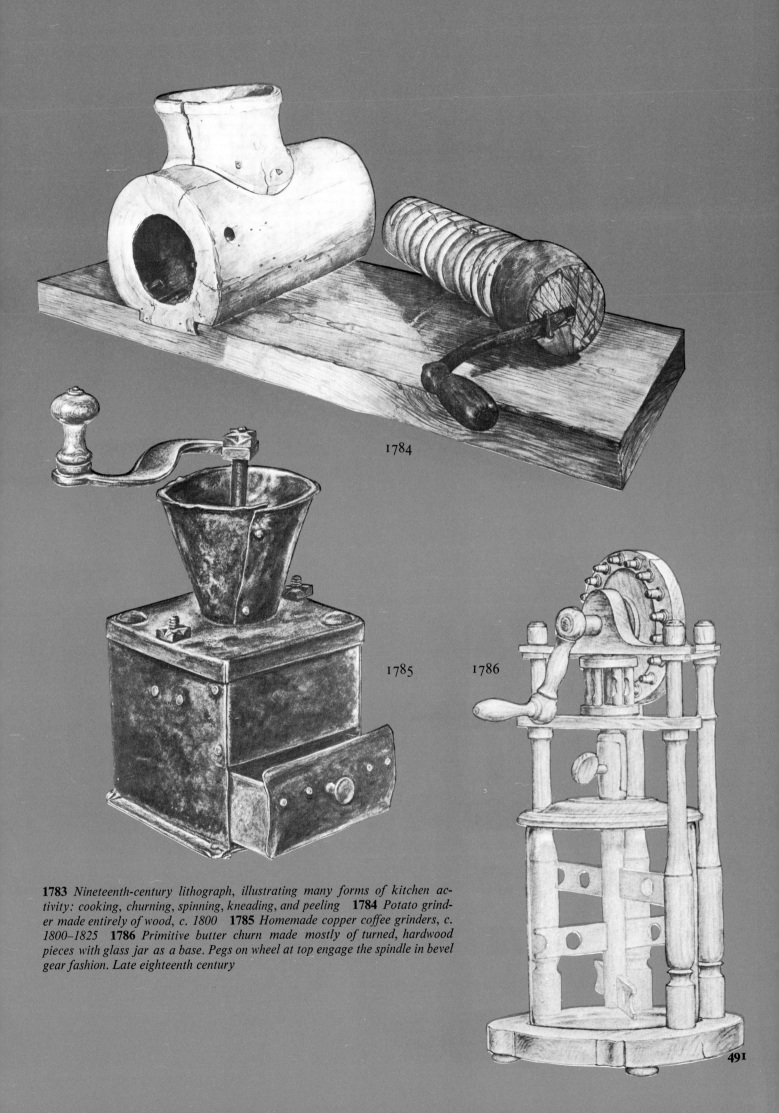

1783 *Nineteenth-century lithograph, illustrating many forms of kitchen activity: cooking, churning, spinning, kneading, and peeling* **1784** *Potato grinder made entirely of wood, c. 1800* **1785** *Homemade copper coffee grinders, c. 1800–1825* **1786** *Primitive butter churn made mostly of turned, hardwood pieces with glass jar as a base. Pegs on wheel at top engage the spindle in bevel gear fashion. Late eighteenth century*

1784

1785

1786

1787   1788

1789

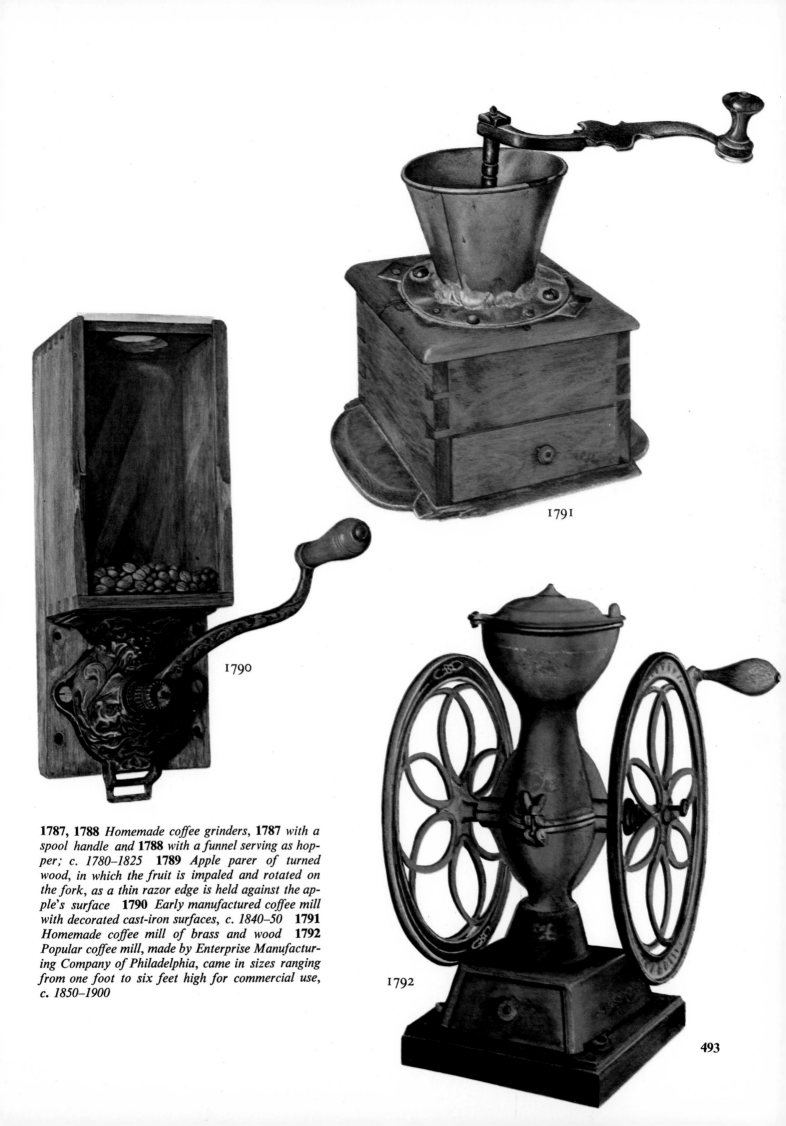

1791

1790

1792

1787, 1788 *Homemade coffee grinders,* **1787** *with a spool handle and* **1788** *with a funnel serving as hopper; c. 1780–1825* **1789** *Apple parer of turned wood, in which the fruit is impaled and rotated on the fork, as a thin razor edge is held against the apple's surface* **1790** *Early manufactured coffee mill with decorated cast-iron surfaces, c. 1840–50* **1791** *Homemade coffee mill of brass and wood* **1792** *Popular coffee mill, made by Enterprise Manufacturing Company of Philadelphia, came in sizes ranging from one foot to six feet high for commercial use, c. 1850–1900*

493

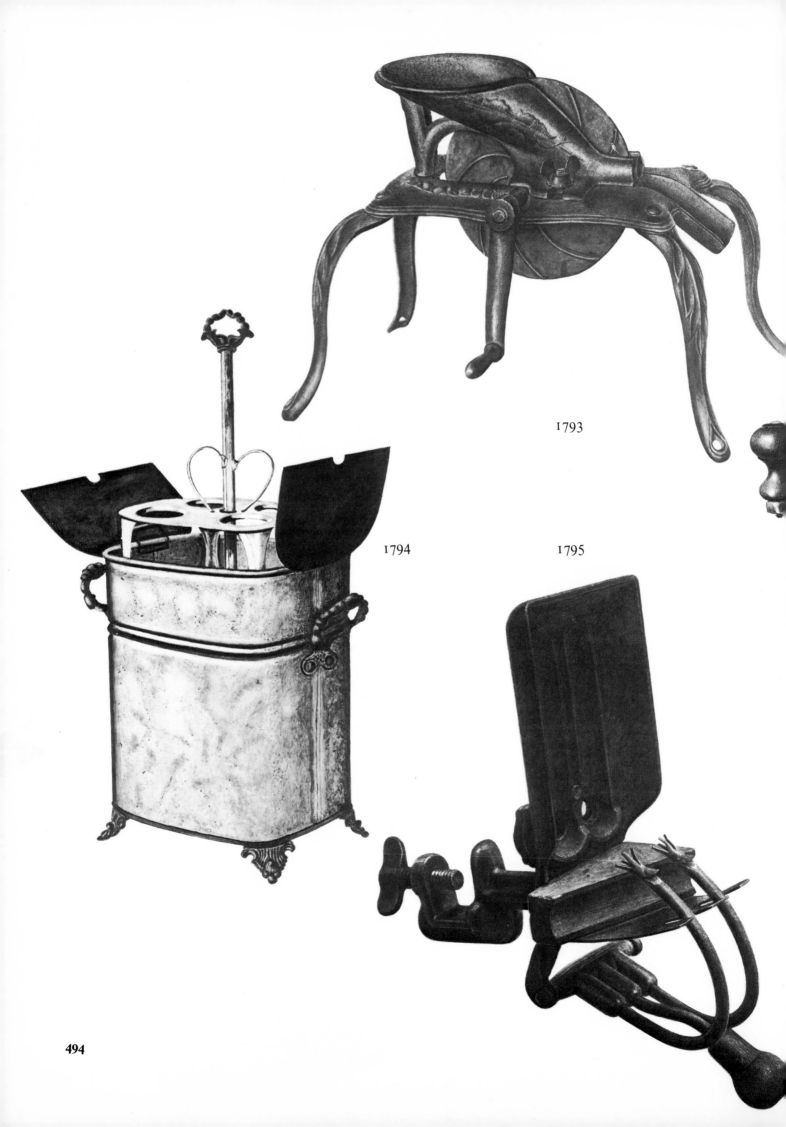

1793

1794

1795

494

1793 Cast-iron cherry pitter, with legs resembling furniture supports, decorated with acanthus foliage, c. 1860 **1794** Tin egg boiler with cast-iron legs **1795** Cherry pitter designed to fasten over table edge **1796** Box-type coffee grinder, popular because the operator could sit on a chair and hold it between the knees while grinding. Delicately ornamented cast-iron parts date this mill, c. 1850–80 **1797** Homemade, wall-type coffee mill, requiring user to hold a vessel underneath to catch the ground beans. Made in Louisiana in 1846 **1798** Dog-shaped cast-iron nut cracker, c. 1860–80

1796

1797

1798

495

1799

A Trivet for the Hot Pot

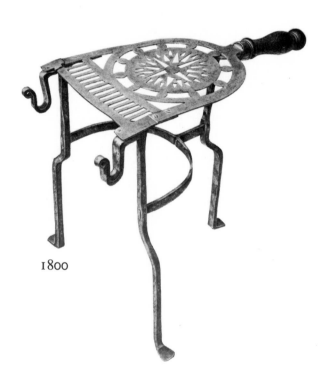

1800

1801

THE TRIVET WAS FIRST introduced into the Colonies from England in the seventeenth century. It was a three-legged or occasionally a four-legged stand for resting pots or kettles and stood on the stone hearth. It was made of wrought iron, but its flat top was a piece of highly polished brass, in a pierced design. The earliest forms used the owner's initials, often worked into attractive motifs in the current Stuart, Chippendale, or Georgian styles. The trivet was sometimes called a spider because "spiders," or frying pans, were also three-legged. Fireside trivets were made with a turned wooden handle, as well as hooks on the forward end, so that they could be hung on a fire bar when not in use. The use of brass for the top plate gradually disappeared, and the entire form was fashioned from wrought iron by the local blacksmith. At times the shape was crude, but later examples show a variety of forms and decorated bases. The tall

1799 *Flatiron stand or trivet with design representing exuberant Victorian taste, incorporating a vase out of which grows a tree of life, scrolls, and floral and foliate forms. Latter half of the nineteenth century* **1800** *Maple-handled, high-legged trivet showing English influence. Brass top with compass motif is supported by wrought-iron legs, c. 1775–90* **1801** *Flatiron holder with design showing an eagle poised atop a heart within a circlet of laurel leaves. Made in the Zoarite Community, Zoar, Ohio, mid-nineteenth century*

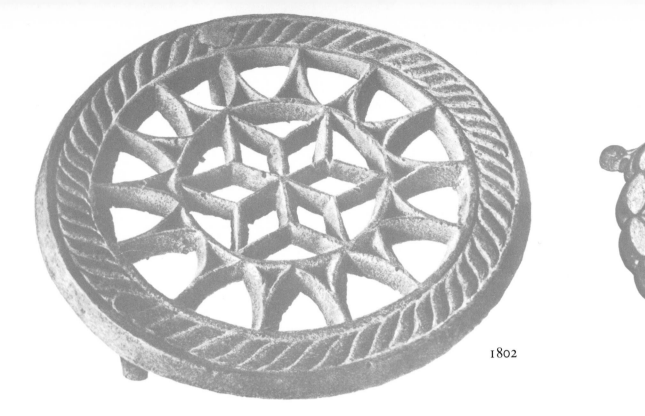

1802

18

legs eventually gave way to short ones no more than an inch or two in height.

The three-legged construction influenced the overall design, for in its simplest form the trivet was a triangle with a handle at the blunt end. However, the smith had an opportunity to exhibit his ingenuity when he shaped and formed the metal in its molten state. The feet and handle were affixed when the body shape was completed, unless, of course, the handle was an extension of the base.

Another related form produced by the smith for kitchen use was the gridiron, a circular footed shape, the top, flat surface of which was marked by parallel bars or by honeycomb, wavy, or serpentine crosspieces in various arrangements. The revolving grill

pivoted around a center pin so that it could be turned easily when used for broiling meat. Wrought-iron trivets and gridirons were made throughout the Colonies during the seventeenth and eighteenth centuries. Those produced in Pennsylvania were heart-shaped or incorporated hearts, fylfots, or common barn symbols in their designs.

Iron stands for flatirons were also called trivets, and were made for use on a ledge, shelf, or ironing board. Like the trivet, they were usually three-cornered to accommodate the similarly shaped flatiron. With the development of foundries, both flatirons and

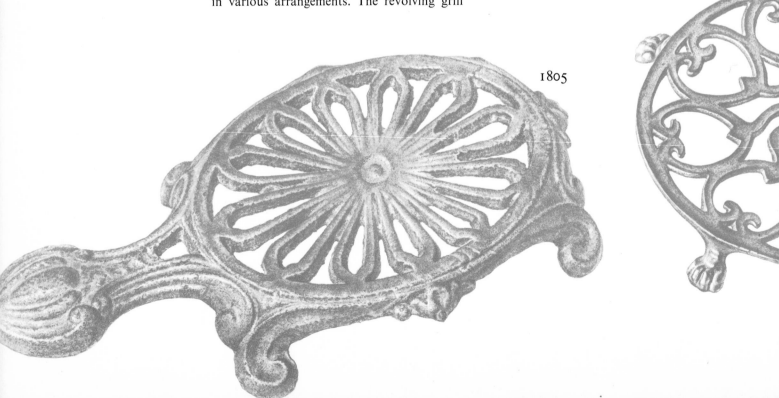

1805

1804

trivets were made in a great variety of designs. This trend began about 1830, and by 1850 trivets of cast iron had almost completely replaced their wrought-iron predecessors. Instead of being crafted by a blacksmith who had been the designer as well as the maker, the newer cast-iron products resulted from a partnership of patternmaker and foundryman. While earlier cast-iron trivets had featured hearts, eagles, stars, and scrolls, as well as such patriotic motifs as George Washington and Miss Liberty, after 1850 the designs became more involved, expressing the prevailing Victorian taste for ornate forms. Naturalistic leaves and flowers, grapes, pineapples, cherubs, and lovebirds were common motifs, as somewhat later in the century were manufacturers' initials and company marks. Borders incorporating mottoes also came into vogue and included popular sayings such as "Good Luck," "Purity, Truth, and Love," and such trade phrases as "Best on Earth."

1802–1807 *Circular-shaped flatiron holders, with or without handles, were found more versatile than the three-footed trivet because there was less chance of their tipping over. Geometrical designs, generally centering around stars, sunbursts, or open centers, predominated*

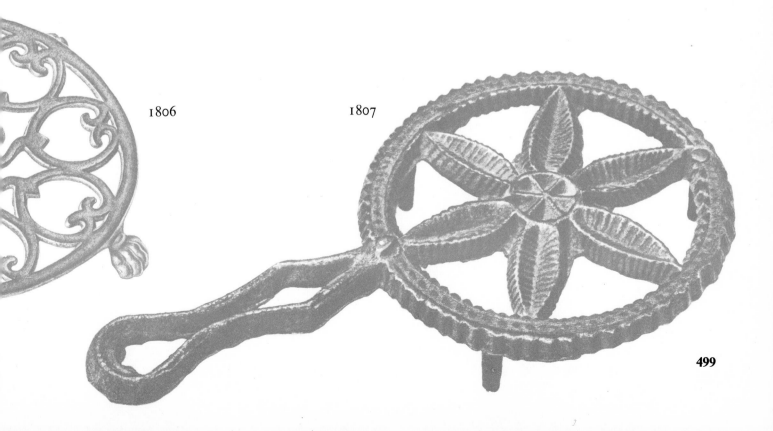

1806   1807

1808

1809

1810

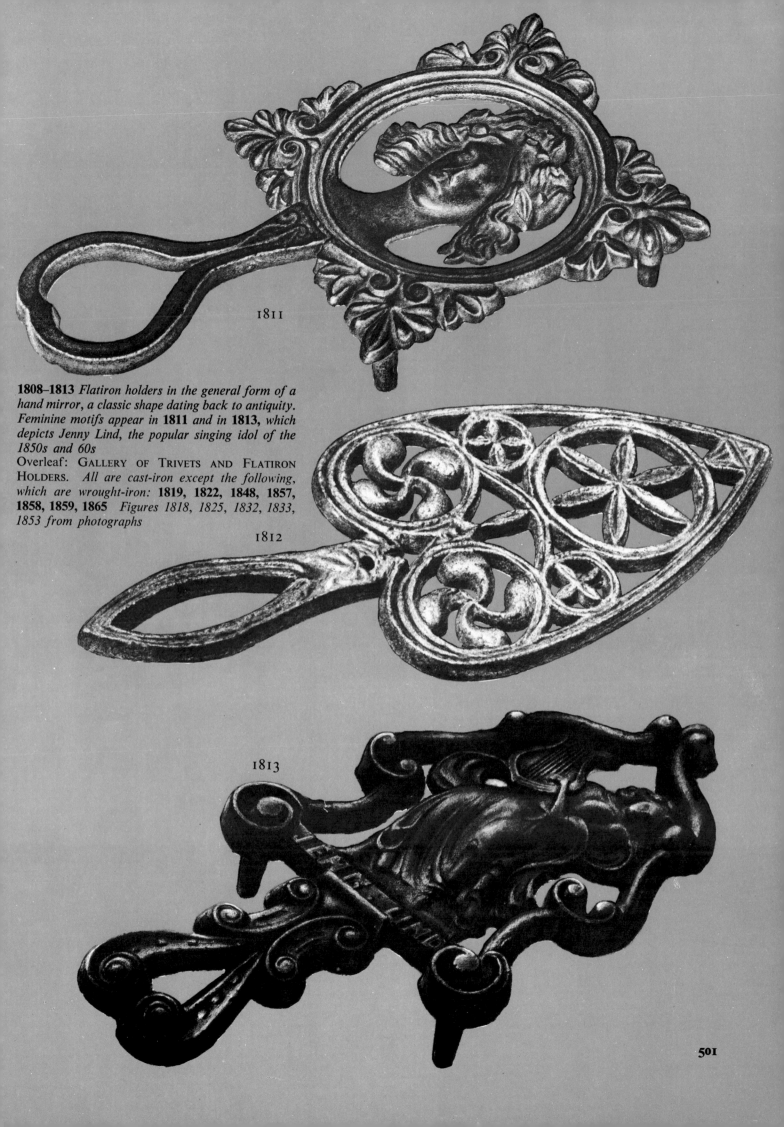

1811

1808–1813 *Flatiron holders in the general form of a hand mirror, a classic shape dating back to antiquity. Feminine motifs appear in* **1811** *and in* **1813**, *which depicts Jenny Lind, the popular singing idol of the 1850s and 60s*
Overleaf: GALLERY OF TRIVETS AND FLATIRON HOLDERS. *All are cast-iron except the following, which are wrought-iron:* **1819, 1822, 1848, 1857, 1858, 1859, 1865** *Figures 1818, 1825, 1832, 1833, 1853 from photographs*

1812

1813

501

1814

1815

1816

1817

1818

1823

1824

1825

1826

1832

1833

1834

1835

1840

1841

1842

1843

1849

1850

1851

1852

1853

1858

1859

1860

1861

1819

1820

1821

1822

1828

1829

1830

1831

1836

1837

1838

1839

1844

1845

1846

1847

1848

1854

1855

1856

1857

1862

1863

1864

1865

1866

1867 *A well-equipped Colonial kitchen stocked a variety of cake and cookie boards, vigorously carved of maple, walnut, and oak for hard wear and to withstand the oven's heat. Many of these can be seen on the shelf above the brick oven. Photograph courtesy Colonial Williamsburg* **1868** *Maple butter mold, with strawberry design* **1869** *Walnut cookie board, with realistically carved fruit, floral, and crown motifs, used for molding holiday sweets similar to marzipan cakes and springerle. Made in Ohio by Swiss immigrants*

Cake Boards, Cookie & Butter Molds

1868

1869

IF A PRESENT-DAY housewife decided to decorate her supply of butter with an interesting design, she would probably be accused of "gilding the lily." A few generations ago, however, when every rural family did its own churning, butter was seldom served unadorned; it was taken to the table in the form of animals, birds, tulips, or hearts, "just for fancy," as the Pennsylvania Germans expressed it.

This custom of embellishing everyday products has been observed in many countries from early times. From the decoration of food containers, it was a short step to decorating the food itself. The simplest means of creating a decorative design was by impressing it with a stamp or shaping it in a mold. The custom of decorative molds for butter was of Conti-

nental origin, particularly practiced by the farmers and peasants of Scandinavia, Switzerland, Germany, and the Alsace region. When this tradition was practiced in the Colonies, the butter was referred to as "print" butter, a term still in use although as a general practice this charming custom has long since been abandoned.

Unfortunately, there is scant record of the use and design of butter molds. They were considered artifacts of lowly origin and as such were very much taken for granted—as was the case with most of the simple artifacts from the early Colonial period. Thus there was no conception that they had value as objects of art. What little information exists is the result of piecing together acquired facts with observations of the objects themselves,

1870

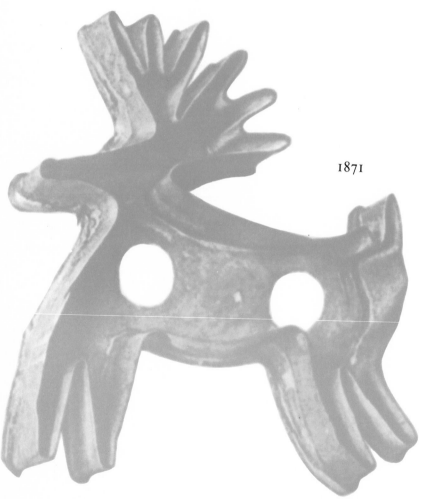

1871

based on a close examination of their carving characteristics. Since the molds were the work of untutored whittlers who practiced a simple technique called "chip carving," this art was limited to simple cuts and twists executed quickly with a sharp knife. Most butter molds were either of pine or poplar, as these were easily carved; however, cherry, maple, and walnut were also used. The earliest extant butter molds were made between 1775 and 1825 and were carved from native woods found in Pennsylvania, New York, and the New England states. The molds show crudely whittled designs in disks about three inches in diameter that are reminiscent of European patterns and hex symbols. At first the molds did not have handles; later, crude handles were inserted into the disks.

Regional traits manifest themselves not so much in carving technique as in motifs. British motifs appear in the New England molds, while the influence of the southern European Palatinate is apparent in the Pennsylvania German ones. British butter molds, although more symmetrical and formal than those of New England, incorporated naturalistic forms, carefully spaced on the face of a mold, and were bordered with various well-defined patterns. The British carvings seem closely related to the designs of contemporary cabinetmakers. British designs included strawberry plants, fruits, and flowers and revealed the mark of a professional wood-carver, not the hand of a farmer who decorated his molds spontaneously, as was the case with the New England molds. Foliate motifs, with curving lines and asymmetrical patterning, imbue the New England molds with an unsophisticated charm. They are the product of artisans familiar with birds, animals, trees, and fruit, whose art experience was limited but whose design sense in this folk-art form was great.

A tradition of fine craftsmanship is evident in the work fashioned by the immigrants from the Palatinate, who settled along the Delaware River and in the regions to the west. Their work displays an admirable knowledge of wood carving and expresses a vigorous simplicity. Comparatively few motifs were employed; these included the conventionalized tulip; the heart and star, which appear in nearly all their decorations; and sheaves of wheat, acorns, and crescents. Frequently the pineapple, a symbol of hospitality, was used.

Since the eagle appeared as a popular decorative motif during the Federal period, it is not surprising that it is found in many forms on butter molds. The cow with milk-filled udder standing serenely under a tree and beautiful elaborations of the hex mark, a symbol of protection, are also frequent motifs. Skilled and versatile carvers wrought a great variety of design versions of each motif. Often graceful leaf forms filled empty spaces and herringbone patterns made other areas more interesting. The outer borders of the butter molds were contained within notched or striated edges.

In the marketplace the butter producer was identified by his design, which thus took on a trademark value. The superstitious farmer took every precaution to maintain the quality of his product, including placing a horseshoe over his springhouse door or a huge hex mark on his barn. One enterprising buttery introduced a note of advertising by adding the

1872

1870–1872 Cookie cutters, fashioned of tin ribbons and then soldered to a flat base, were designed in many forms. Illustrated are the American eagle, a deer, and a horse and rider. Pennsylvania German, nineteenth century 1873 The pie cupboard or "safe," a ventilated wooden cupboard with perforated tin doors, was used to store pies and cakes, protecting them from marauding children before mealtime. Made in Pennsylvania

1873

1874

1875

1876

508

words "Good butter . . . Taste it" to its moldmark.

Butter molds were either cup-shaped or boxed. When cup-shaped, the decoration was placed on the bottom of a plunger used to eject the butter. The butter mold was dipped in scalding, then in cold, water before the butter was packed into it. One unusual mold opened in the form of a Maltese cross with a different design on each of the five hinged sides. Molds were made in various sizes: pounds, halves, quarters, and eighths, although some, probably at a later date, were made to produce individual pats for table use. The designs on both stamps and molds were usually incised so that a raised impression resulted, although there are a few instances of a carved design which resulted in an intaglio impression.

It is rare to discover a field of fundamental design as rich and fertile as that represented by these molds, which until quite recently were overlooked by collectors of Americana. The recognition of their importance as a folk art demonstrates how neglected arts frequently have much to offer students of design and those interested in national traditions.

1874 *Semicircular butter mold with palmette motif* **1875** *Cake boards of a European type known as springerle molds. Varied subjects and precise detailing with razor-like tools reveal domestic details as well as love of farm animals. Made in Pennsylvania, c. 1835* **1876** *Walnut springerle board in which the twenty squares constitute a nursery catalogue of familiar forms and figures, c. 1805– 25*

1878   1879

1877 *Love of birds, expressed in twelve squares depicting the hen, rooster, owl, ostrich, duck, swan, grouse, pheasant, and others, Pennsylvania German, 1843. Photograph* **1878** *Raised tin cookie form, featuring farm and folktale subjects. Nineteenth century. Photograph* **1879** *Maple-sugar mold with semi-abstract carved floral forms*

1880

1881

1882

1883

1884

1885

1886

1887

1888

1889

1890

1880–1890 *Poplar, oak, and maple butter molds representing folk art at its best. "Print" butter displayed the maker's mark, to distinguish it from butter marketed in tubs or crocks and brought higher prices. Eagles and other fowl and barnyard animals were popular motifs. These mostly Pennsylvania German make, except for molding box,* **1888,** *from Wisconsin, c. 1880*

513

1891

1892

1891–1898 *Pennsylvania German butter molds, revealing individuality in choice of motif—the tulip being predominant—and a confident chip-carving technique. Parallel cuts and nicks added interest to the leaf forms; cross-hatching, as in 1893, produced a patterned surface. Striated cuts to resemble feathery forms contribute to the liveliness of the eagle in 1894. The "hex" sign, a common symbol in the region, appears in 1895* **1899–1905** *Butter molds employing leaf and plant forms, especially the tulip, pineapple, and wheat sheaf, demonstrating strong influence of early settlers from Switzerland—a country of butter makers and woodcarvers. Pennsylvania German, first half of nineteenth century. Photograph*

1893

1894

1895

1896

1897

1898

1899 — 1905

515

1906

1907

1908

1909

1906 *Cast-iron cake or cookie form. Photograph* **1907, 1908** *Semicircular butter molds, one featuring the wheat sheaf, and the other the strawberry* **1909** *Acorn motif combined with striated leaf forms. Photograph* **1910–1913** *Abstract leaf forms with serrated edges and V-cut grooves, designs dictated by the cutting tool*

OVERLEAF: GALLERY OF BUTTER MOLDS *Abstract and hex symbols:* **1916, 1920, 1925, 1931, 1932, 1936;** *acorn:* **1914;** *animals and birds:* **1924, 1927;** *eagles:* **1915, 1918, 1922, 1929, 1933;** *plant forms (including tulip and other flowers),* **1917, 1919, 1921, 1923, 1926, 1928, 1930, 1934, 1935, 1937.** *Figures 1914, 1916–1918, 1920–1923, 1925, 1929, 1933, 1936 from photographs*

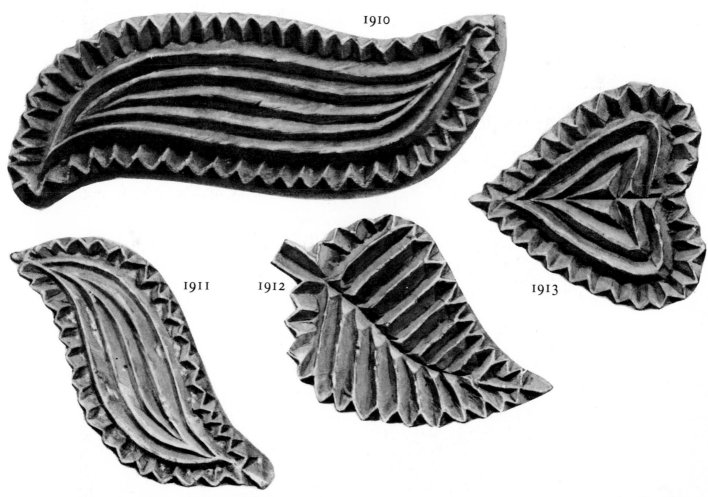

1910

1911   1912   1913

1914　　　　　1915　　　　　1916

1920　　　　　1921　　　　　1922

1926　　　　　1927　　　　　1928

1932　　　　　1933　　　　　1934

1917 1918 1919

1923 1924 1925

1929 1930 1931

1925 1926 1927

519

Bandboxes for Milady's Bonnets

1939

PAPER-COVERED BANDBOXES for ladies and hatboxes for men were lightweight traveling adjuncts that have no exact equivalent today. On the Continent, during the eighteenth century, bandboxes were used to transport and store elaborately starched ruffs and other personal finery. When the ruff lost its appeal and was replaced with the soft lace collar, the bandbox remained a popular and convenient repository. Ladies found it ideal for storing and transporting jewelry, ribbons, artificial flowers, hairpieces, and a myriad of bagatelles. These early boxes were so delicately constructed and fragile that it is surprising that any have survived the century and a half since they were first fashionable in the United States. However, when yesteryear's travelers boarded coaches for perilous overland journeys, they clung tenaciously to their bandboxes, not entrusting them to coachmen; this habit and the fact that many of them were stored in dry attics may account for their survival.

The American bandbox boom started dur-

1938 *Array of bandboxes stacked in a bandbox room, a common adjunct to a millinery shop in cities and large towns during the second quarter of the nineteenth century. Photograph by Einmars J. Mengis, courtesy Shelburne Museum, Shelburne, Vermont* **1939** *Octagonal bandbox, more costly than oval or circular boxes, since the corners had to be especially reinforced*

1940

1941

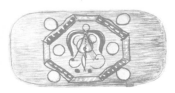

1942

522

ing the second quarter of the nineteenth century, paralleling the development of new means of travel. However, the earliest colored papers for these boxes were probably imported, most of the finely decorated ones coming from France and England. When the box fad gained momentum, the domestic paper printer, using woodblocks, began to design gay and boldly colored papers rather than waiting for the latest imported designs. The earliest use of wallpaper-covered boxes is noted in an advertisement of 1789 by John Fisher of Baltimore, and a fragment of paper from a bandbox owned by Abigail Adams is preserved in the Cooper-Hewitt Museum in New York, noted for its large bandbox collection.

The 1830s and '40s witnessed a steady growth of industrial employment, with women being accepted into the labor force for the first time. This was especially true in New England mill towns, and there was a marked upswing in purchasing power. Girls who had previously not earned anything were now earning two or three dollars per week and thus had the power to purchase such luxury items as bandboxes, which sold for twenty-five or fifty cents each. An enterprising Yankee named Hannah Davis, of Jaffrey, New Hampshire, built a sizable business specializing in the production of bandboxes to cater to this new demand. She started her venture by exchanging boxes for goods and services, but before long it had mushroomed. In order to market large quantities of boxes, she hired a horse and wagon and journeyed to the busy textile towns where the female labor force would buy her out on the spot. For proof of Hannah Davis's business acumen one had only to watch the factory girls as they left the mill towns for their visits home, "riding on the tops of the old stagecoaches . . . with Aunt Hannah's bandboxes around them like satellites around a sun."

With the opening of the Erie Canal in 1825, linking Buffalo and the Great Lakes to the Hudson River and the Atlantic, a great new territory was serviced by canal and river traffic; and only a few years later, in the early thirties, the first iron rails were being laid in various parts of the East. With the availability of these new avenues of transportation, it was not long before many Americans developed a restless desire to travel. American middle-class society decided it was time to visit its historical shrines, to pay homage to patriotic heroes, and to absorb a bit of culture. Hotels and wayside hostelries catering to the new breed of footloose Americans en route to Niagara Falls, Saratoga Springs, the White Mountains, and other well-advertised spots made the journey more enjoyable. Whatever the method of conveyance, leather luggage, carpetbags, and an array of bandboxes were always in evidence, and the bandbox became the symbol of traveling America.

Although some of these boxes were constructed of thin, bent wood, the majority were made of pasteboard, covered with printed designs and lined with newspapers, thus providing an accurate date of manufacture. The

1943

designs were printed from woodblocks, with inks in three or more colors, in the manner of Japanese prints, though more crudely rendered. There was little need, however, for fineness in detailing or fine registry in color printing, since color and gaiety were all that were needed to attract the buyer's eye. The subject matter selected for the coverings varied greatly from floral and geometric patterns to mythological, Classical, historical, and topical scenes. From studying these designs, one gains an excellent insight into social history, for the modes, manners, and events that characterized American taste and temperament are reflected in the decoration of the bandbox.

Prominent design motifs were scenes commemorating historical events. New York's City Hall, Castle Garden, and Merchant's Exchange, as well as hotels and other institutions, were also featured. National figures, including George Washington, William Harrison, Andrew Jackson, and Zachary Taylor, appeared in gay designs. Many fascinating designs give us a picture of what travel was like: by canal boat amid lively country settings; by fully rigged sailing ship, or the newer steamship *Great Western*; by paddlewheel riverboat; by stagecoach at tavern stops; via "The Windmill Railroad"; and via Clayton's Balloon Ascension. Nothing could be more prophetic than an 1840s' design called "A Peep at the Moon," providing a nineteenth-century version of human efforts in outer space.

Romantic and Neoclassical designs ran the gamut and included gardens of love, lute players, Turkish harem scenes, baskets of flowers, garlands of fruit, the four seasons, castles in Spain, children's games, and rural chores. Birds, beasts, and sea serpents supplied a large number of design motifs, with many of the beasts so freely rendered as to defy description. Scenes of the hunt, which included stags at bay, game warden and poacher, lunch in the fields, and the end of the hunt, were perennial favorites. By far the greatest number of motifs were floral and naturalistic. These were derived from contemporary wallpaper patterns and did not require special tailoring. It was merely necessary to cut enough paper to fit around the box and to select appropriate portions for use on the top.

Most bandbox factories were located in the larger cities. New York, Philadelphia, Boston, and Hartford boasted about thirty of these plants. However, the vogue for bandboxes did not last, and most of these factories were out of business by mid-century. The passing of the stagecoach era and the growth in travel by boat and train called for stouter luggage. Hatboxes which could hold half a dozen hats were made of heavier fabric and reinforced construction, and leather luggage, which could better withstand rough handling at depots, was preferred. Thus the bandbox, which had seen its best days, gradually faded into oblivion.

1944

1945

1946

1940 *Hand-painted Pennsylvania German bride-box of thin spruce, bent to shape around a pine base* **1941** *Pennsylvania bandbox with fruit and leaf motifs, early nineteenth century* **1942** *Bandboxes were invariably lined with newspapers, thus enabling us to date them if no date appears on the box* **1943** *Gentleman's hatbox covered with printed design, c. 1830–40* **1944** *Floral-print wallpaper used for box covering* **1945** *Wallpaper for box covering, featuring a chariot drawn by griffons, c. 1830* **1946** *Box paper with rural scene including church, homes, and birds, c. 1830–40* **1947** *Box paper displays Fire Engine Number 13 in action. Printed in Philadelphia, c. 1831–36*

1947

1948

1949

1950

1951

1952

1953

524

1954

1955

1948–1958 *Paper coverings for bandboxes were either all-over patterns, usually floral, or scenic designs, in which case the motif was tailored to fit around the box. The former were more easily adapted to the box surface, being used for both sides and top with only the addition of an edging on the lid. Scenic designs were printed on a long strip of paper from wooden blocks and then glued on, with the seam at the back. Typical scenic designs include: "Windmill Railroad," 1949, commemorating the advent of the railroad (c. 1830); scenes of rural life, 1950 (c. 1830), and 1957 (c. 1835); 1956, log cabin with riverboat and sunburst (c. 1840); and 1958, a handsome public building, here an asylum for the deaf and dumb*

Overleaf: GALLERY OF BANDBOXES. *Designs of Classical or mythological origin:* **1961, 1970, 1970;** *transportation scenes:* **1960, 1968, 1973;** *eagle:* **1967;** *floral and decorative:* **1959, 1976, 1978;** *historical:* **1963, 1975;** *pastoral:* **1962, 1964, 1965, 1969, 1971, 1974, 1977;** *scenic:* **1966**

1956

1957

1958

525

1959

1960

1961

1964

1965

1966

1969

1970

1971

526 1974

CASTLE GARDEN.

1975

1976

1962

1963

1967

SANDY - HOOK

1968

1972

1973

1977

1978   **527**

Hand-hooked for the Home

1980

MAKING RUGS from scraps, strings, and bits of wool and yarn woven together according to personal taste was one of the crafts allocated to the household. The rugs showed the creative instinct of the cottage dweller, and for the long hours of painstaking detail there was a noble satisfaction when the final stitches were put in place.

Experts seem to agree that the art of hooking rugs is an American development, originating in the northeastern section of New England and in the neighboring maritime provinces of Canada. It was brought to these shores by the Scandinavians. The French, English, Welsh, and Scots adopted it during the latter part of the eighteenth century. A long period of gestation occurred; few examples appeared much before 1820. The technique of hooking may be traced to the old method of "thrumming," that is, "of fastening thrums, short cut-off pieces of yarn or cloth, to a background of fabric so as to give a heavy nap. This was usually accomplished by poking the thrums through holes or mesh, so that the two ends showed on one side." The background material was either homespun linen, factory-woven cotton, or burlap. Cloth strips were cut from leftover woolens or scraps, and a metal hook was used to draw the strips through the background fabric into loops. The loops were either cut or left uncut and their length determined

1979 *Universally acknowledged to be one of the rarest of all early American handmade carpets, the famous Caswell rug at the Metropolitan Museum of Art in New York City is an object lesson in native handcrafts. It was made in Castleton, Vermont, in 1835 by Zeruah Higley Guernsey and became known as the "Caswell Carpet" because of her subsequent marriage to Mr. Caswell in 1846. Often referred to as the "Blue Cat Rug" because of a whimsical book about it, it is made up of numerous squares embroidered in what was called "double Kensington stitch," on firm homespun. Its floral motifs, birds and cats, fruits and foliage reveal an exuberant spirit. The portion shown here represents about a quarter of the rug; some two years were spent in the making, from shearing the wool to the dyeing and final embroidery. Its design is a treasure trove of homely inspiration in the best native tradition of needlecraft* 1980 *The bridal couple, only one of almost eighty squares, is a complete, self-contained gem in the Caswell carpet, one of many*

the softness of the pile.

Early hooked rugs show an engaging naiveté of design. With no academic art training, rugmakers ventured into a field involving artistic decisions. The rug area became a canvas on which design, form, color, and texture were combined with skillful needlework to produce a picture. The designer was called on to exercise taste at every turn, a test of blending artistry with manual dexterity.

In the making of hooked rugs, the housewife could select from an abundant range of subject matter. Animals, birds, and buildings required a sense of proportion and scale; geometric and floral designs did not present such problems and thus dominated rug decoration. In the 1850s a rapidly growing interest in rugmaking developed. This became so intense in the East that an enterprising Yankee named E. S. Frost saw vast commercial possibilities in supplying designs.

Frost, a returning Union soldier who had been wounded in the war, was forced to assume an outdoor life for reasons of health. Working as a tin peddler, he soon noticed that his patrons on farms and in New England villages were busily making hooked rugs for their homes. They asked for rug designs, which he and his wife supplied from their own handiwork. Frost shrewdly reasoned that the production of such designs by stenciling could lead to greater sales. His ingenuity was evident from the start: in order to produce a stencil he flattened an old copper boiler and fashioned his stencil outlines with a cold chisel and file, and then printed the design on burlap. His contribution to the hooking of rugs was in the making of patterns, many of which became available to workers throughout the country. He popularized a rural art form for which women of all areas had long shown an aptitude. Whereas Frost's designs were welcomed by many women, mass-production unfortunately robbed them of originality, spontaneity, and individual interpretation.

The art was carried a step further along commercial lines when the demand for wool strips led to their production by factory methods. The frugal housewife no longer had

to salvage cast-off garments and patiently shred them into usable strips. If anything, the ease with which one could purchase woolen strips helped speed the making of more rugs by more housewives.

The life of a hooked rug is short; its longevity depends on the base through which the strands are pulled. Antique rugs were hooked into a background of linen or hemp sacking, stronger than jute or burlap. The linen or hemp was then stretched on a tambour, or wooden frame, and the pattern marked with ink or charcoal. Rugs which covered the floor were necessarily short-lived; others designed as bedspreads were subjected to less wear. Several prominent museum pieces of this type date from the late eighteenth century.

In rugmaking the designs and patterns may run the gamut from the abstract and geometric, and the floral and naturalistic, to the pictorial and illustrative, such as scenic, historical, and patriotic bits of Americana. In the first category there are basketweaves, blocks, frets, wavy lines, zigzags, and the guilloche (interlaced bands, the openings of which are filled with round ornaments). Variants and combinations of these—in color, design, and juxtaposition—depended on the designer's versatility. Where the accumulation of cloth remnants did not permit the matching of colors, the crazy-quilt approach gave free rein to the creator's imagination. Mosaic work, inch squares, and the popular quilt motifs offered a wide choice of patterns, depending on shading and color variations. Geometric shapes—circle, square, triangle, diamond, and star—presented numerous possibilities.

Floral motifs, in formal or informal arrangements, loose sprays, garlands, and festoons used as either central medallions or border offered almost unlimited potential for originality. The floral bouquet has been the dominant design theme of thousands of hooked rugs, and the free interpretation of the floral forms often resulted in young, fresh designs. Many hundred-year-old hooked rugs look as if they have just emerged from the studios or workshops of today's avant-garde artists.

1981

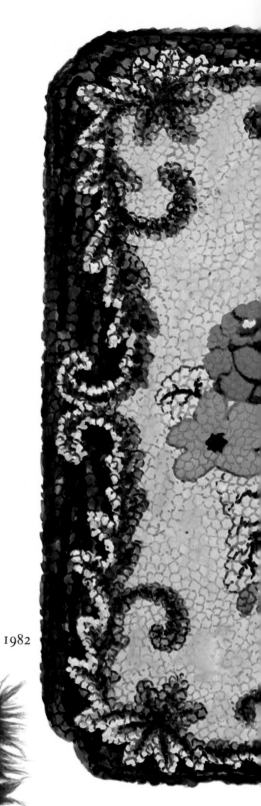

1982

1983

1984

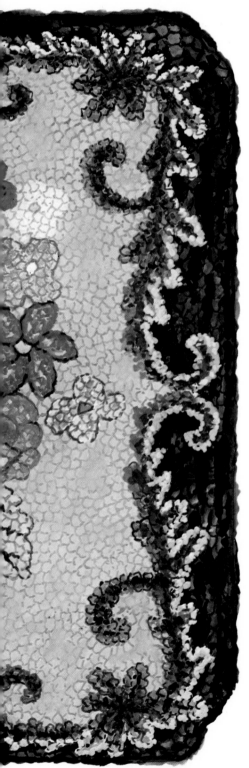

1985

1981–1985 *Florals are favorites. The universal appeal of flowers, their profusion of color, and the ease with which they can be drawn and hooked account for floral popularity in the design of hooked rugs. The more successful rugs involve a schematic plan such as those in which an outer arrangement forms a border, as in* **1982** *and* **1985,** *or a series of concentric ovals, as in* **1981**

1986

1988

1987

1989

1990

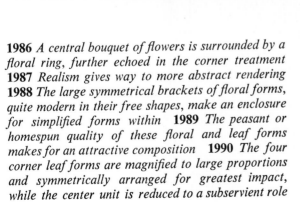

1986 *A central bouquet of flowers is surrounded by a floral ring, further echoed in the corner treatment* **1987** *Realism gives way to more abstract rendering* **1988** *The large symmetrical brackets of floral forms, quite modern in their free shapes, make an enclosure for simplified forms within* **1989** *The peasant or homespun quality of these floral and leaf forms makes for an attractive composition* **1990** *The four corner leaf forms are magnified to large proportions and symmetrically arranged for greatest impact, while the center unit is reduced to a subservient role*

1991

1992

1993

1994

1991 *In the field of geometric design the simplest motif involves a series of small squares repeated with variations in color treatment* **1992** *A combination of straight-line borders, cut corners, and oval center-piece* **1993** *An original scroll design in which opposite curves from a floral center create counterbalance* **1994** *Borders of straight lines and corner pieces contrast with a scalloped enclosure*

537

1995   1996

1997

538

1998

1999

2000

1995 *A simple and honest composition in which horse and fencing tell the story* **1996** *Eagle and shield are loosely rendered, with stars and circles adding extra decoration, c. 1800* **1997** *Pair of roosters framed in a charming border of leaf-clad serpentine vines. Made in Pennsylvania* **1998** *The dog is rendered in a flat tone, with no attempt at anatomical details* **1999** *Many birds, hens, horses, stars, and flowers blend into an unusually pleasant composition* **2000** *Two elephants, a house, circles, and patches of bushes are combined with originality into a crazy-quilt arrangement, 1897*

Heirlooms from Old Looms

2002

THOSE WHO SPIN and weave by hand find themselves part of the continuity of history, as textile processes are among the oldest and most important inventions of ancient man. To this continuous record, the women of America have made a lasting contribution. From the earliest days to well into the nine-teenth century, Colonial women, starting with the shearings of sheep and the cuttings of flax, wove the coarse fibers into articles of beauty and utility.

Hand spinning is the process of converting fibers into a form of yarn, thread, or string. The best-known animal fibers in Colonial America came from sheep and rabbit fur. The

2001 *Eighteenth-century loom on which the home weaver made her homespun bedspreads, cover-lets, floor runners, and other materials was a crudely built affair, yet substantial enough to withstand the continual stresses of the weaving process. The professional weaver, working in his shop, used the same general type of loom. His, however, was equipped with more harnesses—from four to as many as twelve. Photograph courtesy Colonial Williamsburg* **2002** *Ever-popular rose motif in symmetrical design scheme, c. 1840* **2003, 2004** *Woven on Jacquard looms, these coverlets are typical; large central area carries borders on four sides of the bedspreads, c. 1835–40*

2003　　　2004

2005

2006

2007

2008

only vegetable fibers grown were flax and hemp. Yarn was a loosely spun fiber, while thread designated a fiber more tightly spun and twisted. More accurately, the product of man's earliest attempts to make thread may be described as string, which resulted from separating fibers with the fingers and twisting them into the strength or thickness needed. Without spinning there could be no weaving; without fibers there could be no spinning. Fortunately, early laws produced an abundance of the basics for spinning and weaving. In Massachusetts, for example, an ordinance of the 1640s made it compulsory for each Colonial family to spin a given quantity of yarn every year or face a penalty of heavy fines. Growing flax and raising sheep were urgent economic necessities. At home the making of cloth was both essential and inevitable. Sir Henry Moore, governor of New York in the 1760s, wrote: "Every house swarms with children who are set to work as soon as they are able to Spin and Card, and as every family is furnished with a Loom, Itinerant Weavers then put the finishing hand on the work."

In every Colonial home there was the sound of the whirling spinning wheel. To prepare wool for the high, or "walking," wheel on which it was spun into yarn, the heavy winter fleece of the sheep was processed through an arduous succession of cleaning, carding, and combing. The spinning was done on a large wheel; flax was spun on a smaller wheel, also known as a Saxon wheel, a tiring chore often performed by the man of the house. The desired flax fibers were separated by soaking, pounding, scraping, or combing. After the woolen yarn was spun, it was wound into hanks on a wooden frame called a niddy nod-dy, about two feet long.

The large loom on which the yarns or threads were woven into cloth was usually the work of the local carpenter. It occupied a space in the attic, a separate shed, or a special loom room. When space was at a premium the contrivance, sometimes built by the master of the house, was placed in the kitchen, where it occupied about the area of a four-poster bed. The mysteries of weaving—of warp and woof, of heddle and shuttle—were carried on for long hours in order to produce the simple fabrics needed to clothe the members of the family, or to provide the basic material for all bedding and coverlets.

The simplest loom consisted of a frame into which pegs or nails were driven at top or bottom. The warp threads, stretched vertically, were the strongest, and usually made of a better grade of thread than the crosswise threads, called the woof or weft. The warp threads were fastened on the loom like strings on a harp; the woof threads were then worked in and out or across with the fingers, a needle, or a shuttle. In a more advanced type of loom there was a mechanism which separated the warp threads. This action formed a shed, or V-shaped trough, through which the shuttle containing the weft thread was passed from side to side. The warp threads of the trough then recrossed each other to make a new shed. Each time the warp crossed, it locked and held the weft thread just placed in the trough. On some hand looms and on all mechanized looms, the shuttle carrying the weft thread was attached to a spring or propelled by one so that it was shot through, or seemed to fly through the shed instead of being pushed through. This was a fly-shuttle loom, on which it was possible to weave much faster.

The weaving of patterns, in contrast to simple unpatterned fabrics, called for more than two sets of heddles and harnesses and threads of different colors. The foot loom, introduced during the early seventeenth century, had various pedals with which to work the crossbars, thus leaving the hands free to manipulate the shuttle. The draw loom was invented to produce intricate patterns. Here the many sets of heddles were operated by cords pulled by a small boy, who had to swing about precariously, monkey-fashion, atop the large loom. In 1784 Edmund Cartwright invented the power loom, which performed all the operations of moving the heddles and shuttle in any manner desired. This English clergyman, with no knowledge of weaving and very little of mechanics, made a major contribution to lessening the burdens of the tedious hand operations.

The coloring of the fabrics and yarns used by Colonial women was often done by the overworked housewife, who used dyes concocted from various plants in her garden. Red came in various shades and hues as produced by the pokeberry, dogwood, sumac, cherry, and bloodroot; the latter was a favorite with the Indians, who used it to paint their faces and decorate their clothing. Orange came from bittersweet and sassafras bark, yellow from onionskins. Blue, always a popular color in Colonial needlework, usually came from the

2009

indigo plant, either grown domestically in the South or imported. Green was derived from the pressed blossoms of the goldenrod; purple came from blueberries and iris petals. "Butternut brown," the term invariably used to describe the early settlers' garments, was obtained from the bark of the butternut tree. Thus, with the exception of indigo, practically all colors came from indigenous plants. Indigo, a permanent dark blue, was a perennial favorite, especially for coverlets and linsey-woolsey. It was in such demand that special "indigo peddlers" earned their living selling it from door to door.

In the early Colonial period, all cloth required by the average family was made by the housewife, with the help of the children. Later, a great deal of weaving was carried on by traveling journeymen. (The term derived from the fact that the "journey" represented a day's work; in other words, these craftsmen were paid a day's wages.) They relieved the housewife of her tedious weaving and also helped somewhat in pottery making, carpentry, tailoring, and various other crafts. They were an enlivening influence throughout the Colonies, and were depended upon to supply vivid gossip about neighbors an other places. Finally, the weaving shop and the professional weaver became a part of each community, and women ordered fabrics from the weaver though they still furnished him with yarn.

2010

2011

2005–2012 *Details selected at random from woven coverlets show many favorite motifs: conventionalized tree and gateposts, basket of fruit and flowers, lion, eagle with motto, horses, tree, plowman from coverlet called Farmer's Fancy, and eagle with stars*

2012

2013

The patterns for weaving, sometimes recorded on paper, were called "drafts," and were passed from family to family, generation to generation, and town to town. These patterns, like folk stories and legends, were modified gradually by the more creative persons until the originals were changed beyond recognition—a process of evolution common to all arts and crafts. Originally these drafts were brought to this country by immigrant weavers from Britain, Scotland, Germany, and Scandinavia, where weaving and needle-craft were particularly strong. Except to an expert weaver, the elaborate written instructions were meaningless. To the weaver they spelled out the rhythm and pattern one feels in musical compositions.

Handwoven coverlets, whether made at home by members of the family or by the professional or journeyman weaver, may be classified into several categories, according to type and technique involved. These are, in order of their complexity, the overshot, also known as float weave; the summer-and-winter weave; the block or double-weave geometric; and the so-called Jacquard weave.

2014

The overshot weave was one of the earliest and was of three-thread construction. There was one warp, usually a two-ply linen or cotton; a binder weft, in the same material as the warp but often a single ply and slightly smaller in grist; and the pattern weft, which was a colored woolen yarn. The pattern of the over-shot was three-toned: dark, light, and a half-tone. The dark spots or blocks forming the real design were composed of several wefts, where they overlay the basic linen or cotton ground. These are called floats, skips, or overshots. Most frequently this type of coverlet is in a four-block pattern. The overshot design has produced some of our finest and most interesting pure geometrics.

Coverlets woven in the summer-and-winter weave were so named because of their reversible two-toned pattern. They did not have as wide a distribution as the overshot weave and were to be found primarily in the Pennsylvania and New York areas, brought over originally, it is said, by the German immigrants of the early eighteenth century. Because of the intricacy of the patterns, the looms on which these coverlets were woven used eight or sixteen harnesses and called for expert weaving techniques. Indigo blue was favored, contrasting white or natural linen with the dark blue motifs; the design which appeared in blue on one side was reversed and appeared in white on the opposite side. The pattern was still geometric but more intricate than the overshot. The threads were bound together tightly, and it was structurally sounder than the overshot weave. This type of coverlet disappeared at an early date because of the extreme complexity of its execution.

The professional weaver, whether he was an itinerant journeyman or conducted his affairs in his own shop, was responsible for the type of coverlet called block or double-woven geometric, since an elaborate loom was required. These block coverlets, produced mainly from 1820 to 1840, were often the work of German or Scottish weavers, who had pattern books in their native lands featuring the designs; a few of these books were brought over to America. For coloration, they followed the popular style of that day, favoring indigo blue woolen yarn, usually supplied by the

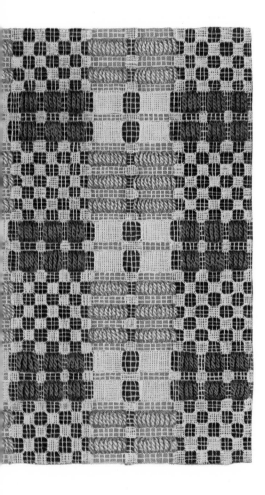

2013–2015 *Pure geometric patterns result in an infinite number of variations as produced in the overshot technique of weaving. Dark wool lies on the light warp, skipping a number of threads; hence the name "overshot." Heavy weft threads and thin warp produce an uneven surface, so that there are textural as well as pattern variants*

2015

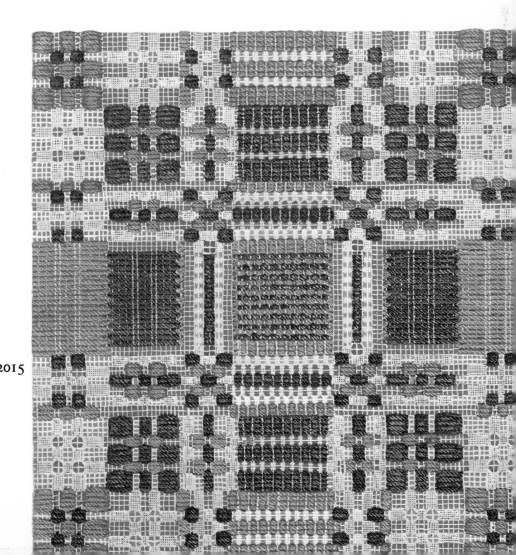

2016

2017

housewife, combined with a factory-made, natural-colored cotton yarn which the weaver supplied. Red and blue yarns were sometimes used together, giving a patriotic aspect to the coverlet.

The fancy flowered coverlets, the Jacquard, include some of the most magnificent designs in the field of American weaving. These first appeared around 1820, particularly in New York and Pennsylvania, later spreading westward into Ohio, Kentucky, Indiana, and Illinois. It is the opinion of most students that the early examples were produced by professional weavers on the draw loom, while later ones were made on hand-operated looms with the aid of the Jacquard attachment. Featured in this general type of coverlet was a wide variety of floral motifs, employed both in diapered arrangements and freely chosen groupings of roses and tulips, laurel, and other leafy ornaments. The borders on the drop sides of these spreads were elaborate and striking, utilizing many finely rendered patriotic motifs. There were stars, shields, eagles, ribbons, mottoes, and figures of George Washington, as well as Mount Vernon and the

2018

546

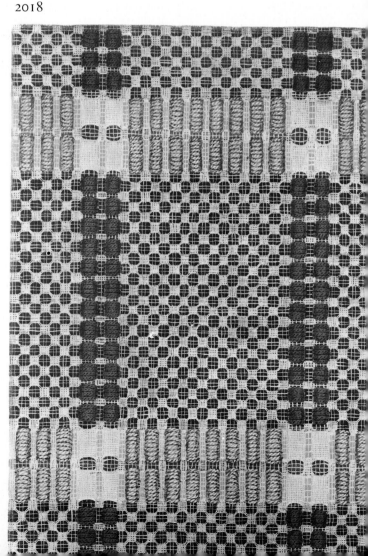

Capitol. Accompanying these were strong chauvinistic urgings: "United We Stand, Divided We Fall," "Under this eagle, we prosper," "Agriculture & Manufactures Are the Foundation of our Independence." It was customary for the weaver to place the date and his name, or that of the individual for whom the coverlet was made, in a corner of the border. In many cases, both names were included, as well as the town or county where the coverlet was woven. This invaluable imprimatur has eliminated all guesswork about the coverlet's provenance.

2016–2021 *Woolen coverlets woven by women from Maine to Georgia and west into Indiana and Illinois were given names as picturesque as the diversified regions in which they were made. Some small idea may be gained by listing just a few: Indian March, Braddock's Defeat, Cuckoo's Nest, Maid of Orleans, Bonaparte's Retreat, Broken Snowballs, and so on. Names were changed to suit the temperament and dialect of each region. A pattern called Sea Star or Seashell in one part of Tennessee became Isle of Patmos and Gentleman's Fancy in another. When such liberties are taken and such differences occur, it is impossible to identify any overshot pattern by a specific name*

2019

2020

2021

547

2022

2026

2022–2029 *Coverlets made from Jacquard weaves are usually reversible, one side light and the other dark. The weaver's name was often woven into one corner, with his address and the date. If the coverlet was made to order, the*

548

customer's name would be included. Motifs were many and included tulips, hearts, roses, stars, birds, peacocks, and the eagle. These designs, except **2026**, are from coverlets woven in Pennsylvania from 1832 to 1846

2030

2031

2030–2037 *Patriotic motifs appear on many coverlets; the eagle is always present, sometimes accompanied by stars, a figure of Washington, or slogans and mottoes,* **2033, 2035, 2036.** *The well-known Boston Town pattern appears in* **2030,** *with yet another adaptation of this in* **2034.** *Florals, paired peacocks, and rose clusters are shown in* **2031, 2034,** *and* **2037,** *dated 1840 to 1858*

2034

2035

2032

2033

2036

AGRICUL
TURE&MAN
UFACTURES
ARETHEFOUND
ATIONOF
OURINDE
PENDENCE
JULY4.
1823

2037

EMAN
UEL
ETTING
ER
ARONS
BURG

1 8 4 0

2038

2038 The Quilting Party, *painted by an unknown artist, c. 1840–50. It pictures an important social event; the final sewing into place of the many blocks and friendship pieces of the quilt. It was an occasion for festive animation, a time for the gathering of young and old in meetinghouse or schoolroom. Courtesy the Abby Aldrich Rockefeller Folk Art Collection, Williamsburg, Virginia* **2039** *The spinning wheel was a fixture in every Colonial home. After the winter fleece was sheared from the sheep's back, it was processed through many stages of cleaning, carding, and combing. Then the loose fibers were deftly twisted at the wheel into continuous strands for weaving* **2040** *Quilts were made up of units like this, sewn together for a large bedspread. This is a mosaic calico piece, made in 1810 near Corning, New York*

The Quilting Bee

2039

2040

No WOMAN EVER quilted alone if she could help it. The quilting bee provided an opportunity for women to gather and gossip. When the bee was held in a grange hall or church vestry room, as many as twelve women could attend. Usually, however, the number of guests was limited to seven, who, with the hostess, made up two quilting frames, the equivalent of two tables of bridge. Good quilting in earlier times was a social requisite, and it behooved the ambitious woman to be an expert with her needle.

The quilting frame was a simple homemade affair, much like today's curtain stretcher. The frame held the patchwork securely so that the decorative top quilt, the inner lining of cotton or wool, and the backing could be sewn together. The quilt was "rolled" from each of the four sides until the center was reached and the quilt completed. Often several quilts were finished in a single session which lasted all day. These sessions ended with a supper of roast chicken or turkey. The men usually arrived in time for the feast, after which there followed singing and dancing. Like so many well-

2041

2042

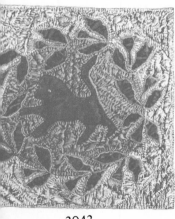

2043

established rural customs—apple-paring bees, corn-husking contests, and barn-raising parties—the traditional quilting party carried with it all of the social amenities. The event marked the successful completion of many months of laborious handiwork.

Several forms of coverlet were derived from European backgrounds; they followed traditional patterns and displayed regional variations. The patchwork quilt, however, made from cotton, calico, and silk fragments, was a distinctly American invention—an economic necessity. The need to salvage every scrap of material and to piece these scraps together to form attractive patterns of beauty and ingenuity constituted an original folk art. Whereas affluent women could import bolts of English materials or patronize specialty shops, those with limited resources had to improvise, making patterns from their carefully hoarded remnants. These are the prized heirlooms in today's needlecraft collections.

There were many techniques of quilting. Pieced or patchwork quilts, first made in the latter part of the eighteenth century, are those in which the patterns follow geometrical designs—mosaics laboriously contrived of hundreds of small squares and diamonds. At first these small pieces were sewn directly onto a fabric backing, but by 1800 women had developed a more practical method and made the quilt parts in block units, each a portion of the overall design scheme. These blocks were pieced together in rows or diagonal bands, with strips of latticework or alternate white blocks between them. When plain white blocks were used as alternate separations, they were also elaborately quilted.

The patterns for quilting were indicated on the material by pencil, chalk, or charcoal, depending on the color of the fabric. Since it was easier to seam two straight edges, the geometric pattern evolved along straight lines running laterally or diagonally or emanating radially from a central point. Thousands of designs resulted and each had its own fanciful name. Often a single pattern was given different names in widely separated regions, nor was it uncommon to find the same name applied to several unrelated designs. For example, Bear's Paw in Ohio, or Duck Feet in

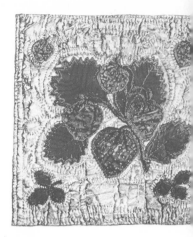

2044

2045

2046

2041

2042

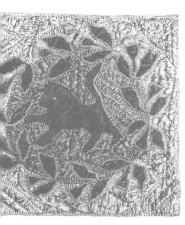

2043

the Mud on Long Island, became Hand of Friendship in Pennsylvania. There are star patterns named for every state in the Union derived from the basic Star of Bethlehem, an eight-pointed star found in numerous interpretations. Entire volumes have been devoted to describing these quilts with quaint and charming names, which included such whimsies as Hen and Chickens, Flying Geese, Stepping Stones, Birds in the Window, Delectable Mountains, Rose of Sharon, Flying Dutchman, Cats and Mice, Turkey Tracks, Jacob's Ladder, Drunkard's Path, Road to California, Robbing Peter to Pay Paul, Young Man's Fancy, Philadelphia Pavement, Jack-in-the-Pulpit, Chimney Swallows, Hearts and Gizzards, and Rolling Stone.

The patchwork counterpanes of the nineteenth century were usually made of solid-colored or printed cotton fabrics, alternating with white for contrast. A favorite color scheme combined turkey red with green cotton, appliquéd on white. Quilted stitching on the white background—perhaps in a lozenge diaper pattern or in squared criss-crossing—provided textural interest to the plain areas. No matter how elaborate the patchwork designs, the stitching of the quilted portions greatly enhanced the attractiveness of the spread. This was the gauge by which quilts were judged in contests. Quilting rather than piecing required the highest degree of needlework. Some women were superior in cutting and sewing the patches, but could never quite master the quilting techniques, which required true ambidexterity. The ultimate in skillful needlework often appears on the all-white counterpanes, where, in the absence of color and bright designs, only the delicate finesse of expert needlecraft is evident.

Toward the middle of the nineteenth century, the social aspects of quilting and the popularity of quilting parties resulted in group

2041–2046 *Quilt blocks were a practical solution in the making of a large spread; the small panels were easily manageable and could be assembled at the quilting bee, if necessary. It was the custom for makers of separate "friendship blocks" to sign their names to the pieces, an added sentimental remembrance for the quilt owner. Dated 1870*

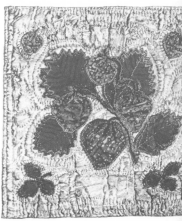

2044

2045

2046

2047

2047, 2048 *The Star of Bethlehem, an intriguing pattern involving difficult piecing and endless patience, has had great attraction for oldtime quilt makers. The making of the star called for thousands of diamond-shaped pieces of chintz, calico, and copperplate fabrics, carefully chosen for color blending and harmony. The eight-pointed star had four corners and four triangles to be designed and pieced according to personal whims, but the dominant motif of the Star held real fascination*

2048

needlecraft for the making of signature, friendship, autograph, bride, album, and presentation quilts. Each quilt was generally intended for a special person or special occasion and conveyed the sentiments of the well-wishers. The donor or originator of the quilt planned the basic outline and assigned separate blocks to friends in the group. When the blocks were completed, the group gathered for a sociable afternoon to assemble the quilt, with its embroidered signatures or good wishes. The honored guest might have been a minister or his wife, an esteemed citizen, or a bride. The variety of designs and expressions of a dozen or more women produced a most interesting memento. The interrelationship of the separate pieces created an ensemble of rare loveliness, quite revealing as an exercise in original folk arts and crafts.

The technique of producing appliqué quilt-

2049

2050

2049 *Quilt involving twenty-five squares proved a challenging invitation for the quilt maker to express her decorative talents* **2050** *Sixteen component floral units, bordered by a swag motif with tulips, show a genuine sense of design and originality* **2051** *Appliqué motifs consist of red flowers and green leaves on white muslin. The central motif of hearts forms a star, in turn encircled by two whirling wheels of leaf and floral forms, typically Pennsylvania German, 1848* **2052** *Friendship quilt in which the outer squares are cut into halves as an interesting variant* **2053** *Floral wreaths and plants decorate this quilt, including a lemon and an orange tree flanking the central diamond, which is a pictorial motif of the owner's house and garden* **2054** *Baskets of flowers and posies of gay-colored chintzes are further embellished by gracefully twisting vines* **2055** *Appliquéd units of calico and chintz are composed of large, flat masses simply outlined* **2056** *Mexican Rose pattern is executed in brilliant red, yellow, and green on white field of shells and feathers*

ing differed somewhat from that of patchwork, though often the two methods were combined in a single spread. Strictly speaking, patchwork produced a mosaic textile; appliqué was constructed from individual pieces which were sewn to a background fabric. The central part of the design sometimes contained a large single unit like the Tree of Life. More often, a smaller unit was repeated in diaper fashion four, nine, or sixteen times to cover the quilt area. Chintz or other printed cotton was cut up to form the decorative elements and added lively interest to the plain fabrics. The Rose of Sharon was a design favorite as it was a

2051

2052

2053

2054

bride's quilt, the final piece in her hope chest. The beauty of this design echoed the tender good wishes of those who made the quilt and presented it to the bride.

By 1850 appliquéd patchwork had become so elaborate that it was too precious for everyday use. The quilts became counterpanes or showpieces, ceasing to serve as coverlets. The pristine condition of many outstanding examples testifies to their limited use and these owe their survival to that custom.

A study of the more intricate appliquéd quilts will show why years often went into their making. Smaller units like the Orange Peel, Caesar's Crown, Basket of Tulips, Little Red Schoolhouse, or, for that matter, any unit repeated forty or fifty times for the quilt's central area involved the most work. The completion of such a quilt could easily have taken hundreds of hours. During the Civil War and the period that followed, there was a decline in quilt making. The introduction of machinery in the textile industry eliminated the need for such tedious needlework. The friendship quilt and its sentiments, along with woven coverlets and appliquéd masterpieces, became treasured heirlooms, testaments to a folk art that has all but vanished.

2055

2056

2057

2057 *Floral wreath, horn of plenty, and basket of flowers are further embellished with the introduction of the flag and eagle, pineapple, Bible, doves, and lyre—a complete grammar of decoration
expressing the sentimental lore of midnineteenth-century life* 2058–2063 *Squares of calico show
the simple elements of which large spreads were composed* 2064 *Floral wreaths, always, popular,
enabled the quilt maker to express her love of color and imagination in a garden fantasy* 2065
Basket of flowers, a perennial favorite in patterns, arranged with geometric simplicity

2058

2059

2060

2061

2064

2065

2062

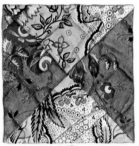

2063

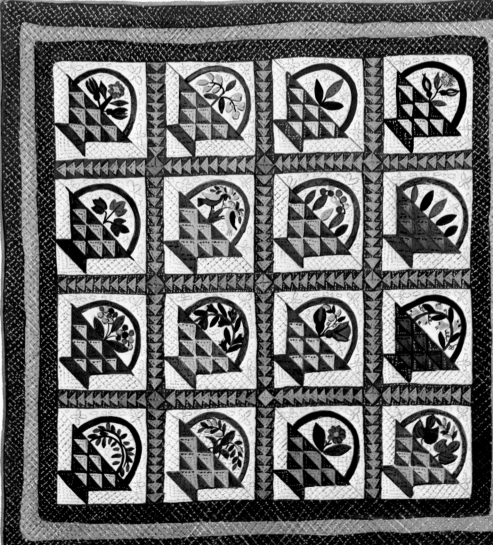

2066

2067

2066 *Basket of flowers, in appliqué, is outlined in quilting on white muslin background, 1820* 2067 *Appliquéd motifs in flat, solid pieces—reds, greens, and browns* 2068 *Morning-glory design in padded appliqué, with festooned border; quilted eagle on white, c. 1857* 2069 *Symmetrical flower-and-stem pattern in an all-over arrangement, within festooned*

2068

2069

2070

border **2070** *Padded quilting creates low relief in monochrome* **2071** *Sawtooth pattern called Delectable Mountains, with border of eagles, 1810* **2072** *Patchwork quilt of sunburst design, within border of swags and bow knots, c. 1840. From photographs except 2066, 2071, and 2072*

2071   2072

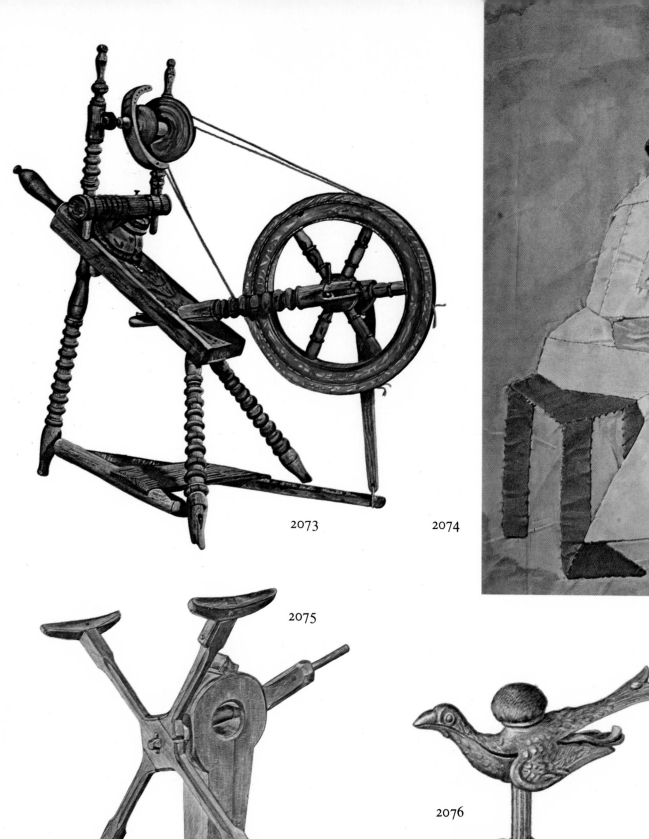

2073　　　　　　　　2074

2075

2076

2077

2078

2079

2073–2079 *Many accessories were needed to speed the work of spinning, weaving, and sewing. The spinning wheel,* **2703,** *is an essential prototype, varying only slightly in different models. The spinning reel,* **2075,** *was used for winding yarn into hanks. Among the quaint and decorative sewing objects,* **2076,** *the sewing bird of cast brass was used as a clamp for the edge of a table. The pads were for pincushions, while the springed beak could hold a piece of cloth till needed. The sewing machines shown,* **2077** *(1860),* **2078** *(1867), and* **2079** *(1858), are but a few of the dozens of new ones patented between the years 1850 and 1870. They were all of cast-iron construction, often gilded and decorated as if to apologize for the intrusion of a piece of mechanism into the Victorian household. The appliquéd piece, called "Gossips,"* **2074,** *introduces a humorous commentary in needlecraft by Eunice W. Cook, of Vermont*

566

2080

2081

2082

2083

2084

2085

2086

2080–2089 *Sewing tables, or work tables, as they were called, were made in a great number of styles. The delicately reeded model in the Sheraton style, **2080**, has a small top drawer and large compartment below; its top lifts at the front. The walnut sewing table, **2081**, with cabriole legs, is dated 1750–79. On the skirted models, a sliding shelf pulls out to expose the bag, **2085**, while the top sides lift up, **2086**. Sewing stands and spool racks are shown in **2082–84**. Sewing birds of wood and brass are to be seen in **2087–89***

2087

2088

2089

Teach Me To Feel Another We
To Hide The Fault I See
The Mercy I To Others Show
That Mercy Shows To Me

Priscilla Nelsons Sampler Wrought In The
14 Year Of Her Age January 23 1837

A B C D E F G H I J K
L M N O P Q R S T
U V W X Y Z

Sentimental Samplers

2091

T HERE IS a fascinating naiveté about folksy samplers. Students of early needlework have found a world of whimsy and frivolity in the untutored expressions of young girls exhibiting their sewing skills, displaying their knowledge of the Bible, or sharing their homespun philosophy. These pieces of handiwork became a part of a girl's dowry, traveled with her throughout life, and were willed to a favorite relative.

Before a young girl attended school to learn the three Rs, she was expected to be proficient in plain sewing, embroidery, and cross-stitching. She helped her mother with hems and seams, and filled in with minor needlecraft chores. At school she had rigid lessons in all techniques of needlework. By the time she was eight she was ready to start displaying her mastery of difficult stitches, her printing and handwriting, her sense of rhythm and composition on a canvas. The sampler was a rou-

2090 *The sampler provided a young girl with a great opportunity for self-expression. This exercise demonstrates her ability to handle the alphabet, adding a bit of doggerel and a pictorial scene—all enclosed in a decorative floral border, made in 1837* **2091** *Stitching embroidery on coarse buckram or canvas imparted some geometrical limitations that added charm and style to the sampler*

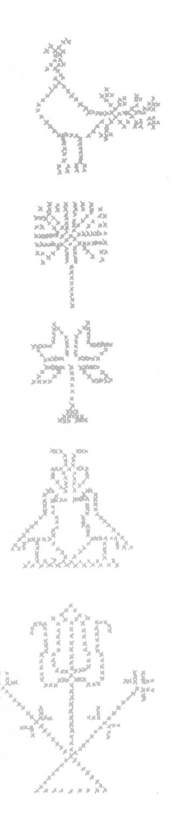

tine part of every Pilgrim daughter's upbringing, proof of her spelling ability and her parents' spiritual influence.

One of the earliest extant samplers, dated 1653, was the work of Lora Standish, daughter of Captain Miles Standish. Very few seventeenth-century samplers survive today, but we have much evidence of diligent handicraft from the 1750s until about 1840. The first samplers were on long strips of handwoven linen about eight inches wide, and the alphabet was almost invariably the dominating element. Fruits and flower sprays were used as borders or to fill in a short line. Horizontal bands made full use of vines and serpentine scrolls interspersed with stylized units. Birds, animals, figures, and architectural facades served as main themes, sometimes dominating the lettering. As time passed, the emphasis changed and alphabetical arrangements were supplanted by essentially pictorial formats, especially in the more ambitious efforts of older children and adults. Beginners had to stick to their ABCs until they acquired proficiency in both composition and needlecraft. Favorite motifs included the Tree of Life, fleur-de-lis, trefoil, Indian pink, pineapple, strawberry, acorn, and various common tree forms.

Typical eighteenth-century samplers, most of which were made in New England, show several different styles of the alphabet, sometimes as many as five. Roman letters were common. A more florid or cursive set of capital letters sometimes preceded those; then, for greater variety, an alphabet of script letters followed. Numerals were sometimes shown if a line needed filling. The most important test of mastery of letter forms came with the handling of a motto or inscription, the fillip that gave expression to the creative spirit and added a literary touch.

Quotations from the Scriptures, the Lord's Prayer, the Apostles' Creed, and the Ten Commandments were used frequently. Other verses dealt with themes of love and friendship, maidenhood and chastity, death and

sorrow. Late nineteenth-century samplers follow the prevailing sentiments of the Victorian era, elevating the sanctity of the home, the sweetness of friendship, familial unity, and heavenly protection. Mottoes could be sternly moralistic or graciously benevolent: "Give us this day our daily bread"; "Thou, O God, seest all"; and "Remember the Sabbath day to keep it Holy." Simple and effective as these mottoes were, they did not adequately afford full expression of sentiment. The young Victorian lass preferred verse, which seemed to her more expressive. There were many source books that served as exemplars of sampler verse: *Godey's, Harper's Magazine,* the many editions of the *Ladies' Album,* and Isaac Watts' *Divine Songs for Children.*

The central theme of the sampler took on greater importance toward the middle of the eighteenth century. As early as 1709 the Adam and Eve motif, a perennial favorite, appeared; another example is dated 1741. In both of these the main figures are nude. In another treatment of the celebrated couple, in 1760, they appear in Quaker costume; the scene also includes a Brown University building and a doctor's gig and horse. Other samplers show further variants of this motif, with fig tree, flowers, and animals. Many Biblical scenes were stitched, among them Noah's Ark and the Holy Land. The hunting scene was one more popular pictorial device that could show to advantage a variety of animals, birds, dogs in pursuit, and stags at bay. An unusual sampler suggesting a family record features a charming pattern of decorative squares in which sprays of flowers alternate with pious sentiments.

About the middle of the eighteenth century, a house or church became the central feature around which a composition was planned. Gardens, trees, and picket fences offered opportunities for interesting color treatment. An architectural motif in the hands of a young and unsophisticated artist could become a joy in

Jesus permit thy gracious name to stand
As the first effort of a youthful hand
And while her fingers oer the canvas move
Engage her tender heart to seek thy love.

Mary. S.C. Burchfield. East Liberty:

2092

2093

its simple rendition, reflecting the contemporary scene with sincerity. Buildings appear frequently beginning about 1745 and continuing for about a hundred years. There was a tendency to illustrate mansions rather than humble cottages. Whether this indicated that the makers were residents or whether it merely represented their hopes and aspirations is a matter of conjecture. One of the most masterful treatments was achieved by Anna Pierce of Oxford, Massachusetts. Her sampler features the typical dwelling of her day, complete with elliptical fanlight over the handsome doorway

I do not ask that city spires
May round my mansion rise
But that my home may be where trees
Are pointing to the skies

Isabella. P Burchfield. East Liberty. June 23 1851

2094

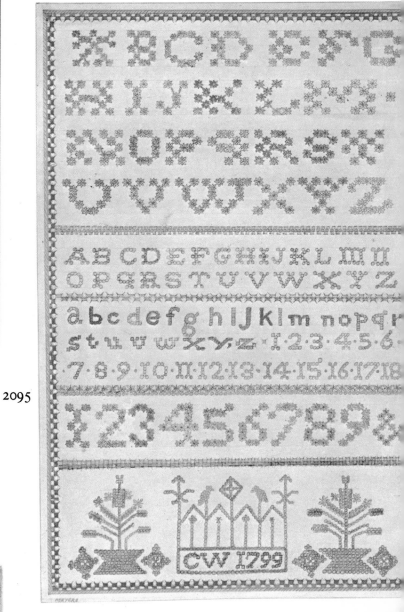

2095

2092 *The most popular form of sampler combined the alphabet, some pictorial representation, a decorative border of nature motifs, and the maker's signature* **2093** *Sampler in crewel stitching with woolen threads on linen, dated 1851* **2094** *Sampler on canvas base embroidered in silk floss and twist, c. 1795* **2095** *Sampler of linen needlework, c. 1799* **2096** *Sampler embroidered on linen scrim, c. 1821*

2096

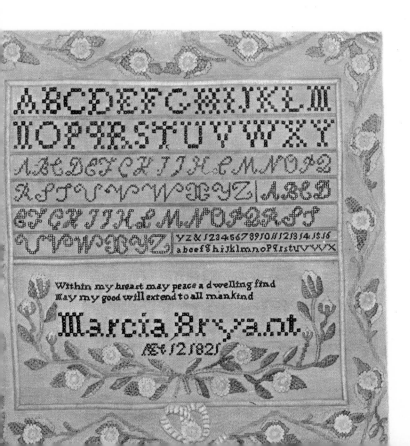

and a white picket fence. Many a young artist had difficulty with perspective and drew the sides of the house with total disregard for its principles, but therein lies some of the charm. Schoolhouses and public buildings also proved of interest. New York's City Hall, topped by a six-line verse, is the subject of a large pictorial sampler. Although the architectural details were highly stylized and fenestration greatly simplified, the representation is faithful and unmistakable.

Mary S. Smith
wrought this
Sampler = 1851
Carlisle

School Nº 8

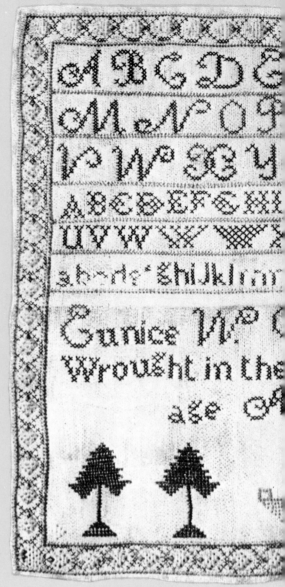

Eunice Mᶜ
Wrought in the
age

2097

2098

2099

2100

574

2101

2102

2097–2102 Sampler designs varied as much as the personalities that made them. Some samplers were composed merely to display skill in handling the alphabet in Roman or script letters, both capitals and minuscules, **2098** and **2100**. Others show preference for ornamentation or pictures, **2099, 2101, 2102;** the last is almost tapestry-like in effect

575

2103

2103 *Printed textiles on a political theme were a way of popularizing a president or a nominee. In this all-over pattern printed on cotton, c. 1830, the first seven presidents of the United States appear, with dates of their administrations. This was based upon an earlier French toile inscribed "Les Présidents des États-Unis," but the original does not show the portrait of Jackson nor does it have the spread eagle at the left or the frigate* Constitution *on the right. These adaptations exemplify the copying of historical subject matter from engravings* **2104** *Literally hundreds of commemorative designs were printed on cotton, linen, or silk depicting portraits of George Washington or scenes from his life*

2104

Commemorative
Cotton & Chintz

THE ICONOGRAPHY of American history on cloth probably started within a year of the Revolution, in 1777, possibly with a cotton kerchief attributed to John Hewson of Philadelphia depicting George Washington as commander in chief of the Continental army. As with most textile prints of the period, it was not an entirely original creation; it was based upon a published engraving by C. Shepherd dated September 9, 1775.

There was an active coterie of at least twenty copperplate engravers producing paper prints in the Colonies before the Revolution. Immediately following the war their numbers increased rapidly, as the demand for historical engravings in the young republic continued to grow. The later engravers concerned themselves with recording the heroes and battles of the Revolution, and thereafter the War of 1812. Plate after plate glorified the exploits of the infant navy. When Jackson managed to win the only major land victory, at New Orleans, that triumph was celebrated with prints by four different engravers.

The ease with which engravers could turn out prints on single sheets of dampened paper could not be achieved in printing bolts of cloth; for this it was necessary to engrave the designs on calenders or rolls.

Reflecting the vogue abroad, printed cottons of all types were in use in America as early as the middle of the seventeenth century, but they were imported from England, which strictly prohibited the manufacture and printing of cottons in the Colonies. By the early part of the eighteenth century, however, many Colonists fretting at the restrictive policy openly violated the ban. Benjamin Franklin's elder brother James, in 1720, advertised in the *Boston Gazette:* "Linnens, Calicoes, Silks, etc. printed in good figures, very lively, and durable colors, and without the offensive smell which commonly attends the linens printed here." Not only were there frequent press notices showing that competition was keen in this trade, but textile printing tools were advertised. Francis Dewing, a Boston engraver, had let it be known in 1713 that he "Engraveth and Printeth copper Plates, likewise cuts neatly and printeth Calicoes."

Most ships arriving from England carried a substantial cargo of dry goods, which were bought up as soon as they were unloaded. Colonial visitors to Britain rarely failed to purchase prints for room furnishings, curtains, bed hangings, or materials for a lady's costume. Another early reference to copperplate prints comes from Benjamin Franklin in a letter to his wife from London in 1758: "There are also fifty-six yards of cotton, printed curiously from copper plates, a new invention, to make bed and window curtains; and seven yards of chair bottoms, printed in the same way, very neat. This was my fancy, but Mrs. Stevenson tells me I did wrong not to buy both of the same color."

The early designs from abroad had followed the traditional floral patterns and other themes of nature. When the Revolution stimulated a market for commemorative subject matter, the printers of cotton goods at first concerned themselves with portraits and with episodes in the life of Washington, the Revolution, and the Federal period. Then followed the War of 1812, genre subjects on the American theme, transportation and the conquest of the West, and political campaigns of the forties and fifties. Pictorial maps, the Civil War, and finally, late in the century, expositions supplied material for broadsides, kerchiefs, and yard goods. But the popularity of such subjects waned as each event slowly passed into history. The designers of cotton goods often took their cue from current best-selling Currier and Ives lithographs; in repetition there was safety.

The limited parallel between graphics and print goods ends with the matter of subject interest. As color and fashion trends changed, the mills of New England, in order to keep abreast of competition, found it expedient to gauge their markets carefully to insure survival, and it was the role of the industrial designer to make his contribution to this end.

2105 *Historical print on buff-colored linen called* The Apotheosis of Franklin, *made c. 1780–83*

2106

2107

2106–2111 *Cottons, especially chintzes and calicoes, in an endless variety of patterns and color schemes were being produced in great yardage by the third decade of the nineteenth century. The process of textile printing had made giant strides and centered around a few mill towns in Massachusetts, particularly Merrimac, whose works employed hundreds of hands. Expert craftsmen imported from England included designers, engravers, printers, color mixers, and chemists. Historical designs continued in great demand, changing in content with new presidents, campaigns, and slogans, and with the coming of the Civil War. In addition to the topical themes, such colorful subject as florals, agricultural scenes and settings, and homely episodes based upon everyday life were popular*

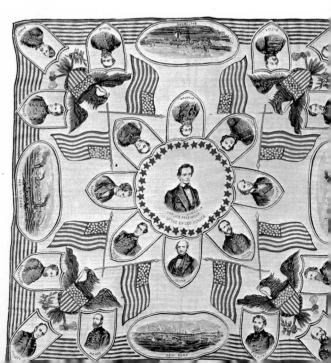

2108

2109

2110

2111

2112

2113

2114

2115

2116

2117

2118

2119

2120

2121

2112–2122 *The constantly recurring use of George Washington as a theme, 2112, 2113, 2117, and 2122, is a testament to his immortality as a design symbol. William Penn's treaty with the Indians is featured in 2120. William Harrison, the military hero, is shown in 2116, while his log cabin at North Bend, Ohio, is depicted in 2115, on a cotton printed in 1841. Scenes from the Mexican War and Zachary Taylor at the Battle of Palo Alto are shown in 2114 and 2121. Transportation in a country gaining an awareness of its magnitude is featured in the scene of the canal boat with passengers and the Mississippi river scene, which pictures a stern-wheeler with cotton fields in the foreground, c. 1825–30*

2122

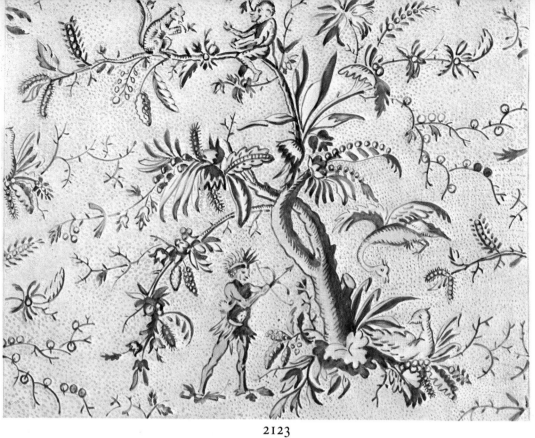

2123

2124

2125

2126

2123–2128 *Floral prints and fabrics used for a variety of household drapery and chair coverings, bedspreads, and children's dress goods display in infinite variety the garden favorites of roses, carnations, peonies, tulips, daisies, morning glories, and many others. Realism is favored except in the whimsies pictured in 2123 and the stylized version of a coverlet in 2124. The eagle spreads his wings in 2127 and 2128*

2128

2127

2129

2130

2131

2132

2133

2134

2135

2136

2137

GALLERY OF TEXTILES. *All-over patterns,* **2130–2140,** *achieve a continuous harmony by repetition of the same unit. The pleasant ornamental effect depends upon a rhythmic flow of decorative elements, blending and weaving into one another. Foliage, vines, and arboreal motifs, interspersed with floral sprigs and leafy sprays, with the introduction of birds or animals for added realistic excitement, were perennial favorites for home use. In* **2137** *and* **2138,** *a badminton court and winter-sports scenes illustrate the occasional use of genre subjects*

2138   2140

2139

BOOK
FIVE

Children's World

BOOK FIVE: *Children's World*

591

2141

2141 The Circus *was painted in 1874. by A. Logan, National Gallery of Art, Washington, D.C. Gift of Edgar William and Bernice Chrysler Garbisch.* **2142** *The circus wagon* The Golden Age of Chivalry, *designed by George Lawrence of the Sebastian Wagon Company, was built c. 1887–89*

The Circus Comes to Town

2142

H urry! hurry! hurry!" has been the raucous cry of the big-top barker ever since John Robinson hauled the first traveling show, consisting of three wagons, five horses, and a tent, beyond the Alleghenies in 1824. Before the nineteenth century ended, the American circus had become not only "The Greatest Show on Earth" but a big business which involved dozens of touring troupes, thousands of performers, and animals from all parts of the globe. This was the heyday of the circus, roughly from 1875 to 1915, with its dazzling three rings, its freaks, and its spangles, glitter, and noise.

The magnificent prologue to the main show was the mile-long parade in a slow, well-ordered procession from the railroad yards to the big tent. The brightly decorated circus wagons carried clowns, musicians, lady per-

ZENZENY & TAVERNIER

594

formers, and animal cages. The steam calliopes sounded a brassy cacophony, and the clumsy, ten-ton *Two Hemispheres* wagon was drawn by a team of forty horses, while dozens of elephants, from midget to jumbo, marched linked together tail in trunk. Phineas T. Barnum inaugurated this parade of colorful circus wagons with the attendant ballyhoo. Favorite parade themes included allegories, legendary heroes of the golden age of chivalry, and Orientalia.

The few remaining circus wagons found today in museums and circus collections are reminders of those spectacles. These ponderous show pieces were created for glamour and showmanship; the over-ornamentation and excessive use of gilded scrolls were designed to captivate the eye. Yet beneath the tinsel and gilt were finely carved figures, symbols of the circus during its apogee. While the whole town usually turned out to see the "super-colossal, transcendentally amazing and electrifying feats of the most stupendous exhibition ever exploited," the gaudy show wagons bore silent testimony to the skills of wood-carvers and gilders.

Wood-carving served a special function in the circus world. The wood-carver, working on contract, turned out wagons with little of the glamour associated with a wood sculptor. The carvings on the wagons were not intended to be studied closely, but were designed primarily as a part of the passing spectacle. They reflected the influences that produced the eclectic and Baroque decorations of that day. Most circus carving was the work of untrained artists; it was not folk art but "popular art." The lavishly ornamented, highly colored wagons stimulated the visual senses and were the keynote of a transient style.

Barnum, Bailey, Cole, Forepaugh, and other circus owners were continually in need of new equipage because their wagons were exposed to all kinds of weather. The cost of the huge wagons could amount to thousands of dollars. Few firms, therefore, could be entrusted with these commissions. Samuel Robb of Canal Street, New York, and the Sebastian Wagon Company, also of New York, built the majority of the wagons. Other builders were located in Chicago, Leavenworth, Kansas, Germantown, Pennsylvania, and Tonawanda, New York.

Robb, sometimes working alone, built wagons and also carved figureheads and cigar-store figures. Later he worked for Sebastian, carving most of the important circus figures. He is known to have carved a series of nursery-rhyme and fairy-tale characters—Bluebeard, Cinderella, Mother Goose, Sindbad the Sailor, Red Riding Hood, and the Old Woman Who Lived in the Shoe—for the Barnum circus parade. Robb employed a few hands, among them Thomas White, who copied Classical statuary, producing a Greek slave and an Adam and Eve.

Many of the finest wagons were designed and built by Jacob Sebastian, a skilled carriagemaker who came to America from France in 1854. At the time of his death in 1880, his shop had grown to include a staff of carvers, figure painters, gilders, and letterers, in addition to carpenters, wainwrights, and wheelwrights. Until the decline of circus fortunes resulted in bankruptcy, Sebastian's son John continued the business, maintaining the staff and some vestige of his father's reputation.

In the construction of the wagons, oak and hickory were used for the structural members and frames and yellow pine and whitewood for most of the carvings. The softer woods were more vulnerable to exposure; this played great havoc with the carved figures, resulting in splitting, cracking, and the loss of arms, fingers, and noses. It is surprising, therefore, that any of these figures have survived. Van Amburgh's *Great Golden Chariot* was among the most lavish wagons. It was a richly carved structure which featured a helmeted, steel-armored noble slaying a lion with his lance,

4

2143 The Circus Coming into Town, *wood engraving by the illustrator team of Paul Frenzeny and Jules Tavernier, appeared in* Harper's Weekly, *October, 1873*

2144

surrounded by Romanesque scrolls. The Colmar brothers' prize wagon had a lifesize nude on each corner; these gilded showgirls never failed to create a stir in the audience. The Wallace Circus had a steam calliope with a high driver's seat flanked by ornate scrolls from which emerged a female figure driving stylized lions. Adam Forepaugh's steam calliope featured four over-lifesize figures of dancers and musicians holding tambourines and clarinets. The sides were ornamented with stylized eagles and snakes, or dragons. Barnum and Bailey's hand-carved calliope topped them all. The pipes emitted both steam and music and showed clearly through the latticed side panels, which had elliptical center medallions surmounted by carved cherubs riding on the spread-winged birds.

2145

2146

2144 *The circus wagon* United States *is one of the most magnificent examples of circus carving, replete with symbols of the American spirit. Figures and allegories proudly display the flag and the eagle. In the central panel the Goddess of Liberty stands flanked by Indian maidens. Every square foot is covered with architectural framework, arches and pilasters, arabesques and storied details designed to instill patriotic fervor in the hearts of spectators, c. 1875* **2145** *Seated lion carved in relief for a Sparks circus wagon, c. 1900* **2146** *Relief carving of figure with pipes of Pan, from circus wagon, c. 1900*

2147   2148

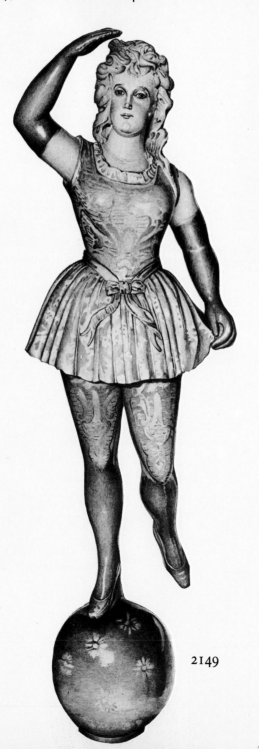

After the Barnum and Bailey show completed a successful five-year tour of Europe, Bailey decided to commemorate its triumph with the biggest and most elaborate gilded wagon in circus history, *Two Hemispheres*. The contract was awarded to Sebastian; its construction took almost a full year. One side of the wagon represented the eastern hemisphere and carried the emblems of Great Britain, France, Belgium, Spain, Italy, and Russia. On the other side, the United States, Canada, Mexico, Brazil, Argentina, and Chile were shown. A replica of the two hemispheres, guarded by a lion and a bear, was in the central portion. On the front, two American eagles appeared with outstretched wings, and on the rear were two elephant heads with uplifted trunks.

In a giant circus parade, at least a dozen wagons were drawn by matched teams of stallions in gay plumage and merrily tinkling bells. The bulk and weight of these circus wagons, so difficult to store and costly to maintain, have led to their destruction. Fortunately, a number of the wagons were stored on an empty farm lot outside of Bridgeport, Connecticut, some years ago. When storage charges

2149

2150

2151

began to mount and the circus company could not meet the payments, the wagons were put up for sale. At that time William Warren, state director of the WPA Federal Art Project, acquired the lot and its contents, thus salvaging many fine circus figures, which have since been acquired by collectors.

In addition to the few existing show wagons, numerous posters exist—from small handbills or throwaways with black-and-white engraved illustrations to gigantic four-sheet posters—which convey some of the grandeur and opulence of the circus in its heyday. The circus poster, never admired for its high level of artistry, was the only contemporary medium that adequately portrayed the details of the parades and the events of the circus.

2147–2150 *Circus wagons were designed to sparkle and glisten in the parade of floats and vehicles. Carving was in high relief; wagon sides were usually divided into architectonic units separated by pilasters, arches, and draped decorations. A special theme was assigned to a wagon:* **2147** *and* **2148** *show the Dolphin wagon. The Sparks wagon,* **2150,** *features a lyre and a winged head, with jesters behind and draperies at the sides. From photographs* **2149, 2152** *Calliope figures carved in the round, c. 1895* **2151** *Head carved by Sebastian Wagon Company for one of Barnum's circus wagons, c. 1885*

2152

2153

2154

2155   2156

2153, 2154 *Pair of dancing figures from Spark's circus wagon. Probably made by Moeller Brothers Wagon Company, Baraboo, Wisconsin, c. 1900* **2155, 2156** *Pair of draped figures, one with a lyre, the other holding a flower. They adorned the sides of Barnum and Bailey circus wagons made by the Sebastian Wagon Company of New York. Possibly carved by Samuel Robb, about 1880*

2157

2158

2159   2160

2157, 2158 *Pair of figures draped as muses, corner decorations on Barnum and Bailey circus wagon, c. 1880* **2159, 2160** *Figures carved by Samuel Robb of New York, noted for his cigar-store Indians of the same period, c. 1880*

2161

2162

Merry-Go-Round Menagerie

2163

THE FIRST REVOLVING platform with the carrousel figures we know today was built in the little town of North Tonawanda, New York, in 1879. The improvements, which included elaborate ornamentation and fanciful animals, heralded a new era. Previously, merry-go-rounds had featured only prancing horses and chariot seats. Carrousels, an entertainment feature of every fair here and abroad, were also an essential part of the circus, and they became the major attraction in amusement parks throughout the country, their numbers expanding rapidly during the closing years of the nineteenth century. Almost a dozen companies were kept busy turning out a veritable menagerie of wooden figures.

2161, 2162 Carrousel figures of a rooster and a lion. Photographs courtesy the Smithsonian Institution, Washington, D.C. Eleanor and Mabel van Alstyne Collection 2163, 2164 Galloping animals seemed more popular with older children, while the very young felt safer with the static figures. Deer and rabbit, c. 1890

2164

Leavenworth, Kansas, was the home of the important Parker Carnival Supply Company. Riverside, Rhode Island; Delphos, Ohio; and Germantown, Pennsylvania, each supported a company, while in North Tonawanda two manufacturers of carrousel equipment thrived as a result of the town's unique position in the field. Chicago, Milwaukee, and New York were also centers of merry-go-round activity, as most carvers of this type of work were found in large metropolitan areas. Some makers of carrousel figures were found in the smaller towns where amusement parks were built.

Carrousel animals and circus-wagon figures were related; both supplied the carnival atmosphere, yet there were some differences. On the wagons the figures formed an integral part of the overall decorative theme; the focal points were accentuated in high relief, a contrast to the low-keyed scrollwork. The figures were rarely free-standing or carved in the round. Their backs were flattened so that they could be attached to the wagon sides or to panels. This is the reason for many of the static poses, which were planned as part of an architectonic arrangement with strict spatial limitations. Carrousel figures, on the other hand, were independently carved, since each unit—horse, lion, giraffe, goat, or other animal—was intended for a separate rider. The animal could be viewed from all sides and could be removed without disturbing the surrounding facade. The fast-moving platform provided a forward thrust that determined the action of the animals. Figures in static poses were meant for young children, who were strapped into position. The other figures, usually on the outer rim of the platform, were designed for more daring riders, and the brass ring also attracted older children to the outside positions. In later years, the up-and-down action of the animals provided an extra thrill.

Softwoods, especially white and yellow pine, were most suitable for the carrousel animals. Pine was easily worked, and greater speed of execution meant the figures could be produced quickly in great numbers. Little sanding or polishing was necessary in the detailing of the head, mane, and tail portions. The rounded areas of the body which required sanding were turned over to assistants and apprentices. Finally, the figure was ready for

painting and gilding. These carrousel animals received the same bright-colored treatment as the circus wagons. Frequent refurbishing was necessary to maintain their attractiveness, and often much of the original intention of the artist was obscured.

In the shops where most of this work was done, the carvers worked anonymously. Occasionally, the name of the artist is known, either because of his reputation or from extant billing records. Charles Louff, working in Riverside, Rhode Island, made a name for himself, starting about 1880. Louff carved a number of horses and other animals, including lions, panthers, goats, pigs, deer, and rabbits. They were vigorously executed and notable for detailing. His handling of a horse's mane and tail deviated from the regular grooved hairlines. He introduced locks of hair which curled in various directions, giving each animal an unusual Baroque look. Saddles and blankets also had fancifully carved border designs. Instead of the stereotyped horse in action, with extended forelegs, Louff varied the attitudes to obtain greater originality. He introduced a pair of birds hanging on the hind part of the horse as though the rider were just returning from the chase. In all, Louff's animals were well conceived, realistic, and appropriate to their purpose and function. When removed from carrousel platforms and placed in collections of folk art, they become works of art in their own right.

Bob Crandle, a wood-carver with a small factory on Third Avenue at Thirtieth Street in New York, specialized in hobbyhorses, velocipedes, and merry-go-round horses. The horse bodies were made from large pine-tree trunks, while the limbs were carved separately and doweled into position. Painting produced a variety of equine figures; some were spotted to look like piebald horses and pintos, or even striped to look like zebras. Crandle also carved some lions and giraffes.

The horse was by far the most popular carrousel animal. It was treated in a variety of colorings to imitate the pinto, sorrel, palomino or the spotted white charger, a favorite among young riders. Lions, tigers, giraffes, dogs, roosters, ostriches, and many other exotic members of the menagerie appeared on the colorful carrousels.

2165

2166

2167

2168

608

2165–2172 *The galloping steed was the carrousel's most popular animal, even though some of the more dangerous animals like lions and tigers attracted the daring youngsters. Stirrups were provided, but two- and three-year-olds had to be hoisted into their saddles by parents, who stood alongside. American carrousels with revolving platforms first appeared in 1879. Made in North Tonawanda, New York, between 1880 and 1900*

2169

2170

2171

2172

2173

2174

2173 *Pair of walking panthers yoked together, c. 1890* **2174–2175** *Carrousel goats Louff of Rhode Island. His animal figures were boldly conceived and vigorously carved, suggesting intense liveliness* **2176** *Carrousel whippet; harness treatment provides opportunity for decoration and gilding*

2175

2176

2177

2178

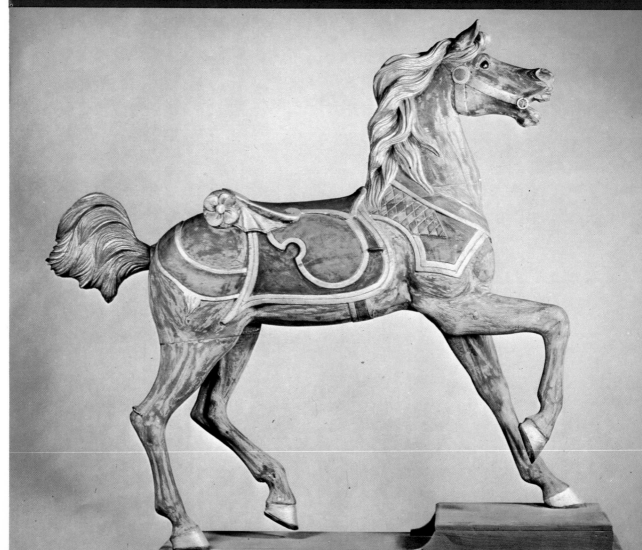

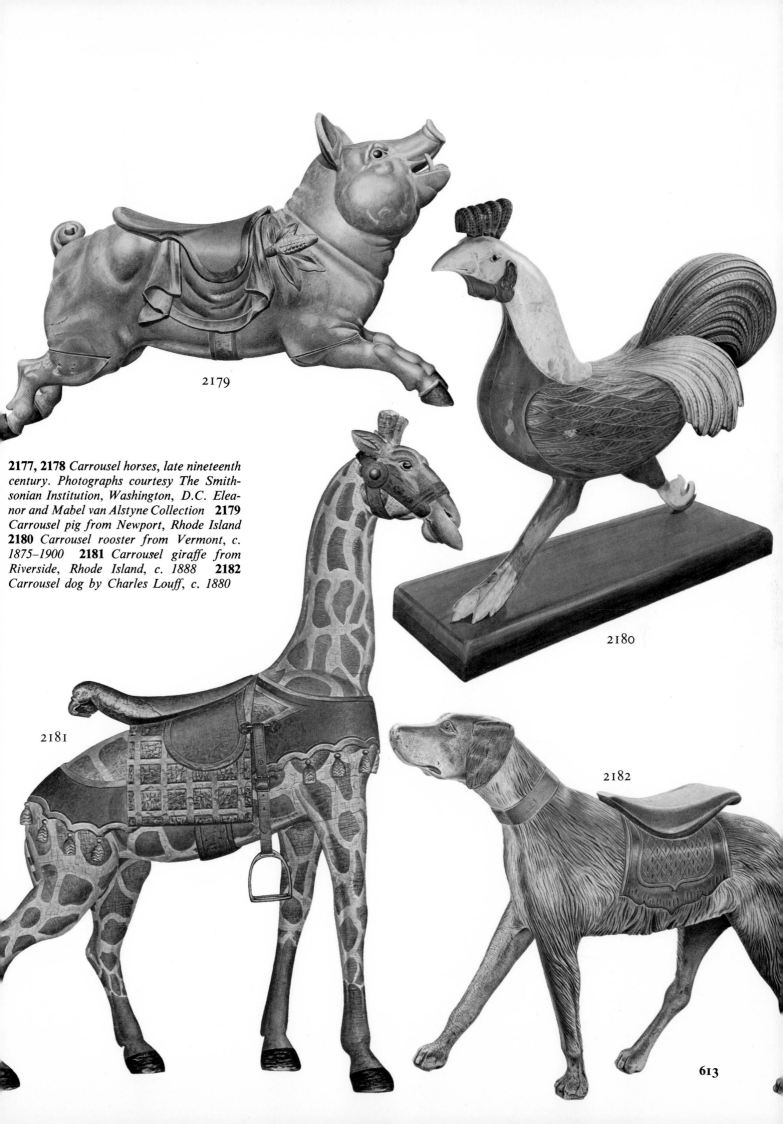

2177, 2178 *Carrousel horses, late nineteenth century. Photographs courtesy The Smithsonian Institution, Washington, D.C. Eleanor and Mabel van Alstyne Collection* **2179** *Carrousel pig from Newport, Rhode Island* **2180** *Carrousel rooster from Vermont, c. 1875–1900* **2181** *Carrousel giraffe from Riverside, Rhode Island, c. 1888* **2182** *Carrousel dog by Charles Louff, c. 1880*

2179

2180

2181

2182

2184

2186

2183

2185

2183–2190 *The gay carnival spirit of the carrousel found expression not only in the dynamic action of galloping horses and other animals but in the decorative headpieces used for adornment on the merry-go-round structure, benches, and chariots. Horses' heads,* **2185** *and* **2190**, *are all that survive from full figures. The lions' heads,* **2183**, **2186**, *and* **2188**, *were popular architectonic devices whose counterparts are to be found in the work of the figurehead carvers as well.*

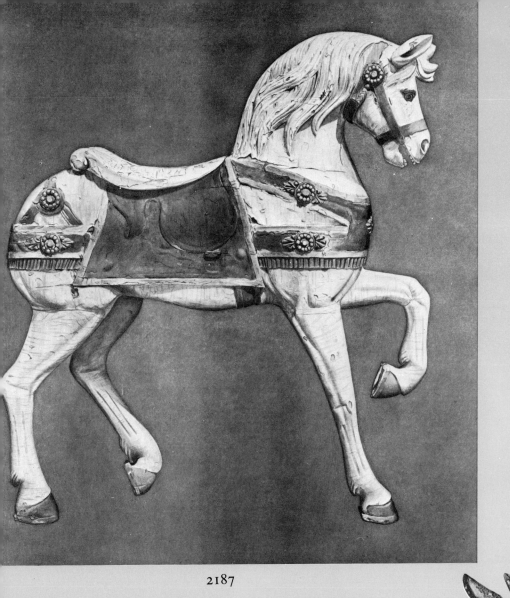

2187

2188

Occasionally the forms of other animals were introduced, as in the wolf's head, in **2189**, obviously a derivative from historic ornament. All these were products of the Parker Carnival Supply Company, made about 1890 at Leavenworth, Kansas. The carrousel horse, **2184**, is the work of Charles Louff of Riverside, Rhode Island. It is distinguished from the average run of figures by such spirited and extravagant mannerisms as the tilt of the head, the placement of the horse's legs, the Baroque treatment of the mane, and the decorations on blanket and saddle. All these details, carefully studied and well executed, add to the animation and exuberance of the animal and to the over-all effect

.2189

2190

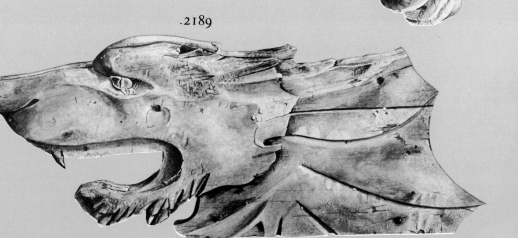

2191

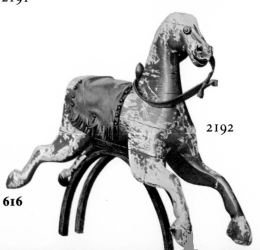

2192

616

2191 The Hobby Horse *was painted about 1840 by an unknown artist in Massachusetts. National Gallery of Art, Washington, D.C. Gift of Edgar William and Bernice Chrysler Garbisch* **2192** *Semicircular hoops provide unusual base for this hobbyhorse* **2193** *Leather horse and rider, c. 1880* **2194** *Musician nods his head and moves his bow in mechanical music box, c. 1890*

Playthings & Pastimes

2193

CHILDREN'S TOYS mirror the tastes and trends of their times, and the toys of the early Colonial days in turn reflect the unfrivolous nature of that period. Very often there were no toys at all and imagination served to turn sticks and stones into games; children who lived along the seashore played with shells and pebbles. By the end of the seventeenth century, some English toys were being imported, but they were available to only a small fraction of the population. For the most part the early settlers fashioned crude playthings out of pine, oak, maple, and cherry wood from the forest.

The rocking horse, or hobbyhorse, was the most popular form of amusement for all children. Its design and construction presented a real challenge to the artisan—an opportunity to demonstrate imagination in contriving it from a single plank or shaping it sculpturally. Collectively, a group of hobbyhorses reveals the wide range of skills found among amateur craftsmen. The back and saddle of the horse

required clever design for comfortable seating and the runners had to be sturdy enough for constant rocking over long periods. Realism in equine features was a matter of the toymaker's patience and ability; the lack of it in cruder models certainly did not hinder the child's fun. The plank forms, thin and elongated in their more economical construction, had the universal appeal of all primitive things. The more elaborate, full-bodied shapes approach carrousel figures of a later day and represent the handiwork of skilled carvers rather than amateur craftsmen. Hobbyhorses were forthright examples of folk carving and ingenuity, from the leather ears tacked into position to the genuine horsehair tails.

In New England villages the making of toys became a sideline for carvers and carpenters. In Pennsylvania German counties, where toymaking descended from the distinctive wood carving of the homeland, there was an abundance of charming miniatures—animals, birds, and other figures. Noah's Ark, with its full complement of paired birds and beasts, was

2194

2195

2196

2197

particulary attractive to children. In addition there were the traditional Christmas decorations—the crèche and nativity scenes. Celebrated itinerants included the German carvers Wilhelm Schimmel and Aaron Mountz (often spelled Mounts) and the Swiss George Huguenin. Although Schimmel was especially noted for his birds, his most elaborate creation was the Garden of Eden, of which he made a number of copies. Here he stood Adam and Eve in the shade of a tree, surrounded them with a variety of animals, and enclosed the whole ensemble within a picket fence. He covered all this with heavy coats of whatever paint was available at the farmhouse, most often a barn red.

The wooden figures, although faithfully executed, still had one drawback: they lacked the animation so necessary to a child's sense of play. Out of this urgent need there developed other wooden toys, articulated with moving parts and mechanical arrangements of the simplest sort. Whirligigs, tall, attenuated figures with arms pivoted through the shoulders, revolved about a central axis. Windmills were built in miniature and mounted on boards to spin freely when the wind reached sufficient velocity. Other mechanical contrivances involved watermills with overshot wheels. Still another was a figure balanced on a horizontal bar actuated by a crank handle. Again, the Pennsylvania Germans devised all manner of revolving mechanisms—music boxes with many figures mounted on a spinning platform, stamping mills in which hammers pounded and clattered, and figures whirling around a maypole, all colorfully designed and attractively painted. Carved wooden pieces in which balls were imprisoned within bars constituted an exercise for the whittler's own amusement. Often the tour-de-force was a wooden chain of many links.

The vast variety of wooden toys included sets of miniature furniture with which to equip an entire dollhouse. There were chairs, tables, benches, stools, chests, beds, lowboys, and highboys. Some of these pieces, especially those made by a cabinetmaker for his children, are our finest examples of diminutive woodworking. Welsh dressers and corner cabinets provided display pieces in which to show off the child's precious bits of miniature china and porcelain. An important addition to doll equipment was an American creation: the doll carriage. It came in every possible style and size and was usually a sideline of baby-carriage makers. Later on, in the second half of the nineteenth century, reed and wicker bodies replaced the wooden ones, which had been heavier and sturdier. The doll carriage was subjected to constant use and frequently handed down.

As tin toys followed those made of wood, in about 1840, a new realm opened up for the toy makers. Dies could easily stamp out all shapes and forms, which could then be crimped together at the seams for extra strength and rigidity. Mechanical playthings, a constant source of amusement for children, now also gained a new dimension. Though simple actions had been known as early as 1825, the windup, or clockwork, toys with spring action came in with the popular wave of tin toys. These mechanisms could be installed to make a figure dance a jig, play an instrument, or—in the case of dolls—simply walk. They could produce locomotion in steam engines, paddle-wheelers, and fire trucks. Windup toys included capering clowns, music boxes, revolving tables on which monkeys danced, and a thousand and one novelties ideally suited to tin because of its lightness and the low cost of its manufacture. The present scarcity of tin toys from the seventies and eighties is incomprehensible when one remembers the record-breaking output of the toy makers in their heyday. One single manufacturer is known to have produced forty million tin toys annually in the 1870s.

Fortunately for today's collectors, the cast-iron variety, which came in a bit later than tin, had a better chance for survival. Although

2195–2200 *Design, construction, and rocker action vary greatly. Very low horses, sometimes called rocking chairs, are for tiny tots under two. The primitive horse, 2198, was made in Minnesota, 1902. The horse and rider, 2200, is only a toy*

2198

2199

2200

2201

2203

2202

2204

620

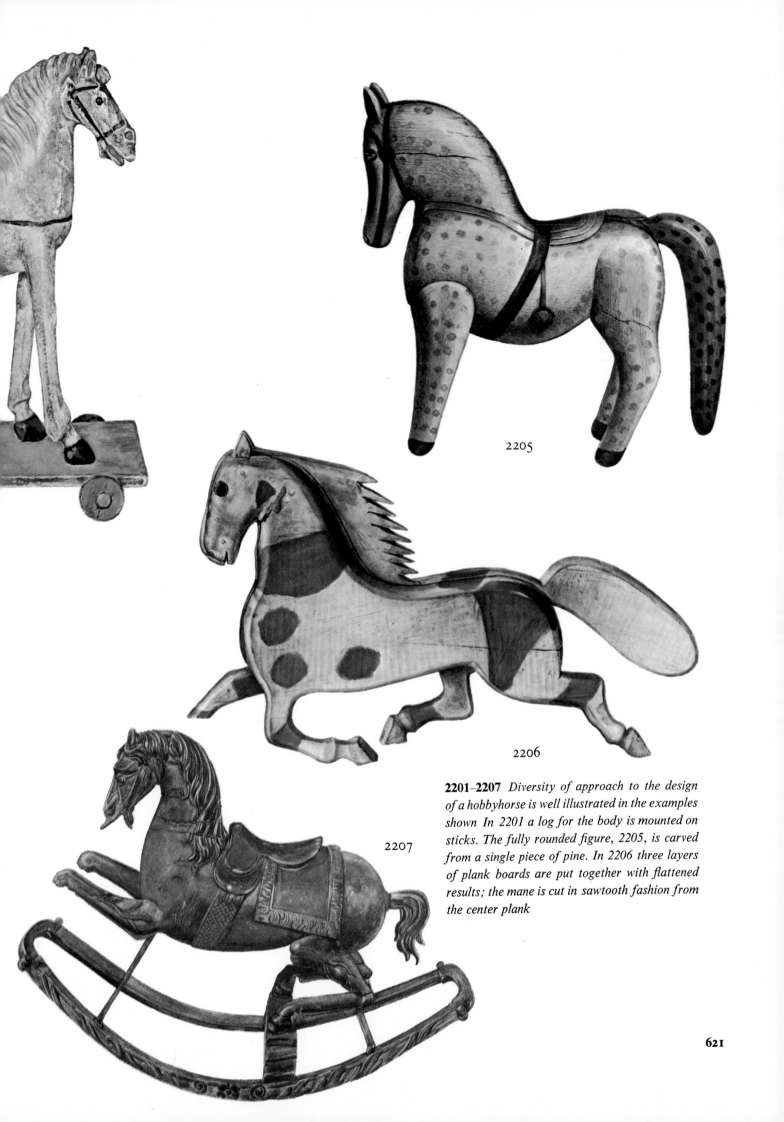

2205

2206

2207

2201–2207 *Diversity of approach to the design of a hobbyhorse is well illustrated in the examples shown In 2201 a log for the body is mounted on sticks. The fully rounded figure, 2205, is carved from a single piece of pine. In 2206 three layers of plank boards are put together with flattened results; the mane is cut in sawtooth fashion from the center plank*

2208 2209 2210

2211 2212

622

2208 *Whirligig, Sailor Jack, made in the eighteenth century* **2209** *Wooden toy, hand operated, c. 1800* **2210** *Bouncing jack made of oak, c. 1800–1830* **2211** *Lumberjack carving of pine and oak, c. 1885* **2212** *Wooden dachshund with movable joints, c. 1880* **2213** *Wooden toy with revolving horses and riders* **2214** *Windup toy of wood and cast iron in which boxers box* **2215** *Building a Noah's Ark was an exercise in shaping many wooden animals*

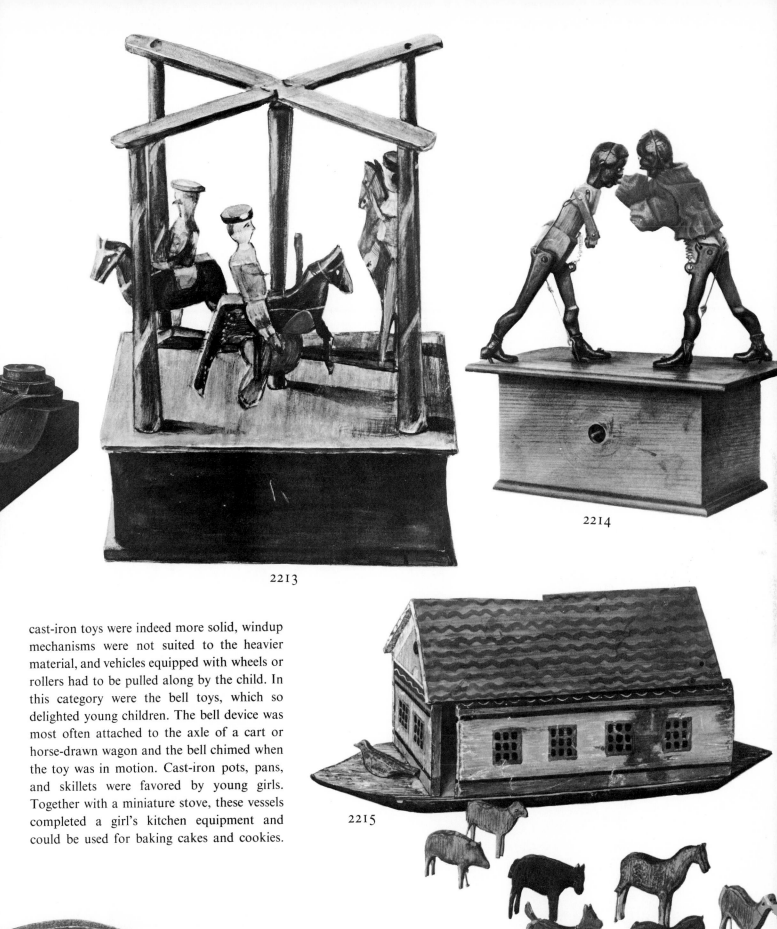

2213

2214

cast-iron toys were indeed more solid, windup mechanisms were not suited to the heavier material, and vehicles equipped with wheels or rollers had to be pulled along by the child. In this category were the bell toys, which so delighted young children. The bell device was most often attached to the axle of a cart or horse-drawn wagon and the bell chimed when the toy was in motion. Cast-iron pots, pans, and skillets were favored by young girls. Together with a miniature stove, these vessels completed a girl's kitchen equipment and could be used for baking cakes and cookies.

2215

623

2216–2222

2223

2224

2225

624

2226　　　　　　　2227　　　　2228

The perennial favorites for boys were transportation models, which the toy makers built with endless ingenuity. The early prototypes of vehicles were jigsawed of wood and often had lithographs pasted over the flat surfaces to lend color and interest. With the advent of new methods and materials everything was possible: farm wagons and circus wagons, sailing vessels and steamboats, fire engines and delivery trucks, trolley cars and trains; a cow catcher heading a locomotive was a distinctly American feature. Trains and locomotives were eventually extended to an entire railway system of tunnels, bridges, depots, switches, and every other known accessory which could be made in miniature.

2216–2222 *Set of ninepins probably carved by a settler in the Pennsylvania German region, midnineteenth century* **2223, 2224** *Toy stamping mill of trip-hammers and revolving mannequins in music box. Made in Pennsylvania, c. 1840* **2225** *Carved wooden housewife with movable joints* **2226–2228** *Wooden costumed figures* **2229** *Carved statue of farm couple*

2229

2231

2230

2232

2233

2230–2236 *The saga of American transportation, at a time when great progress was being made in every direction, is reflected in a cavalcade of vehicular toys fashioned of wood, cast iron, and tin. The progression starts with the team of oxen, 2230, and the covered wagon, 2231, followed by the fire engine, 2232, the cast-iron train set, 2233, the tin omnibus, 2234, and the tin steamboat side-wheeler, 2236. Typical of cast-iron bell toys is the Pony Bell Ringer, 2235. Figures 2230 and 2235 from photographs*

2234

2235

2236

2237

2238

2239

2240

2241

2242

2237–2244 *Wheeled toys of many different types were favorites at the turn of the century. There were many animals mounted on platforms with wheels, engines and vehicles in great variety, coaches, wagons and omnibuses. Besides the cast-iron kinds to be pulled about, there were wind-up toys of tin and the automobile, at first imported from Germany and France, was among these. Within a few years American toy autos were being made*

2243

Overleaf: GALLERY OF TOYS. *Carvings:* **2251, 2253, 2255, 2258, 2259, 2262, 2264, 2266, 2269, 2273, 2280,** *dolls and carriages:* **2254, 2257, 2265, 2271, 2282** *gun:* **2283** *horses* **2245, 2249, 2261, 2268, 2274, 2284, 2286** *kitchen range:* **2260** *mechanical action toys:* **2246, 2252, 2275, 2276** *top:* **2246;** *wheel toys and vehicles:* **2247, 2248, 2250, 2256, 2261, 2263, 2267, 2270, 2272, 2274, 2276, 2277, 2279, 2281**

2244

629

2245

2246

2247

2248

2253

2254

2255

2256

2261

2262

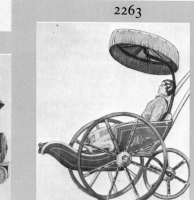

2263

2264

2269

2270

2271

2272

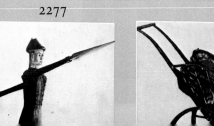

2277

2278

2279

2280

2249

2250

2251

2252

2257

2258

2259

2260

2265

2266

2267

2268

2273

2274

2275

2276

2281

2282

2283

2284

2285

2286

631

2287

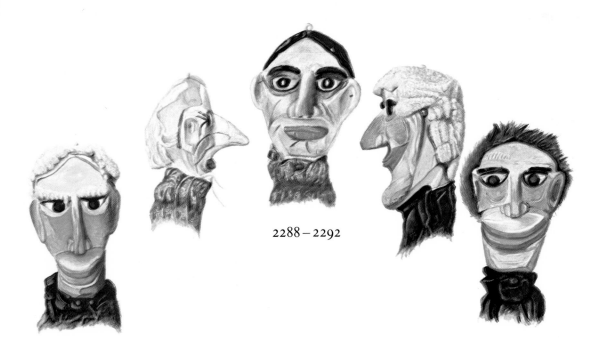

2288–2292

Dolls, Puppets

& Marionettes

2293

DOLLS, PUPPETS, and marionettes have always figured largely in the child's world of fantasy. Fortunately, their size and shape have not mattered, for in the early days of the Colonies the homemade dolls were crude indeed. One of the earliest, which was called—because of the obvious similarity—a bedpost doll, was simply a rounded stick with a face painted on it. In some regions children learned from friendly Indian tribes how to make simple puppets out of buckskin. But the universal favorites, on the farm and in the city, were rag dolls, which could be made by anybody who

2287 *Marionette Chinaman made to be operated by strings from a position above the stage. Head carved of black walnut and painted, costume of silk with rhinestone buttons, and papier-maché ball. Made by puppeteer Oliver Lano, c. 1870* **2288–2292** *Painted puppet heads of carved walnut. Wigs were made of fur and wool by Oliver Lano, c. 1870* **2293** *Hand puppet, Judy, has stick in the body to hold up head. Painted wooden face and hands, velvet cap, and cotton clothing, c. 1870*

2294

owned an extra bit of cloth; often a clothespin was used for the body. In an era of make-do they became cherished possessions.

The popularity of rag dolls eventually led to the manufacture of dolls in quantity. The pattern was made by stamping or printing a design on two separate pieces of cloth, one for the front and the other for the back. These were then cut out, sewn together, and stuffed.

Rag dolls were dressed in pieces of calico, muslin, linen, or silk left over from a dress or an appliqué bedspread. Occasionally a doll might be clad in Quaker costume, but on the whole regional dress was not in evidence. There were, however, marked variations in doll construction, with cornhusks and nuthead dolls prevailing in rural areas.

Gradually dolls became more elaborate. The importation of papier-maché heads started in the early nineteenth century. These were mounted on canvas, linen, or kid bodies stuffed with sawdust. China heads from Austria and Germany came next, followed by wax heads from England. Unclothed dolls' bodies could be bought and costumed to suit the current taste. Of even greater interest to the ladies were the so-called milliners' models, fashion replicas sent from abroad as an advance showing of the new styles.

Innovations constantly appeared on the doll market. In the 1870s a Yankee inventor named Joel Ellis came up with the mortise-and-tenon joint, by which wooden pieces could be inserted and fastened, or made movable. The practicability of these for doll construction led Ellis to the formation of a Vermont company for the manufacture of dolls that could assume all sorts of odd positions and perform acrobatic stunts. His success inspired the invention of the ball-and-socket joint for doll movements and many other improvements. After the walking doll came the talking doll, a by-product of Thomas Edison's work on the phonograph.

Puppets and marionettes have followed a very different pattern, since they are completely handmade, from the fashioning of the heads and facial expressions to the articulation of the figures and their costuming. Puppeteers make a clear distinction that sometimes comes as a surprise to the layman. In the true meaning, puppets are manipulated directly by hand, or sometimes with a stick from underneath; marionettes are controlled by strings or wires from above. The puppeteer often conceives, writes, and directs the play, designs the stage and costumes, and creates all the sets and stage appurtenances in his own workshop. The miniature theater offers a rare form of self-expression in which artist, craftsman, stage director, and actor are combined in a single personality.

The lineage of the puppet show may be traced to ancient times in Rome, Greece, Egypt, and India, where costumed figures and effigies were carried in awe-inspiring religious processionals and on festive occasions. During the Middle Ages, puppets played their roles in miracle and Passion plays. As the repertory broadened they started to appear in secular entertainment, taking on native forms in different countries. In France the favorites were called Guignol and Polichinelle. In England and America we know them as Punch and Judy. The English Punch entertained his audiences by telling of his marital troubles with Judy and by his impertinent antics. The portraits of Punch and his fellow players are so excellent that the characters seem almost human and have served as models for many a subsequent play. As W. H. Chesson expressed it, Punch is made "a goggling miscreant, whose hump is a rigid and misplaced tail and whose military hat, above a crustacean face, completes a rather melancholy effect of mania." Almost a hundred years ago this figure, like that of the wooden Indian, stood outside many tobacconist shops, his big nose suggesting the fragrance of cheroots and the spice of snuff. While Punch was the perennial villain, low-browed, vile, and murderous, Judy was pictured as a beauty, the continual butt of her husband's machinations and anger. Cruikshank, the English illustrator, has given us a fine set of twenty-four watercolor drawings of Punch and Judy.

There have been few improvements in the technique of the puppet theater since Punch began his travels in England, almost three centuries ago. The methods of puppetry have a basic simplicity and honesty which do not encourage innovation. The stage is formed within a portable wooden framework which is covered with cloth or decorated alfresco. At the bottom edge of the stage opening, which generally comes just above the puppeteer's head, is a projecting shelf on which the properties may be placed. Sometimes there is a flap below the main opening out of which the devil may make a surprise appearance. Scenery is painted simply on cloth drops or board cutouts; for the purpose of the average Punch play a garden or any scene will serve. Furniture is not generally used. The gallows are set up by pegging the base of the gibbet into a hole in the shelf.

The puppets are hung upside down by loops in their skirts on a row of hooks inside the booth. The puppeteer plunges his hand into the opening of the hollow costume, slips his index finger into the neck of the puppet, his thumb into one arm and his second finger into the other, and brings the figure onstage right side up. It is held at arm's length over his head. Punch is always on the right hand and the other characters change on the left hand while Punch holds the attention of the audience. Sometimes extras, an army or a mob, are held up on a forked stick.

The roving puppeteers who delighted children on street corners or village greens in seven-

teenth-century England, or at country fairs or in taverns of New England two centuries later, had a universal appeal to people of all ages. Nathaniel Hawthorne, thrilled by such a performance, wrote in 1838: "After supper, as the sun was setting, a man passed by the tavern door with a hand-organ, connected with which was a row of figures, such as dancers, pirouetting and twining, a lady playing on a piano, soldiers . . . all these keeping time to the lively or slow tunes of the organ. He had come over the high, solitary mountains where for miles there could hardly be a soul to watch his players and hear his music."

The marionette makers have a long tradition of creativity; many families engaged in puppetry have handed down their knowledge and experience for generations. One such outstanding group was the Lano family, whose forebears had trundled puppet shows about the streets of Milan in a handbarrow. Oliver Lano, the son of Alberto Lano, came to the United States in 1825. In their heyday the American Lano puppets traveled in the frontier country playing in obscure places, often with hastily improvised settings and impromptu programs. Teamed with circuses and medicine shows, puppet plays were only one number on a variety bill. Casual, leisurely, and unpretentious, the Lano puppets were fairly typical of wandering shows before the days of organized theater. Like other small shows on the frontier scene, they were welcomed in remote places as a great event. Their repertory included many scripts of the Punch and Judy variety as well as performances about David and Goliath, Robinson Crusoe, and other perennials. The Lano characters are known as fine examples of dramatic caricature. Their facial expressions were deeply carved for extreme emphasis, then painted with great imagination. Erwin Christensen, in his book *Early American Wood Carving*, describes them as follows:

2294

2295

2296

The judge who presides over Punch's trial for his life is truly menacing in his ghostlike pallor, and the Devil himself glows with his red cheeks and green eyes reflecting the tortures of hell. For color is as varied as shape, and both together are used with gusto. One looks in wonder at these raucous characters, broadly grinning, or open-eyed, teeth showing and chins pushed forward as if prepared for a savage attack. Devices like the shoe-button eye are in the tradition of the craft itself.

Carving and painting merged to produce an effect of grotesque fantasy well suited to slapstick comedy.

The puppeteer puts his heart and soul into carving the facial features of his puppets; the face symbolizes the entire character. Regardless of the puppets' actions, one sees only the helpless look of the heroine or the snarl of the villain. In the final analysis, it was the well-defined facial structure, fashioned with economy, that spelled success for the puppeteer.

2294–2299 *Marionettes as various characters in plays by the Lano family, well-known puppeteers, c. 1870. The Cannibal is shown in 2297, and the Sultan's Choice, a fan dancer, in 2299* **2300, 2301** *Puppets Punch and Judy, made by the Lano family, c. 1880*

2297

2298

2299

2300

2301

2302

2303

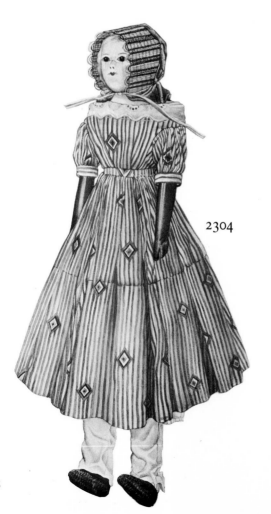

2304

2305

2306

2307

2302–2309 *Costumed dolls reflect the mood and manner of a particular era and were dressed according to the materials available, usually dressmaking remnants. Limbs were mostly cotton sewn together and stuffed, sometimes containing sticks to make them rigid, c. 1850–90*

2308

2309

2310

2311

2312

640

2313

2314

2315

2316

2317

Overleaf: GALLERY OF DOLLS AND PUPPETS. *Most of the examples shown may be classified as costume dolls whether they are clad in rags or silks and whether or not they are stuffed. Heads are made of muslin, yarn, wax, wood, or bisque. Others include Indian dolls: 2351, 2365; male dolls: 2330, 2347 (General Grant); 2352, 2358; manikins: 2341, 2554 (Indian); marionette: 2325; puppets: 2322, 2344 (witch lantern), 2346, 2349 2350, 2356, 2361, 2364, 2366; undressed: 2334*

2310–2312 *The doll maker exercised much ingenuity in the construction of head and face when imported wax or bisque heads were unavailable. Cornhusks, nutheads, papier-maché, woven yarn, and stuffed cottons were a few of the materials pressed into service* **2313, 2314** *Pair of Indian dolls with carved wooden heads, stuffed bodies, and buckskin costumes. Made by Marie Rose of the Montana Cree Reservation* **2315** *Rag doll Tilly, made about 1880* **2316** *Negro doll with carved wooden head and stuffed body, made about 1870* **2317** *Hand-painted doll's cradle, made in Pennsylvania, c. 1780*

2318   2319   2320   2321   2322   2323

2330   2331   2332   2333   2334   2335   2336

2344   2345   2346   2347   2348   2349

2356   2357   2358   2359   2360   2361   2362

2324   2325   2326   2327   2328   2329

2337   2338   2339   2340   2341   2342   2343

2350   2351   2352   2353   2354   2355

2363   2364   2365   2366   2367   2368   2369

2370

A Penny Saved....

2371

THRIFT WAS among the virtues that nineteenth-century parents tried to instill in their children. Every primer and Bible tract emphasized the value of saving a penny: "Resolve not to be poor; whatever you have, spend less and save more." "It is saving, not getting, that is the mother of riches," Benjamin Franklin had put it earlier. Proverbs and sermons of thrift at home or in Bible school were not entirely effective, however. It took the inventiveness of the small iron foundries to hit

2370 *Cast-iron and polychromed Uncle Sam mechanical bank made its debut shortly after the Centennial Exhibition. It became one of the most popular toy banks of its day* **2371** *A penny deposited brought the promise of action and a faint bark from the Speaking Dog bank, patented in 1885*

on a method of combining thrift with fun. Between 1850 and 1910, millions of mechanical banks were made by a handful of foundries.

Large copper pieces were first issued by the government in 1793; this led to improvised forms of the piggy bank made from gourds, clay, seashells, and some even whittled from wood. Such contrivances were followed by glass and china banks in a variety of shapes—houses, chickens, ducks, turkeys, wild and tame animals, public characters, and historic landmarks, including Plymouth Rock and the Liberty Bell.

By 1857, when the minting of large copper pennies was discontinued, manufacturers turned to the production of painted tin banks that looked like churches, gabled houses, drums, and bandboxes.

Just after the Civil War the first iron banks appeared. They were modeled after the square bank buildings, with a cupola and a "Savings Bank" inscription over the door. This plain bank building, unfortunately, offered little opportunity for novelty. Then the insertion of a simple spring action brought life into the still bank. Patent applications for the new designs have provided us with a record of the various types of mechanical banks. From about 1870, the intricate movements became increasingly popular, reaching a peak in sales before the close of the century. A single penny deposited in the slot brought a ticket of admission—a sideshow, a bit of amusement enjoyed by children and adults alike. The toy soldiers bowed, the mule kicked his heels, and the eagle flapped its wings. This approach to thrift proved more effective than stern admonitions

and moralizing maxims.

Less than a dozen firms produced these mechanical banks. A leader among them was the J. & E. Stevens Company, Cromwell, Connecticut, whose 1873 catalogue listed about two dozen distinct patterns. Other companies were located in Philadelphia and Lancaster, Pennsylvania; Kenton, Ohio; and Buffalo, New York. As each new volume or bit of research on this subject is completed, the total number of patterns increases. The latest count records about six hundred designs. The banks were manufactured in forms that made up a veritable Noah's Ark, complete with frogs, turtles, rabbits, owls, pigs, horses, elephants, and lions. The American eagle feeding its young was a favorite. Others included a Punch and Judy theater, baseball batter and battery, the Old Woman Who Lived in the Shoe, a bowling alley, ping-pong players, fortunetellers, wood-choppers, and the like. Comic situations also had appeal: a boy being thrown by his mule or turning a somersault.

Current events played their part in influencing the choice of subjects. At the time of fairs and celebrations, such forms as Uncle Sam, the Liberty Bell, and Independence Hall were produced by different foundries. Novelties were issued for special occasions, such as the Columbian World's Fair in 1892 and the Pan-American Exposition in 1901.

Although hardly an expression of folk art, the mechanical banks represent another field in which the patternmaker, molder, and colorist combined their talents to create articles of mass appeal.

2372

2373

STUMP SPEAKER

2374

2375

2376

2377

2372 Spring action in the gun of William Tell sent the penny flying at the apple on the boy's head, 1896 **2373** Black Sambo characters were a product of the 1880s **2374** For a penny the mule cart tipped upward, sending the mule into midair **2375** Growing interest in baseball made this Dark Town Battery a favorite in its day, 1888 **2376** A coin is placed on the clown's hand, the lever is pressed in the back, and presto, the coin is swallowed **2377** A cannon shoots the coin into the pylon of this Artillery Bank, 1892

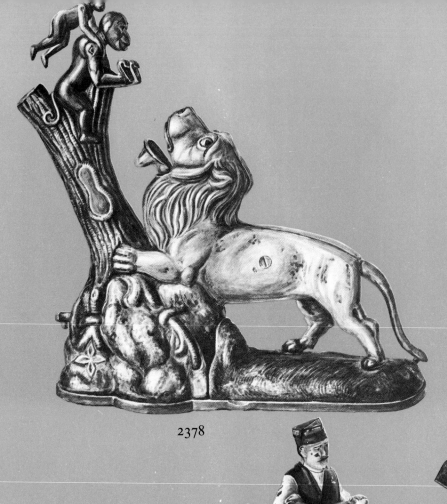

2378

2379

2380

2381

2382

2383

2378 The monkey throws the coins right into the lion's mouth every time 2379 Hod carrier and bricklayer supply the simple action in this mechanical bank 2380 As the mother eagle dropped her coin into the waiting young beaks she flapped her wings and there was a chirp from within 2381 Teddy and the Bear celebrated an incident in one of Roosevelt's hunting expeditions. As the coin is shot into the tree trunk a bear's head pops up 2382 Bank titled "Always Did 'Spise a Mule" rears hind legs as sitter falls forward in astonishment 2383 Rooster bank is activated by lever in tail, causing head to raise and crow while coin is dropped into slot, c. 1875

2384

2385

2384 *Jonah banks his coins in the wide-open mouth of the whale, 1888* 2385 *When the right forefoot is pressed, the frog's mouth opens wide to receive coin, 1872* 2386 *The bear and hunter, in many versions, shoot the coin into a pouch for safekeeping, c. 1895* 2387 *After coin deposit mule swings around to kick over watching boy (see 2382)* 2388 *Organ Bank plays a tune as monkey doffs his hat and drops coin into slot* 2389 *Trick Dog jumps through the hoop and lands coin in the barrel*

2386

2387

2388

2389

ORGAN BANK

TRICK DOG

653

654

2390

2391

2392

2393

2394

2395

2390 *"Still banks" rely more upon design than action. The Liberty Bell bank appeared at the time of the Philadelphia Centennial* **2391** *The Statue of Liberty obliges with a peal when a penny is deposited, c. 1885* **2392** *Independence Hall bank appeared just before the Centennial of 1876* **2393** *Santa Claus obligingly dropped his penny into the Christmas chimney* **2394** *Many coin banks were modeled on the architectural forms of the bank building* **2395** *Corpulent receiver of coins was called the Tammany Bank*

2396

2397

656

2398

2399

2400

2401

2402

2396 *The swinging acrobat provides the action in this mechanical bank, c. 1875* 2397 *Punch and Judy bank provides action in the stage setting, 1884* 2398 *Circus Elephant performs as follows: coin is placed between rings at lower right, ball held by acrobat at left is pulled back, clown turns at waist, and elephant's trunk flicks coin into slot, 1882* 2399 *Figure in bank building turns to make deposit* 2400 *Trick Pony takes coin in his mouth and bends his head to drop it into feedbox* 2401 *The clown seated on a globe does a turn as coin is placed into*

slot 2402 *The miser holding bills waves his arms in this bank of very limited action, c. 1875*

Overleaf: GALLERY OF COIN BANKS. *Animals and birds:* 2403, 2408, 2412, 2418, 2423, 2424, 2426, 2429, 2430; *buildings:* 2407, 2410, 2413, 2414, 2417, 2428, 2431, 2435, 2438; *mechanical action banks:* 2404, 2406, 2409, 2415, 2416, 2419–2422, 2427, 2432, 2433, 2436, 2437; *patriotic:* 2405, 2434. *From photographs except* 2405, 2407, 2409–2411, 2413–15, 2417, 2421, 2424–26, 2428–30, 2432, 2434, 2435, 2438

2403

2404

2405

2406

2411

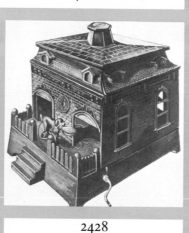

2412

2413

2414

ORGAN BANK

2419

2420

2421

2422

SPEAKING DOG

2427

2428

2429

2430

2435

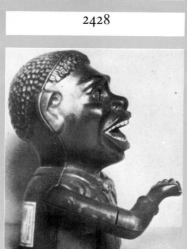

2407

2408

2409

2410

2415

2416

2417

2418

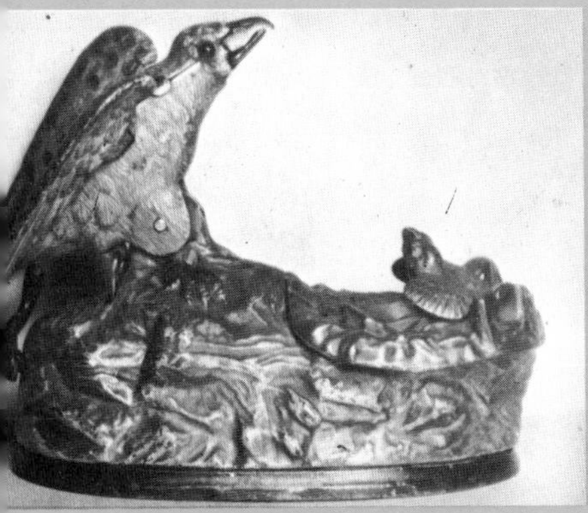
2423

2424

2425

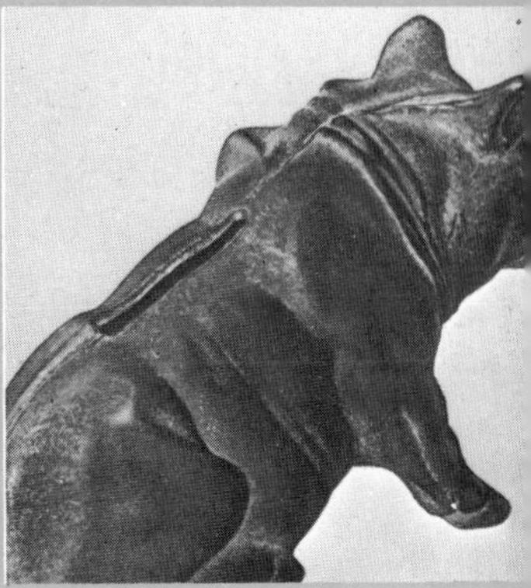
2426

2431

2432

2433

2434

Hudson River Valley, Sunset, *painted c. 1850 by Thomas Chambers. Little is known about the artist except that he was born in England in 1808 and came to the United States in 1832. Primarily a painter of marine views, landscapes, and portraits, he lived and worked for long periods in New York, Boston, and Albany. There are no records of his later career, or of the place and date of his death. Many of his landscapes are said to have been inspired by engraved views of American scenery similar to those done after the watercolor paintings of William H. Bartlett. Another version of this scene, with changes in the river boats, indicates some duplication in his dozen works so far identified. National Gallery of Art, Washington, D.C. Gift of Edgar William and Bernice Chrysler Garbisch*

BOOK SIX

Across the Nation

BOOK SIX: *Across the Nation*

2439

2439 *The Conestoga wagon, so called because it originated in the Conestoga Valley of Lancaster County, Pennsylvania, was a landmark achievement in pure American utilitarian design. It was ruggedly constructed to withstand the strain of overland travel and to carry several tons' cargo in addition to the large families of its owners. The ingeniously contrived curved wagon bed prevented cargo from rolling and spilling when traveling the uphill terrain of the Alleghenies or when fording rivers en route. Strictly functional in every detail, the few places where native crafts could find expression were in the toolbox lids of wrought-iron hardware, hinges and hasps, or the decorated brake shoes. As generations of German families pushed westward, starting as early as 1755, the familiar Conestoga became the symbol of the frontier settler seeking to make his fortune in America's unconquered regions*

2440 *Carved wooden bag stamp used to identify a farmer's homespun grain bag at the miller's* **2441** *Egg cup of turned wood made and decorated by G. Lehn, a retired farmer. Late nineteenth century*

From the Rhineland
to Penn's Land

2440

T HE PROMISE of freedom of worship brought the first immigrants from the German Palatinate to America during the fall of 1682. Through the efforts of William Penn and his Quaker agents for the German Land Company, the wooded regions bordering the Delaware valley and an area hundreds of miles to the west were opened to them for colonization. Here the immigrants could settle, free from endless war, religious persecution, and excessive taxes. This immigration from Germany grew steadily until the middle of the eighteenth century. In 1738, for example, some nine thousand persons landed in the busy port of Philadelphia.

Many of the new immigrants came over as indentured servants, with contracts to work from two to seven years to repay their passage. Not all, however, were peasants or farm people—some were much-needed artisans and craftsmen such as masons, carpenters, tanners, bakers, butchers, and blacksmiths. The members of this group of Colonists who prospered most were the husbandmen who knew best how to farm the Pennsylvania fields.

The German settlers in America either belonged to the Lutheran and Reformed churches or followed the more austere beliefs of the Anabaptists. Among the latter were the Amish and the Mennonites, called "the plain people," who renounced all worldly frills,

2441

quirks of fashion, and modern inventions. To this day, they wear distinctively plain clothes, shun the automobile, and exclude all superfluous ornament from their simple farmhouses.

With a stubborn tenacity, the Amish and Mennonite pietists resisted any and all outside influences and attempts to assimilate them into American life. They constituted a self-reliant enclave, self-supporting and self-governing, yet never antagonistic to the laws of the land. Their own press published their newspapers and journals in their native German tongue; publishers issued or imported German books and Bibles for use in the schools, and English was all but unknown. As late as 1911, it was necessary to make English compulsory in the public schools of the region. The possible consequences of entertaining a large group almost immune to Americanization were noted early by Benjamin Franklin, who wrote: "Unless the stream of their importation could be turned from this to other Colonies . . . they will soon so outnumber us, that all advantages we have will not (in my opinion) be able to preserve our language."

This never happened, yet the ways and habits of the Pennsylvania Dutch (a misnomer derived from the word *Deutsch*, meaning "German") linger after almost three centuries. It is estimated that about a third of a million people, both here and in Canada, still speak with pronounced traces of the original dialect.

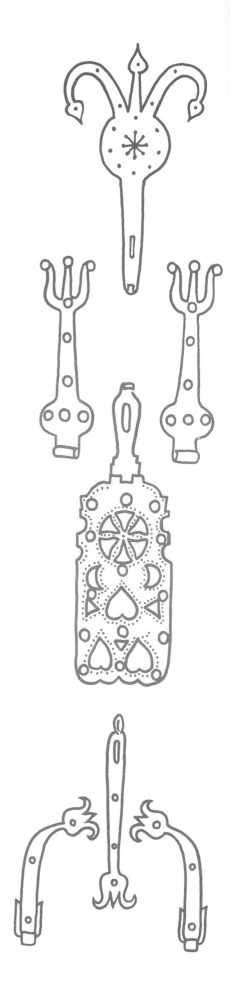

This very insularity has also preserved a heritage in the arts and crafts that is without parallel for originality, purity, and diversity.

In establishing themselves on virgin soil, the transplanted German farmers banded together in groups with artisans in order to furnish all necessary articles, the design of which was rooted in the medieval German culture. When a farmer could not build what he needed, he turned to his brethern. Craftsmen equipped the early settlers with essentials. Thereafter, other skilled workers, such as cabinetmakers, coppersmiths, and silversmiths, added grace and beauty to the simple homesteads.

The decorators and craftsmen of the region were not original designers. They adapted and intelligently applied decorative motifs almost identical to those of the Rhineland Palatinate. They used the unicorn, a fabled symbol of purity, to decorate many fine chests that were crafted in Berks County. The peacock, a symbol of resurrection, appeared on ceramic plates and pottery as well as on *Fraktur* birth and wedding certificates. The tulip, basic to the decorative vocabulary of the region, first bloomed on the Continent at Augsburg in 1554. It was brought into the Western world from Turkey, and its popularity spread thoughout Europe. The tulip became an important decorative motif in southwestern Germany, and subsequently appeared on many fine examples of Pennsylvania German furniture and folk art.

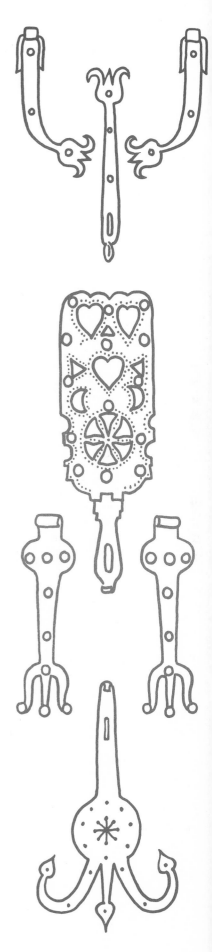

2442

668   2443

2442 *Displayed on the open shelves of this Pennsylvania German pine cupboard of the eighteenth century are earthenware plates, jars, and jugs with slip and sgraffito decoration. Photograph courtesy the Henry Francis du Pont Winterthur Museum, Winterthur, Delaware*

To a Bit of Clay
They Added Beauty

2444

PENNSYLVANIA GERMAN settlers from the Rhine Valley inherited a love for ornamental kitchenware which reflected Old World techniques and traditions. The abundance of native red clay, the endless supply of fuel, and the ease in setting up a kiln were ideally suited to the continuation of their pottery handicrafts.

Directly beneath the rich, fertile soil of eastern Pennsylvania, especially in Montgomery, Bucks, and Berks counties, a good quality of potter's clay was found. Once a potter located a supply, he stripped the top layer of soil to a depth of about six inches in an area

about five by ten feet. The clay was then dug and hauled to a homemade kiln. When one clay pit was exhausted, the potter had no difficulty in finding another close at hand.

Kitchen articles were the first to be fashioned from this clay—plates, pots, bowls, and baking dishes. The potter also produced red roofing tiles, reminiscent of his European homeland, a practice that has continued into the twentieth century. All potters made nests of pots in graded sizes for apple butter and milk; covered earthenware jars for pickles and preserves; mixing bowls, jelly molds and colanders; and handled jugs for cider and vinegar,

2443 *Covered earthenware dish of pierced work required extreme care in the cutting. Such work was often performed by potters who sought to impress their prospective employers with their skill* **2444** *In this sugar bowl the lid has a unique decoration of many-tiered beaded flanges and scrolls* **2445** *Covered jar from southeastern Pennsylvania shows the sgraffito treatment of conventional tulip-and-leaf design. Made in 1830*

2445

which were stoppered with corncob stumps. Many potters turned out red clay teapots, dark-brown coffeepots, cups, thick mugs of quart capacity for ale or spirits, and pitchers in varying sizes. There were enormous platters in oval, round, or octagonal shapes and casseroles with ornamental covers.

Aside from kitchenware, many other household articles were supplied by the potter: washbowls, candlesticks, lamp bases, hot-water bottles, soap dishes, shaving mugs and bowls, vases, flowerpots, and hanging baskets. Smaller objects included inkstands and sanders, toys, pipes, and coin banks. For the most part these were crafted in simple forms and shapes, strictly utilitarian and unadorned. However, when the homemaker wanted something special, "just for fancy," the potter produced his version of fashionable imported Staffordshire mantel ornaments or Bohemian bric-a-brac, such as little figurines, birds, and animals. These were crude and quaint, yet they satisfied the aesthetic standards of those who remembered the earthenware knickknacks of the homeland. These fancy pieces were by no means numerous; at best, they represented a small fraction of the potter's output. They survived because they were given a place of honor in the home.

The most prized pieces of pottery today are the highly original ornamental ware made in the European tradition by a few Pennsylvania potters. Their mastery of ceramic techniques attained a level of artistic excellence difficult to match in the vast field of American folk arts. Presentation pieces were commissioned as gifts for weddings, birthdays, or anniversaries.

Much care was taken with the design and embellishment of these pieces, and elaborate inscriptions and pertinent sayings were an integral part of a decorative theme that often included the recipient's name and occasionally that of the potter.

With a masterful sense of design, the potter organized an elaborate ornamental vocabulary that included such flowers and fruits as the familiar pomegranate, tulip, fuchsia, olive leaf, forget-me-not, and lily of the valley. Decorative patterns relied heavily on favorite animals and birds—dove, deer, rabbit, fish, eagle, rooster—and the horse and rider. Appropriate inscriptions of humorous homespun philosophy were introduced by the creative potter as a foil for his decorative treatment.

The potter used two essentially related techniques to apply his patterns to the flat or rounded surface of his wares; slip decoration and sgraffito. Both methods have been known since ancient times, and descended into the hands of the Pennsylvania Germans by way of central European ceramic artisans. Slip decoration was applied by means of one or several goose quills that fed a thin clay fluid from a slip cup. The potter manipulated this cup deftly until the fluid flowed in scrolls, squiggles, or dots to delineate his design. The thin white or creamy solution was a special type of clay, or "slip," imported from New Jersey. As the potter worked his slip cup, his deft movements produced a calligraphic language, not unlike writing done with a broad-pointed nib. He was also able to make thin hairlines with which he would outline figures and decorations. Great skill was required in this operation, as the craftsman's strokes, once applied to the surface, were permanent. When fired, the slip became a light cream or buff color, which contrasted with the darker background of the base.

The second method of decorating pottery surfaces is sgraffito, a term derived from the Italian *sgraffiare*, "to scratch." This technique was used extensively by the Pennsylvania German potters and involves incising a design into a semiwet clay surface by means of a thin sharp-edged wooden tool. First a cream or golden-yellow slip color was applied, then the hairline design was scratched through it, exposing the rust color of the redware; then the piece was fired. The potter worked to achieve a simplicity and clarity of expression —every line, floral form, bird, or figure was rendered with a minimum of strokes.

An entirely new pottery form was created in the process of filling requests for gift ceramics: the circular dish or pie plate. Because of the many variations of the popular tulip motif that decorated this kind of plate, it came to be called tulipware. Created as display pieces, tulipware offered an excellent opportunity for the ceramic craftsman to exhibit his talents. Peacocks, eagles, roosters, and leaf and floral designs in infinitive variety were rendered with a freshness and unmistakable naiveté that came to be characteristic of the work of the Pennsylvania region. Another distinctive feature of these concave dishes was the use of concentric outer rings. They invited the use of pertinent sayings that added an extra fillip to the decorative scheme. Johannes Neesz inscribed one thus: "Luck and misfortune is every morning our breakfast." As a border for a bird and tulip design John Leidy wrote: "Every bird knows to rest for a short hour after eating." The same potter inscribed this sentiment about independence: "Rather would I single live than my wife the breeches give." Another bit of sly humor accompanies a courtship scene: "God hath created all the beautiful maidens. They are for the potter, but not for the priests." The drinking mug, often elaborately decorated, presented a more difficult problem for inscriptions. One noted piece reads: "I say what is true, and drink what is clear." These expressions were penned in the Pennsylvania German dialect.

Quite by accident, about the turn of this century, this dialect led to the first scholarly interest in these charming pieces. Dr. Edwin Barber, then curator of the Pennsylvania Museum, discovered one of these curious plates in a junk shop. He assumed the piece to be of European origin, but, on deciphering the inscription, realized that instead of High German, this was indeed one of the local dialects, and that the object had been made in a nearby pottery at least a hundred years before. A search was undertaken to locate additional ware to form the basis for a museum collection. After scouring the countryside, Barber was able, from conversations with descendants of potters and their families, to reach a new appraisal of his discovery. Barber also found that the folk traditions displayed in the pottery handicrafts of the Pennsylvania German settlers were the result of a strong cultural heritage that resisted the whims of fashion and preserved those values that suited the settlers' temperaments.

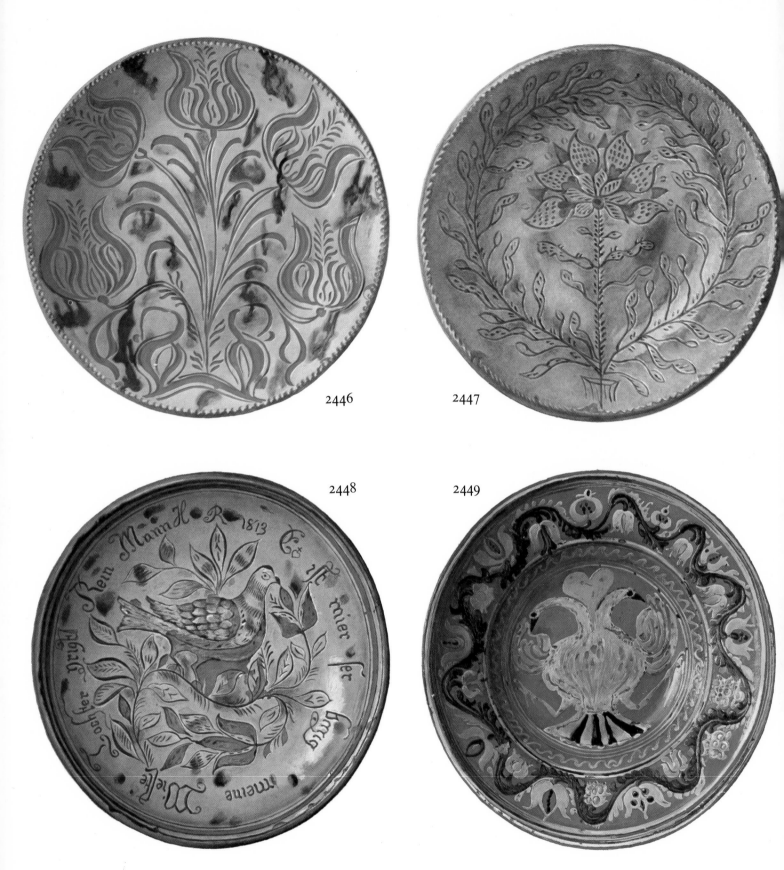

2446   2447

2448   2449

2446 *Tulips, in both natural and conventionalized forms, figured conspicuously as the most prominent decorative motif on Pennsylvania earthenware* **2447** *Feathery leaf and floral forms are an inspired improvisation of the potter with a flair for decoration* **2448–2453** *Fanciful bird forms often are a central feature of these ceramic plates, surrounded with circular borders of flowers, mottoes, or geometric elements. A wide variety of aviary favorites are shown, including the eagle,* **2451** *(c. 1830), the dove,* **2448** *(1813), the peacock,* **2452** *(1812), the parrot,* **2453** *(1808), and the imaginary double bird,* **2449**. *"Deer's Chase,"* **2450** *(c. 1800), was the work of David Spinner*

2450

2451

2452

2453

2454   **2455**

2456

2457

2458

2459   **2460**

2454–2467 *Many of the pie plates of Pennsylvania potters are recognizable by design, composition, lettering, or other characteristics. David Spinner of Bucks County,* **2454** *(c. 1810), drew figures of soldiers, cavaliers, fashionable women, and picturesque hunting scenes. John Leidy,* **2462** *(1786), was an outstanding craftsman who decorated in sgraffito and the more difficult technique of slip painting. Johannes Neesz,*

2463, 2465, *may have been associated with David Spinner, as his work bears a close resemblance. Georg Hübener,* **2461** *(1786), was a master decorator and skilled at lettering; his handsome inscriptions often carry a comic valentine message. Samuel Troxel,* **2457** *(1826),* **2459** *(1828), had a fondness for birds, specifically the American eagle; he always dated his pieces, often to the very day*

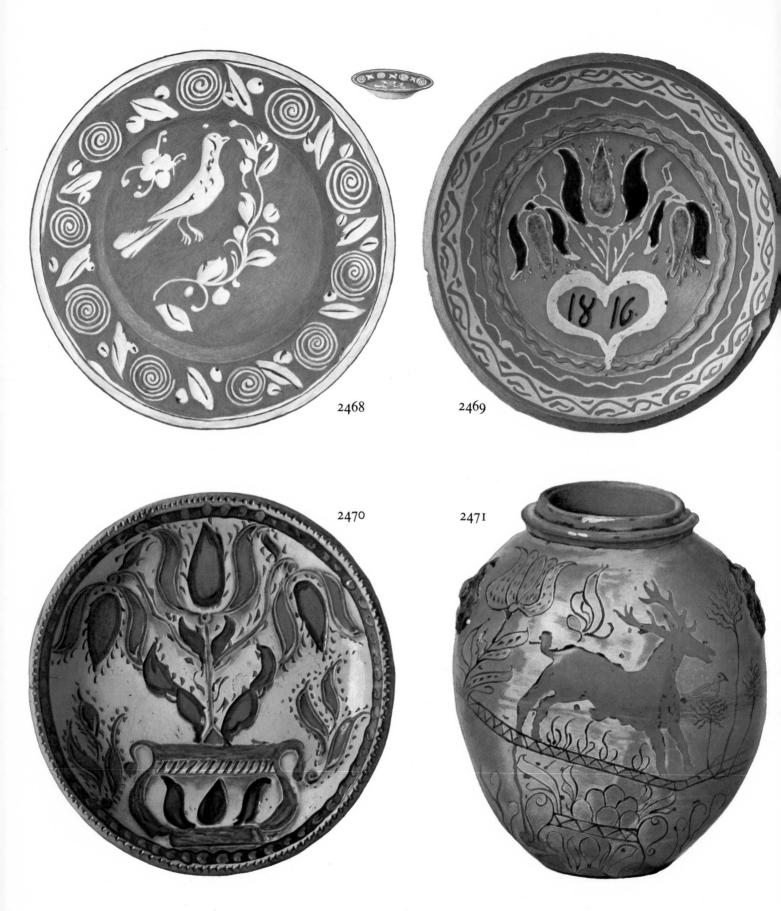

2468

2469

2470

2471

2468–2475 *Slip-decorated ware was made by trickling liquid clay, called slip, through a quill attached to a cup, and required a sure sense of design and direction. True slip is usually distinguished by light-colored ornamentation upon a darker ground, the resultant design taking on a light relief. In contrast, sgraffito ware is the result of incising lines into the soft clay surface before firing. The lines thus depressed, or intaglioed, show dark against a white or yellowish field. Slipware plates are* **2468, 2469, 2472, 2473;** *sgraffito-ware pieces are* **2470, 2471, 2474, 2475**

2472 2473

2474 2475

Overleaf: GALLERY OF CERAMIC PLATES AND DISHES. *Animal motifs:* **2492, 2502, 2504, 2522, 2526;**
birds: **2481, 2483, 2484, 2500, 2514, 2515, 2518;** *decorative and floral:* **2476, 2478, 2480, 2482, 2485–
2491, 2493–2499, 2501, 2503, 2505–2512, 2516, 2517, 2519, 2523, 2525;** *figures:* **2479, 2524;** *linear:*
2477, 2513, 2520, 2521

2476

2477

2478

2479

2480

2484

2485

2486

2487

2488

2494

2495

2496

2497

2504

2505

2506

2507

2513

2514

2515

2516

2517

2481

2482

2483

2492

2493

2489

2490

2491

2502

2503

2499

2500

2501

2509

2510

2511

2512

2519

2520

2521

2522

8

2523

2524

2525

2526

679

2527

2527 Polychromed rooster carved in the well-established tradition of the Pennsylvania German wood-carvers. Every detail in this exquisite piece suggests the hand of a master. The haughty position of the head, sinuous curves of the neck and breast, the peacock-like spread of the splendid tail feathers, the delicate patterning of surfaces, all combine to create an outstanding expression of the whittler's art of the nineteenth century. Photograph courtesy the Abby Aldrich Rockefeller Folk Art Collection, Williamsburg, Virginia

2528

2529

Whittled for Pastime & Profit

WHITTLING HAS BEEN described variously as a pastime for boys, as everyman's natural instinct, or as a sophisticated way of producing wood shavings. With a sharp knife, anyone can use his leisure time to fashion miniature objects such as mantel decorations, kitchen accessories, toys, and fanciful pieces that have no practical purpose.

The output of the amateur Pennsylvania Dutch whittlers was tremendous, although only a few were above the ordinary. Among these were Wilhelm Schimmel, Aaron Mountz,

Noah Weis, and George Huguenin, all of whom were active during the latter part of the nineteenth century. Whether their professional competence is related to their Alpine and Bavarian backgrounds, or whether it indicates a skill developed by experience and observation, the results are worthy of serious study.

The names of most whittlers are unknown, but in some instances their identity has been preserved either by an occasional marking or a recognizable technique. A general design characteristic or possibly the incisional manner of chip carving may also provide a clue to the whittler's identity.

2530

2528 Eagle carved by Wilhelm Schimmel follows a very personal formula—a crisscross decorative pattern simulates body feathers, while the wing-feather structure consists of rugged prismatic forms serrated at the ends 2529 Eagle and squirrel on nest of leaves, surrounded with buds; another subject of which Schimmel carved a small number 2530 Eagle carved from single block of pine by Aaron Mountz, latter part of the nineteenth century

The work of these folk craftsmen falls into several categories according to the treatment of the wood: carved, whittled, scratch-carved, or turned. One of the most skilled carvers was Wilhelm Schimmel. He used a naive cross-hatched patterning scheme when simulating feathers on a bird or the shaggy mane on a horse or dog, creating a surface more characteristic of the peasant approach to stylization than an accurate representation.

Aaron Mountz was a friend and disciple of Schimmel's, and began whittling with his encouragement. Both carved the same general type of subject, such as birds, barnyard animals, squirrels, dogs, and sheep. Whereas Schimmel often affected a rough manner, Mountz's style was painstaking and precise.

Another noted carver was George Huguenin, a descendant of a French-Swiss family, who arrived in this country about the middle of the nineteenth century. He brought with him the wood-carving skill of his native Switzerland, its technique and traditions, customs and subject matter. Most of his time was devoted to making figures for miniature crèches that were usually placed at the base of the Christmas tree. Huguenin's toys were in the European tradition. His barnyard creatures were realistic, particularly his sheep, on which he glued woolly coats. Often he made a barn to hold the flock as well as other toys.

More utilitarian but no less decorative are the surface carvings in wood made for kitchen articles. Wooden cake and cookie molds and marzipan boards were used as matrices for *Lebkuchen* and gingerbread cookies. The springerle boards were subdivided into from six to twenty-four squares, and each one had a different design. The motifs for the boards may have been inspired by nursery fables, animals and birds, or even by Biblical scenes in the more elaborate pieces. The finest examples of these springerle boards were the work of professional carvers and can be found in today's antique markets.

In addition to flat cookie boards, designs were carved on cylindrical rollers which were fitted with handles and looked like rolling pins. Another type of surface decoration related to the cake and cookie boards is found on

butter molds. These might be the property of a single household for its own table use or might be found on print butter that was sold at the local market. The mold designs often became a trademark by which the buyer could distinguish one brand from another. Molds were carved in varying forms, from rectangular to circular. The butter was packed into the circular form with a paddle, and then ejected by a simple plunger which left its imprint. The design, carved in intaglio, appeared in relief on the butter. Designs varied greatly. One of the most interesting motifs is the star-shaped symbol of the sun, which was used to protect the butter from spoilage.

Wood carving also appeared on sugar mortars, dippers, bowls, ladles, and paddles. In addition to carved kitchen utensils, there were clock frames, spoon racks, mirror frames, weathercocks, gateposts, and a myriad of other objects which appealed to the craftsman.

It is worth noting the marked contrast between the peasant carving of the Pennsylvania farmland areas and those of the New England region. In the former group, we find the minor decorative arts: toys, mantel ornaments, cake and butter molds, and a Noah's Ark filled with animals and birds. Occasionally a sculptured figure appears in the round, like that of Blind Justice, a rare example of pure three-dimensional carving, attributed to John Fisher of York, Pennsylvania. No architectural carving existed because the farm dwellings, mostly of native stone, did not permit exterior ornamentation; the hex signs on barn exteriors were the only notes of decoration to be found. On the New England seaboard, however, cities enjoyed a flourishing trade with Europe and naturally developed a broader cultural base. Garden statuary, decorations designed for architectural placement, figureheads and marine decoration in all its many phases, trade signs, and all manner of lesser types of carved work were found throughout the area. Trade and other dealings with foreign sources encouraged an exchange of ideas and skills, whereas the farmland regions maintained their insularity and, with it, a limited horizon in arts and crafts. Both regions, however, have contributed significantly to the mainstream of decorative art in America.

2531

2532

2533

2534

2535

2536

2537

2538

2539

2540

2541

2542

2531–2543 *Domestic birds, especially the barnyard variety, were among the favorite subjects of the traveling whittlers of the Pennsylvania countryside. Hens and roosters, robins and parrots, were second in popularity only to the favored eagle. The many renditions of the rooster were more realistic than those of the eagle, possibly because the latter was rarely available for close study, and so became more idealized. If some birds are difficult to identify, it is because of a design formula the carver adopted*

2543

2544

2544-2549 *Aaron Mountz, a disciple of Schimmel and undoubtedly influenced by him, nevertheless developed his own individual style. He was more painstaking and precise. While many of Schimmel's birds defy recognition, a work by Mountz is clearly distinguished by its naturalistic approach. Yet his manner is stylized too, dominated by a strong sense of patterning in the feather treatment. His subjects included eagles, parrots, owls, herons or cranes, and poodles—and even the last carried the crosshatching of fur and mane*

2545

2546

2547

2548

2549

687

2550

2551

2552

Wandering Wood-carver

THOSE CARVERS who traveled extensively in order to peddle their wares seem to have attained greater competence than those who did not. For one German settler in the Pennsylvania region, Wilhelm Schimmel, carving odd bits became a way of life. Little is known of Schimmel's background, but he may have come from the Black Forest or Bavarian section of southern Germany, where wood carving had been practiced for centuries. Schimmel came to live in the Cumberland valley, near Carlisle, shortly after the Civil War, and from then until his death in 1890 he shuttled over the countryside, going from house to house peddling his talent with a jackknife. Sometimes he carried little birds and animals ready-made for quick sale. At other times he would ask for any large piece of pine lying about, offering to transform it into

2553

2550, 2551 *The rugged rough-hewn character of Schimmel's eagles is a reflection of the man himself, who was noted for his temper as well as for his excellent handicraft. Figure 2550 from a photograph, courtesy the Smithsonian Institution, Washington, D.C.* **2551** *Eagle carved by Schimmel carries the unmistakable characteristics of outstretched wings, serrated feather ends, small body, and large head with a tuft* **2552** Garden of Eden *is Schimmel's naive attempt at storytelling, replete with fence, figures, apple, snake, and tree embellished at the top with pine shavings. The carver made several of these* **2553** *There is a strong suggestion of the parrot in this upright eagle, particularly due to treatment of head and beak*

an eagle that might measure as much as three feet across. When he came to town with a basket of birds, he traded his handiwork for meals or just for pennies. Sometimes he would pass a splendid carving across the bar in exchange for a pint of whisky.

Schimmel was said to be surly, blasphemous, and ill tempered. Children learned to avoid him, but a few people understood and befriended him. John Greider, a miller and farmer living just west of Carlisle, opened his doors to the rude itinerant carver. After Schimmel had made one of his tours of the neighboring towns, he would return to the Greider homestead and volunteer to help with the farm chores.

The technical marks of Schimmel's handiwork are obvious and easy to detect. He first shaped the body of a bird, then carved the wings as separate members. These were pegged or doweled into position. When finished with the detailing, Schimmel applied a coat of gesso, a plaster wash he preferred to use before applying the final coat of paint, in order to brighten his birds and beasts. Black, brown, red, and yellow ocher were his favorite colors, though his palette often depended on what the farmer had available, whether barn red or an indiscriminate leftover.

Schimmel's fame rests particularly on his eagles, which are now in leading public and private American collections. He also executed all types of barnyard animals and occasionally wild ones such as lions, wolves, and foxes of indefinable features; toy soldiers were also among his creations. Just before his death he fashioned an Adam and Eve before the tree where they were tempted; the grouping was surrounded by a picket fence with corner posts mounted on a rectangular base. This and other Biblical scenes were popular with the people of the region, but Schimmel's character did not favor lessons from the Bible; he was more at home with the eagles and roosters on which his fame rests.

2554 *The pose of this Schimmel eagle differs from his favorite attitude, shown below. Wide wingspread and low body are unusual, yet all other characteristics of the carver are in evidence, including crosshatched patterning on body, coarse carving on wings and parrot-like beak structure. Photograph*
2555 *Crosshatching on the tail of this squirrel by Schimmel gives more of a pine-cone than a fur effect*
2556 *At least two dozen of this Schimmel eagle are now in the hands of collectors and museums*

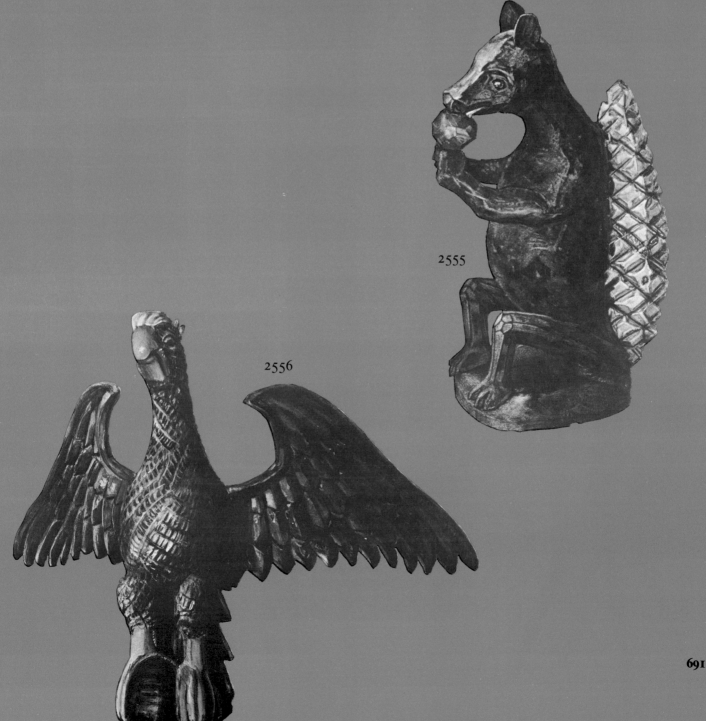

2555

2556

692   **2558**

2557 *In the eighteenth-century parlor of the Kershner house in Berks County, Pennsylvania, is furniture typical of the period and region. Grouped about the walnut sawbuck table are side chairs described as Moravian and an armchair at the table's end, a country version of the Philadelphia Chippendale form. In the corner stands the traditional German wardrobe usually included in the bride's dowry, and, next to it, the leather-covered armchair that belonged to self-styled "baron" Henry Steigel, the glassware manufacturer. The blanket, or dower, chest is dated 1774, and on its top is a Bible box with a 1748 German Bible. The tall clock, with inlays, is by Jacob Graff, of Lebanon. The table is set with wooden plates, horn cups, pewter tankards, and green glass bottles. Photograph courtesy the Henry Francis du Pont Winterthur Museum, Winterthur, Delaware*

2560

Furniture

"Plain & Fancy"

THE VAST WOODLANDS of the Pennsylvania colony, from the fertile rolling countryside bordering on the Delaware westward over the mountainous regions reaching to the Monongahela, were rich in softwoods and hardwoods suitable for fuel, fencing, construction, and furniture. The supply was so abundant as to justify calling the Colonial era in America the "age of wood."

After several generations of working with woods that were new to them, both joiner and cabinetmaker had learned their individual peculiarities, their textures, strength, grain, their staining and polishing characteristics. Cedar resisted moisture and thus was suitable for fence posts, shingles, pails, tubs, and cisterns. Woods like pine and oak had many uses, not only for furniture but as joists, sills, and rafters in the construction of barns and

2558 Pennsylvania plank chair featuring stylized tulip heart 2559 Wall cupboard with central panel carved with birds and gouge marks 2560 Spoon rack with decorations of chip-carved Frisian lunettes

buildings. Ash and hickory were ideal for tool handles and where great strength was needed. For the making of furniture, pine and whitewood, that is, tulip poplar or yellow poplar, were most used among the softwoods. Fine cabinetry called for hardwood such as black walnut, cherry, and maple; their bird's-eye and tiger-striped variants were the result of a particular way of cutting and sawing. Mahogany, so extensively used by the Philadelphia cabinet, makers for the formal pieces in the style of Chippendale and Hepplewhite, were not used in the style and period under discussion here.

By the middle of the eighteenth century, many of the agricultural settlements of eastern Pennsylvania were emerging from their primitive conditions. Farmers were now able to order better furnishings for their homes from the local cabinetmaker. Moderately affluent

pioneers tried to recapture the amenities of their homelands and to create heirlooms that could be passed down to their children.

Tables and chairs were made first, then a *Schrank* (wardrobe) for storing clothes, as closets were virtually unknown. Cupboards and dressers came next in the succession of things most needed, followed by smaller objects like Bible chests and wall racks for spoons, stools, and occasional pieces. The priorities varied, naturally, according to the Colonist's circumstances, and also depended on the local craftsman and the extent of his commitments. Family custom among the early Pennsylvanians dictated that a daughter should have a dowry at the time of her marriage. The dower chest, of simple dovetail construction and decorated in styles that varied from county to county, headed an inventory of items that

2561 *Poplar wagon seat with splint webbing, splayed, ring-turned legs, and cresting rail with pierced heart, c. 1780*

2561

included a wardrobe, table, bed, and a stated number of quilts and coverlets woven by the bride to be. These essential country furnishings became the nucleus around which the bride's future home was built. Fortunately, because of the great care with which these chests were designed and treasured, they survive as a record of a way of life of two centuries ago, rich in detailed notations and documentation.

A cursory glance at the table setting and furniture of the Kershner parlor, typical of a family in moderate circumstances, shows a marked parallel with room furnishings of contemporary southern Germany. The local craftsman, like his patron living on a farm or in a small village isolated from the outside world, reflected the prevailing Baroque taste. Hardly a trace of contemporary fashion filtered through to him, and thus his design concepts were uncontaminated by the whims of the day, especially the popular acceptance of the masters of English cabinetry. Thus the Germanic prototypes were reproduced as closely as memory allowed in the earlier years of colonization and, as recollection served, well into the nineteenth century.

The plank-seat chairs in the Kershner parlor followed a Moravian type, with sharply splayed legs, heavy flat seat, shaped splat back silhouetted in graceful outline. A reinforced crosspiece under the seat served to anchor the legs. The massive armchair for the head of the table had front legs that were turned in simple fashion and heavy arms that sometimes ended in a knob or scroll. It had a flat back with a shaped splat, a solid seat, and square-shaped shaped splat, a solid seat, and square-shaped rungs. The sawbuck table, which was often very long, had thick crossed legs held rigidly in position by a central stretcher and pegged pins for tightening at both ends. This table type antedated the four-legged tables that were usually equipped with drawers under the plank tops for storing linens and cutlery.

The huge wardrobe, or *Schrank*, was an important piece that took on mammoth proportions. It, too, followed closely along the lines of central European pieces. It rested on corner brackets and had a heavy cornice, large double doors, and several drawers at the bottom. The facing of doors and stiles was hippaneled or treated with stained or painted moldings. Often the entire surface of the wardrobe was decorated with exquisite traceries of familiar folk motifs, painted with superb skill or inlaid by a rare technique called "wax inlay," in which the wax hardened and mellowed to resemble ivory.

Corner cupboards and open-shelf dressers were built to display choice bits of decorated pottery and pewter. It was customary to notch the edge of one of the open-dresser shelves to form a spoon rack. Hanging wall cupboards, chests of drawers, and smaller items such as Bible boxes, candle boxes, spice holders, pipe racks, and mirrors were usually decorated rather than left as plain wood surfaces.

A favorite among the Pennsylvania cabinetmakers was the straight-grained black walnut. It became very dark when highly polished, however, and this darkness accounted for fluctuations in its popularity. Where black walnut was not available, both yellow and black cherry wood were used. When well aged, black cherry approaches mahogany in color, and its workability is quite similar.

Characteristic of all this region's furniture was its strictly utilitarian quality. Sturdy construction was never sacrificed, even in dower chests that were meant to be embellished. A fondness for color and gaiety in furnishings nevertheless manifested itself, not only in the decorated dower chests, but in cupboards, dressers, and smaller objects that could be treated more intimately. Such furniture may be said to be "paint decorated." It received several coats of a base paint which acted as a preservative, and then the decoration was added, "just for fancy." It is most difficult to draw the line between "plain" and "fancy," but generally the love for conceits and whimsies appears more often in minor objects that lent themselves to ornamentation than in functional pieces of furniture.

2562

2563

2564

2565

2562 *Peasant-type walnut table (c. 1730–40) with shaped square legs supported by heavy stretchers. The apron is richly decorated with curvatures. Wide table-top planks are held together with cleats* **2563** *Oak sawbuck table (c. 1750) with cross side supports of heavy stock held together by center stretcher and pegged darts at ends. Foot rests also serve to give additional support as stretchers* **2564** *Decorated Pennsylvania dresser with glass doors, reeded quarter columns at corners, and hand-painted ornaments, including figures of angels taken from birth certificates, c. 1828* **2565** *Corner cabinet with open shelves at top; door and side panels with painted decorations*

2566

2567

2568

2566 *Oval-top pine table shaped in the traditional provincial form, with splayed legs and bottom stretchers. Apron decorated with typical curves and scrolls of the region. Dated 1750* **2567** *Hanging corner cabinet of pine is graced by an especially delightful display area at top, delicately scrolled and topped by fitting cap molding, c. 1750* **2568** *Open kitchen dresser for the display of plates, kitchenware, and spoons. Decorated cresting under cornice and on side pieces shows heavy plank construction*

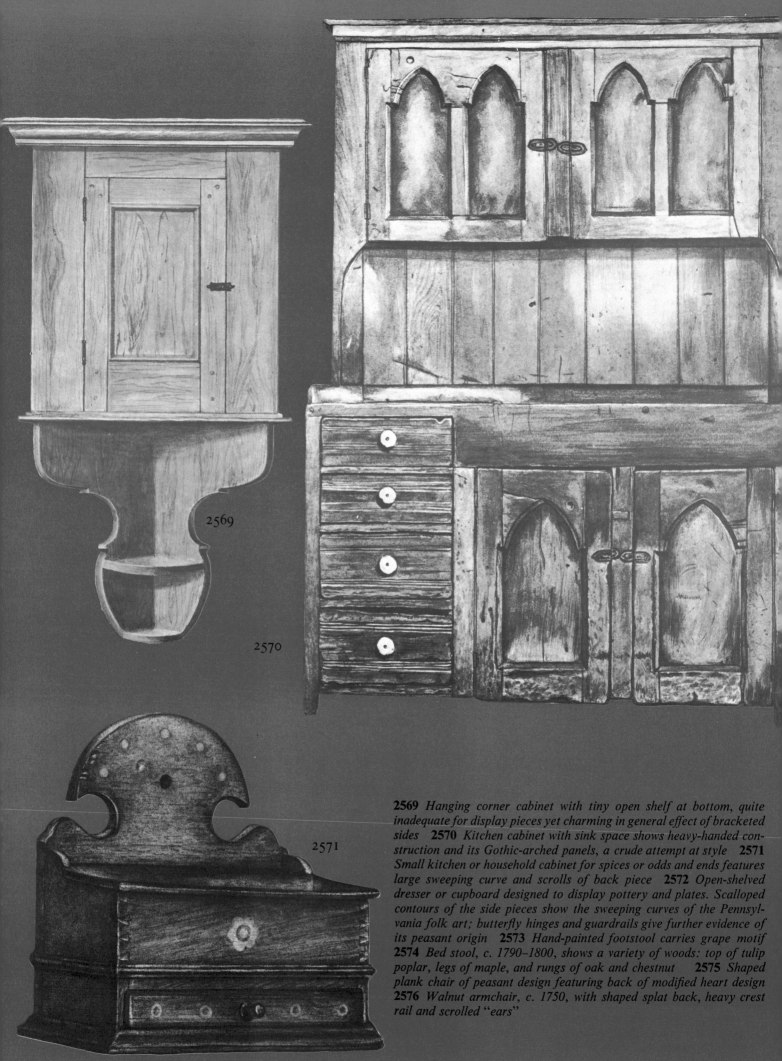

2569

2570

2571

2569 *Hanging corner cabinet with tiny open shelf at bottom, quite inadequate for display pieces yet charming in general effect of bracketed sides* **2570** *Kitchen cabinet with sink space shows heavy-handed construction and its Gothic-arched panels, a crude attempt at style* **2571** *Small kitchen or household cabinet for spices or odds and ends features large sweeping curve and scrolls of back piece* **2572** *Open-shelved dresser or cupboard designed to display pottery and plates. Scalloped contours of the side pieces show the sweeping curves of the Pennsylvania folk art; butterfly hinges and guardrails give further evidence of its peasant origin* **2573** *Hand-painted footstool carries grape motif* **2574** *Bed stool, c. 1790–1800, shows a variety of woods: top of tulip poplar, legs of maple, and rungs of oak and chestnut* **2575** *Shaped plank chair of peasant design featuring back of modified heart design* **2576** *Walnut armchair, c. 1750, with shaped splat back, heavy crest rail and scrolled "ears"*

2572

2573

2574

2575

2576

699

2577

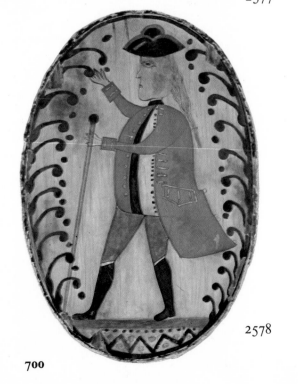

2577 *The traditional Pennsylvania German style of decoration is much in evidence in this Fraktur room, so called because of the many baptismal certificates, house blessings, and framed sentiments written in Fraktur calligraphy. Typical also in this Berks County room are the two hand-painted dower chests at the rear. Second half of the eighteenth century. Photograph courtesy the Henry Francis du Pont Winterthur Museum, Winterthur, Delaware* **2578** *Of the same period is this painted splint box, showing a man in a red coat with cane and tricorn hat and suggesting the festive occasion when this type of box was given* **2579** *In many dower chests the architectonic division of space into panels effectively separated decorative elements. This one, made in 1787*

2578

Decorated for Dowry

2579

THE DOWER CHEST was a traditional part of every maiden's
world; she began to fill it with
linens and laces the moment she
learned to sew. When she stitched her first
sampler or embroidered her first linens, these
were carefully stored in the chest until she was
married. Dower chests were the first hope
chests designed to serve both a utilitarian and
a romantic function and great care went into
their construction and decoration. They were
generally three to four feet long and were
placed in either the parlor or the bedroom.
Some chests contained a built-in drawer or

two, but this was not typical. To raise the chest
off the floor and give it a more convenient
height, various supports were used—the shoe
or trestle foot, the ball foot, the ogee bracket,
or ordinary bracket foot could be placed at the
four bottom corners. All of these could easily
be constructed from flat stock with a scroll or
fret saw.

The woods most used for dower chests were
pine, poplar, and walnut. The large expanse of
the front and top surface of each chest invited
the hand of the decorator, and at the same time
a painted surface made the soft wood more
durable. The farmer-carpenter, however, rarely

attempted to decorate the chest himself, but preferred to wait for the itinerant decorator to make his accustomed rounds.

The painted chest of the Pennsylvania Germans varied little from eighteenth-century European peasant furniture which was made of inexpensive pine and decorated in color. The favorite background color was a soft blue; dark green, brown, and even black were used on occasion. On this background, the decorator deftly applied vases of flowers, stars, tulips, daisies, birds, angels, and unicorns. The front panel was often divided into an architectonic arrangement of two or three arched areas. The end panels utilized the same architectonic forms to extend the impact of the front facade. Often the decorator designed an interplay of motifs which extended from the front areas to the end panels.

In Pennsylvania, the tulip recalled the distant gardens of the Rhineland and was used extensively. The fuchsia and carnation were also popular. The heart, symbol of love, appeared in every medium employed by the folk artist. The huge star featured on the com-

modious barns in Lehigh and Montgomery counties appeared as a favorite motif in chest decoration. The unicorns on Berks County chests are a carry-over from medieval days, when they represented the guardians of maidenhood. The peacock, stitched on hand towels and painted on chests and toleware, was a respected weather prophet.

Most chests were painted to order; often the owner's name appeared with the date and year of execution. The lettering on many of these chests was often in the Germanic or *Fraktur* style, using Gothic letter forms. Christian Selzer (1749–1831) inscribed and painted some of the finest dower chests in the Pennsylvania region.

Another fine decorator was Heinrich Otto, who also had a printing shop in Ephrata. His favorite design motifs were parrots, peacocks, animated birds with twisted necks, floral forms, and leafy vines.

Except for a few names, the painter-decorators whose works are now on display in museum collections or in private homes remain anonymous.

2580

2581

2582

2580–2585 *All marriage chests had lift lids; some featured bottom drawers, but otherwise their construction varied little. There is great ingenuity in their scheme of decoration, however, and diverse motifs are used. Double-arched panels, as in* **2581, 2584,** *and* **2585,** *and triple arches, as in* **2582** *and* **2583,** *assist in well-ordered design schemes in which urns, flowered arrangements, and unicorns appear.*

2583

2584

2585

2586

2587

2586–2591 *In the dower chest for Ann Beer (1790), the decorator floats a pair of mermaids holding sprays of flowers. Geometric elements characterize* **2589;** *plants and floral forms dominate in* **2587, 2588, 2590,** *and* **2591** *with unicorns, hearts, and tulips interspersed. Most of these chests were made and decorated before 1800*

2588

2589

2590

2591

707

2592

2593

2592–2597 *The floral sprigs and plant forms of Pennsylvania dower chests exhibit an informal boldness and sprightliness. Feathery leaves and twisting stems are the rule, and where the ornament is confined to a panel, it generally grows from an urn or vase and takes a symmetrical shape. The human figure is rare, but can be seen in* **2594** *and as a rider in* **2595**. *Unicorn chests (see* **2596**), *named after their dominant motif, are often intricately ornamented*

2594

2595

2596

2597

2598

2599

2598–2603 *A group of chests made and decorated between 1775 and 1787 follows no rigid scheme. Swirling petaled blossoms in* **2600** *almost suggest a child's pinwheel. The all-over repetition of small units,* **2598,** *is quite unique; the introduction of shells and insects,* **2602,** *is unusual in this region. In* **2599** *and especially in* **2603,** *the exceptionally elaborate use of flowers and birds creates panels with a quality of fine tapestry. Wherever escutcheon plates are used, they are often available furniture forms and thus not compatible with the peasant character of the chest*

2600

2601

2602

2603

711

2604

2605

For Bibles, Books & Bibelots

2606

2607

2608

2609

2604–2610 *The small box or chest came in many forms and has variously been called a desk box, Bible box, gift box, and treasure chest. Lids were either hinged or sliding tops. Floral decoration was lavish. The ubiquitous tulip form was employed, and occasionally geometric devices, as in* **2607** *and* **2608**. *The candle box,* **2606,** *combines the best of many favorite motifs. The casket with domed lid,* **2608,** *is covered with wallpaper. A salt box for the kitchen is shown in* **2609**

2610

2611

2612

2613

714

2614

2611–2616 *The four sides and top of the carved trinket chest,* **2611,** *are embellished with birds and floral sprigs. Painted candle boxes,* **2613** *and* **2616,** *were also used to hold jewels. End panel,* **2612,** *is decorated with flowers, buds, and leafy vines. The dough trough of poplar,* **2614,** *was decorated by Christian Selzer. The decorator of the domed casket,* **2615,** *has departed from traditional motifs in favor of abstract devices of rings and cusps, vigorously painted*

2615

2616

2617

2618

716

2619

Scribe & Scroll

THE PENNSYLVANIA DUTCH followed the ancient practice of recording vital statistics in family registers, using excellent handmade paper and illuminated inks, tints, and dyes so that the records would survive. This tradition encouraged the creation of lively, original genealogies in forms that are authentic and artistic.

Much credit must be given to the Pennsylvania papermakers, for without their skill, these beautiful writings and records would have been lost. Among a group of Mennonite colonists that settled there was William Ritten-

house, who was descended from a long line of German papermakers. With the help of German workmen, Rittenhouse set up a mill on the banks of the Schuylkill River. Paper was in demand in all the Colonies, especially because of the uncertainty of shipments from overseas, and local printing houses needed it for printing currency and for their other work.

The highest grade of paper was made from linen and cotton rags and remnants, by a slow process of disintegration, fermentation, and the beating down of the textile fibers. The rags were macerated between two millstones and immersed in troughs of water. After being

2617, 2618 *Birth and baptismal certificates, called* Taufschein, *are intricately lettered and embellished in the traditional* Fraktur *style* **2619–2621** *Details from* Fraktur *paintings show a love of floral and naturalistic ornament*

2620   2621

thoroughly cleansed, the whole was beaten into pulp by large wooden hammers until a homogeneous mass resulted. The mass was then put into a wooden frame with a base of woven wire netting that permitted only water to drip through. The skilled papermaker then manipulated the frame so that the fibrous particles of pulp were evenly deposited and became a thin layer on the frame. The basic sheet of wet paper was then removed by a woolen web, or felt, and dried.

The beautiful records of the Pennsylvania Dutch are done in *Fraktur. Fraktur-schrift*, as it was called in Germany, was a form of creative calligraphy named after the sixteenth-century *Fraktur* typeface. The latter was a crude imitation of the current manuscript writing styles, more cursive than the stiff Gothic black letter, and was cut in metal by the German type founders shortly after Gutenberg's time. When the Germans settled in southeastern Pennsylvania, the writing of family records, *Taufschein,* or birth and baptismal certificates, *Bücherzeichen*, or bookplates, house blessings, and valentines continued. Highly ornamental, hand drawn and colored, these calligraphic pieces were executed by the educated members of the community, the schoolmaster and the clergyman, or by itinerant artists.

The schoolmaster was expected to be versatile. He prepared legal papers, wrote letters for people who could not write, and executed the hand-written documents, especially those pertaining to births and baptisms, that were in constant demand.

To teach writing and the styles of the alphabet and at the same time to demonstrate his skill as a penman and decorator, the schoolmaster prepared a *Vorschrift*, or handwritten model, that was the forerunner of the nineteenth-century copybook. From the *Vorschriften*, pupils learned how to form numerals and letters of the alphabet in German script and *Fraktur* writing. An ever-present feature was

the large ornamental German capital, heading a well-lettered pious German text. The schoolmaster frequently signed his name to the *Vorschrift* to testify to his fluent craftsmanship. The *Vorschrift* was often presented to a pupil as a reward and token of the instructor's regard. It was framed with other examples of the calligrapher's art, and hung on the family walls. The *Haus-Segen* (house blessings) were treasured wallpieces, for devout Germans felt more secure when they could follow these religious invocations daily.

Each *Fraktur* practitioner seems to have adhered closely to his own style of drawing and decoration, and this repertoire of motifs became identifiable over a period of time. As long as his decorative idiom was acceptable, the practical workman saw no reason to introduce new elements, and he would expect a promising pupil to copy them too. But because the copyist's imitation was never exact, and because, as he became more proficient, he made changes of his own, there was always an infusion of fresh ideas.

Painting and drawing at Sunday afternoon sessions were permitted, although all other forms of amusement and entertainment were strictly forbidden. Invariably the finely executed religious precepts in *Fraktur* were set before the young scriveners to copy. A kind-hearted schoolmaster would often present a drawing of a bird or flower as a prize for diligence and good conduct. These little tokens were carefully preserved from generation to generation.

The Pennsylvania German style decorations on the *Fraktur* manuscripts cover a wide range of subject matter. The renditions, however, take on distinct technomorphic variations because the sharp-pointed pen made linear characteristics quite different from those translated by the brush or the sgraffito incisions on ceramics. Greater detail, more minute and microscopic handling of leaf and floral forms, accompany the letter forms on *Vorschriften,*

Taufschein, Haus-Segen, and *Bücherzeichen.* Floral motifs were generally conventionalized, except for the tulip; its shape was close enough to botanical form to be recognizable.

The *Fraktur* artist's inspiration came from many sources, including textile pattern books published in Switzerland, Germany, France, and England in the period from 1580 to 1750. Highly stylized decorative birds—parrots, peacocks, doves, hens and chickens, and eagles—and particularly the *Distelfink* (gold-finch), were favorite motifs. Animals included lambs, lions, and deer. The unicorn and other motifs were borrowed from heraldic sources. Strangely enough, these aristocratic symbols represented the very classes from whom the freedom-loving Germans had escaped. On occasion, other motifs appeared, such as stags, mermaids, and angels, though the human figure was rare because a higher degree of skill was required for its delineation.

Like many other Colonial craftsmen, the scriveners were often itinerants who made a meager living traveling about peddling their handiwork. Often they prepared their documents before setting out, leaving blank spaces to be filled in according to the purchaser's needs. Ornamental examples of their work, like quotations from the Bible, blessings, and hymnals, were framed, and often the only pictorial objects on farmhouse walls. Of the itinerants, a latecomer to the fertile Pennsylvania countryside was August Bauman, a Hungarian by birth who adapted to the German customs. Late in the nineteenth century, he traveled by horse and buggy from village to village, plying his craft and catering to a fast-disappearing demand. This outmoded profession was his sole source of livelihood, and the fact that he was able to pick up commissions indicates the strength of the tradition.

There are a number of outstanding names associated with *Fraktur* arts and crafts. One of the best known is that of Francis Portzline, who was born in Düsseldorf, Germany, in 1771, and lived to be ninety-six. Hundreds of birth and baptismal certificates were made by Portzline; many of them are signed, but even those that are not are unmistakably his. The basic large heart-shaped cartouche, or enclosure, was designed to bear the text, with an interlaced Celtic knot at its lower tip. Surrounding the heart was an assortment of floral and animal motifs that were fairly consistent throughout his long career: tulip sprays, parrots, naturalistic birds, conventionalized hex symbols, and a sprinkling of smaller elements. All were rendered with a sure line and with bold drawing and coloring; the spatial relationships were almost as well studied in later life as in his prime. A noted example shows the *Hausfrau* at the bottom of a certificate, in well-tailored costume and apron, holding a floral wreath on which is perched a bird.

Heinrich Otto, of Lancaster County, was a contemporary of Portzline, a decorator whose broad interests included not only *Fraktur* work but the painting and decorating of chests and other furniture. He extended his medium by designing and cutting woodblocks with *Fraktur* motifs, and then printing *Fraktur*-type broadsides which he colored by hand. Printed specimens dated as early as 1784 show a prolific sense of design; movable floral and animal blocks are incorporated and juggled in a variety of arrangements that are rarely repeated. The cherub's head, parrots and peacocks, flowers and wreaths, provide restless, expressive language.

Unfortunately, Otto's ingenuity in devising printed shortcuts for the hand-drawn illumination eventually led to the demise of *Fraktur* writing. By the end of the nineteenth century, very few calligraphers were still practicing their art because the printing press had become an increasingly strong competitor. On the wall of the Bucks County Historical Society hangs a touching memorial to the art of *Fraktur*—it shows a paintbox belonging to one of the early illuminators of the county.

2622

2623

2624

2625

2626

720

2627

2628

2629

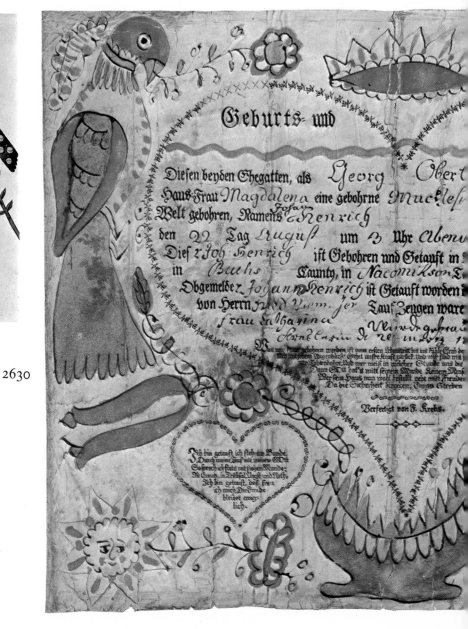

2630

2622–2630 Fraktur *is distinguished by an elaborate
system of embellishment in which intricate calligraphic arrangements are incorporated with floral
and animal decoration. The heart was used wherever
panels were called for, often as a dominant cartouche
around the message, baptismal record, or blessing*

2631

2632

2633

2634

2631 *Elizabetha Schlosser's birth certificate is set in a beautiful composition of hearts and flowers, recorded in 1808* **2632** *Manuscript and miniature illustrating selection from a hymnal, dated 1797* **2633** *Drawing of peacocks and parrots found pasted inside a chest of similar design, 1782* **2634** *Birth and baptismal record executed by Martin Brechall, an excellent penman and teacher, 1806* **2635** *Birth certificate, dated 1766, which*

2635

2636

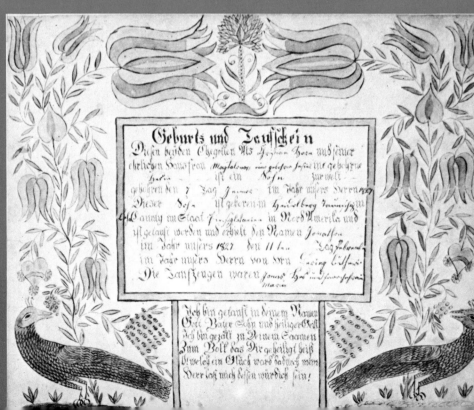

2637

2638

freely uses naturalistic forms and peacocks **2636** Drawn and colored on wrapping paper, this birth certificate of Lea Herold is an original composition of floral and plant forms **2637** Handsome composition of birds, tulips, hearts, and urns with no inscription, may have been merely an exercise of the decorator's skill **2638** Tulips, plant forms, and birds decorate this birth and baptismal record, dated 1827

Forgings & Fireplaces

2640

AMONG THE EARLIEST SETTLERS in the Pennsylvania territory were much-needed artisans, including an appreciable number of ironmasters and blacksmiths. They readily found employment and opportunities for setting up their own iron plantations. The region was rich in limestone for flux and timber for making charcoal, and the iron ore often lay just beneath the rusty soil. Little digging was needed to reach the ore, and only a few tools besides a pickax and a crowbar.

Setting up an iron plantation required a location in the midst of several thousand acres of timber, which was then felled to keep the furnaces going. At the time of the Revolution,

there were already eighty-one ironworks operating in Pennsylvania, including blast furnaces, forges, rolling mills, plating mills, steel furnaces, and bloomeries. This is remarkable in view of the British Parliament's Iron Act of 1750, which attempted to prohibit such ironworks in the Colonies so that this valuable trade would remain in British hands. The law was openly flouted, and during the Revolution the well-established foundries were able to supply cannon, mortars, shells, and shot to the American army.

Iron plantations were planned as great self-supporting woodland estates that sustained all the workers in the community. Skilled laborers included woodcutters, teamsters,

2641

2639 Pat Lyon at the Forge *was painted in 1826 by John Neagle of Philadelphia. It shows the black-smith in his shop. A glimpse of the jail where Lyon was falsely imprisoned can be seen through the open window. After his release he used the money paid him as restitution to commission this painting by the artist. Museum of Fine Arts, Boston* **2640, 2641** *Decorative wroughtiron hardware and hasps adorned the box lids on Conestoga wagons in eighteenth-century Pennsylvania*

2644

2642

2643

2642 *Cast-iron stoveplate, dated 1751, cast by John Potts, Pottsgrove Furnace. The Biblical reference indicated is "Judge Not." Photograph* **2643** *Stoveplate cast by George Stevenson, 1763, at the Mary Ann Furnace, York County. Photograph*

charcoal burners, colliers, smiths, and iron-workers of all types. The women did the weaving and spinning, the haying and harvesting, and the planting and tilling of the soil, in addition to their housekeeping chores.

In this community the patriarchal blacksmith was a man of substance, skilled in his craft, respected and in great demand. The smith forged axes and tools for clearing the forest, nails and hardware for homes, metal implements for working the soil, iron rims for wagon wheels, and axles for all manner of vehicle. Decorative hasps and hinges were used on Conestoga wagon toolboxes, waffle irons, and fireside equipment such as spits, trammels, brackets, cranes, and pothooks.

The farmer and ironmaster were closely allied because of the constant need for fuel. The smaller furnace owners bought their wood from farmers, who cut it from their timberland. When a farmer had accumulated sufficient capital, he might venture into the lucrative iron industry, providing his land contained enough ore deposits.

As the needs of the settlers grew, some degree of specialization developed among the several hundred smiths. Most were busily engaged in making essential tools and in supplying household needs. The fashioning of bits of hardware and kitchen utensils encouraged some latitude in shapes and forms. Those smiths with a flair for improvisation created functional ironwork with a touch of grace and ornament. Their products show an originality in the adaptations of favorite

2645

2646

2644, 2645 *Wood engravings of the "Iron-Founder" and the "Blacksmith" from Edward Hazen's* Panorama of Professions and Trades, *1836* **2646** *Stoveplate or fireback cast by the Colebrookdale Furnace, near Pottstown, 1763. Photograph* **2647** *Front of jamb stove cast by Henry William Stiegel at Elizabeth Furnace, Manheim, Lancaster County, 1765*

regional motifs such as the tulip and heart, and other indigenous forms.

Molten iron does not permit fumbling or hesitation, and the smith had to be a man of decision. He could not work from paper designs but had to carry in his mind a clear picture not only of the final form but the steps necessary in arriving at this design. The tools he needed—hammer and punches, tongs, and chisels—were carefully racked in order, conveniently within his grasp as he worked at the anvil. An apprentice operated the giant bellows which furnished the draft for the fire as the smith forged his piece of iron, gracefully turning and twisting it on his anvil until a latch or delicate fork took shape.

The "village blacksmith" managed somehow to survive until the twentieth century, but today he is a rarity. To recapture the picture of this vanished American, restoration villages have introduced the blacksmith shop as a curiosity along with the country store and the one-room schoolhouse.

While the blacksmith produced individual pieces, the iron-caster's products resulted from pouring molten metal into sand molds, and

2647

2648

thus many casts were created by repeating this operation. A patternmaker was responsible for design of the cast-iron pieces. The patterns were made from wood, lead, or pewter, but the majority were of wood since this could readily be cut, carved, or chiseled to provide the details of decoration and lettering which often accompanied a design. Most patternmakers had a feeling for ornaments and figures and had mastered the Roman alphabet, for inscriptions and quotations were an integral part of Pennsylvanian stoveplates and firebacks. Fine sand provided the ·material into which the pattern was imbedded, thus forming a matrix into which the hot metal flowed. For the casting of pots and other kitchen utensils, the sand-flask method was used in conjunction with clay molds.

Among the better-known ironmasters were the celebrated Henry W. Stiegel, the self-styled "baron" who operated the Elizabeth Furnace; Thomas Rutter, who started Colebrookdale Furnace in 1720, the earliest in this territory; Thomas Maybury, who operated the Hereford Furnace; and the various members of the Ege family, who owned works in the Cumberland valley: the Mount Holly Iron Works, Carlisle Furnace, Charming Forge, and Pine Grove Furnace.

2649

2648 *The fireback pictures "The Highlander" and was cast at New York in 1767, although there are no records to prove a foundry existed on the island of Manhattan at that time. The plate is adorned with a rich Flemish border surmounted by dolphins. Photograph*

2649 *Cast at the Mary Ann Furnace in York County, 1763. The doubled, arched design, supported by twisted columns and enclosing a floral pattern, is a peculiar convention followed by most Pennsylvania furnaces after they abandoned Biblical scenes in about 1750. The origin of this decoration is unknown, but with minor variations it persisted, as if a trademark, among most furnaces in the region*

Firebacks and stoveplates were produced in great quantities throughout the eighteenth century. The former, usually decorative, were designed to reflect heat from the fireplace into the room. Their efficiency was so questionable that Benjamin Franklin was prompted to design the Franklin stove.

Invented in 1742, the Franklin stove was, in effect, a portable lightweight cast-iron fireplace with back and sides and an extended floor. It could be readily placed into any existing fireplace with piping to connect it to the nearest flue. Thus Franklin's stove provided all the joys of an open fire in addition to the comfort of greater heat; and it used less fuel. On many of the stoves that were produced, the large front face above the opening enabled the patternmaker to do his best ornamental handiwork. Perhaps the best-known decorative styles were those that incorporated the inscriptions "Alter Idem" and "Be Liberty Thine."

The true fireback, commonly used in the area, was positioned at the rear of the fireplace wall, usually higher than wide, with a raised crest or curvature at the top. Its overall shape is similar to that of many gravestones. These were cast for the German immigrants by English and Welsh foundries. The iconography of the German fireplates incorporates a language of devices and floral patterns: tulips, lilies, stars, lozenges, hearts, wheat sheaves, and sunbursts combined with artful imagination. Their designer or designers, the most original of the stoveplate carvers, produced a series of plates that were highly stylized; they were derived from established motifs yet were uniquely different from the European versions. The Renaissance framing, the use of arches, columns, decorative spandrels, the form of the date cartouche, the style of lettering and

2650

2651

2650 Almost a companion piece to "The Highlander," in 2648, the figure of a maiden is accompanied by the word Frühling, *meaning Spring. Photograph* **2651** *Stove plate made by Stiegel at the Elizabeth Furnace in 1769 bears a portrait in relief of Stiegel, "The Hero"*

2652

2653   2654

numerals, and the use of banded inscriptions point to earlier plates that were cast both in Germany and in other parts of this country.

The firebacks were cast in single pieces, but the elaborate construction of cast-iron stoves afforded an opportunity for the designer to display his virtuosity. Most popular, at first, was the five-plate stove, a device set into a wall of the fireplace which extended into the adjoining room behind. It had no fuel door or smoke pipe and was fed through the wall from the front. This stove is representative of the first of American-made iron stoves. Jamb stoves, as they were also called, were common in Germany, and many sets of plates were brought to Pennsylvania, where they served as patterns. Biblical subjects with German titles dominated the decorative themes. These stoves were manufactured in the eastern and central part of the colony from 1741 to 1768.

The Biblical pictures attributed to Pennsylvania furnaces date from 1741 to 1749, a period of only eight years if we except two extremely crude examples done in 1760. Comparatively few Bible stories were illustrated on stoveplates cast in America: twenty-three were from the Old Testament, and only ten from the New Testament. Neither the Nativity nor the Passion was represented. The most popular subjects were the Miracle of the Oil (2 Kings 4:1–7) in ten versions, and the Miracle at Cana (John 2:1–11) in eleven versions. These two events often decorate the same stove.

The only known eighteenth-century Pennsylvania stove patternmaker was Hen Snyder (1722–1767). All other designers of the cast-iron plates of this era are anonymous, so that there is still much speculation about them.

2652 Franklin stove, *following the inventor's plans, was not made during his lifetime. This design in the Adam style shows festooned decoration with the heads of Franklin and George Washington, made c. 1800–1810. Photograph* **2653** *Fireplace backs were cast in decorative patterns; this shows a very ornate handling of acanthus-leafed centers, with oak and acorn meanders.* **2654** *Fireplace iron casting in the Dumbarton House, c. 1790. Photograph* **2655–2659** *Forged wrought-iron hardware made in the eighteenth century in eastern Pennsylvania. The "double dragon" designs are shown in 2657 and 2658. Conestoga wagon toolbox-lid hardware is shown in 2659*

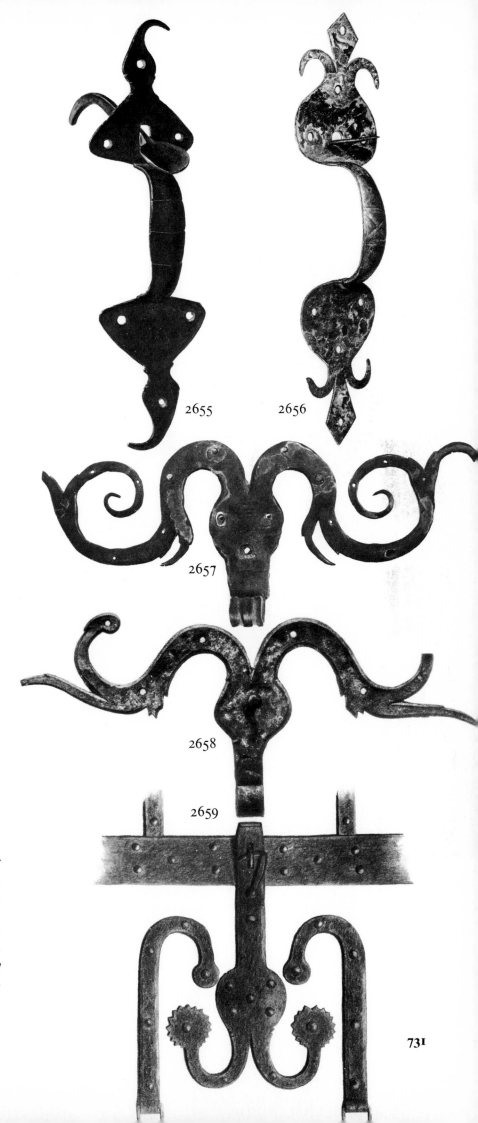

2655   2656

2657

2658

2659

731

2660

2660 *The stark simplicity of this Shaker room shows austerity carried to the point of fanaticism. Shunning all suggestion of decoration as an invitation to pleasurable experience, the Shakers fashioned every chair, table, bedspread, and cabinet to combine "strength, sprightliness, and modest beauty." Restraint is a characterizing feature, exemplified by the Brethren's rocking chair made about 1830 in New Lebanon, New York, the largest and most important Shaker establishment. The cast-iron stove is in marked contrast to the ornate products of contemporary foundries of that era. A long dining table, the built-in drawers, and closets are also consistently plain. The Millenial Laws of the sect directed that "floors in the dwelling houses, if stained at all, should be of a reddish-yellow," traces of which still show on the bare floors*

2661 *This unusual small table exhibits some slight deviation from the Shaker simplicity in the turned beadings on the pedestal and in the form of the tripod legs*

2661

Purity of Form ...
the Shaker Credo

FUNCTIONALISM DECREES that any article shall be designed according to the purpose it is meant to fulfill, and by the same token eschews ornament as a disingenuous effort to conceal honest structure. Acting on these principles, the Shakers made a rare contribution to American design. Their furniture shows a most revealing insight into pure form, underlined by their belief that the utmost beauty lies in harmony, regularity, and order.

The communal group called the Shakers, originally the Shaking Quakers, were properly known as the United Society of Believers in Christ's Second Appearing. The sect was founded in the 1760s by Ann Lee of Manchester, England. In 1774 the founder and a small group of followers emigrated to America, where they first settled near Albany, New York. Despite many hardships, the sect prospered after the Revolution; within a few years of its founding, it boasted some eighteen

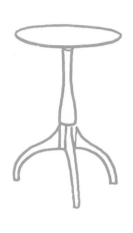

communities scattered throughout Maine, Massachusetts, Connecticut, New Hampshire, New York, Ohio, and Kentucky. The early converts to Shakerism came mainly from poor and simple folk. As their numbers increased, the Shakers had to depend on their own ingenuity and skill to fill the need for communal dwellings, barns, workshops, and mills. Before they could start to build, they had to fell trees in the forest, learn the properties of the different woods, and dam streams for waterpower to run their sawmills. They were fortunate in having wood in abundance and variety. The greater part of the built-in furniture—cupboards, chests of drawers, shelves, and wardrobes—was made of pine, which was easy to work and durable. After pine the wood most commonly used for furniture was hard, or rock, maple. There were also the so-called fruitwoods: cherry, pear, and apple. Cherry was favored for tabletops because it took a beautiful and lasting polish. Rock maple was the standard wood for slender articles that had to bear the strain of continuous use—pegs for the pegboard, spools, bobbins, and reels in the workshops, and drawer knobs—and also for posts, slats, rungs, and chair legs. Ash and hickory were valuable for the making of curved pieces. They are the "bending" woods, easily steamed to any shape. An example of the results of skillful steaming and bending, as practiced by the Shakers, was an oval box fabricated of two kinds of wood: pine for the top and bottom, and maple, cut to the thinness of an eighth of an inch, for the rounded sides. These boxes came in many sizes and were usually sold in nests of six or twelve.

The Shakers made both built-in and movable pieces of furniture. The built-in pieces became an integral part of the architectural scheme of the interiors: conceived in stark, simple terms, flush with wall surfaces, and designed to give maximum storage efficiency. Their movable furniture may be divided into two categories: those pieces intended for membership use in the dwelling houses and churches, and those built for the workshops, including spinning wheels, looms, cobblers' benches, and worktables of various kinds. But when the term "Shaker furniture" is used today, it usually refers to tables, bedsteads, benches, and especially chairs.

Shaker chairs were outstanding for their lightness, durability, and graceful beauty. The chairs had to be light because they were hung from pegs on the wall moldings whenever the floors were cleared for religious ceremonies. Like the tables and benches, the very earliest chairs were painted or stained a dark red. Later, the preference was for light stains and varnishes, which allowed the grain of the wood to show its natural beauty. No veneers or heavy lacquers were ever used; veneer was considered a sinful deceit and was strictly taboo. The earliest chair seats were rush, splint, plaited straw, or leather. Perhaps the single most distinguishing mark of the Shaker chair is the delicate finial at the top of each back post. These finials, like stylized pine cones, formed perfect extremities for the slender frames. Although they differed slightly from one community to another, they were always in harmony with the chair frame.

Shaker beds were very simple, hardly more

than cots. They were three feet wide, had short headboards and sometimes shorter footboards, all painted green, and were equipped with large wooden rollers. The "retiring rooms" were often fitted with rocking chairs or a variation called a "tilting chair," which was invented at New Lebanon, New York, about 1825; this afforded a pleasant tilting motion with no danger of slipping. The Shakers were probably the first people in this country to produce and use the rocking chair on a large scale. Intended originally for aged and infirm sisters and brethren, it was not long before rocking chairs were assigned to every retiring room, evidence that Shaker asceticism did not exclude some modicum of comfort. Rockers were made both with and without armrests, but followed no fixed pattern. They may be arbitrarily classified into mushroom-post, scrolled-arm, rolled-arm, cushion-rail, and sewing rockers. The mushroom post, used almost exclusively in the later Shaker chairs and rockers, was also common at an early period. At first the wide, gently crested, flat-bottomed mushrooms were turned in the same piece with the rest of the front post; later on, the mushroom was turned separately and attached by a hole bored into the arm post. As the Shaker rocker continued to grow in popularity, there were serious questions concerning its proper place in that inflexible society. During the great revival of 1840, one Philemon Stewart asked, "How comes it about that there are so many rocking chairs used? Is the rising generation going to be able to keep the way of God, by seeking after ease?"

It has been charged that since the Shakers used simple forms inherited from the plain country style of early New England, they originated no new designs and cannot be considered a creative people. In a limited sense this is true; theirs was a gift of simplification and refinement. By discarding all unnecessary artifice and embellishment, the Shakers reduced these early designs to their essentials of form and proportion and achieved distinctly beautiful results. The conformity to an accepted design was one of the basic tenets of the Shaker approach.

Although an individual's efforts were subordinate to the common welfare, it cannot be said that the Shakers stifled personal expression. As a matter of fact, individual development was encouraged. When it was seen that a member was proficient in a specific craft, that worker was permitted complete freedom of performance. Many Shaker cabinetmakers were known by name even though they were not permitted to sign their pieces. When the Shaker communities were enjoying their greatest prosperity, in the period roughly from 1820 to 1870, the master craftsmen produced an amazing assortment of "sprightly" furniture. Personalities of exceptional skill, among them James Farnum, Gilbert Avery, John Lockwood, George Wickersham, Benjamin Youngs, Thomas Fisher, and Robert Wagon, attuned to the spirit of simplicity, designed and executed hundreds of fine, unpretentious pieces. These were either copied exactly by apprentices or were altered to fit particular needs: the master craftsman became the designer and executed the prototype, which

2662

2664

736

2663

2662–2666 *Since the Shakers believed that "True Gospel simplicity . . . naturally leads to plainness in all things," it affected every design, whether in architecture, furniture, or textiles. The winding stairway,* **2662,** *exhibits this restraint, its graceful lines merely tracing the form of its architecture. Cabinets and closets invariably had wooden knobs, never metal. The mushroom rocker,* **2666,** *with its four slats and cone finials, became the archetype widely copied in many areas. To the Shakers must go credit for popularizing the rocking chair. The bedstead,* **2665,** *is very similar to a type to be found in the Zoar community, in Ohio*

2665

2666

was reproduced in such quantity that mail-order sales became possible in the 1880s.

Religious fervor and a high degree of dedication motivated every member in the pursuance of his daily work. Whether the excellence they attained is attributable to religious impulse or was the result of the true craftsman's attitude to the task in hand, the end product carried its own reward. Surely, the perfecting of utility and the designing of forms so pure were made possible only by a high quality of skill, technical ability which, in the words of Joseph Conrad, embraced "honesty and grace and rule in an elevated and clear sentiment, not altogether utilitarian, which may be called the honor of labor."

737

2667

2668

2669

738

2670

2671

2667–2671 *Efficient use of storage space followed strictly the precepts of Mother Ann, the founder, that "care and management of temporal things" was a cardinal principle. It followed that domestic order and neatness were the individual responsibility of every occupant of a communal dwelling. Order necessitated the construction of a great number of chests, cases of drawers, cupboards, and closets, as all bedclothes, clothing, textiles, and utensils were required to be put out of sight. Built-in drawers and overhead cupboard space were architecturally incorporated for maximum efficiency,* **2668**. *The white porcelain knobs on the secretary,* **2671**, *distinguished storage space for smaller knickknacks*

2672

2673

2674

740

2675

2676

2672–2677 The pie safe, 2672, shows twenty panels of tin, simply perforated to permit ventilation. The sewing table, 2673, has delicately shaped legs. The large dining table, 2674, has a pine top four feet wide and trestles made of birch; frequently such tables measured twenty feet long. The crib, shown in 2677, appears in both Shaker and Zoar communities

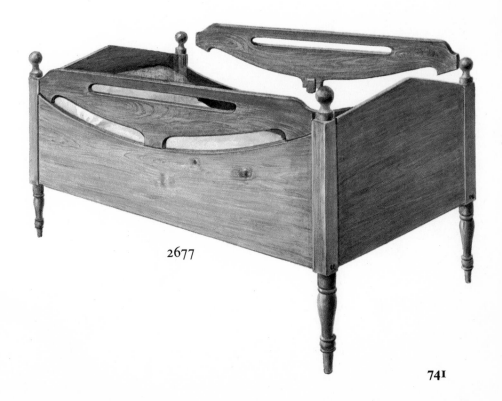

2677

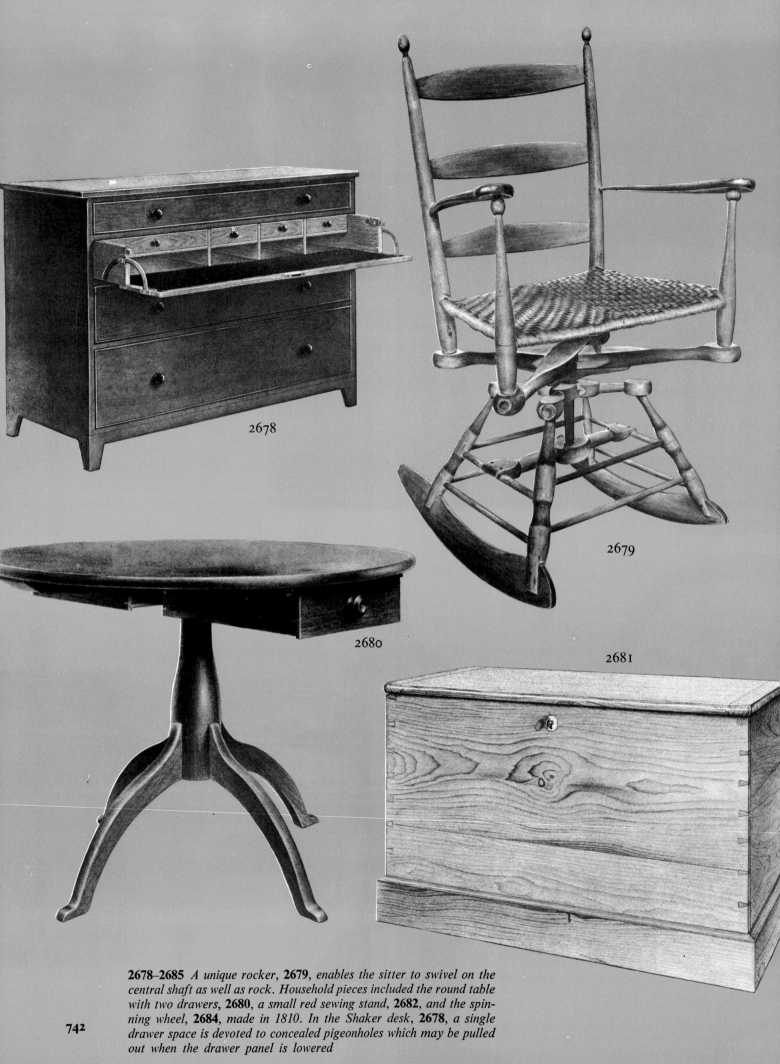

2678

2679

2680

2681

2678–2685 *A unique rocker,* **2679**, *enables the sitter to swivel on the central shaft as well as rock. Household pieces included the round table with two drawers,* **2680**, *a small red sewing stand,* **2682**, *and the spinning wheel,* **2684**, *made in 1810. In the Shaker desk,* **2678**, *a single drawer space is devoted to concealed pigeonholes which may be pulled out when the drawer panel is lowered*

2682

2683

2684

2685

743

2686

2687

2688

2689

The Separatists of Zoar

HISTORY RECORDS some three hundred experiments in communal living in America during the past three centuries. For the most part, they were based on religious rather than economic tenets. One of the longest-lived and most successful communities was founded by a band of Pietists in Tuscarawas County, Ohio, in 1817. Aided by wealthy and sympathetic Quakers and led by Jacob Bimiler, they built a little village which still stands, almost untouched by time.

Bimiler was a strange genius who combined the position of religious leader with that of business agent. He was quick to see the market for the group's excess products in the surrounding countryside. Bimiler sold the community's farm products, developed the mineral resources of the land, and eventually operated the general store, which carried practically everything needed in a frontier settlement. He did not hesitate to hire outside artisans and craftsmen for extra help in the community. The combination of agriculture and industry brought fame and fortune to the town of Zoar. One result of the economic success was a commodious community building known as King's House. This twenty-one-

2686 *Plank chair showing influence of traditional German peasant furniture of the seventeenth and and eighteenth centuries* 2687 *Perpetual calendar with movable dials indicating in German not only the days and months but also the times of sunrise and sunset and the fixed holidays. Hand-painted decorations on wood show flowers and castles reminiscent of native Germany* 2688 *In this Zoar furnace floriated panels are set into sides and front facing, repeated on tinplate below, 1835* 2689 *Frame for baptismal certificate built up of spool sections, c. 1817–37* 2689A *Butter mold of five-branched swirl design* 2690 *Thread holder, made near Zoar, Ohio, c. 1825–45*

2690

2691

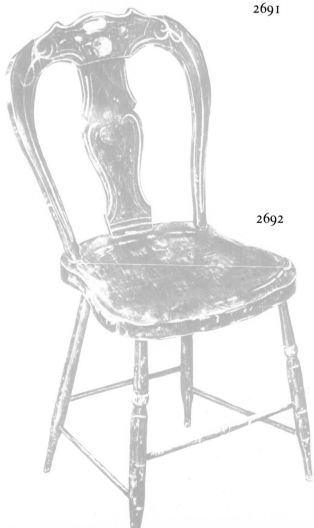

2692

room brick structure, today a museum, was erected in 1843, and Bimiler died ten years later. He left no adequate successor, but the well-established industries continued to run along without interruption. In 1898, no longer able to compete with modern methods and tired of the rigid discipline, the members finally disbanded. At the time of dissolution, property valued at over a million dollars was divided among the hundred and thirty-six surviving members.

The Zoar craftsmen brought with them a strong German tradition, which manifested itself in furniture design and in the decorative arts and crafts. Although they were separated from their neighbors by custom and religion and were admonished to keep to themselves, they still allowed outsiders to influence them. The well-defined Germanic style of their earliest work became diffused, and from this cross-breeding there resulted a selection of motifs and styles thoroughly typical of Midwestern, mid-nineteenth century America.

Zoar furniture styles ranged from sixteenth-century European designs to walnut parlor pieces of the 1880s. The first furniture made at Zoar was purely Germanic in its derivation: plank-seat chairs, large wardrobes, and small cupboards. The hanging cupboards, painted a gray-blue color, were a favorite form which, according to tradition, concealed ornamental glass and china behind heavily decorated doors. Later the furniture showed traces of prevailing period styles, such as German Biedermeier, Hepplewhite, Sheraton, and American Empire. These were attributable to such outside cabinetmakers as John Leser, George Hagney, and I. Fritz, whose names were accurately recorded in daybooks from 1836 to 1858.

It is interesting to observe that the work of outsiders was encouraged for purely economic reasons. Furniture made for members was severely simple and often rather heavy, with slight German accents. Tables were seldom the drop-leaf type, so popular throughout the Midwest; they were more likely to be tavern tables with pinned-on tops. Stands, chests of

2691 *Bonnet cabinet of cherry with decorated panels, made in Zoar, Ohio, c. 1836* **2692** *Painted and decorated Zoarite chair, c. 1860–70* **2693** *Black walnut hanging cabinet, known in the Zoar Schwabian dialect as* Haube-Kaeschtle, *1836* **2694** *Rocker made in Zoar, with shaped seat and arrow spindles*

drawers, beds, "kitchen Windsor" chairs, and slat-back chairs were all made for use at Zoar. Cherry was the favorite wood, but poplar or tulipwood and some walnut, pine, maple, and hickory were also utilized. Rather than the traditional German painted decoration, the craftsmen preferred red or a gray-blue color which was often given the appearance of wood grain.

Over thirty-five trades and crafts were practiced in the Zoar community, including printing and binding. The iron foundry, the woolen mill, and the pottery were the most significant commercial enterprises. The new settlers were quick to avail themselves of the good clay on their property; surprisingly, their first products were roof tiles of the North European type. Their pottery, for the most part, was unglazed redware. Some examples show soft orange-red clay under a light coating of glaze, and some were coated with yellow slip before glazing. Decoration was simple, usually plain incised lines. Less often there was slip decoration, thinly applied in contrast to the heavy slip of the Pennsylvania potters. A few pieces of Rockingham and yellowware are ascribed to Zoar; the hard, stony brown glaze characteristic of much Ohio pottery was also used.

Many other trades were carried on at Zoar. Conrad Dienman, an expert woodturner, probably made many of the spinning wheels sold in the general store. A wagonmaker, a cooper, and a watchmaker all worked in the community and served outside customers. A tin shop, operated by John Moffatt from 1837 to 1860 or later, made tea- and coffeepots, buckets, dippers, measures, funnels, boxes, candle molds, covered cans, and some attractive cookie cutters. Most of this toleware was unadorned; the general store was interested in quick sales at modest prices.

The quality of Zoar workmanship was always honest. The simple products lacked the purity of the traditional Shaker output and the decorated works did not display the flair and originality the Pennsylvanians demonstrated. Even so, Zoar craftsmanship remains an example of the results which can be achieved in a well-knit community which is sustained by group discipline and sensitive to neighboring influences in the mainstream of American folk arts and crafts.

2693

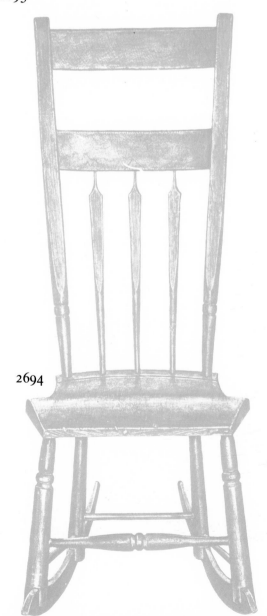

2694

748

2695

Lorenzini '38

Icons & Images of the Santeros

2696

F RANCISCO DE CORONADO first explored the Southwest in 1540, pushing northward from Mexico in search of the fabled Seven Cities of Cibola. Many other Spanish conquistadores followed in this period of exploration, but not until the closing years of the sixteenth century was any attempt made at colonization. In 1598, accompanied by a group of missionaries and colonists, Juan de Oñate established the first permanent settlement in the Southwest. By 1610 Santa Fe had become the capital of the region that encompassed Arizona, New Mexico, Colorado, and western Texas.

The territory of New Spain extended all the way from Mexico and Central America, including the hundreds of Caribbean Islands, up through that region. In the course of time the frontiers pushed eastward to include all of Texas and westward to cover all of California. Although a settlement had been established in St. Augustine in 1565, there had been no large-scale attempt at colonization in Florida and two hundred years of occupation failed to leave any permanent cultural imprint. In the Spanish Southwest, however, the more serious drive had a lasting effect upon the arts and crafts of the area. After Oñate's conquest the Pueblos lived in virtual servitude for some eighty years. They finally rebelled in 1680, causing the massacre of about four hundred Spaniards. Their freedom was short-lived; in 1692, De Vargas crushed their revolt with a fierce tyranny. The battles of those days wiped out early Spanish Colonial artifacts; hardly a trace of the decorative crafts has survived from

2695 Retablo *painted on wood with gesso ground, dated 1783. San Jose, California* **2696** Saint George and the Dragon, *carved of pine by Celso Gallegos, c. 1920. Like the work of the earlier* santeros, *such fanciful figures and subjects in relief were used not only to decorate graves but also as* santos *for the home*

the period antedating 1700. After the reconquest of the area, the mission of San Xavier del Bac was established and became the first outpost in Arizona; San Antonio emerged as the center of the small colony in Texas. The last thrust of the Spanish empire was the string of Franciscan missions set up by Padre Junipero Serra. In 1769 he founded his first mission in San Diego, and in 1823 his last. In 1821 Mexico's break with Spain encouraged secularization and effectively destroyed the mission system. Thereafter, large numbers of American settlers began to arrive in Texas, coming by covered wagons which rolled westward from Missouri on the Santa Fe Trail. By mid-century the great rush was on to the California goldfields; the entire Southwest territory had become part of the United States, ending three centuries of Spanish domination.

The California missions became citadels of artistic culture, as well as centers for the conversion of the Indians and protective presidios aimed at thwarting British and Russian encroachment. Each mission was a self-sustaining community with grainfields and orchards, a water-supply system, and quarters for Indians and soldiers. The natives were taught weaving, pottery, tanning, soap making, and the production of other marketable commodities. Every effort was made by the padres to make the Indians self-reliant, but they were slow to adopt new ways. By the time of the Mexican Revolution, the period of cultural development had not been long enough for distinctive new art forms to flourish. Thus, the California heritage became an admixture of Mexican art, local workmanship based on Mexican and European designs, and a remarkable blending of Spanish and Indian elements.

In contrast to the coastal regions, where intercourse between settlements could be conducted by crude, ox-drawn carts along El Camino Real or by sailing vessels visiting the important harbor towns, the New Mexican

areas were markedly separated from Mexican culture; distances were vast and the terrain forbidding. To the south, the Spanish superstructure was simply imposed upon the Pueblo Indian base which was already well established when the Spanish colonists came. These *pueblos* (towns and villages) were situated mainly in northern New Mexico along the upper Rio Grande; consequently, the first settlements sprang up in this region. The Indians' communal way of life was sedentary, agrarian. The Indians were also skilled in weaving and basketmaking. In these isolated mountain hamlets, after a long period of germination, the folk art of New Mexico developed. Some Mexican influences on the Indian culture can be detected, particularly in sculpture and wood carving.

Historically, the crafts and folk arts of the Spanish Colonial Southwest may be divided as follows: the period of Spanish rule dating from the reconquest of New Mexico to the Mexican Independence (1692–1821), the Mexican Republic (1823–48), and the American period, commencing when these territories came into the Union (1848). It was the Spanish missions that first gave the style of the Southwest its essential character. In the ranch period, distinguished by the formation of the great landed estates of California (1820–50), no more new missions were added to the chain. Separated from the control of the Church, they lost their influence and fell into decay. The Indians who had attached themselves to the mission communities were dispossessed and became peons or cowboys. The craftsmen who survived practiced outside the church or mission community, and with the coming of industry their folk art gradually disappeared.

At the very outset of the Spanish infiltration, architecture and crafts were brought to the Southwest from Mexico by the Franciscan priests. Under their tutelage local workers learned new techniques: how to work in

metals, principally silver and tin; how to carve and build in stone; and how to use paints in the European manner. All of the teachings of the priesthood were designed to inculcate the spirit and fervor of the Church, and thus the *santero* school of painting, wood carving, and sculpture was born. The *santo* (saint) was a holy image. To Spanish-speaking New Mexicans *un santo* means any religious image, whether in wood, stone, metal, plaster, painting, or print. In recent years the New Mexicans have appropriated the term to mean indigenous folk images. A maker or repairer of *santos* is called a *santero*, and his products fall into two categories: pictures painted on wood panels, called *retablos*, and figures carved of wood, covered with a gesso base, and painted, called *bultos*.

California missions possessed numbers of paintings imported from Mexico, where they had been done in the European manner; in New Mexico oil canvases were virtually unknown. The native *santeros* were taught by the priests to paint directly on panels of cottonwood or pine which were first treated with gesso. Only a small number of these *retablo* paintings were signed. Father García, serving in New Mexico (1747–79), Father Pereyro (1798–1818), José Aragón (1822–35), and Father Molleño (1828–45) are a few whose works are identifiable by signature or stylistic mannerisms. The earlier *retablo* paintings were the inspired oeuvre of the priests themselves and were used to decorate church walls or altarpieces. The paintings were characterized by lively gestures and expressive features. Although the native *santeros* attempted to follow in the footsteps of their instructors, their works were less animated. No longer designed as statues, carved figures became images for the home; each adobe had its patron saint. Through stylization these figures assumed a simplicity of form and a naive monumentality.

The native *santero*, after learning his craft

from a teacher-priest, usually decided to sell his *santos* for a livelihood. He traveled from town to town and, much like his distant cousin the Yankee peddler, offered his wares at the household door as bringers of good luck. To the native the image was the source of supernatural power that would heal the sick, cure the lame, and insure a bountiful harvest. There were also amateur *santeros* who did the work as an exercise in religious devotion, one that was certain to yield blessings.

The *bulto*, a small free-standing statuette of a single saint or group, was carved in the round. Made of cottonwood roots more often than pine, the *bulto* served for daily reverence, general decoration, and as a talisman. If the posture called for outstretched arms or limbs in other extended positions, these were carved separately and pegged into the body, following which the body was smoothly covered with gesso ground and painted. For realistic drapery, cotton folds were applied to the figure after being dipped into wet gesso. The earlier figures, antedating 1800, followed the Mexican Baroque style. The so-called Cordova *bultos*, named after the village of their origin, are thought to be the work of José Rafael Aragon, a *santero* working in the period of 1830–50. These figures are tall and elegant, with faces finely chiseled and clearly colored. The Mora type of *bulto*, named for the Mora river and valley district, shows highly stylized modeling and dates from about the Civil War period.

The timeless aspect of the culture of the Southwest stands out in the architectural base which the Spanish settlers inherited from the Indians. The Pueblos had been building multistoried apartment dwellings since about 700 A.D. Some were tucked away in cave openings like the Cliff House near Flagstaff; others, like the North House of Taos, stood on open, sunbaked plains. The Spaniards did not destroy this Indian way of life but adopted it, using their own tools and techniques to create a

2697

2698

2699

2700

2701

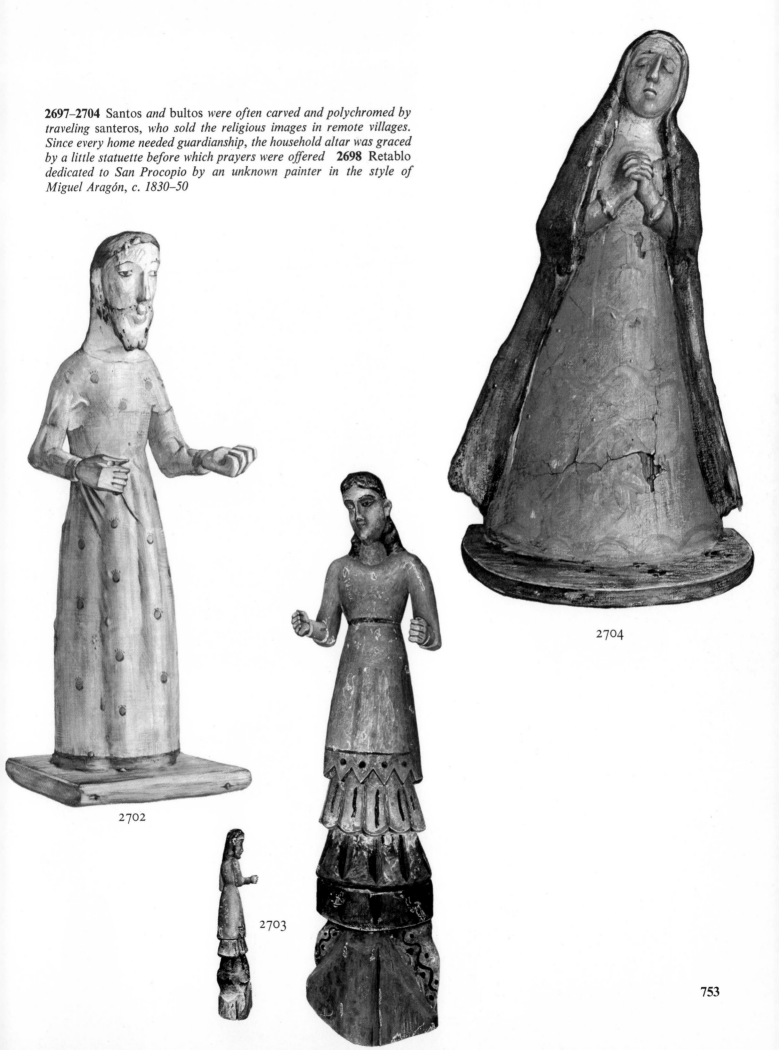

2697-2704 Santos *and* bultos *were often carved and polychromed by traveling* santeros, *who sold the religious images in remote villages. Since every home needed guardianship, the household altar was graced by a little statuette before which prayers were offered* **2698** Retablo *dedicated to San Procopio by an unknown painter in the style of Miguel Aragón, c. 1830–50*

2702

2703

2704

753

2705

2706

blend that became the unique style of the region. Indeed, tools and implements were among the rarest of commodities. There was no real progress in the building arts until the settlers arrived with planes, saws, bits, and augers. Further advances were made when the railroad was extended to this area.

Adobe, which is mud mixed from the clay-and-gypsum desert soil and baked by the sun, served as the universal building agent. By piling up layers of adobe, the Indians built their homes of many stories to make a *pueblo*, or town. The Spaniards improved this crude method by mixing straw with the adobe and baking it into bricks. On their cattle ranches they limited themselves to single stories of wide adobe construction, which developed into the contemporary ranch style.

2707

2708

2709

2710

The generously proportioned plaster walls of the missions presented an opportunity for the Indian painters, who covered them lavishly with religious themes—the Crucifixion and stories of the saints—adding ancient Indian symbols and using the exuberant colors developed in their ceremonial paintings. Mission art work was a unique fusion of European architecture with the kind of crude Indian motif that appears in the petrographs, or rock paintings, of the region. The artists also produced large easel paintings, such as the Stations of the Cross, which are exceptional in regional folk art.

2705 Retablo *of a type common to New Mexico, painted between 1750 and 1850. A pine board covered with gesso, then painted in tempera* **2707** Bulto *from the church at Ranchos de Taos, made between 1830 and 1850. Clearly copied from a print or small painting, as evidenced by the artist's inability to cope with the upper ends of drapery* **2706, 2708, 2709** *Pine or cottonwood crosses used as grave markers show great variety and ingenuity in the silhouette designs. Decorative effects were obtained in zigzag cuts in the outlines, rarely with carvings on the flat surfaces. In 2708 there are appliquéd ornaments of tin and the wooden surfaces are decorated* **2710** Retablo *of the Holy Ghost painted in the region of the Rio Grande valley* **2711** *The Immaculate Conception was declared the principal doctrine of all Spanish possessions, including those in the New World. This carved and painted* bulto *was made in New Mexico, 1830–50*

2711

2712

2714

2713

2712-2717 *Painted chests, especially the front and top panels, were often gaily decorated with floral designs, figures, and tableaux suggestive of fiesta pageantry. Bright colors, exuberant figures, and lush vegetation combined to convey the lively Latin temperament. The general feeling of design of these chest panels, painted in New Mexico in the first half of the nineteenth century, is derivative of an influence traced to Mexico, in the area of Chihuahua* **2714** *Embroidery in which floral and leaf forms are handsomely designed and competently executed*

2715

2716

2717

2718

2718–2721 *Representative of a group of about forty chests similarly painted and decorated, these display amazing freshness and colorful vitality. The pictorial theme might be a handful of dragoons in boats, odd-shaped and without oars,* **2718**, **2720**, *a pair of tropical birds in gay plumage,* **2721**, *or a pair of animals of uncertain species. But always the background areas are completely covered with rosettes, lunettes, and an assortment of rich foliage rendered in bright hues that delight the eye*

2719

2720

2721

2722

2723

2722 Santo *enshrined in an enclosed setting. Made in New Mexico, nineteenth century* **2723** *Ceremonial candlestick of carved native pine, polychromed over gesso base. Made in the Spanish-Californian Mission style, c. 1815* **2724–2727** *The chest on stand,* caja en mesita, **2724**, *was often massively proportioned for a large adobe house. Carvings of inset panels are identified with the style of Taos. The base shows the pronounced sawtooth motif characteristic of effects obtained with limited tools, c. 1870. In* **2725**, *corner stiles are simply carved as legs. Hasps and hinges of wrought iron are of local origin, though often these were imported from Mexico; made in northern New Mexico, c. 1850. Trinket box,* **2726**, *has deep carving on all sides, buckskin hinges, c. 1860. The small chest,* **2727**, *made in the vicinity of Taos, c. 1800, is decorated with fanciful scrolls and abstract forms*

2724

Furniture & Furnishings of the Southwest

2725

2726

2727

2728

2731

2729

2728–2730, 2733 *The* colcha *is a typical form of New Mexican needlework in wool using a long stitch crossed at a 45-degree angle by a short holding stitch. The term* colcha *is derived from the classical Spanish for "stitch"; the New Mexican quilt is called a* colchone. *Embroidered wool bedcovers date from the 1840s and represent a form of folk needlecraft. Characteristic of this type are the florets and nosegays of carnations, pomegranates, and other flowers and foliage, done in vibrant colors of warmth and gaiety. An enlarged detail from the corner of* 2729 *is shown in* 2733. 2731 *Bedspread of cotton embroidery showing crewel stitch on closely woven canvas, c. 1870–80* 2734, 2735 *California Indian basketry has been considered the finest of its type ever woven. The designs combine motifs like blocks, diamonds, chevrons, and, as in* 2735, *conventionalized renderings of the Spanish royal coat of arms, castles, and lions. An inscription woven into the border tells of its maker, Anna Maria Marta of the Mission of Saint Bonaventure. The basket is woven in the usual Indian fashion of coils covered with rush and sewn together*

2730

762

2732

2733

2734

2735

763

2736

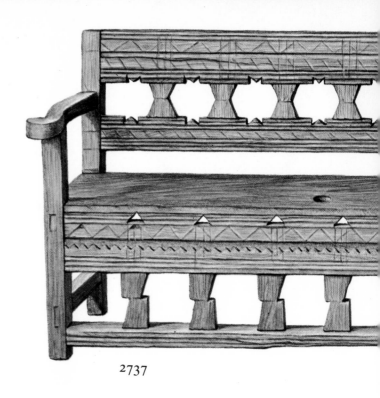

2737

2738

2736–2740 *Chairs of the Southwest, while of definite Spanish influence, with carved details and leatherwork embossed and covered with large brass heads, were primitive in their lines. They follow rigid construction, using square posts as legs and flat, unupholstered seats. Stretchers are either carved or plain. The monk's chair,* **2740,** *was not designed for comfort; the back splat shows the sawtooth design found in many of the plainer examples of this region. The long bench,* **2737,** *also shows the simple saw-cut motifs, a most primitive attempt at introducing decoration* **2741** *Carved and painted redwood cabinet, with wrought-iron hinges. Made by an Indian craftsman at the Mission San Juan Bautista* **2742, 2744** *The picture frame,* **2742,** *and the wall sconce,* **2744,** *show a type of decorative tinware indigenous to the Southwest, derivative of the finer silverware of similar design. However, instead of chasing and tooling for ornamentation, the worker in tin used punches, embossing, and piercing to obtain results* **2743** *Lock plate features the double eagle. Its inspiration could be both Mexican and American*

2739

2740

2741

2742

2743

2744

765

2745

2746

2747

2748

766

2749

2750

2751

2745–2752 *An array of furniture of the Spanish Southwest demonstrates the paucity of working implements. Chests and tables were square and squatty, with a massive quality of heavy workmanship. Often the introduction of a decorative stretcher or apron, as in* **2747** *and* **2748**, *results in a scallop or sawtooth design as one of expediency. The monstrance,* **2745**, *achieves a decorative note from simple cutouts and drilled holes and the addition of moldings. The turned candlestick,* **2749**, *is brightly colored in orange with cool greens and blues. A more ornate treatment above the opening of the confessional,* **2751**, *attempts to glorify, with simple means, the special purposes of this religious piece. The mission chimes,* **2752**, *have a homespun quality; the same may be said of the candelabra,* **2746**, *made of tin with arms twisted in all directions*

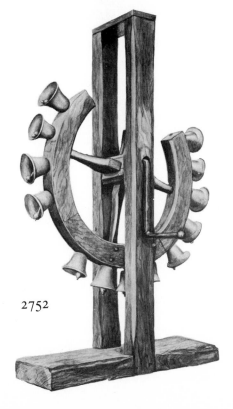

2752

2753

2753 Branding Scene, *painted by S. Morgan Bryan. Kennedy Galleries, New York* **2754** *Proprietary marks made on various parts of the calf's hide by knife cuts and slashes*

Heraldry of the Range

2754

Like so many other traditions and customs in the cattle industry, branding can be traced back to the arrival of the Spanish conquistador Cortés. When Cortés and Pizarro were building a new empire that stretched from Mexico to Peru, Cortés branded slaves and animal stock alike with the sign of the Three Christian Crosses. Spaniards had traditionally put their house marks on everything they owned since medieval times, and the brand was simply a declaration of ownership. From this simple assertion of authority there developed a system of marking untold millions of cattle, a complicated code of laws and regulations, and a fascinating array of tools and techniques.

Brands were placed on livestock with a stamp iron or running iron soon after calfing time, when the young heifers had to be marked and counted. It was a dirty, dusty business, requiring the combined efforts of a half dozen cowhands to rope and hold the cantankerous beasts, tend the fire in which the irons were heated, and burn the mark into the tender young hide.

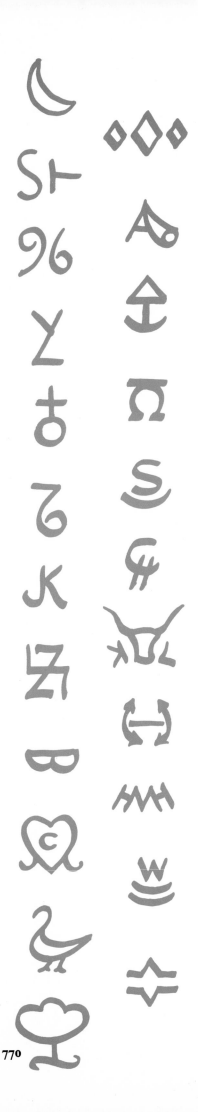

After years of violations and cattle theft, the ranchers decided that some form of legal registration was necessary, so the brand of each ranch was entered in an official brand book at the county seat. Even so, it was difficult to create a design that could not be altered. The brand might be composed of any combination of letters, numerals, or abstract shapes. Some of the more unusual included the Walking R, Rocking H, Lazy Y, Cut and Slash, Forked Lightning, Man in the Moon, and Crazy Three. Literally thousands of these were registered across the West.

To make a brand the ranch blacksmith would turn to his forge and deftly twist a few small bits of iron into the required shape, beating the joints into a single form and fixing it to a long poker handle. The stamp enabled the brander to burn the mark into the hide in a single operation.

When an animal was sold to another ranch the new owner placed his brand on it. To make the transfer legitimate, the original owner vented (from the Spanish *vender*, to sell) his brand—usually by burning a bar across it. The hide of the unfortunate horse or cow that had been sold a number of times began to resemble an informal brand directory or a well-traveled piece of luggage.

In later years, when leather became a more valuable commodity, the practice of defacing the hide declined. An elaborate system of earmarking was substituted, with slits and cuts devised in endless combinations. The extensive glossary of terms used to describe earmarks is a language that only the experienced rancher understands. Such descriptive words as "overslope," "swallow fork," "jingle bob," or "over-and-under bit" testify to the ingenuity of the cowhands in overcoming difficult assignments on the range.

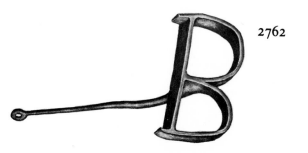

2762

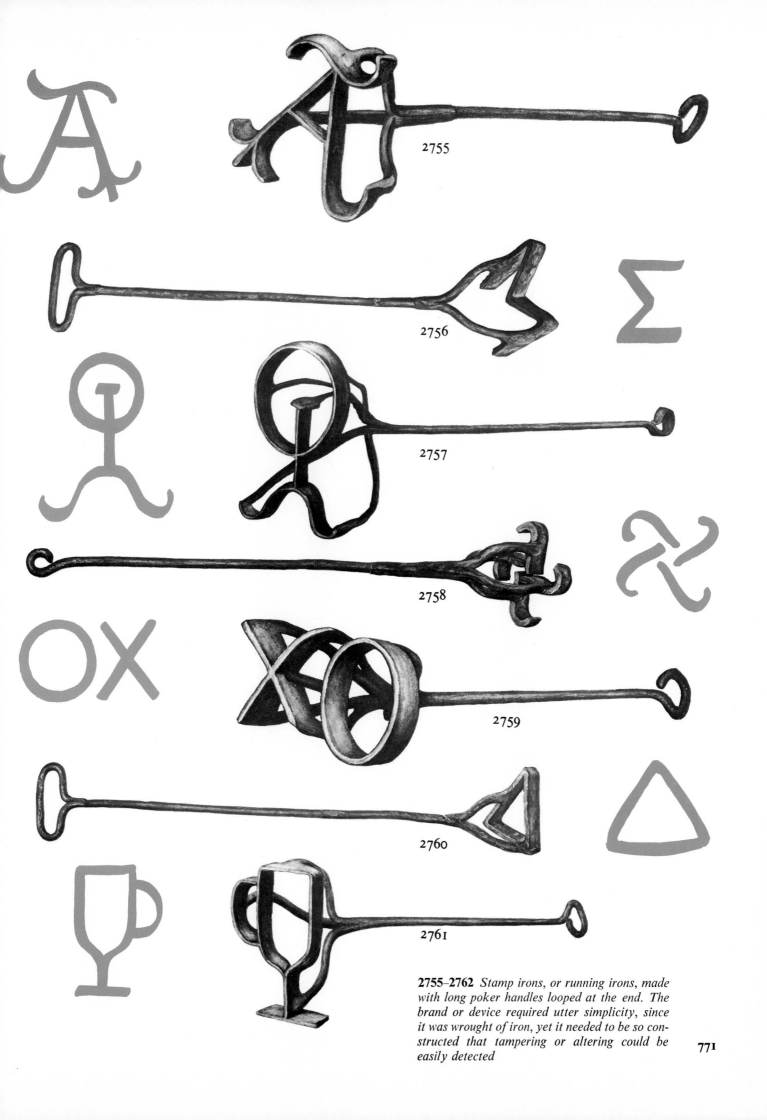

2755

2756

2757

2758

2759

2760

2761

2755–2762 *Stamp irons, or running irons, made with long poker handles looped at the end. The brand or device required utter simplicity, since it was wrought of iron, yet it needed to be so constructed that tampering or altering could be easily detected*

771

2763

Bridles, Bits & Spurs

2764

2765

I N THE RIDING gear of the cattleman hardly a square inch of the metal or leather surfaces is free from some form of decoration.

Like so many other Western traditions, this can be traced to Mexican practices and beyond that to origins in medieval Spain. During Spain's Golden Age, a style of extravagant decoration developed in which floral designs were freely interspersed with figures and animal motifs set in bold relief.

The trend toward unrestrained opulence reached its height during the Renaissance, and by the time Philip II ascended the throne in 1556 there was a positive lust for effusive ostentation. The plateresque style, distinguished by a richness of ornamentation suggestive of silver plate was the style of the day, and it was this love of embellishment that formed the heritage of every craftsman in the Southwest, whether he worked in iron, silver, or leather.

2763 *The hackamore bit is a prime tool, especially useful when taming or training a colt. Side pieces are often gaily decorated. This one features the female form in outline, brand marks on the silver crosspiece, and a serpent below. Bosal at top is of woven thongs* **2764, 2765** *Bridle bits forged of iron, including chain, links and tassels on crossbar*

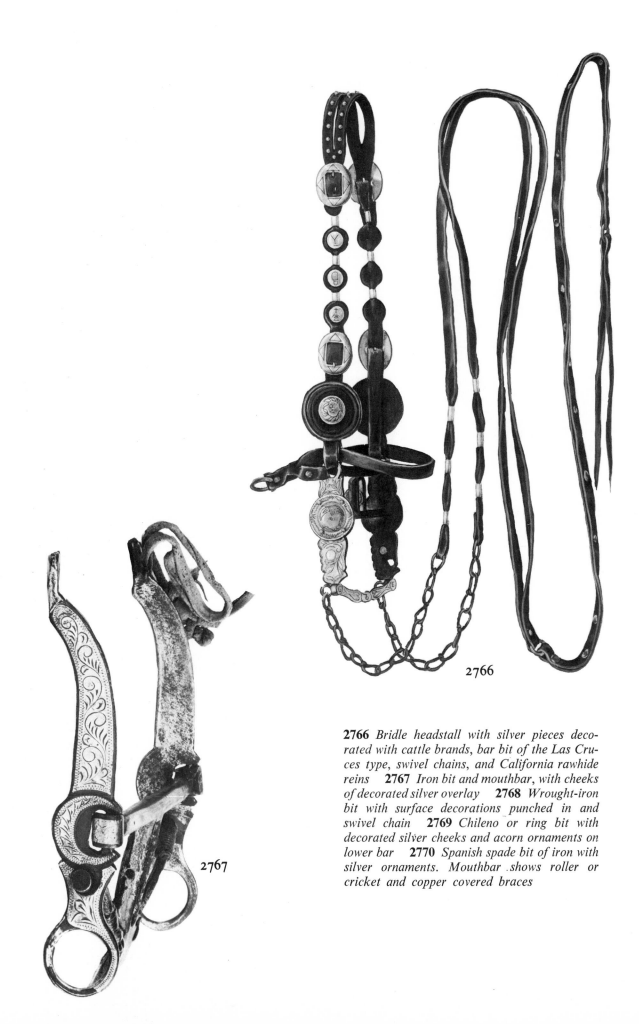

2766

2766 *Bridle headstall with silver pieces decorated with cattle brands, bar bit of the Las Cruces type, swivel chains, and California rawhide reins*   **2767** *Iron bit and mouthbar, with cheeks of decorated silver overlay*   **2768** *Wrought-iron bit with surface decorations punched in and swivel chain*   **2769** *Chileno or ring bit with decorated silver cheeks and acorn ornaments on lower bar*   **2770** *Spanish spade bit of iron with silver ornaments. Mouthbar shows roller or cricket and copper covered braces*

2767

The bridle headstall, or headgear of the horse, enabled the *caballero* to display all the skill and artistry of the craftsmen of his ranch. The many parts of the bridle—crownpiece, browband, throatlatch, cheekpiece—invited the decorative touches that lent glamour to the headpiece. The cheekpieces were ornamented with spots and *conchas* (shell-shaped disks of silver). Dangling chains, though noisy, were added because they were believed to provide entertainment for the horse. Bits offered the greatest opportunity for imaginative treatment, and an endless variety of fanciful designs that combined fine steel and silver were produced.

The spurs worn by all *rancheros* can be traced back to the ancient prod or pryck. From this simple pointed spur the revolving rowel developed. It was made in many forms from long, sharp-pointed stars to sawtooth and smoothly rounded rowels designed to inflict less pain on the horse. The spur shank, button, heel band, and heel chains were integral parts that could be richly embellished. The status of the horseman could be gauged by the amount of ornamentation on his boots and spurs as well as on his horse's saddle and bridle.

Every detail of the cowboy's equipment tended to the ornate rather than to functional simplicity, a tradition that continues to this day. The virile cowhand never disdained fancy clothes, and his chaps, belts, and hat were often encrusted with silver ornaments.

2769

2768

2770

775

2771

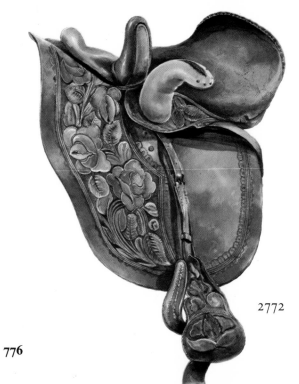

2772

2771 Bronc on a Frosty Morn, *painted in 1898 by Charles Marion Russell. The setting is the Judith Basin, Montana, where Russell spent many of his early years as a cowpuncher* **2772** *Tooled-leather sidesaddle with rose and leaf decorations; seat and cantle feature stitched decorations*

2773 *Saddle with horn decorated with a star and the name "Whitby." Cantle of hand-tooling showing the initials "O W," side pouch with decorated lid, silver mounts, and tie strings*

Tools & Trappings of the Cowhands

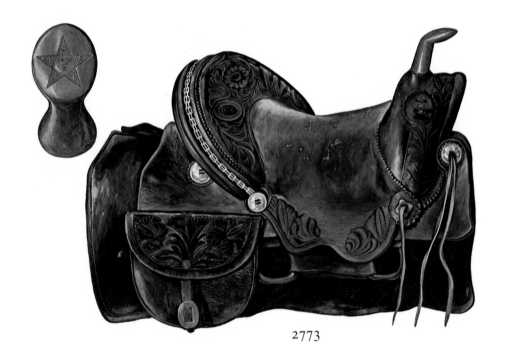

2773

CATTLE TENDING in the Southwest dates from the early sixteenth century when the Spanish conquistadores under Hernando Cortés introduced longhorns into Mexico. The descendants of these early adventurers operated large estates known as *haciendas*, or, in the case of smaller operations, *ranchos*. The men employed on every ranch, large or small, to handle the cows were called *vaqueros*, meaning cowboys. (The American equivalent "buckaroo" is simply a corruption of the Spanish word.) Slowly the great herds drifted northward, where grazing conditions were superior. In Texas the herds were incredibly vast, and mustangs and cattle which ran wild could be had for the taking. Thus the classic cowboy of the Southwest was born of Mexican

tradition and American necessity. With him came all the Spanish terminology for cowboy gear and cattle herding, along with picaresque characters and legends of the Old West.

The accessories of the range and cattle tending, as well as the cowhand's personal accouterments, consisted of leather goods and ironware. The metalwork was wrought in simple, functional forms, yet, where practicable, these were made to yield an ornamental twist. Typical of the region's metalwork were: branding irons in many designs, since each ranch needed its own distinctive brand mark for quick identification of cattle; silver bridle bits, wrought with great delicacy and artistry in fanciful designs; steel stirrups, trimmed and overlaid with silver; steel spurs, often with mountings and other details of chased silver; and a great variety of wrought hardware— such as picket pins for tethering a horse— needed for use on the ranch. Thus an important place on every large ranch was the smith's shop, where there was not only constant shoeing to be done, but also the making of the hundred-and-one requisites of the range. In addition to the blacksmith's efforts, the local silversmith contributed his glistening bit to ornament the dull wrought-steel pieces. Working separately or as a team, these two craftsmen were responsible for all the hardware, plain or decorated, for which the Southwest was justly famous.

Pen and ink sketches of bronco busting by Edward Borein, from his book Borein's West

2774

2774 *Child's sidesaddle, c. 1820, by an unknown craftsman from Monterey, California. Handsomely embroidered in silk, the velvet-upholstered seat shows Diana, protectress of maidens, in a chariot drawn by two goats. The cornucopias embroidered on both sides are logical Neoclassical attributes, for this goddess was identified with fertility rites and was honored at harvest time. The border design and workmanship are of superior quality, suggesting older centers of the craft in Mexico* **2775** *Oxbow stirrup with American eagle in chased-silver mounting* **2776, 2777** *Spurs with decorated leather straps, iron shanks with silver mountings. Rowels have rounded prongs*

Saddles & Stirrups

2775

O VER THE CENTURIES the saddle evolved from a simple invention designed to facilitate remaining on a horse to a highly specialized tool in a major industry. By the time the conquistadores moved into America, saddlery itself had acquired the status of a folk art that was often carried to extraordinary extremes. A Spanish *caballero* was a gentleman, and he would not consider outfitting his horse with unadorned gear.

The most painstaking attention was focused on the construction and leatherwork of the Andalusian saddle, a distinctly functional form that was enhanced by the expert hand-tooling and stitching that had long been Spain's special pride. The wooden framework of the saddle, known as the tree, was wrapped with rawhide to prevent splitting. Stirrups were attached directly to the tree, and the frame was then covered with leather. The saddle had a high pommel—a most important part, as it

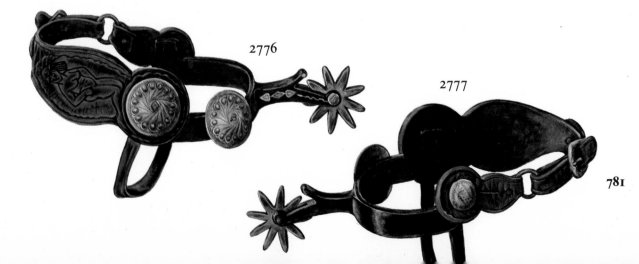

2776

2777

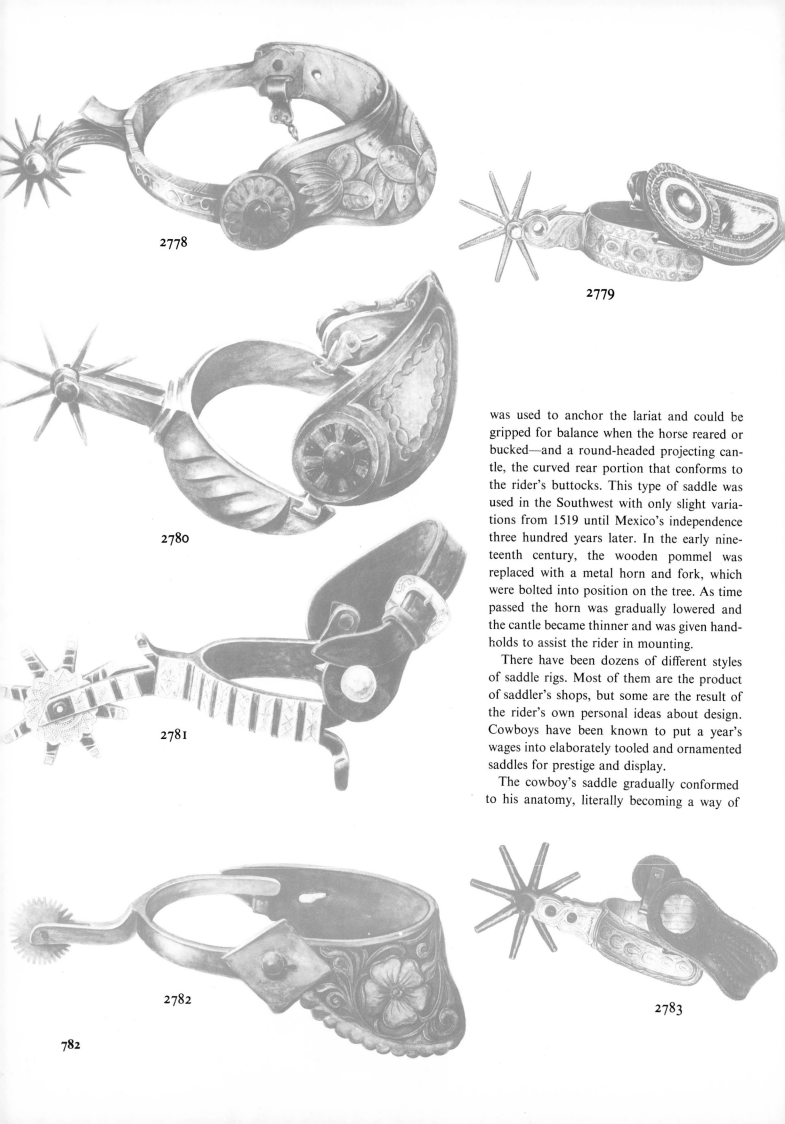

2778

2779

2780

2781

was used to anchor the lariat and could be gripped for balance when the horse reared or bucked—and a round-headed projecting cantle, the curved rear portion that conforms to the rider's buttocks. This type of saddle was used in the Southwest with only slight variations from 1519 until Mexico's independence three hundred years later. In the early nineteenth century, the wooden pommel was replaced with a metal horn and fork, which were bolted into position on the tree. As time passed the horn was gradually lowered and the cantle became thinner and was given handholds to assist the rider in mounting.

There have been dozens of different styles of saddle rigs. Most of them are the product of saddler's shops, but some are the result of the rider's own personal ideas about design. Cowboys have been known to put a year's wages into elaborately tooled and ornamented saddles for prestige and display.

The cowboy's saddle gradually conformed to his anatomy, literally becoming a way of

2782

2783

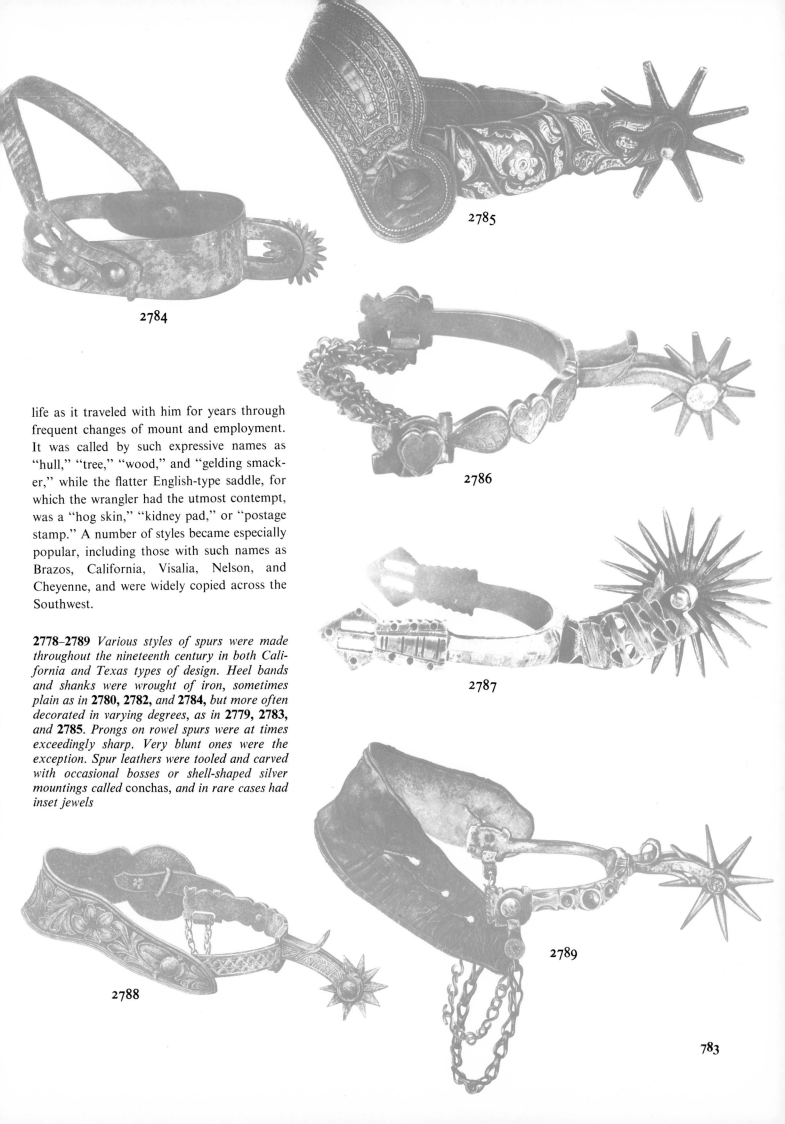

2784

2785

2786

2787

life as it traveled with him for years through frequent changes of mount and employment. It was called by such expressive names as "hull," "tree," "wood," and "gelding smacker," while the flatter English-type saddle, for which the wrangler had the utmost contempt, was a "hog skin," "kidney pad," or "postage stamp." A number of styles became especially popular, including those with such names as Brazos, California, Visalia, Nelson, and Cheyenne, and were widely copied across the Southwest.

2778–2789 *Various styles of spurs were made throughout the nineteenth century in both California and Texas types of design. Heel bands and shanks were wrought of iron, sometimes plain as in* **2780, 2782,** *and* **2784,** *but more often decorated in varying degrees, as in* **2779, 2783,** *and* **2785.** *Prongs on rowel spurs were at times exceedingly sharp. Very blunt ones were the exception. Spur leathers were tooled and carved with occasional bosses or shell-shaped silver mountings called* conchas, *and in rare cases had inset jewels*

2788

2789

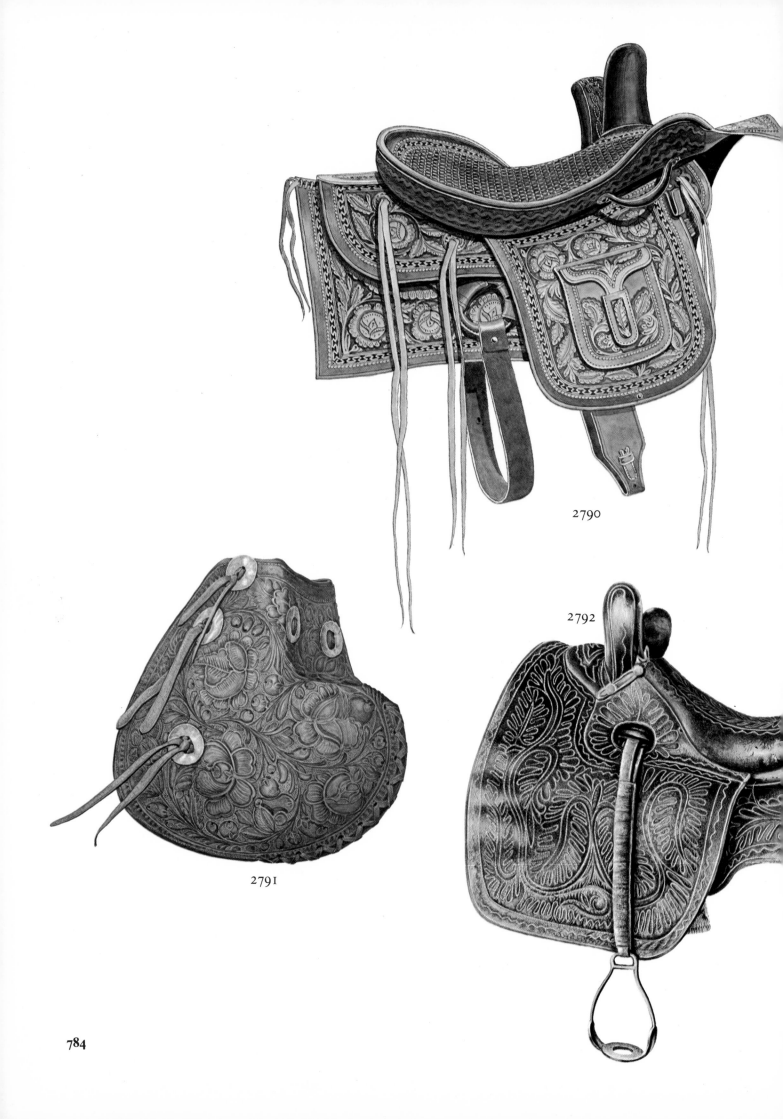

2790

2791

2792

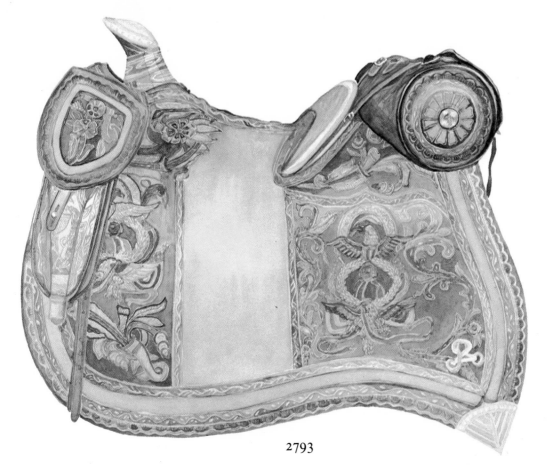

2793

2794

2790 *Sidesaddle of richly carved leather with low cantled seat, extra pouch on side flap, leather tie strings. A product of the 1880s* 2791 *Full leather stirrup decorated and tooled with roses, petals, and foliage patterns* 2792 *Lady's sidesaddle from California. Rich all-over decorative effect produced entirely by skillful stitching of palmettes and meanders* 2793 *Officer's saddle with roll pouch behind low cantled seat and pistol holster at pommel. Decorated with American symbols including eagles and head of George Washington, c. 1860–65* 2794 *The fine art of the saddlemaker is shown in the delicate tooling of naturalistic roses and rosebuds in this child's saddle, c. 1860*

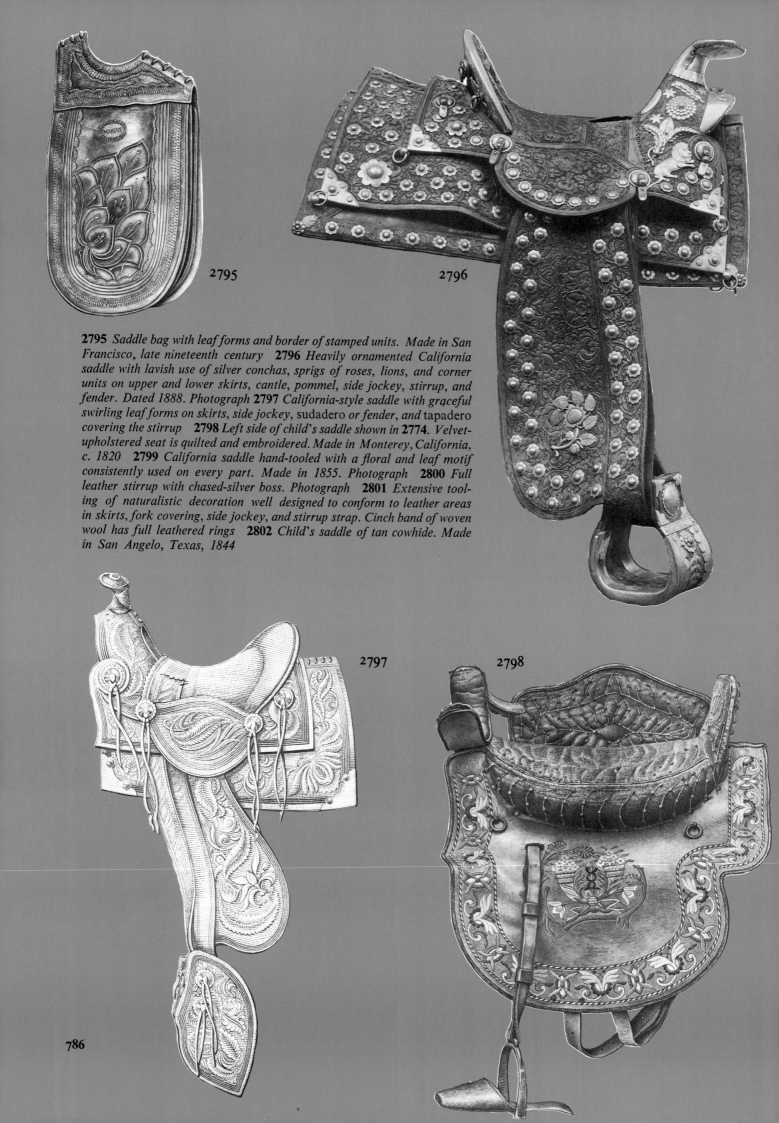

2795 *Saddle bag with leaf forms and border of stamped units. Made in San Francisco, late nineteenth century* **2796** *Heavily ornamented California saddle with lavish use of silver conchas, sprigs of roses, lions, and corner units on upper and lower skirts, cantle, pommel, side jockey, stirrup, and fender. Dated 1888. Photograph* **2797** *California-style saddle with graceful swirling leaf forms on skirts, side jockey, sudadero or fender, and tapadero covering the stirrup* **2798** *Left side of child's saddle shown in* **2774**. *Velvet-upholstered seat is quilted and embroidered. Made in Monterey, California, c. 1820* **2799** *California saddle hand-tooled with a floral and leaf motif consistently used on every part. Made in 1855. Photograph* **2800** *Full leather stirrup with chased-silver boss. Photograph* **2801** *Extensive tooling of naturalistic decoration well designed to conform to leather areas in skirts, fork covering, side jockey, and stirrup strap. Cinch band of woven wool has full leathered rings* **2802** *Child's saddle of tan cowhide. Made in San Angelo, Texas, 1844*

2799

2800

2801

2802

787

The Squire of Mount Vernon

2804

No other american hero has been as much revered or variously represented as George Washington. Our first president seems to have been a willing and gracious sitter in spite of his busy schedule, for during his lifetime some twenty-seven different artists painted or sculpted his likeness. Gilbert Stuart alone did about one hundred portraits of Washington. Charles Willson Peale and members of his illustrious family pursued their idol with great tenacity, and on one occasion all joined in at once to sketch the president from every angle. France's noted

2803 General Washington on *a* White Charger, *painted by an unknown artist in New York, c.1830. National Gallery of Art, Washington, D.C. Gift of Edgar William and Bernice Chrysler Garbisch*
2804 *Carved oval plaque of George Washington by Samuel McIntire*
2805 *View of the river front of the mansion at Mount Vernon as it originally looked. The modest dwelling was remodeled and enlarged several times, beginning in 1757. Photograph courtesy Mount Vernon Ladies' Association, Mount Vernon, Virginia*

2805

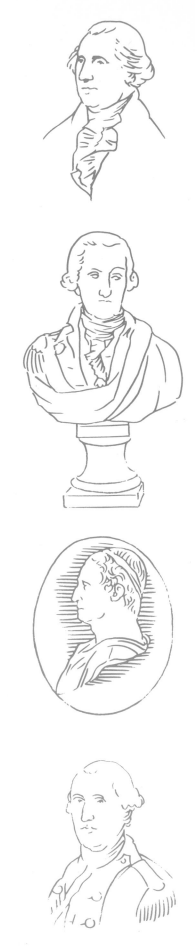

sculptor Jean Antoine Houdon was sent by his government in 1785 to produce the familiar bust that has served as the model for a great many stamps and coins. When Washington visited Salem, Massachusetts, in 1789, the famed architectural woodcarver Samuel McIntire sketched him as he addressed the townspeople from the courthouse balcony. From this informal model the artist was able to carve an excellent oval plaque that measured approximately three feet by five.

It is only natural that the man who led the Revolutionary forces with such skill and courage should have become a legend in his own day. During the trying times of his administration and through the years of retirement this reverence continued to gain in intensity and the citizenry came to endow him with godlike qualities. Manifestations of this adoration are to be found in any survey of the handicrafts of the time. In the backwoods of New England, Vermont housewives devoted long evenings to hooking "Father of Our Country" rugs, while in the southern Highlands Carolina carpenters whittled busts out of pine planks.

Upon Washington's death in December, 1799, this reverence assumed renewed vigor, and he became a symbol of national unity and patriotism. Engravings, cotton goods, medals, bills and coins, and a great variety of memorabilia were produced. Craftsmen and folk artists alike were spurred to a feverish pitch of activity, perpetuating Washington's image in statues, busts, andirons, porcelain and pottery, quilts and coverlets, cretonnes, and wallpaper patterns. When pressed glass became popular, Washington's likeness appeared on bowls, dishes, and flasks, and the development of Currier and Ives' famous prints eventually made it possible for even the poorest family to display his likeness.

To catalogue the ways in which the first president's face and figure have appeared over the years would require an encyclopedic study. Unlike the American eagle, whose popularity varies with the mood of the country, the Washington mystique remains unchallenged and unwavering, as solid as Plymouth Rock.

2806 *In 1823 Rembrandt Peale painted a portrait of Washington which became known as the "port-hole" portrait because of its circular frame. This mid-nineteenth-century mezzotint showing the full bust surrounded by an oak wreath, the whole engraved to represent a sculpture in stone, was done by Adam B. Walter, after the Peale painting. Courtesy New York Public Library, New York City*

PATRIÆ PATER

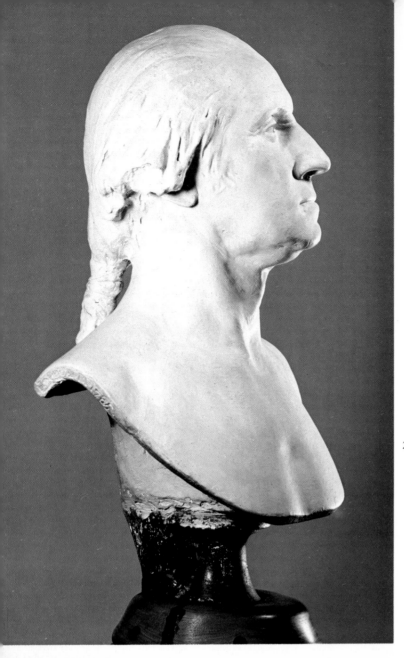

2807

2808

2807 *Bust of Washington by Jean Antoine Houdon, executed during his visit to Mount Vernon in 1785. Photograph courtesy Mount Vernon Ladies' Association, Mount Vernon, Virginia* **2808** *Cotton-printed textile featuring Washington and the newly elected president Benjamin Harrison, 1889* **2809** *Printed textile showing profile of Washington in a wreath of flowers*

2809

2810

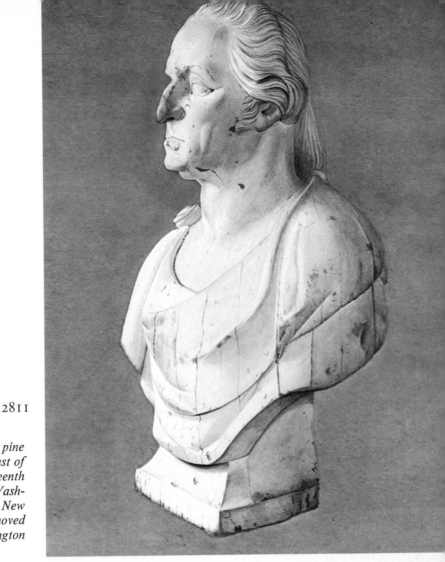

2811

2810 *This equestrian figure, carved in low relief on a pine plank, is the work of a native craftsman, 1902* **2811** *Bust of Washington carved in pine and painted white. Late nineteenth century* **2812** *Polychromed wooden statue of General Washington carved in 1776. It was erected in Bowling Green, New York, after the statue of King George had been removed* **2813** *Printed textiles showing portraits of George Washington were issued throughout the nineteenth century*

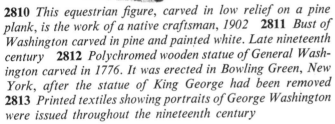

2812   2813

2817   2814

2815   2816

794

2814 *Detail from the printed textile after a copperplate engraving entitled* The Apotheosis of Franklin. *The commander in chief stands in the leading chariot by a seated female figure holding the legend "American Independence 1776." Probably printed in France, c. 1783* **2815** *Cast-iron garden figure made in New York by the Mott Iron Works. Latter half of the nineteenth century* **2816** *All-over pattern of Washington in an oval alternating with shield design reading "Peace"* **2817** *Cast-iron andiron with Washington's figure on pedestal. Mid-nineteenth century* **2818** *Cast-iron andiron shows Washington in squat, robust form rather than the usual heroic proportions* **2819** *Cotton printed kerchief with full-length portrait of Washington. A portion of the Farewell Address is at left, a eulogy at right, and the eagle, a square rigger, and the British Lion at the bottom, c. 1806* **2820** *Figure of Washington by an unknown sculptor follows the pose of the well-known statue by Ward on the steps of the New York Subtreasury Building. It is painted with blue uniform and yellow breeches and closely follows minor details of buttons and waistcoat wrinkles, a sign of the folk artist rather than the professional*

795

2821

2821 *Three-foot high seated figure of Liberty, by Eliodoro Patete of West Virginia. The artist's familiarity with Italian religious art is revealed in the academic attitude of the figure, which suggests a Madonna. The books, stars, diadem, and especially the inscriptions are all characteristic of folk-art expression, c. 1865* **2822**, *Cast-iron Liberty Bell coin banks produced at the time of the great Philadelphia Centennial in 1876* **2823** *Statue of Liberty coin bank, a type very popular following the statue's unveiling in New York harbor in 1886*

2822

Symbols of Freedom

BEFORE THE AMERICAN colonies became independent, on festive occasions, when custom called for a display of colors, the Union Jack was unfurled and images of Britannia were in evidence. With the Revolutionary War and the Declaration of Independence, these symbols of English domination were, of course, abandoned: the new republic required its own official emblems, a flag and a state seal.

On June, 14, 1777, Congress adopted a new flag, but various flags were used during the Revolutionary War. For example, beneath a banner of crimson and silver with the legend "Conquer or Die!" the embattled farmers at Concord Bridge fired "the shot heard round the world"; beneath the Pine Tree banner the battle of Bunker Hill was lost and won; and beneath the Rattlesnake flag the American fleet won its first victory. Hence, to sever the last link that bound the Colonies individually to England, the Stars and Stripes was created as a symbol of national unity. The thirteen red and white stripes, one for each of the states, had been a feature of an earlier flag that included the Union Jack in the upper left-hand quadrant, but the resolution on the design for the new flag replaced the small Union Jack motif with thirteen white stars, symbolizing a new constellation. (These stars were usually arranged in a circle, but placement varied.) It was this flag that represented the new country when Lord Cornwallis surrendered in 1781, and it had already become such an accepted symbol that it was displayed widely and figured importantly in paintings, carvings, needlecraft, and metalwork.

While the flag was adopted within a year of Independence Day, the Great Seal with the American eagle required longer deliberation.

2823

At the beginning of the Revolution, Congress appointed a committee of prominent citizens —among them George Washington, Benjamin Franklin, Thomas Jefferson, and John Adams —whose task it was to devise and design a seal, or official coat of arms, that would incorporate the ideals, aspirations, and unity of the young republic. They met on the afternoon of July 4, 1776, a few hours after the signing of the Declaration of Independence. Some of the designs discussed for the seal were quite fantastic; for example, Thomas Jefferson suggested a seal that would depict the Israelites crossing the Red Sea and the Pharoah's army being destroyed. Six years elapsed while committees met and disbanded, and one design after another was proposed and rejected. In May, 1782, a third committee submitted to Congress a design by William Barton, an authority on heraldry. Barton's design incorporated an eagle—"the Symbol of Supreme Power and Authority, signifying the Congress." The Continental Congress did not consider this design acceptable either, however, and Charles Thompson, secretary of that body, took over. Thompson eliminated the allegorical figures which had appeared on previous designs and made the eagle—specifically the American bald eagle—the central motif, "holding in his dexter talon an olive branch [symbolizing peace] and in his sinister a bundle of arrows [representing war]." (Barton's eagle had held a sword and a flag.) Over the eagle's head was a constellation of thirteen stars and in its beak a scroll bearing the motto *E Pluribus Unum*. This motto was the one feature surviving from the design submitted by the first committee. The verso side showed a pyramid symbolizing stability and permanence with the Eye of Providence at its top. After some additional changes by Barton—he supplied thirteen alternating white and red vertical stripes below the rectangular blue field on the eagle's breast—the seal was adopted by the then revolting Colonies on June 20, 1782. It was later approved by the Philadelphia Federal

Constitutional Convention of 1787, and was in common use by the time of George Washington's inauguration in 1789.

To date, there have been seven dies of the Great Seal. The fourth and fifth dies, cast in 1841 and 1847, were criticized because the eagle's left talon did not hold the thirteen arrows specified in the original legislation passed by Congress. In 1884, at the request of Theodore Frelinghuysen, secretary of state, Congress appropriated a thousand dollars for the preparation of a new die. A new seal showing the correct number of arrows was made the following year by James Horton Whitehouse, chief designer for Tiffany and Company. His design is the one in use today.

The Stars and Stripes, along with the Great Seal and the American eagle, provided artists, designers, and craftsmen with emblems that have been used for almost two centuries. The eagle, whose use as a symbol descended from antiquity, proved a particularly versatile decorative motif. Without studying, much less submitting to, the artistic conventions governing heraldry, American artists and craftsmen intuitively recognized that there were few limits to the decorative potential of the newly adopted national symbol. Thus a profusion of decorative eagles appeared from the time of the War of 1812 through the Civil War.

Other popular patriotic emblems included the figures of Columbia and Uncle Sam—the former a poetic, the latter a comic, symbol of the United States—and of Liberty, the Liberty Bell, Independence Hall, and likenesses of George Washington.

During the closing years of the eighteenth century and the first decades of the nineteenth, artists and craftsmen used these national symbols to express the period's patriotic fervor. In the works of folk artists these motifs were given a fresh and earthy vitality. More, perhaps, than in any other period of American history, such folk works seem to spring directly from the heart and thus are exceptionally effective expressions of the ideals of freedom and unity.

2824

2825

2826

2827

2828

2829

2830

2824 *Carved eagle in which natural proportions have been sacrificed to emphasize head, beak, and talons* 2825 *Sheet-brass powder horn displaying elaborate military motif. Late eighteenth century* 2826 *Painted cast-iron mirror frame topped by an eagle. Patriotic motifs include flags, shield, officer in medallion, 1862* 2827 *Carved and painted pine sea chest, combining maritime symbols—anchor and fisherman's head—with patriotic motif of eagle and shield. Made in Massachusetts, c. 1840* 2828 *Stamped sheet-brass eagle, used as decoration on parade floats and platforms, 1840–50* 2829 *Columbia weather vane with thirty-two-star flag. Made of cast zinc, sheet copper, and brass, c. 1865* 2830 *Painted eagle appears on many regimental drums of Civil War vintage*

2831

2832

2831 *Bronze plaque of head of Lincoln, c. 1862* **2832** *Carved figurehead from the packet ship* Congress, *depicting the seated figure of Liberty with shield and eagle. Late eighteenth century* **2833** *Ship's bell cast in bronze, with eagle, shield, and military symbols, 1846* **2834** *Cast-iron gates and fencing around the Washington Monument in Baltimore* **2835** *Elaborately carved cake mold representing America's triumph over England: at the right, an eagle and shield with cornucopias, Columbia, and a helmeted warrior facing the defeated forces of Britannia. The victorious American eagle surmounts the design* **2836** *Castbrass bootjack, with the shield and motto from the Great Seal* **2837** *Printed cotton with all-over pattern of the eagle and seals of the states. Late nineteenth century* **2838** *Liberty weather vane of sheet copper, c. 1885–90, Figures 2833–35 from photographs*

2833

2834

802

2835

2836

2837

2838

803

U. S. Custom House. 1805.

2840

The Eagle Spreads Its Wings

THE EAGLE HAS long been the most popular American motif in the decorative arts and crafts. Thousands of artists and craftsmen have interpreted its image. Soaring and circling far above the earth, plunging like a meteor from the sky, screaming defiance at a storm, or fiercely striking its prey—to men of every age the eagle has embodied freedom and power. This image has been emblazoned on the chariots of warriors and on the shields of knights from the time of Caesar to the battle of Iwo Jima.

A bald-headed eagle of the American species with outspread wings and legs is prominently displayed on the Great Seal of the United States, which was approved by Congress on June 20, 1782. The use of the bird followed ancient precedents. Three thousand years before Christ the eagle had been guardian deity of Mesopotamia and had also represented Babylonia, depicted in a pose similar to that on the Great Seal.

In ancient Greece and its colonial states, the eagle, holding a thunderbolt or its prey, was for long a favorite emblem on coins. It also appeared on Roman coins, medals, and gems, often with a palm branch in its talons. The standard of the Roman legions was a spread eagle, encircled by a laurel wreath and grasp-

2839 *Eagle signboard with the owner's name, J. Procter, hung outside the entrance to the Red Lion Inn at Red Lion, Delaware. Washington is known to have stopped here, for an entry in his diary for March 1791 notes that he gave his horses "a bite of Hay at the Red Lyon" on his way to Mount Vernon. Photograph courtesy the Henry Francis du Pont Winterthur Museum, Winterthur, Delaware* **2840** *Painted pine eagle clutching arrows and shield. Carved by Samuel McIntire in 1805. From the customhouse at Salem* **2841** *Pine sternboard eagle with foliated scrolls or rinceaux. Early nineteenth century*

2841

ing a thunderbolt in both talons. During the Middle Ages, eagles with either single or double heads flourished as heraldic devices. Thus the selection of the eagle as a national emblem was influenced by medieval and Classical models, the latter of which were simultaneously very influential in other areas of art, notably architecture.

The eagle on the Great Seal was by no means the first emblematic eagle to make its appearance in the American Colonies. As early as 1700, one was stamped on a New York token of lead or brass; in 1776 it was featured on a Massachusetts copper penny within a semicircle of thirteen stars; and in 1778 the State of New York included an eagle perched on a globe as part of its official coat of arms. However, the eagle of the Great Seal is the first specified as being of the American bald-headed species, "bald" in the older sense of the term, meaning white.

A bald-headed American eagle was also incorporated in a design by Major l'Enfant for a badge for the Society of Cincinnati, a group founded in 1783 by members of the American revolutionary army. Benjamin Franklin, although well-informed in a wide variety of fields, was apparently no ornithologist, and on seeing the badge, he wrote to his daughter from France: "I am, on this account, not displeased that the figure is not known as a bald eagle but looks more like a turkey. For in truth, the turkey is in comparison a much more respectable bird and withal a true original native of America. Eagles have been found in all countries, but the turkey is peculiar to ours. . . . He is, besides, (though a little vain and silly, it is true, but not the worse emblem for that) a bird of courage, and would not hesitate to attack a grenadier of the British guards, who should presume to invade his farmyard with a red coat on." In the preceding paragraph Franklin had expressed the

wish that "the bald eagle had not been chosen as the representative of our country; he is a bird of bad moral character; he does not get his living honestly . . . too lazy to fish for himself, he watches the labor of the fishing-hawk, and when that diligent bird has at length taken a fish, and is bearing it to his nest for the support of his mate and his young ones, the bald eagle pursues him and takes it from him . . . like those men who live by sharping and robbing he is generally poor, and often very lousy. Besides he is a rank coward; the little kingbird, not bigger than a sparrow, attacks him boldly and drives him out of the district."

In *The American Eagle, A Study in Natural and Civil History*, Francis Hobart Herrick comes stoutly to the defense of the national bird, clearing him of Franklin's charges. Herrick suggests that the accusations may have been inspired by pique, since Franklin's own design for the seal—he had been chairman of the first committee—had been rejected. Herrick describes the bald eagle as a native who has never been known to leave the continent of his own volition, who nests as near the sun as he can get, "like a true bird of Jove and messenger of the star of the day," and as a model parent, devoting six months or more to rearing his young. "He does not live entirely or mainly by 'robbing' or 'sharping,' as Benjamin Franklin seemed to believe, but is an expert fisherman in his own right, and he will not rob the osprey unless this bird is heedless in giving him the chance, or, as it were, offers him the challenge . . . above all the eagle is no rank coward, as Franklin also mistakenly supposed. Contrary to that savant's opinion, he is never driven from the neighborhood by the little kingbird, or by any other living being excepting a man armed with a gun. . . . Woe to any impudent marauder who assails the castle of the king of the air when eggs and eaglets are in danger. . . . The truth of the matter is that the eagle has learned from bitter experience that he is king of birds only, and that where man

807

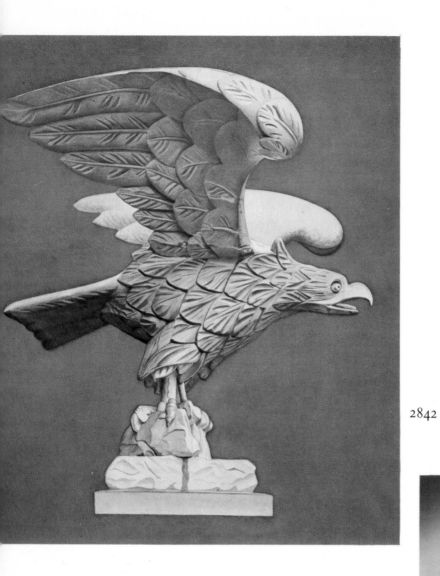

2842   2843

2844   2845

808

2847

2846

2848

2842 Carved pine eagle, probably made in Newport, Rhode Island, c. 1830 **2843** Ribbed whisky flask with eagle in oval. Made by Louisville, Kentucky, glassworks **2844** Cast-brass eagle, mounted on an acorn-shaped walnut base **2845** Pine eagle, nearly five feet tall, said to have served as a signboard for an unidentified "Eagle Tavern" in Rhode Island. Feathers on breast, wings, and back, individually cut in high relief, reveal powerful carving, c. 1850–75. Photograph courtesy Colonial Williamsburg **2846** Ceramic eagle used as a mantel decoration **2847** Snare drum of bent-wood with painted eagle, mid-nineteenth century **2848** Coverlet with woven design including eagle, the most popular motif in the first half of the nineteenth century

enters the picture, caution and circumspection
are the price of life, liberty and independence."
Herrick adds that if the eagle had possessed
the brains of the dodo, he would have been
virtually extinct by the end of the eighteenth
century.

After the adoption of the Great Seal, a
variety of eagles appeared on other seals and
insignia, including those for departments of
the federal and state governments and the presidential seal, and on coins. Frequently, as on
the presidential seal, the eagle turns its head to
the left, whereas on the Great Seal the head
turns toward the right, which is considered the
correct position. Other variations include
placing arrows in the right claw and the olive
branch in the left, reducing the number of
arrows or of stripes in the shield, and placing
the eagle on the shield instead of the shield on
the eagle. Some people condemn these revi-
sions for not conforming to heraldic law.
Various eagles, especially those on coins, have
also been criticized for being of alien breed, for
example, for having the long feathered trousers
characteristic of the golden eagle; whereas the
American eagle, except in its juvenal stage, has

2849

2850

bare or half-bare shanks, extremely conspicuous because they are bright yellow.

At Washington's inauguration, the eagle's popularity increased. After taking office, Washington made a triumphal tour of the thirteen states and was greeted everywhere with eagle transparencies traced on starched and whitewashed windowpanes, behind which blazing candles produced dramatic effects. At balls in the President's honor, fans and ribbons displayed painted eagles, and men's lapels carried engraved ones in brass. Washington himself had become a confirmed eagle lover; a spread eagle was perched on the finial of his desk at Mount Vernon, and an eagle was carved above his pew in St. Paul's Church. Within a few years, the eagle had become the country's most popular decorative motif. The War of 1812 produced another patriotic upsurge, fanned by the fervor of renewed activities against Britain, that expressed itself in the arts and crafts. After the war, craftsmen worked the bird of freedom into an extraordinary number and variety of designs. Subsequent nineteenth-century presidential campaigns, patriotic celebrations, and national

2852

2853

2849 *Cast-iron eagle, nineteenth century* **2850** *Soldered sheet-brass eagle torch, used in the Mexican War, 1848* **2851** *Cast-iron eagle pin tray, c. 1870–80* **2852** *Brass eagle door knocker, c. 1850* **2853** *Brass eagle door knocker, c. 1840–50*

2851

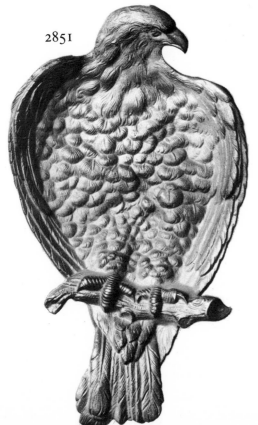

2854

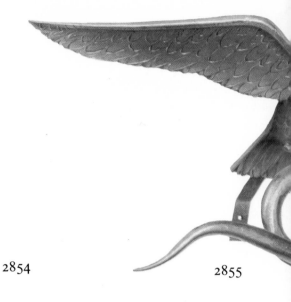

2855

2856

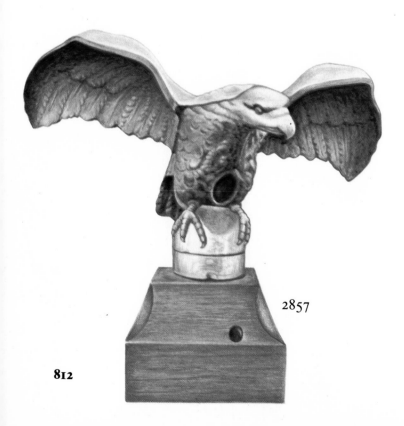

2857

2854 *Eagle weather vane, nineteenth century. Photograph courtesy the Smithsonian Institution, Washington, D.C.* 2855 *Gilded wood eagle and snake, nineteenth century* 2856 *Carved eagle with shield and arrows. Photograph courtesy the Smithsonian Institution, Washington, D.C.* 2857 *Cast-iron eagle flagpole holder, 1856* 2858 *Carved eagle ornament. Photograph courtesy the Smithsonian Institution, Washington, D.C.* 2859 *Carved eagle figurehead, early nineteenth century* 2860 *Cast-iron eagle desk ornament* 2861 *Eagle with realistically detailed feathers and proportions revealing a strong Napoleonic influence, especially in the bolts of lightning clutched by the talons*

2858

2859

2860

2861

2862

2863

2864

emergencies brought forth new crops of eagles.

With appropriate democratic impartiality, the eagle lent itself to the decoration of porcelain dinner services—which were imported from England and China because an American porcelain industry was slow to develop but which used American motifs—and kitchen crockery. It was impressed into whisky flasks and Sandwich glass, woven into curtain and upholstery fabrics, and perched as a finial on mirrors, clocks, and weather vanes. It was carved into butter stamps and delicately inlaid in drawing-room furniture, painted on tavern signs and cast into flatiron holders, and even stitched in quilted counterpanes, complete with arrows, olive branch, scroll, and overhead stars. The eagle was also minted in a number of forms, but its image on coins and paper

2865

money is not nearly as varied as are its manifestations on other types of objects.

Throughout the nineteenth century, the eagle was a favorite motif for stoneware. Early examples were small and crisply incised; the later ones were large, brushed on in cobalt blue with bold calligraphic strokes, or molded in relief. Pennsylvania German potters some-

2862 *Cast-iron eagle standing on cloud formation. Made by the Meeker Foundry in Newark, New Jersey, c. 1850* **2863** *Cast-iron stove urn with eagle finial, c. 1850. Photograph* **2864** *Wooden eagle, carved in low relief as marine decoration* **2865** *Gilded copper eagle ornament, nineteenth century*

2866 *Powder flask with eagle, crossed pistols, and motto* E Pluribus Unum. *Made in 1778.* **2867** *Cast-iron eagle ornament. Photograph*

2866

2867

2868

2869

2870

2871

816

2872

2873

2874

2875

2868–2875 *Eagles were usually carved from pine, which is easily cut and gouged. Those of wide wingspread generally necessitated carving the wings as separate pieces, which were then supported and strengthened with metal cleats (**2869** and **2875**.) More static poses, as in **2872** and **2873**, were used on flagpoles or weather vanes. Nineteenth century*

2876

2877

times incised the eagle in pie plates, in celebration of presidential candidates. Handsomely stylized eagles appeared on wooden butter stamps of Pennsylvania German origin. These were carved by folk artists, usually in intaglio so that the design impressed on the butter would appear in relief.

Spirited and beautiful eagles were introduced in pieced, knotted, and other types of quilts which exhibit skilled craftsmanship and the creativity of many generations of American women. Weavers were not content simply to make the eagle the central motif of the coverlet, but worked the bird into elaborate borders in repeat patterns. Commemorative textiles featured the eagle and told the nation's story through pictorial scenes and symbolic motifs. Some of these celebrated the Mexican War,

2878

2879

others commemorated the Philadelphia Centennial, and still others were issued at the time of Benjamin Harrison's inauguration in 1889, which was also the centenary of Washington's election and the year in which the state of Washington was admitted to the Union.

The most interesting and beautiful eagles are found among those carved in wood, either in relief or in the round, as decorative panels for sofas, chairs, and mantelpieces; over the doorways of public buildings or private dwellings; on cupolas and gateposts; as shop or tavern signs; or as figureheads. This medium—mahogany and pine were the preferred woods—attracted both self-taught folk artists and trained sculptors, architects, and cabinetmakers. Fine marquetry eagles were inlaid in mahogany, satinwood, and maple

2880

2876 *Carved wooden eagle, attributed to Samuel McIntire, c. 1800. Photograph.* **2877** *Copper eagle weather vane, mid-nineteenth century* **2878** *Colored and gilded eagle, carved from mahogany, c. 1800–1810, by the noted sculptor William Rush. In Independence Hall, Philadelphia. Photograph* **2879** *Eagle figurehead with eighteen-foot wingspread. Carved by John Haley Bellamy for the U.S.S.* Lancaster, *c. 1880–90* **2880** *Eagle and banner, carved in low relief. Conventional style of execution with a minimum of incised strokes. Made by John Haley Bellamy* **2881** *Carved eagle, gilded and polychromed. Feather treatment approaches acanthus foliation*

2881

2882

chests, slant-top and tambour desks, secretaries, tall clocks, knife boxes, and tilt-top tables. The number of inlaid stars in a piece was usually the same as the number of states in the Union at the time, which helps to date the piece.

First among the untrained craftsmen was the Pennsylvania German whittler Wilhelm Schimmel, who worked during the post-Civil War years. Of the academicians, one of the most distinguished was America's first native-born sculptor, William Rush (1756–1833), among whose surviving works are two magnificent eagles carved as emblems, one for a church and the other for a fire company. Samuel McIntire, born a year after Rush, has been called the most celebrated of the craftsmen-architects of America. He was fond of making an eagle in relief against a background of stars the central motif of his exquisite mantelpieces, and of cresting the rails of his equally beautiful mahogany sofas with the emblem. He also executed eagles in the round

with closed wings and eagles perched on globes as ornaments for gate arches and cupolas. Among his works is a noble spread eagle which was placed over the door of the Old Custom House in his native Salem. McIntire's New York contemporary, Duncan Phyfe, like other cabinetmakers of the period, made charming mahogany chairs with eagle splats for distinguished clients.

Another outstanding artist-craftsman of a more recent period was John Haley Bellamy (1836–1914) of Kittery Point, Maine. He devoted most of his life to carving eagles, finding his chief employment with the Boston and Portsmouth navy yards and the government. He made ornamental eagles for public and private buildings and innumerable small spread eagles, many of which were brilliantly painted and gilded and were placed over the doorways of ships' cabins. He developed a special technique for stylizing his eagles, which are extremely graceful and proud, with fierce beaks, usually holding a banner carrying

2883

2884

a patriotic motto. Possibly his most ambitious one is the huge figurehead for the U.S.S. *Lancaster,* carved in 1859. This gigantic bird has a wingspread of more than eighteen feet and weighs about thirty-two hundred pounds.

Cast-iron eagles are probably as numerous and diverse in character as those carved in wood. They range from such small objects as a delicately molded pin tray and a mechanical bank in the form of an eagle feeding its young to a majestic creature with a wingspread of sixty-five inches, once used as a sign. Sometimes these eagles appear to derive from European prototypes and to have been adapted by tradition-loving craftsmen to new patriotic uses. In addition to gold, silver, and bronze coins and medallions which featured the image of the eagle, sheet copper was hammered into eagle weather vanes. In early Pennsylvania food "safes," the tinplate ventilating holes were sometimes pricked in eagle patterns. Furniture mounts, and particularly the finials of clocks, featured many types of brass eagles.

In retrospect, it seems fortunate that the founding fathers chose the eagle, which could be easily rendered and interpreted in most mediums in a great variety of attitudes—perching, preening, soaring, gliding, attacking, and alighting. For the versatility of our national symbol has continued to inspire countless artists and artisans.

2882–2885 *The spread eagle took many forms, with and without accessory decorations, as a motif ideally suited to the stern of a ship. The horizontal extension of the wings varied from five to eight feet. In contrast to the figurehead at the bow, which called for treatment in the round, sternboard eagles were executed in comparatively low relief. Coupled with the eagle were such design elements as flags, drapes, the shield, and the ribbon bearing the motto* E Pluribus Unum. *A fine example of gilded pine carved by Alton Skillin for the U.S.S.* Enterprise *in 1881 is shown in 2882. The eagle and shield in 2883 were carved by John Bellamy*

2885

2886

2887   2888

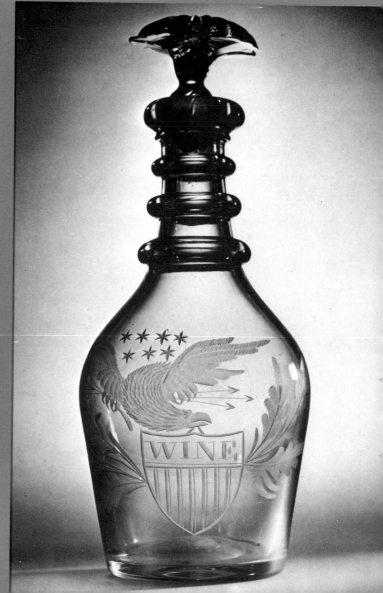

822

2886 *Painted pine eagle, by William Rush, c. 1810. Photograph courtesy Philadelphia Museum of Art* **2887** *Glass plate, with eagle clutching arrows and olive branch as central motif, c. 1830. Photograph courtesy Corning Museum of Glass, Corning, New York* **2888** *Decanter with engraved eagle. Photograph courtesy Corning Museum of Glass, Corning, New York* **2889** *Carved pine pilothouse eagle. Photograph* **2890** *Glass goblet with engraved eagle and motto. Photograph courtesy Corning Museum of Glass, Corning, New York* **2891** *Cup plate with eagle. Probably from Boston & Sandwich Glass Works, 1831. Photograph courtesy Corning Museum of Glass, Corning, New York*

2889

2890   2891

2892   2893

2892–2897 *Coverlets woven 1800–1850. No single motif was repeated as often as the American eagle in nineteenth-century coverlets produced by both housewives and professional weavers. The eagle*

2894   2895

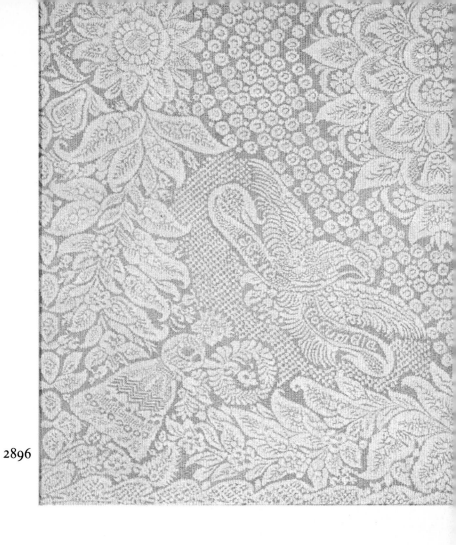

2896

sometimes occupied the central medallion but was more often employed as a corner motif or repeated figure in a border. Designs were derived from weaving drafts that were exchanged throughout the states

2897

2898 2899

826

2900

2901

2898 *Damask weave in red and white which includes several patriotic slogans, the equestrian figure of Washington, and a border of eagles and stars. Made in New York state, 1841* **2899** *Reversible coverlet evidently made from the same weaving draft as that in 2898, though produced in Pennsylvania in 1842. Note how accidental weaving produced a double eagle in the border* **2900** *Bedspread with rare center medallion of the Great Seal* **2901** *Signature of the maker is linked with the eagle, ribbon, and* E Pluribus Unum, *1853*

Basket of Fruit with Flowers, *painted c. 1830 by an unknown New Jersey artist*

STATE
PROJECTS

ALABAMA: Montgomery

ARIZONA: Phoenix

CALIFORNIA

  Northern Division: San Francisco

  Southern Division: Los Angeles

COLORADO: Denver

CONNECTICUT: New Haven

DELAWARE: Wilmington

DISTRICT OF COLUMBIA:

  Washington

FLORIDA: Jacksonville

GEORGIA: Atlanta

ILLINOIS: Chicago

IOWA: Des Moines

KANSAS: Topeka

KENTUCKY: Louisville

LOUISIANA: New Orleans

MAINE: Portland

MARYLAND: Baltimore

MASSACHUSETTS: Boston

MICHIGAN: Lansing

MINNESOTA: St. Paul

MISSOURI: Jefferson City

NEW HAMPSHIRE: Manchester

NEW JERSEY: Newark

NEW MEXICO: Santa Fe

NEW YORK: Albany; New York City

NORTH CAROLINA: Raleigh

OHIO: Columbus

PENNSYLVANIA: Harrisburg

RHODE ISLAND: Providence

SOUTH CAROLINA: Columbia

TENNESSEE: Nashville

TEXAS: San Antonio

UTAH: Salt Lake City

VERMONT: Rutland

VIRGINIA: Richmond

WASHINGTON: Seattle

WISCONSIN: Madison

ARTISTS

ALABAMA

Brock, Teresa, *photographer*

ARIZONA

Brooke, Mary Edith

Chamber, Elizabeth

Davidson, Lloyd A., *photographer*

Johnson, Elizabeth

Jordan, Elizabeth

Upton, Eugene

CALIFORNIA (NORTHERN)

Bailey, Evelyn

Cero, Emil

Dougan, Ethel

Gerke, Rose Campbell

Jackson, Gordena

Nastasi, Lena

Semple, B.

Tallman, Verna

Torell, Pearl

Van Voris, Vera

Westfall, Tulita

Willoughby, C.

CALIFORNIA (SOUTHERN)

Barks, Frank C.

Barnes, Ruth M.

Bartlett, Dana

Blakeley, Hal

Bradleigh, Beulah

Brown, Dayton

Buckley, Anne Gene

Buker, Ruth

Burge, Irene M.

Christoffels, Cornelius

Crawford, Jack, *photographer*

Donahoo, Juanita

Hastings, Florence

Herbert, William

Hobbs, Christopher

Holt, Geoffrey

Jewett, Edward T.

Kieckhofel, William

King, Georgina

Linsley, Margaret

McAuley, William

Miller, Randolph F.

Noble, Raymond E.

Park, Paul, *photographer*

Parker, Gladys C.

Pratt, Albert

Reynolds, Arthur P.

Rhone, George E.

Romano, Josephine C.

Sherman, Howard H.

Swanson, Syrena

Taylor, Robert W. R.

Tierney, Peter A., *photographer*

Towner, Edith

Transpota, Gerald, Jr.

Waddell, Harry Mann

Whiteley, Kay

Willoughby, David P.

COLORADO

Duncan, Polly

Gross, Joseph

Krasnowski, Vincent

Lorenzini, Eldora P.

O'Bergh, Carl

Valle, Maud

Woods, Ranka S.

CONNECTICUT

Boyer, Ralph

Collins, John

DiGennero, Edward

Doerfler, Isabella Ruth

Dolmith, Rex, *photographer*

Elliot, Martha

Engel, Edward F.

Flynn, Lawrence

Galvin, Robert

Gaylord, Marian

Gully, Alvin M.

Hackney, Malcolm, *artist and photographer*

Holden, Ray

Hoxie, Jerome

Kravitt, Samuel, *photographer*

LaRoche, Karl, *photographer*

Lauretano, Michael

Matulis, John

Merriam, Harold

Metelli, Guido

Partyka, Martin

Parys, Alfred

Peterson, Fred

Skreczko, Henry, *photographer*

Smith, Philip

Smith, Rex

Solomon, Miriam Y.

Waterbury, Blanche

Weiss, Fred

Weld, Howard

DELAWARE

Blake, Earl, *photographer*

Brinton, Amos C.

Bukill, Henrietta S.

Crewe, L. S., *photographer*

Edwards, William H.

Fineman, Samuel

Ford, Samuel W.

Frazier, Cornelius

Grant, D. J.
Harding, Donald
Henderer, Regina
Hukill, Henrietta S.
Jackson, Gwendolyn
Lawson, James M.
Loper, Edward L.
Macklem, Leslie J.
Miller, J.
Moll, John B.
Petrucci, John
Price, John
Rosel, Vincent
Saltar, Gordon
Swientochowski, John
Towers, E. A. Jr.
Wharry, Lawrence
White, Gould, *photographer*

DISTRICT OF COLUMBIA
Montgomery, Mrs. Inez
Sterling, Ella Josephine
Stottlemeyer, Margaret
*Stelmach, *photographer*
Prince, Mildred

FLORIDA
Browne, Frank S.
Casaway, J. W.
Fossum, Magnus S.
Hassebrock, Fred
Holme, Maude
Johnston, Annie B.
Keane, Frank M.
Kelton, Maud S.
Merrill, Katherine
Parker, Cora
Runyan, Manuel G.
Walbeck, Alfred

Wilson, Carmel
Wilson, Marguerite

ILLINOIS
Aberdeen, Harry G.
Bates, Dorothea
Bevier, Milton
Blewett, Wellington
Bluhme, Oscar
Bodine, John
Brown, H. Langden
Buecher, Edward W.
Clark, Robert
Grossen, Harry
Kibbee, Edward
Koehl, John
Koehn, Alfred
Long, Louella
Ludwig, William
Mazur, Stanley
McCombs, Orrie
McEntee, Frank
Melzer, Kurt
Navigato, Rocco
Opstad, Adolph
Owen, Mary
Rekucki, Michael
Rudin, Albert
Spiecker, William
Thompson, Archie
Thorsen, John
Unger, Max
Vail, James H. C.
White, Wayne

IOWA
Bashaw, Edward
Brown, George C.
Davenport, F. C.

Dawson, Clarence W.
Diason, G. E.
Durand, Francis L.
Eiseman, Frank
Feidler, A.
Gilson, Robert
Golden, Margaret
Griffith, LeRoy
Hartenstein, Violet
Hightower, Herndon
Hollingsworth, Doris
Kempter, Harley
Marshall, Claude
Mason, Georgine
Merchant, Flora
Nelson, Lelah
Newmann, Raymond
Oldfield, Harold
Roberts, Sydney
Scalise, Gerald
Vernier, Racine

KANSAS
Ayres, Rolland W.
Clement, Clayton
Fritz, E. Allen
Fudge, Frank J.
Gray, Ethel Lillian
Greider, John F.
Henderson, Violet
Kent, M. Louise
Lockwood, Norma
Wear, Verna M., *photographer*

KENTUCKY
Brown, Mona
Carroll, Orville A.
Childers, William Paul
Cronk, Lon

Davidson, Mary C.
Goodwin, Charles Reed
Mowery, Elbert Samuel
Prater, Mary D.
Ulrich, Alois E.
Vezolles, George V.
Williams, Edward D.

LOUISIANA
Arbo, A.
Boyd, Joseph L.
Cannella, Joseph
Curry, Aldous R.
Doria, Alvin J.
Frère, Herbert S.
Mangelsdorf, Hans
Price, Ray
Verbeke, Lucien

MAINE
Avanzato, Dominic, *photographer*
Bartlett, Curry M.
Bent, Mildred
Davis, John
Gale, Harriette
Gray, Rosamond P.
Hentz, Karl J.
Poffinbarger, Paul
Skillin, Alton K.

MARYLAND
Alain, Marie
Arnold, Madeline
Bowman, Charles
Causey, Lillian
Campbell, Douglas
France, Michael
High, William
Meyer, George B.
Montgomery, Inez B.

Mosher, Steller
Philpot, Samuel
Schindele, C., *photographer*

MASSACHUSETTS
Berman, Sadie
Bilodeay, Laura
Broome, Lloyd
Chabot, Lucille
Cohen, Frances
Constantine, George
Cunningham, Eleanor
DeKalb, Beatrice
Dinghausen, Alfred
Domey, Alice
Dorr, Phyllis
*Fisher, *photographer*
Foster, Lawrence
Fuerst, Betty
Gale, Harriette
Ger, Anne
Gilman, Helen
Goldberg, Joseph
Hazen, Willard
Hyde, Hazel
Iverson, Jane
Kelleher, John W.
Koch, Gertrude
McIntyre, Samuel
Merrill, Sumner
Missirian, Zabelle
Moutal, Elizabeth
Muollo, Victor F.
Page, Marian
Peterson, Lawrence
Pollman, William
Rich, Winslow
Richards, A. J., *photographer*
Selmer-Larsen, Ingrid

Smith, Alfred H.
Smith, Irving I.
Stearns, Alice
Van Dunker, Dorothy
Wright, Wynna

MICHIGAN
Brennan, Dorothy
Bush, Rex
Chichester, Beverly
Coleman, Anne
Croe, Eugene
File, George F.
Gray, Frank
Harris, Dorothy
Hiatt, Helmle, *photographer*
Hochstrasser, Walter
Makrenos, Chris
McLellan, James
Ramage, David
Rokita, Florian
Stahl, Lillian
Strzalkowski, Edward
Vance, Vivian L.
Weise, Elmer

MINNESOTA
Heiberg, Einar
Keksi, Karl
Luedke, Mrs. Gene
Quackenbush, Lloyd
Rice, Wilbur
Sharp, Floyd R.

MISSOURI
Barnett, Gerard
Brooks, Adele
Chomyk, Michael
Clement, Clayton
Erganian, Sarkis

Ficcadenti, J.
Finley, William
Gutting, Frank W.
Hagen, Emil
Haupt, Dolores
Kelly, Paul
King, Harry
Makimson, Loraine
Rigsby, Robert
Ritchey, Lionel
Walsh, Hardin D.
Weisenborn, Harold
Williams, Donald
Turnbull, James B.

NEW HAMPSHIRE
Cosgrove, Alice
Herrick, Marion E.
Lacoursière, Lucille
Lewis, Ralph M.

NEW JERSEY
Bernhardt, George
Brush, Julie C.
Buergernaise, Carl
Calderon, Ludmilla
Camilli, Albert
Connin, Peter
Cutting, John
Durand, Francis L.
Famularo, Marie
Fischer, L. Valdemar
Gaskill, Marion
Hall, John
Halpin, Grace
Klein, Samuel O.
Holloway, Thomas
Jennings, Walter W.
Magnette, Edith

Manupelli, Raymond
*Marsh
McIntyre, Marjorie
Meyers, Henry
Miller, Edith
Moon, Roy
Murphy, Vincent
Nelson, Frank
O'Neill, J. J.
Papa, Joseph
Pearce, E. L.
Schuerer, Robert
Schwabe, Erwin
Shane, Charles R.
Simpson, Columeris
Sudek, Joseph
Stevenson, F.
Streeter, Donald
Taylor, Richard
Ward, Paul
Wegg, Arthur
Zuccarello, A.

NEW MEXICO
Barrio, Conrado
Boyd, E.
Claflin, Majel G.
Lantz, Juanita
Marley, J. Henry
Mirabal, Alfonso
Parish, Margery
Reimer, Richard
Thomas, Grace
Wiswall, Etna

NEW YORK CITY
Acampora, Nicholas
Almgren, Jenny
Amantea, Nicholas

Annino, L.
Bader, Herman
Beer, Doris
Benge, Jessie M.
Berge, Virginie
Berner, Mary
Bialostosky, Ruth
Borelli, Francis
Borrazzo, Salvatore
Boyd, Julia
Budash, Frank
Burzy, Vincent
Campbell, Rollington
Capaldo, Ernest
Capelli, Gianito
Carano, Vincent
Cartier, Ferdinand
Caseau, Charles
Choate, F.
Clark, Mae A.
Colgan, J. N.
Concha, Margaret
Cook, Gladys
Crimi, Nancy
Curtiss, Marion
Dana, John
Danziger, Isador
Delasser, Yolande
Dezon, Sylvia
De Wolfe, Henry
Dieterich, John
Doran, Walter
Drozdoff, Leo
Duany, Hester
Dwin, Dorothy
Eisman, H.
Emanuel, H.
Fairchild, Elizabeth

Fastovsky, Aaron

Fenge, M.

Ford, Mildred

Forman, Bessie

Fowler, Catherine

Frankes, P.

Fulda, Elisabeth

Fumagalli, Frank

Garfinkel, Sara

Gernon, Dorothie

Gibbes, Winifred

Gilsleider, Edward J.

Goldberg, Isidore

Gordon, Jean

Granet, Henry

Greene, Minna

Grubstein, Milton

Gussow, Bernard

Hansen, Esther

Harnly, Perkins

Henning, Charles

Herrett, Emery

Hobert, Helen

Hoffman, Melita

Johnson, Arthur

Johnson, Philip

Karlin, Agnes

Kieran, Dorothy

Lacey, Dorothy

Lane, Rosalia

Larzelere, Fanchon

Lassen, Ben

Lawson, Irene

Le Fevere, Jules Z.

Lemberg, Gertrude

Lindermayor, John

Lipkin, J.

Livingston, Rolland

Loughridge, George

Lowry, Mina

Lubrano, Joseph

Maralian, A.

Marshack, Daniel

May, Ada V.

McBride, Hubbell

Mierisch, Dorothea

Middleton, Owen

Mitchell, Marie

Mose, Eric

Mosseller, Lillian M.

Nason, Alfred

Perkins, Arlene

Peszel, Jean

Phillips, L.

Pimentel, Palmyra

Resnick, Benjamin

Riza, Janet

Rothenberg, Joseph

Rothkranz, L.

Roy, Suzanne

Ruelos, Eleanor

Sackerman, Gilbert

Sanborn, Gordon

Sandler, Selma

Shiren, Alvin

Silvay, Van

Sovensky, Isidor

Spicer, Joel

Squeres, C.

Staloff, Jack

Steinberg, Isidore

Szilvasy, May

Tarantino, John

Tercuzzi, John H.

Trekur, Michael

Tuccio, Amelia

Van Felix, Maurice

Von-Paulin, M. Rosenschield

Von Urban, Charles,
photographer

Walton, Kalamein

Wenger, F.

Westmacott, Bernard

Winter, Charlotte

Zaidenberg, A.

NEW YORK STATE

Badin, Ferdinand

Brown, E.

Cavanaugh, John

De Strange, Isabella

De Vault, David S.

Earl, F.

Fitzgerald, Mary

Fletcher, D.

Gausser, E.

Gibbo, Pearl

Glover, Joseph

Lumbard, Howard N.

Luttrell, M.

Matthews, Arthur

Merkley, Arthur G.

Parker, Cushman

Phillips, G.

Plogsted, Louis

Sanborn, Gordon

Schmid, M.

Schmidt, W.

Scrymser, C.

Shearwood, William P.

Sherlock, Geneviere M.

Spangenbergh, G.

Topolosky, A.

Watts, Thomas

Whitaker, R.

Youngs, Jesse M.

Zito, Emilio

OHIO
Barnett, Richard
Boehmer, Fritz
Bronson, Helen
Bulone, Angelo
Cline, Orville
Dadante, Michael
Drake, James
Dyball, Adelaide
Graham, Ernest, *photographer*
Guinta, Jerry
Jennings, Harry
Larson, Carol
Russell, Ralph
Wilkes, John

PENNSYLVANIA
Anderson, Elmer G.
Angus, Charlotte
Antrim, William L.
Brown, Roy S.
Buergernaiss, Carl
Calbick, William, *photographer*
Davis, Betty Jean
Davison, Austin L.
Dingman, Bryon
Fleming, Elmo
Gross, James, *photographer*
Hays, Mrs. May, *photographer*
Iams, J. Howard
Jean, Albert
Kottcamp, Elmer R.
Levone, Albert Jean
Lichten, Frances
McGough, Raymond
Mitry, Joseph
McComb, Inez
Moran, Henry

Moss, Charles, *photographer*
Newswanger, Myra
Ogle, Charles, *photographer*
Poster, D.
Roadman, Charles
Shellady, Eugene
Soltmann, Max
Strehlau, Carl
Syres, Franklyn
Wenrich, Luther D.
White, Edward
Wilson, Eva
Weber, Roy

RHODE ISLAND
Barton, Robert
Donovan, Donald
Gold, Albert
Handy, Dorothy
Murphy, Henry
Pohle, Robert
Riccitelli, Michael
Ryder, Albert
Sullivan, J.
Tomaszewski, Henry

SOUTH CAROLINA
Gordon, Margaret

TEXAS
Bolser, G.
Brennan, Joe, Jr.
Davis, Pearl
Gomez, Rafaela
Guerra, Flora G.
Guillaudeu, Gladys M.
Johnson, Dorothy E.
Lauderdale, Ursula
Liberto, Virgil A.
Molina, Esther

Pena, Jesus
Rivero, R.
Starr, Angela
Ustinoff, Peter C.

UTAH
Cheney, Clyde L.
Mace, Frank J.
Martindale, Esther
Rosenbaum, Howell
Shurtliff, Wilford H.
Smith, Cecil
Truelson, Florence M.

VERMONT
Lovett, Cleo

VIRGINIA
Alward, Linnet
Bodenstein, Molly
Brown, Florence Grant
Burton, Mary Ann
Busey, Rosa G.
Darby, Edward A.
Eubank, Ann Belle
Farrington, Dorothea
Gills, Robert
Goodman, Mattie
Grant, Florence H.
Humes, Mary E.
Ions, Willoughby
Jones, Mamie M.
Kennady, Virginia
Monfalcone, Renee
Pettijohn, Lucille
Powell, Francis W.
Raike, Elizabeth
Rex, Edna
Skeen, Jesse
Styll, Elgin M.

Vaughan, Annie L.

WASHINGTON

Bruseth, Alf
Correll, Richard
Fletcher, William O.
Fossek, Clementine
Haugland, Augustine

WISCONSIN

Anderson, Alexander
*Ballard
Bartz, Eugene
*Beck

*Bernhardt
Biehn, Irving L.
*Daeda
Dooley, Thomas
Faigin, Samuel
Fallon, Michael
Fernekes, Max
Frank, William
Geuppert, Albert
Gielens, Jacob
Lang, William
*Lauterbach
Lemcke, Lloyd Charles

Miller, Eugene C.
Moreno, Alfonso
Praefke, Walter
*Roehl
Secor, Clarence
Stenzel, Erwin
Stroh, Herman O.
Tardiff, Robert
*Thoss
*Volem
Waldeci, H.

839

INDEX

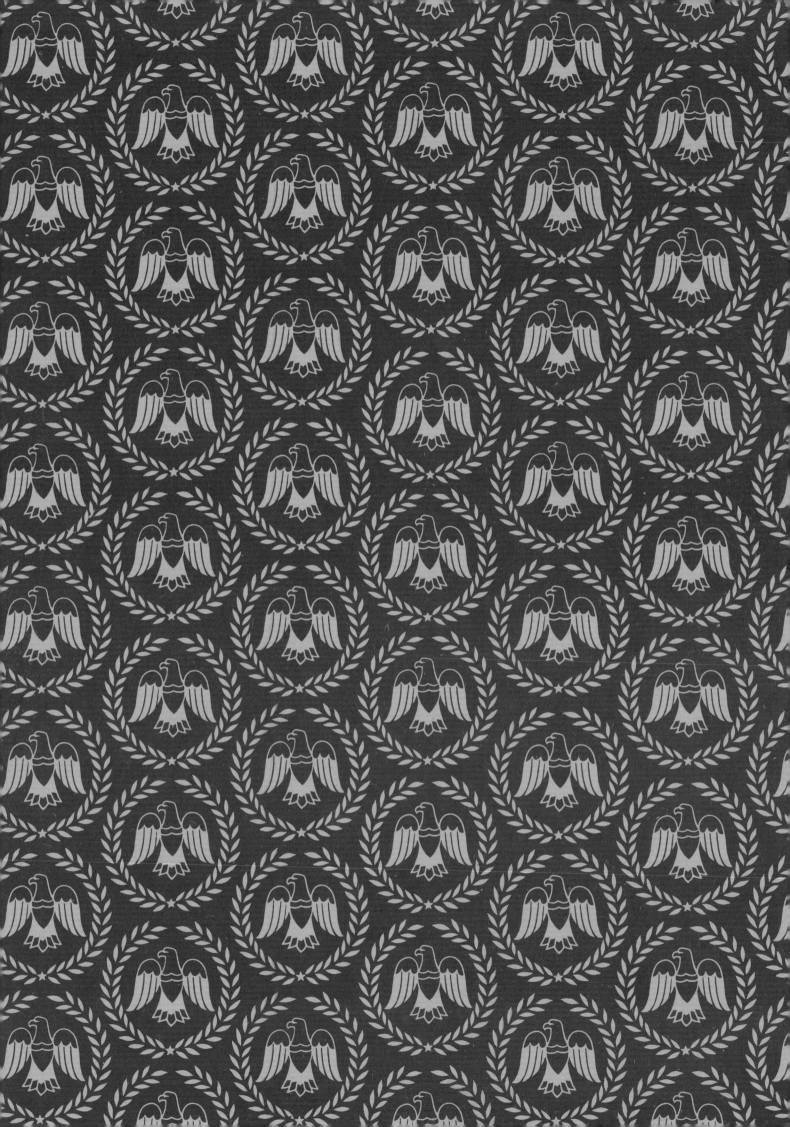